The Making
of a Cook

The Making of a Cook

Madeleine Kamman

Atheneum

NEW YORK

Macmillan Publishing Company
866 Third Avenue, New York 10022

Library of Congress catalog card number 75-162974
ISBN 0-689-70559-X
Published simultaneously in Canada by McClelland and Stewart Ltd.

Macmillan books are available at special discounts for bulk purchases
for sales promotions, premiums, fund-raising, or educational use.
For details, contact:

Special Sales Director
Macmillan Publishing Company
866 Third Avenue
New York, NY 10022

10 9 8 7

Printed in the United States of America

To My Three Men

Acknowledgments

THE UNDERSTANDING of "my three men"—Alan, Alan Daniel and Neil—and the persistence of my students —in particular Carolyn Gusman, Goody Cohen and Selma Kasser— encouraged me to progress from thinking about this book to writing it. Two other factors that helped to prod me were Craig Claiborne's liking for snails and Charlotte Sheedy's fondness for all things French.

My thanks for lifelong teaching go to my mother, Simone Pin, and to my aunt Claire Robert; to Madame Simone Beck, coauthor of *Mastering the Art of French Cooking* and codirector of L'École des Trois Gourmandes in Paris, and to Chef Charles Narses, the great instructor at the Cordon Bleu in Paris, both of whom made formal contributions to my learning; to Chef André Soltner of Lutèce in New York and "Meilleur Ouvrier de France 1969," with whom an informal conversation can turn into a masterly cooking lesson.

My appreciation for their technical advice to Professor Lillian Hoagland Meyer, formerly Head of the Chemistry Department of Western Michigan University, Kalamazoo; Dr. Samuel Gusman, President of Warren Teed Pharmaceuticals, Columbus, Ohio; Bert Porter of the King Arthur Flour Company, Boston, Massachusetts; The National Sugar Refinery Company, New York. To Miss Mary-Lou Welschmeyer of the Product Information Department, Corning Glassware, Corning, New York, my thanks for the dish in which the freezing of soufflés was tested.

My gratitude to Linda Fisher, Gloria Einbender, Ellen Simon and

Lois Ernst, who tested recipes; to Susan Champion, Ann Heitman and Dora Ciparchia for assistance with the manuscript; and to Inez M. Krech for her expert editorial help.

Finally, thanks to Dorothy Parker for her interest and encouragement and for putting up with my "Frenglish."

Introduction

COOKS WHO BELIEVE that "another French cookbook" is just what we *don't* need can be assured that this is a book of a different kind. What we need to keep from French cuisine is the peerless techniques. With those techniques we can create countless new dishes based on American ingredients—corn, sweet potatoes, molasses, brown sugar, pine nuts, pecans, avocados, limes, American wines, Bourbon—which are rarely used in France.

No one has surpassed French cooking methods, and so far they remain the foundation of most Western food preparation. Nevertheless French cooking terms remain mysterious to many women. While I have used some of these specific terms, I have translated them or explained them so that the particular process is quite clear. The techniques and recipes are part of what French food writer Robert Courtine calls *la cuisine des femmes,* in contrast to the *grande cuisine* of chefs. Consequently, although there are some complicated dishes, there is nothing here that cannot be performed in the home kitchen.

It is true that there are born cooks who can serve remarkable meals, apparently without planning or recipes and without spending hours at the stove. Unfortunately most of us need directions, practice and time. In my opinion the directions needed are not so much recipes as solid basic techniques that can be applied to countless preparations. Although this book has recipes for eggs, soups, meats, fish, etc., as most conventional cookbooks do, the internal arrangement is different. The information is organized according to methods or techniques.

For each technique, I have tried to give you an explanation of the chemical and physical changes that take place in the pot while you are at the stove. There are chemical reactions that can be critical for your results in the kitchen, but do not worry—no chemical formulas are to be found in the book.

By giving general principles and proportions which you can apply to many different preparations, I hope to help you to make your own way to creative cookery. By heritage the American cook is creative in the kitchen, more so than her French counterpart. The cook on the farm where ingredients are plentiful provides excellent meals, and in middle-income families where there are no funds for expensive, precooked, prepackaged, catered foods, home cooks produce kitchen miracles. There are fewer miracles in the kitchens that rely largely on packaged foods. I do not make a declaration against the canner or the freezer, for you will see in the pages that follow that I use canned and frozen foods when they contain first-quality products. I am, however, taking a stand against too gimmicky short cuts and against the use of second-rate ingredients.

The recipes that illustrate the techniques are based on the best ingredients—unsalted butter, homemade stock, real cream. Of course you can use margarine and canned stock and you can make other substitutions, but you will discover that the pastry made with margarine lacks the delicious taste of butter, and the sauce made with canned stock will be too salty. The American palate is used to very sweet or very salty foods, not surprising when we remember that sugar and salt were until recently the chief means of preserving foods. If you try a more gentle touch with salt and sugar, if you learn to make your own stock, if you enrich your sauces with unsalted butter, you may discover a new world of tastes.

Most of the recipes are planned to make six servings, with modest-size portions because the food is rich. Of course you can replace some of the rich ingredients and make an edible dish, but it will be a different dish with different taste and consistency. If you cannot prepare meals of rich foods as a daily matter, try to serve a fancy dinner once a week. Besides being an occasion for rejoicing for the whole family, it gives the cook an experience for entertaining with flair and diversity. On this special occasion be merry, enjoy yourself, savour the whole taste of your meal, relax as you dine, and converse during the meal. Discuss the value of the wine you are drinking, the seasoning of the food you prepared; make that weekly beautiful meal something to look forward to, something to make you forget that from Monday to Friday there have been an office, loud children and weight-watchers' meals. During the week while you are using less expensive ingredients, faithfully apply your good culinary techniques.

Some of the formulas assembled come from the kitchens of my ancestors, some from memories of friendly dinners at tables all over the world, but most are my personal way of marrying the cooking techniques of my former country with the delicious ingredients produced by my new one. Just a few are the work of great culinary artists, some long gone, some still young and active. To each of them I have given credit at the beginning of the recipe. Without doubt, I have taken liberties with classic preparations, and both American and French purists may frown, but I have tried to show how the basics can be used to develop a personal style in the kitchen.

Don't believe that "some people will never be cooks." Each of you can develop a personal style. Cooking is not a drudgery; cleaning and ironing are, I must say, quite painful, but cooking, like sewing or painting, is a creative activity, too little practiced and too little enjoyed. It can even be therapeutic: Are you mad at someone? Make a loaf of bread; after ten minutes of kneading, you will be freed from your feeling of annoyance. If something goes wrong in your preparations, relax and try to understand your mistake. If you learn the reasons for the failure, you may be able to rescue the dish; certainly you can avoid the mistake the next time.

My contact with the world of food and gastronomy has been life-long. My French family was a clan of epicureans who could spend a whole Sunday discussing food and wine. One of us was the chef and owner of L'Hôtel des Voyageurs at Château-la-Vallière, a Michelin-starred restaurant. I became an American after my marriage to my Philadelphia-born husband; by the time this book is in print, I will have been "making" cooks in America for over ten years. For me the kitchen is "the fun place" in the house and cookery an art and a joy. In this book I hope to express these feelings of fun and creativity and to share with others my joy in food.

Madeleine Kamman

Contents

I   TOOLS OF THE TRADE   3
(kitchen equipment and how to use it)

II   GOOD INGREDIENTS FOR GOOD DISHES   15
(butter, cream, seasoning, wine)

III   MIRACLES IN A SHELL   35
(egg cookery)

IV   HAPPY MARRIAGES   71
(stocks and soups)

V   A MATRIARCHAL SOCIETY   101
(sauces)

VI   THE TRUE WAY TO THAT MAN'S HEART   151
(meat cookery)

VII   MARINE TREASURES   243
(fish cookery)

VIII   FRENCH ELEGANCE   287
(quenelles, aspic and chaud-froid, pâtés and terrines)

IX   COLORS ON YOUR PLATE   313
(vegetable cookery)

X   JEWELS ON YOUR PLATE   371
(poaching fruits, sugar cookery, fruit sauces)

XI   WRAPPED IN DOUGH   387
      (pastry doughs, pies, tarts, and turnovers)

XII   STAPLE OF LIFE   413
      (yeast bakery)

XIII   LIGHT AND AIRY RELATIVES   435
      (cakes)

XIV   SETS OF TWINS   461
      (baked soufflés; mousses and frozen soufflés; baked cus-
      tards, Bavarian cream, loaves and timbales; pancakes and
      crêpes; cream-puff paste)

      Index   531

The Making
of a Cook

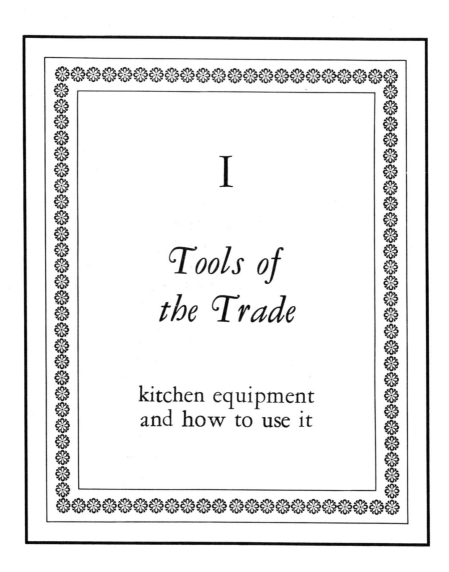

I

Tools of the Trade

kitchen equipment
and how to use it

N O EXTRAVAGANTLY expensive array of equipment is needed to cook well. Many of the essential items can be purchased for very little in a local shop, but if you purchase your equipment in a hotel supply store it will be sturdier and longer lasting.

This list of items may seem enormous. If you are equipping your first kitchen, you will not acquire everything at once. On the other hand, if you are a gadgeteer, you can safely go through your possessions and retire anything not listed here.

POTS AND PANS

The best pots and pans are the old copper beauties. They are heavy and conduct heat evenly, but they are expensive and must be retinned at regular intervals. You can find copper pots lined with stainless steel, which require no retinning; these are worth the large initial investment, but they are made only in limited quantities.

Other excellent pots are those made of cast iron coated with porcelain enamel; there are French, Dutch and Belgian companies who make these. Also there are Danish pots of sheet steel coated with porcelain enamel.

There are good American-made pots. Some of these are thick aluminum pots made by companies such as Wearever (the restaurant line); or pots of Wagnerware Magnalite; or stainless-steel pots coated on the bottom with aluminum made by Farberware; or stainless-steel utensils coated with copper on the bottom made by Revere Ware; or enamelware pots.

The heavier the pot, the sturdier it will be, and the longer it will retain heat, but remember, the pot is not cooking; you are. Regulate your heat according to the thickness of the pot and you will be able to cook even with inexpensive thin-walled vessels.

There are special problems with certain pots. For instance tinned copper pots must be cleaned in a special way. Use soap and water only, never a cleanser or a metal wire pad. A pot lined with a thick layer of scorched or caramelized food can be filled with water containing 1 tablespoon of baking soda per cup of water; prolonged boiling will make the crust lift off by itself.

Aluminum pans should not be used for cooking white sauces or creams, because such preparations require constant stirring. The soft aluminum is actually scraped off the bottom in tiny flakes and thus the sauce becomes tinted gray. If aluminum pots are the only kind you have, be sure to stir with a wooden spoon which will not scratch the bottom of the pan.

These are the utensils you will need. All these pots and pans are used for the various recipes that follow. Of course you will not need a 15-quart stock pot if you do not intend to make large quantities of stock, nor a fish poacher if you don't plan to poach whole fish.

½-quart (2 cups) saucepan

1-quart (4 cups) saucepan

2-quart saucepan

10-inch skillet. If you have one with a heatproof handle, you can use it for preparations that are started on the top of the stove and finished in the oven.

→ 1¼-quart braising pot

4-quart braising pot. Braising pots *must* be very thick; enameled cast iron is especially good.

15-quart kettle or stock pot, for stocks, soups, stews

Double boiler

Hot-water bath (like the bottom of a large double boiler); you can improvise this.

Fish poacher equipped with rack

Steamer for clams and mussels (Or you could steam shellfish in your large stock pot.)

Roasting pan

Broiling pan with rack, unless your stove is equipped with a broiling rack

Small saucepan for dissolving coffee powder, melting gelatin, making caramel

Omelet pan, for omelets only. See Chapter III for more about this.

Crêpe pan. See Chapter XIV for more about this.

Flambéing pan

Metal and asbestos pads for controlling heat under saucepans

Baking Utensils

8-inch flan rings

8- and 9-inch aluminum pie plates

8-inch deep dish for upside-down and deep-dish pies

2 cookie sheets or baking sheets. These come in various sizes: 14 by 17 inches is a practical size. If they are unbendable they will not become warped.

Jelly-roll pan, 12 by 15 inches

Cake pans. These come in many sizes and shapes; those mentioned in the recipes include 8-inch and 9-inch round pans, 10-inch round or square pan, 10-inch springform pan, flat baking pan 13 by 9 inches, tube pan or *Bundtkuchen* pan (best lined with nonstick coating), and many other sizes.

Bread pans, 9 by 5 by 3 inches. You can use these for cakes and for baked custards and loaves also.

Cake racks. Use these as fish broiling racks as well as to cool baked items.

Muffin pans or *brioche* molds

24 small tart pans

9-inch pizza pan

3-cup soufflé dish

6-cup soufflé dish. See Chapter XIV for more about these.

1-quart ovenproof baking dish or casserole

3-quart ovenproof baking dish or casserole

1¾-quart (7 cups) Corning Ware casserole (freezer to stove)

6-cup earthenware terrine

6-cup pâté mold with removable hinges

Individual fireproof casseroles or au gratin dishes

Shirred-egg dishes

Custard cups, 3-ounce or 4-ounce, or individual ramekins, or *pots de crème*

Ovenproof serving casseroles or dishes

OTHER LARGE PIECES OF EQUIPMENT

Large strainer with flat bottom (*tamis*) for puréeing soups and
vegetables

2 medium-size conical strainers, one for sifting dry ingredients,
one for straining stocks and sauces

Wooden pestle to use with strainers

Colander for draining vegetables

Food mill

Electric mixer, standard or hand mixer

Food grinder. Invest in a good one.

Blender. This is a real gift to the serious cook; it puts the old
mortar and pestle to shame. You can even make fresh bread
crumbs with it. Invest in a good blender.

Vegetable slicer. There is an inexpensive version of the French
slicing board (*mandoline*), which is very efficient.

Grater and shredder. With this you can grate cheese, chocolate,
nuts, apples, and you can shred or grate vegetables. Buy the
kind that comes apart for easy cleaning.

2 chopping boards. Have one for pungent foods (onions, leeks,
fish) and the second for other purposes. Wash chopping
boards with soap and water after each use, and dry immediately.

Marble slab. No, this is not essential; a countertop will serve as
well, but if you have a marble slab, by all means use it for
rolling out pastry and many other purposes.

ESPECIALLY FOR FRYING

Electric deep fryer

Electric frying pan or skillet

Frying basket, for lowering foods into hot fat

Noodle-nest frying basket, for potato or noodle nests

Pan with nonstick coating for frying fish

Frying thermometer

FOR STORING AND FREEZING
2 dozen 1 ½-cup Mason jars with dome lids
2 dozen 1-cup Mason jars with dome lids
4½-ounce baby-food jars
Large jars for storing stock
Plastic containers for pungent foods such as shallots
Freezer tape
Plastic wrap
Foil

SMALL UTENSILS
Clock and timer
4 wooden spoons. They do not conduct heat, therefore one can avoid burned fingers. Also they do not scratch the pot bottoms.
Long-handled kitchen fork
4 rubber spatulas, 2 large ones for folding, 2 small ones for scraping every last spoonful from saucepans or bowls
1 large wooden spatula
2 long metal spatulas. You'll use these to lift cooked foods from baking dish to serving platter.
Large serving spoon
Skewers for skewered foods, for testing cooked foods such as fish, and for applying aspic decorations
Wooden food picks
Potato and vegetable peeler
Melon-ball scoop
Larding needle (*lardoir*)
Trussing needle
Rotary hand beater
12-inch balloon wire whip for beating heavy cream
14-inch or 16-inch balloon wire whip, the larger the better, for whipping egg whites
12-inch unlined copper bowl in which to whip those egg whites (optional)
2 small wire whisks for sauces

Small grater for citrus rinds

Small mortar and pestle for herbs and spices

Pepper mill

Meat baster

Plastic pot scrubber for cleaning clams or mussels

Crackers for lobster claws

1 set of measuring cups for dry ingredients. The mark for the measure should be at the top of the cup. To get an exact amount, level off the contents with a spatula.

1 measuring cup for wet ingredients. The mark for this must be below the top of the cup or the contents would spill. In order to get an accurate measure, use a transparent cup of glass or plastic.

4-cup measuring bowl with pouring spout

2 sets of measuring spoons

FOR DESSERT PREPARATIONS

Flour sifter

Mixing bowl for pastries, breads, cakes. Use heatproof glass, pottery, stainless steel.

Rolling pin

Pastry bag with changeable nozzles. Home sets can be found in all hardware stores, but a professional set is a better investment. The most used nozzles are plain round, fluted, star-shaped.

4 pastry brushes 1 inch wide, made of natural bristle, two for brushing meats with fat, two for glazing pastries

Pastry cutters. You can improvise these with the covers of coffee-pots and saucepans.

Candy thermometer (same as frying thermometer)

4-cup Charlotte mold

Molds for Bavarians, mousses and other molded desserts

For extras, you might someday acquire an Italian copper *zabaglione* pan, French *coeur à la crème* baskets, French fluted china pie plates.

KNIVES

Chef's knife with 8-inch carbon-steel blade, for chopping vegetables

Paring knife with 3½-inch blade for paring and boning

Slicing knife with 12-inch or 14-inch blade for slicing meats and cakes

You may already have many other knives, and I could mention others, for instance, chopping and paring knives of other sizes, filleting knife, knife with saw-tooth edge, and so on, but the knives listed are the essential ones.

Carbon-steel blades stay sharper than stainless ones. Two good brands are the German Henckels and the French Sabatier. Use your knives only on a wooden chopping or slicing board to protect the fine edges.

Wash and dry knives carefully and put them out of the reach of curious little hands. If a blade becomes stained, rub it with the bottom of a cork dipped into a little sink cleaner; it will look like new.

HOW TO USE KNIVES

Take hold of the handle of the knife in your right hand, with your thumb placed on the upper right corner of the blade where it joins the handle. Do not extend the index finger over the blade.

To slice vegetables such as carrots and onions: Cut a slice from round vegetables so they will lie flat without bobbing about. Use a guillotinelike motion and move the tip of the knife along the board as you cut thick slices (⅛ to ¼ inch) from the vegetables.

To dice vegetables such as onions and shallots: Cut each onion or shallot into halves. Put each half flat on the chopping board with the root end toward the left. Cut slices ⅛ to ¼ inch thick at right angles to the board, with the point of the knife toward the root end, but do not cut through the root, which will hold all the little pieces together until you have finished.

Next cut similar slices parallel to the board, again not cutting through the root. Last, slice across the onion at right angles to the board, and your onion will be diced.

To cut vegetables into julienne, such as carrots, turnips, potatoes: Cut the vegetables into slices, then into small sticks. For a fine julienne cut sticks ⅛ inch wide, for a large julienne cut sticks ⅙ inch wide.

To cut vegetables into mirepoix or brunoise: Using the same motion as for slicing, cut julienne pieces of vegetables into small cubes. Cubes of ⅙ inch are *mirepoix,* those of ⅛ inch are *brunoise.*

To cut lettuce or other leafy greens into chiffonnade: Roll up together several leaves of lettuce or other greens. Slice the roll at ⅙-inch intervals. The long curly strips are the chiffonnade (from *chiffonner,* to crumple).

To mince or chop into very small pieces parsley, mushrooms, nuts, hard cheeses, chocolate: Hold the knife handle with your right hand in the conventional way. With your left hand apply pressure to the tip of the blade; use the "mounds" of the palm of the hand and leave the fingers extended. (If you hold the blade between the tips of your fingers, you can cut yourself.) Lift the blade with your right hand and press down with both hands in a rapid chopping motion to reduce the food to very small particles.

A few other kitchen necessities:
Kitchen string
Baking and parchment paper
Cheesecloth
Kitchen towels. Paper towels can be used for almost everything, but cloth towels are sometimes better; for instance, thick cloth towels work better for holding lobsters. Cloth towels can be cleaned with laundry soap and bleach.

FREEZER

One other necessary piece of kitchen equipment is your refrigerator, but this you are already using and taking for granted. The freezer is almost as familiar, and it is an important aid to economy in the modern kitchen. I do not agree with the general statement that "frozen foods are dead foods." Carefully defrosted meats are excellent. As a help to your budget, buy whole chickens when they are on sale, and cut them up yourself (see p. 157). If you are only using the breasts for cutlets, freeze the remainder. Buy large joints of meat in the same way; the bones and scraps will give almost costfree stocks. With the freezer to help, you can use every scrap. Store a white-stock and a brown-stock bone and scrap bag in the freezer, and keep accumulating for your stock sessions. In the same way store leftover vegetables; when blended with chicken or beef broth, they will make a better than average vegetable soup. Stocks and sauces take a long time to prepare. With the freezer you can prepare large amounts at one time.

Clarified butter (p. 17) and truffles (p. 28) can be frozen. Completed preparations can be frozen too; you will find many examples in the recipes that follow.

STOVES

Either gas or electric stoves can be used. Electric stoves present one problem; it takes time for a burner to heat to the proper temperature, and it takes time again for the burner to cool off to a lower temperature. Therefore if you are preparing a recipe that requires more than one temperature, use two or three burners so that the pot can be moved from one burner to another. This is important for delicate dishes, especially those made with eggs.

PREPARATION TRAY

In some recipes, there are several different preparations, which are assembled in the end to make a finished dish. You may find it convenient to divide the ingredients for each stage of the recipe. Read the ingredients and the method, then measure the ingredients and transfer them to custard cups or plates for each portion of the recipe. You will need only one set of measuring cups and spoons. Place the ingredients that belong together on a tray to wait until the stage when you use them.

SAFETY POINTERS

When working in the kitchen, wear low-heeled shoes; sneakers are slippery. Don't work in bare feet; a drop of hot fat is painful and dangerous. Tight-fitting slacks can soak up hot spilled liquids, and loose overblouses can catch on fire. A long baker's apron covering you from the shoulders to below the knees is the only fitting garb in a kitchen. Do use pot holders and mittens. Handle all sharp tools with care. Respect gas and electricity, for they are powerful forces even though we have tamed them to use for the most delicate cookery.

II

Good Ingredients for Good Dishes

butter, cream,
seasoning, wine

BASIC INGREDIENTS

BUTTER

UNSALTED BUTTER will give you good results in all your cooking, and this is what I recommend. Although the salted butter sold in supermarkets is generally fresh, it keeps many dishes short of perfection. Salted butter browns foods faster because the sodium chloride in suspension in the fat caramelizes at the bottom of the pan and around the food when subjected to high heat. Food may look somewhat better if sautéed in salted butter, but the natural taste is better preserved when unsalted butter is used.

Unsalted butter is an important ingredient in sauces such as hollandaise and hot butter sauces. As for desserts, use salted butter, if you desire, for doughs and pastries, but only unsalted butter should enter the composition of creams and sweet sauces.

Fresh butter is almost white and has a typical "clean butter" smell. When you buy butter, smell the package; slightly rancid butter can be detected even through 2 layers of paper.

CLARIFIED BUTTER

When heavy cream is churned to make butter, the molecules of fat it contains agglomerate to form blocks of butter floating in a mixture of whey and casein. Although the butter is washed before being packaged, some whey and casein remain in suspension in it. When food is sautéed in hot butter, the whey and casein precipitate at the bottom of the pan and often turn brown and burn so that the sautéed food is pitted with many brown and black dots. Clarifying the butter is the solution to this problem.

Melt the butter over medium heat. Let it stand for 20 to 30 minutes. With a spoon remove the foamy crust (casein) from the top. *Do not pour or strain,* even through a cheesecloth, but *spoon* the deep-yellow liquid butter fat into a jar, and store. The casein may be used in vegetable dishes, but the whey left at the bottom of the pan is unusable. Mixed with the whey is some of the butterfat. To avoid losing it, refrigerate the whole mixture in a custard cup; when the butter has solidified, add it to the jar of clarified butter and discard the whey.

Clarified butter, also known as "butter grease," used for panfrying will give you gorgeous and clean-looking food. Clarifying butter is an old-fashioned procedure not used enough nowadays. To skip the clarification step, modern cooks add unmelted butter to hot oil; the oil helps the butter to reach a higher temperature without burning.

However, it is neither difficult nor time-consuming to clarify butter. To spend even less time at it, prepare 2 pounds of clarified butter at a time. Clarified butter keeps fresh in the refrigerator for 2 to 3 weeks, since whey and casein, both subject to bacterial transformations, have been removed. Or you can store it in 4-ounce baby-food jars, and freeze.

CREAMING BUTTER

Creaming introduces air into butter, which becomes whiter and lighter. The whey is evenly distributed through the butterfat. When sugar is added to the creamed butter, the whey mixes with the sugar to form a syrup emulsified in the butterfat. The whey contained in the butter is often a helpful sugar-melting agent in preparations such as buttercream. Creaming is an important leavening agent in cakes.

To cream, use a wooden spoon, a hand whisk or, best of all, an electric mixer. The butter should be "softened," that is, at room temperature, but not at all melted. If the butter is too hard when you are ready to use it, enclose it in a damp towel and knead it until it is soft enough to handle; or rinse a bowl with boiling water, dry it carefully, and cream the butter in the warmed bowl.

MARGARINE

If the taste of margarine is not always discernible even to the connoisseur, the absence of butter is. If you do use margarine, keep it for your everyday fare, and use butter for special occasions. There are many brands of margarine on the market; I have found several unsalted brands to be good. Margarine will reduce your cholesterol intake but not your caloric intake, since it produces, per tablespoon, 2 more calories than butter.

If you use margarine for dietary reasons, keep in mind that the soft tub-type margarine should be reserved for a spread for bread and for dressing cooked vegetables. It should not be used for panfrying because it burns much too fast.

OIL

Deep frying is done in oil. Most of the oils sold in supermarkets are of above-average grade and may be used for deep frying with excellent results, but in my opinion corn oil is the best. Olive oil should be reserved for salads and for those dishes which need the strong olive flavor.

CREAM

Heavy cream is a mixture of butterfat emulsified in milk. No matter what treatment is given to American heavy cream, Normandy cream will never be produced out of a supermarket carton. However, our heavy cream will make sauces with the correct consistency if the sauces are properly cooked and reduced. American cream is perfect for whipping and produces an absolutely sweet-tasting *crème Chantilly*. Pasteurized cream sold in jars is excellent for sauces but tastes too "cheesy" for desserts.

WHIPPED CREAM

When you whip cream, you build up protein and fat walls enclosing tiny bubbles of air. The more you whip, the stronger and firmer the walls become. If you beat too much, the fat molecules will cling to one another to make butter, and the protein walls will collapse and release water.

Chill the heavy cream and freeze the bowl and beater for 2 hours before whipping so that the butterfat remains quite firm. If the butterfat in the emulsion is warm and fluid, the cream will not foam or thicken. If the surrounding temperature is above 80°F.—and only then—beat the cream in a bowl set in another bowl containing ice. If the cream seems or is too warm, add a few ice chips to the bowl before whipping.

A hand whisk will give more volume to the cream than an electric mixer. Follow the instructions of the maker if you wish to use an electric mixer, but the best whipped cream is hand fluffed.

Whip cream stiff to decorate cakes and fruit cups or custards, and add it to these dishes by piping it through a pastry bag.

Whip cream to the Chantilly stage, i.e., until it barely mounds and still flows from the beater or whisk, for all mousses, Bavarian creams and frozen soufflés (see p. 484).

TO STABILIZE WHIPPED CREAM

When a cake filled with whipped cream is made ahead of time, stabilize the cream with gelatin or cornstarch; otherwise the cake layers will soak up moisture from the cream.

Gelatin Whip 1 cup cream to the Chantilly stage. Melt 1 teaspoon unflavored gelatin in ¼ cup of water in a double boiler. Let the gelatin cool slightly. While continuing to whip the cream, pour the gelatin into the cream in a thin stream until the cream is stiff. Chill.

Cornstarch Mix together ⅓ cup cold milk and 1 teaspoon cornstarch. Thicken over medium heat and let cool. Whip 1 cup cream to the Chantilly stage; mix one quarter of it into the cornstarch mixture. Continue beating the cream until stiff, then fold it quickly into the cornstarch mixture.

To Flavor Cream Add 1 to 1½ tablespoons liqueur per cup of cream only when the cream starts thickening. Use flavoring extracts in the same manner.

FLOUR

The recipes in this book are based on unbleached all-purpose flour. Instantized or instant blending flours are not satisfactory.

Soft pastry and cake flours are not always easy to locate in supermarkets. You can make flour as soft as pastry flour by putting 1 tablespoon cornstarch in an 8-ounce measuring cup and sifting enough flour over it to make 1 cup. To obtain the equivalent of cake flour, increase the amount of cornstarch to 2 tablespoons. With these minor adjustments, you can use all-purpose flour for all your baked products.

To measure flour, use nesting-type measuring cups that contain the measured amount when filled exactly to the brim. Sift directly from the sifter into the cup, letting a mound form; then level the surface of the flour with one stroke of a spatula.

SUGAR

When you cook, you use sugar in its most commonly sold forms: confectioners' sugar for icings; powdered or superfine sugar for sauces, beverages and fruit preparations; granulated sugar for all-purpose use; both light and dark brown sugar. Unless otherwise mentioned in a recipe, sugar means *granulated sugar*. Granulated sugar is cooked with water to make sugar syrups. For information about cooking sugar and sugar syrups, see Chapter X.

GELATIN

Unless otherwise directed in a recipe, use 1 envelope of unflavored gelatin to gel 2 cups of liquid. To add gelatin to a preparation, mix it with 1 tablespoon of cold water and melt the mixture in a small pot placed over simmering water. The melted gelatin will readily blend into any mixture without a chance of forming lumps. Scrape all the gelatin from the sides of the small pot with a rubber spatula.

SPECIAL FOR DESSERTS

CHOCOLATE

There are many good American brands of chocolate; Baker's, Hershey's, Maillard's are some of the familiar names. If any of these are available to you, use them without hesitation. However, in my opinion, nothing gives better results for the very best taste in fine preparations than imported Swiss bittersweet chocolate; there are several brands and you can probably find Tobler or Lindt, to mention two, generally available.

Melt chocolate in the top part of a double boiler; turn off the heat as soon as the water in the lower pot reaches the boiling point. Do not melt over direct heat; more often than not, you will be busy doing something else and the chocolate will overheat, the starches it contains will gelatinize, and it will become hard. You can melt butter with chocolate if the recipe is so arranged, but do not mix spirits with melting chocolate. The heat will evaporate the alcohol of the spirit and half of the flavor will be lost.

Cool melted chocolate before adding it to ribboned egg yolks. If you add the chocolate when it is still hot, the yolks will poach and the later incorporation of egg-white foam will be difficult.

NUTS

Unless you bake professionally, do not buy almonds in large quantities. You can buy small amounts of blanched almonds whole, slivered or sliced in vacuum-packed plastic bags. If you prefer to prepare almonds yourself, it is not difficult.

To blanch almonds: Bring a pot of water to a boil, add almonds, turn off the heat, and let the nuts steep for 3 minutes. Rinse them under cold water. Squeeze the kernel out of the brown skin between thumb and index finger. Let the nuts dry for several hours.

To chop almonds: Use a large chopping knife and chopping board. Hold the knife handle with the right hand and press down on the blunt side of the blade with the left (see: To mince or chop into very small pieces, p. 12).

To grind almonds: Use a nut grater or an electric blender. Add 1 or 2 tablespoons of sugar to the bottom of the blender container to prevent formation of almond paste; the sugar will absorb the almond oil pressed out by the blades.

To toast almonds: Spread almonds evenly in a single layer on a cookie sheet. Roast in a 350°F. oven for 6 to 10 minutes depending on size. Better stay in the vicinity of the oven, because these few minutes go very quickly.

To make almond milk: Grind almonds in an electric blender together with boiling milk or water; let steep together. Squeeze through several layers of damp cheesecloth. Add ¼ teaspoon almond extract per cup almond milk. You can make water-based almond milk in bulk by using ¼ cup whole blanched almonds per cup of boiling water. Freeze in 1-cup Mason jars.

To skin hazelnuts or filberts: Put shelled hazelnuts or filberts on a cookie sheet and bake them in a 275°F. oven for about 10 minutes, or until the skins fall off when you rub the nuts between the hands.

To skin pistachios: Buy natural undyed and, if possible, unsalted pistachios. If the skin does not loosen by itself, blanch the nuts like almonds.

PRALINE POWDER

Praline powder is a delicious caramel and nut powder often used in pastry cooking. To make it, you must first make the praline confection.

> 2 *cups sugar*   2 *cups chopped nuts*
> ¾ *cup water*

Mix sugar and water and cook to the hard-crack stage (310°F.). Add the nuts and let cook to the caramel stage. Pour the mixture onto a buttered cookie sheet or a marble slab and let it cool to a nut brittle. Break the brittle into pieces and pulverize the pieces in the blender; it will take only a few minutes. Store the praline in well-sealed jars. You can make praline with blanched or unblanched almonds, with pecans, or with hazelnuts (filberts). Sometimes a mixture of several kinds is used.

RAISINS

Use the type of raisins called for in the recipe. Soak them first in fortified wine, rum or brandy to plump them and add flavor.

FLAVORING FOR DESSERTS AND DESSERT SAUCES

Citrus fruit extracts may be added to creams or custards, but a finer taste is obtained if grated rinds are added to scalded milk and allowed to steep for about 2 hours; then use the flavored milk to make the cream or custard. The same procedure applies to all citrus fruits.

Orange-flower water distilled from orange blossoms can be found in specialty shops; this is imported from France.

Almond taste is given to a mixture by adding ground almonds and a few drops of bitter-almond extract. The extract is used to compensate for bitter almonds, which we no longer find among the nuts in our markets because they contain prussic acid.

Coffee flavoring is obtained by using instant coffee powder dissolved in a very small amount of water. Even strong prepared coffee is never strong enough.

SEASONINGS

Herbs, spices and minerals are used for seasoning. Our best-known and universally used seasoning is *salt,* which is a mineral. It is obvious enough to think of adding salt to meats, fish, vegetables and so on, but salt is also important in desserts. Any sweet dish should contain a small amount of salt to balance the sweetness of the sugar. Use from ¼ to ½ teaspoon, according to your taste, *never more.* If you bake a cake with salted butter, omit the salt. Recipes for cooked desserts (creams, mousses, soufflés) do not always mention salt because it is considered customary for a cook to remember the "pinch" of salt.

Another seasoning recently used to excess is *monosodium glutamate,* or MSG. Although this has no flavor of its own, it is a flavor intensifier. However, monosodium glutamate should never be used in Western cookery; it belongs in Oriental foods only. Also, it seems that this product may be a health hazard if too much is used.

Herbs are parts of plants, especially the leaves, grown in temperate zones, while spices are parts of plants, especially the dried seeds and barks, grown in tropical zones. Housewives are sometimes too liberal with herbs and spices, sometimes they do not use them at all. Herbs and spices impart wonderful flavors to foods if used with discrimination.

HERBS

It is often difficult to find fresh herbs; fortunately they may be used in their dried state. When flavoring a large amount of liquid (sauce, soup, stock), add the dried herbs directly to the liquid. When flavoring a preparation with a low moisture content (hollandaise-type sauces, for instance), revive the dried herbs by pouring a small amount of boiling water over them; it will restore their elasticity and help them blend delicately in a fine composition. If 1 tablespoon of chopped fresh herb is required in a recipe, you can use 1 teaspoon of the dried herb instead.

Parsley is the most-used herb in our cookery. There are three types: the familiar curly-leafed parsley, the flat-leafed or Italian parsley, and so-called Chinese parsley, which is actually fresh coriander and is also called *cilantro*. Fresh parsley leaves are used for flavoring and for garnish, but you will notice in some of the recipes in this book that *parsley stems* are used. The stems are even more flavorful than the leaves.

Among the other familiar herbs, bay leaf, thyme and celery must be used sparingly; their pungency is apt to ruin a dish. California bay leaf (from a tree) is much stronger than European bay leaf (from a bush), usually labeled Turkish bay leaf. If a recipe calls for 1 bay leaf, use 1 whole Turkish bay leaf but only ½ California bay leaf to obtain the same flavor.

Other herbs used in the preparations that follow are tarragon, a favorite with chicken; basil, rosemary, dill; juniper berries, especially for lamb and venison; caraway seeds, and many others. If using these flavorings is new to you, start cautiously, with very small amounts. It is possible to add more, but impossible to take it away. I may like basil, but will you? If you know you don't like the particular herb listed in a recipe, try another.

You will often see *bouquet garni* listed. A *bouquet garni* is a bunch of herbs tied together; usually it includes bay leaf, thyme, fresh or dried, and fresh parsley stems. *Bouquet garni* flavors all stocks, brown sauces and gravies. Since it is tied together, it is simple to lift out the little bundle at the end of the cooking.

The most-used flavoring vegetables are members of the onion family—garlic, shallots, chives, leeks and onions themselves, including green onions, which are also called scallions.

SHALLOTS

Shallots are little bulbs with reddish skins. They grow in clusters like heads of garlic, but inside of the skin they are somewhat purple in color. They have some of the characteristics of both onions and garlic. Try to imagine French cuisine without shallots! They are fairly expensive. The little bulbs mold quickly if kept in a wet place; on the other hand, too dry storage makes them shrivel to mere skins. Place them in a plastic ice-cream container with a tight lid and store in a vegetable crisper of the refrigerator. No shallots? Use fine-chopped scallions.

LEEKS

Whoever bred the first leek deserves the blessings of all cooks, for nothing else gives basic stocks such superb flavor. Leeks are more difficult to locate than shallots unless you are not too far from an Italian market. If you cannot find leeks, try growing them; they thrive in gardens. In stocks, use whole leeks; for fine cream soups and in fine preparations such as leek pie, use only the white part.

SPICES

Whole spices retain their flavor and freshness much longer than ground spices. This is especially true of pepper, our most-used spice. Freshly ground pepper is much superior, and the whole peppercorns will keep for a long time.

Black peppercorns look brown and shriveled; they have been picked when the berries are unripe and dried. White peppercorns are riper when they are gathered, and they are slightly fermented. After this the outside of the berries is removed to make white peppercorns. White pepper is less powerful than black pepper. Use white pepper in white sauces, so that your sauce has no black specks.

Cayenne pepper comes from another plant. It is made by grinding the seeds and pods of a hot pepper that is related to our familiar green bell pepper. It is extremely hot, so it should be used sparingly.

Cinnamon, cloves, nutmeg, cardamom, vanilla will all be found in the recipes. Use whole rather than ground cloves; stick them in a vegetable (onion or turnip) going in the same pot. Nutmeg, like pepper, is much more flavorful if freshly grated.

VANILLA

Vanilla is used as a flavoring by itself and also as a neutralizer for the taste of egg yolks. A cake may be flavored with a liqueur which will give it its particular taste, but it will also contain a little vanilla to temper the taste of egg yolk.

Vanilla comes from the seed pod of an orchid, and the bean itself gives the best flavor. Scrape the little seeds out of the pod into the liquid of a recipe, or use a section of the pod. However, vanilla beans are not always easy to locate. Instead you may use pure vanilla extract; imitation vanilla extract is not acceptable.

VANILLA SUGAR

Buy 2 vanilla beans, cut them open on the side, and put them in a 4-cup container that can be tightly sealed. Cover the beans with granulated sugar; you will obtain excellent vanilla-flavored sugar. Use it for meringues. Keep replacing the sugar, not the beans.

SPICE MIXTURES

In French recipes for pâtés and meat pies the mysterious ingredients *sel épicé* (spiced salt) and *quatre-épices* (four spices) appear time and again. There is no set formula for either of these preparations, although the base of both mixtures is similar. Every spice company in Europe has its own formula. Recently American spice firms have begun to make their own versions of *quatre-épices*. In the formulas that follow, the balance of salt and pepper follows the recommendation of Auguste Escoffier. The spice mixture is my own, since the master mentions only vaguely "spices."

SPICED SALT (*sel épicé*)

⅓ cup salt	1 teaspoon ground cinnamon
4 teaspoons ground pepper	1 teaspoon grated nutmeg
2 teaspoons ground coriander	½ teaspoon ground cardamom
2 teaspoons ground allspice	⅛ teaspoon ground cloves

Mix the salt and all the spices in a blender jar, and blend on high speed until finely powdered. Put the mixture in small jars that can be tightly sealed.

FOUR SPICES (*quatre-épices*)

1 teaspoon ground cinnamon	2 teaspoons ground coriander
2 teaspoons ground allspice	2 teaspoons finely crumbled dried
⅛ teaspoon ground cloves	tarragon
½ teaspoon ground cardamom	½ teaspoon finely crumbled dried
1 teaspoon grated nutmeg	marjoram

Mix the spices and dried herbs in a blender jar, and blend on high speed until finely powdered. Put the mixture in a small jar that can be tightly sealed.

TRUFFLES AND FOIE GRAS

Truffles are subterranean fungi found near the roots of oak and chestnut trees. They are of two kinds: black and white. The best black truffles are collected from Périgord in France and from Umbria in Italy. Toward the end of the holiday season, the French relieve the demand for truffles by importing some black beauties from Norcia and Spoleto. White truffles come chiefly from Piedmont in Italy.

Truffles deserve respect not only because they are so flavorful, but also because of the vast amount of time and patience it takes to gather them. Truffle hunters spend months training young sows in France, or dogs in Italy, to develop a taste for them. Taken on a collection party, these animals dig down to trace each "black diamond," which the truffle lover pockets swiftly. Truffles have not yet been located in the United States; but some mycologist with a great palate will one day import a trained pig, find them, and become a millionnaire. Meanwhile they must be purchased canned.

Truffles, black and white, must be peeled with a vegetable peeler to remove their tough and rough skin. However, the peelings are very flavorful. Use them to flavor sauces and salad dressings; strain out the peels before serving. The canning brine can be added to sauces. Do not misuse truffles; they have no place in improperly cooked sauces or in so-called pâtés made out of liverwurst.

BLACK TRUFFLES
Buy the largest possible can; it will be proportionally less expensive. Store unused truffles individually in baby-food jars; cover the truffle with melted lard, Cognac, Madeira or port. Freeze truffles only if immersed in port or Madeira.

To revive the taste of canned black truffles, peel them and slice or dice them, and let them steep in slightly warmed port, Cognac or Madeira; then add them to the dish you are preparing.

WHITE TRUFFLES

These are more difficult to handle. Their taste is so very delicate that any strong wine or alcohol, rather than add anything to them, would damage them further. For best flavor, white truffles should be eaten raw, so that one can imagine the effects of canning on them.

To revive white truffles, slice them and let them steep in a few tablespoons of melted chicken or veal meat glaze (p. 79) if available. If not, let them just heat through in the meat juices or sauce they will accompany. They blend beautifully in salads prepared with lemon juice and olive oil.

FOIE GRAS

Foie gras means fat liver. In Périgord, Alsace, Hungary and Czechoslovakia, geese and ducks are kept in very small pens and force-fed. The rich diet and lack of exercise add layers of fat to the birds. Their livers grow to become enormous bloated bags, full of pinkish butter. When the birds are butchered, their livers are processed for *foie gras,* while their bodies are canned and sold as *confit d'oie,* or goose in jelly. To purchase *foie gras,* go to the best fine-food shop; it is extremely expensive. Make sure that the label reads *Foie Gras* or *Foie Gras au Naturel;* in *Mousse de Foie Gras,* the proportion of *foie gras* is so small that it can scarcely be tasted.

WINES AND SPIRITS

TABLE WINES

Natural table wines—wines that have not been fortified—both red and white—are used in sauces. They must undergo a boiling process to allow the alcohol they contain to evaporate. The flavor of the wine used permeates the sauce and gives it an individuality that remains even after cooking. Any amount of uncooked table wine added to a finished sauce makes it harsh and unpalatable.

Choose a good-quality dry wine. For a special occasion, use the same wine to cook a dish that you plan to serve with it at dinner. A dry vermouth never quite adequately replaces a good dry white wine.

French wines bear the name of the plot of land, the village, town or region where they originated. American wines are called *varietal* when they bear the name of the grape from which they were made. They are called *generic* when they bear the name of a French region or village; such wines are intended to be similar in style to the French wine from those places. For example, Pinot Noir is a varietal wine made with as close as possible to 100 percent of Pinot Noir grapes, while an American wine simply called Burgundy is made with some Pinot Noir grapes blended with one or several more types of grapes. In general, American varietal wines are better than generic wines.

California wines are made from *Vinifera* grapes (the European grape) or hybrid grapes (crossbreeds of different species of grapes, some European, some American), while New York State wines are chiefly made from blends of *Labrusca* grapes—the indigenous American grapes—and hybrid grapes. Two producers in New York State make wines from European Vinifera grapes and hybrids. Dr. Konstantin Frank's pure Vinifera wines can definitely compare with some of the best European wines, while Mr. Walter Taylor's Bully Hill wines can, in my opinion, be considered prototypes of wines produced from hybrid grapes.

Labrusca wines cannot be easily used in cooking due to their strong fruity bouquet. However, they are very pleasant to drink. The Niagara, Delaware and Duchess varieties can be used to make excellent sabayon dessert sauces.

There is a false belief among new "connoisseurs" that American wines are not as good as European ones. American wines vary in quality, but when they are produced by reputable houses they are better than the lower quality of wines made in Europe and exported to this country at high prices. An expensive European wine may be very good, but when one is dealing with less expensive bottles, it is often better to use the corresponding American product. Cheap French wines can be the result of unfortunate blending.

Of course wines are produced in other countries besides France. Italy, Spain and Portugal, Germany, Austria and Hungary, Switzerland, Greece, South Africa, Chile—all these countries produce wine, and some of it is splendid. You will find suggestions for wines to accompany the main dishes that follow, and they come not only from

France and the United States but from some of these other places. However, I want to encourage you to become acquainted with American wines. In fact, if you are a novice at this, try to learn about wines from everywhere by reading about wine and trying as many as possible at all prices so as to establish your own personal taste and preferences.

SOME WINE EQUIVALENTS

European Wines	American Wines
RED	RED
Bordeaux	Cabernet-Sauvignon
Bourgogne	Pinot Noir
Beaujolais	Gamay-Beaujolais
WHITE	WHITE
Bordeaux dry (Graves)	Semillon and Sauvignon Blanc
Bordeaux sweet (Sauternes)	no equivalent in United States— Sauterne (without an s) is a generic name for wines made of Semillon grapes
Bourgogne	Pinot Chardonnay, Pinot Blanc
Alsace and Germany	Traminer Riesling Gewürztraminer
Champagne Brut	Korbel Brut, Blanc de Blancs, California Goldseal Brut, New York

Wine is the healthiest beverage, full of vitamins and an excellent tonic, but here's a word of advice: serve Bordeaux wines (clarets) rather than Burgundies to senior citizens; keep the Burgundies for active crowds.

Another point to remember when serving wine is that preparations with acid sauces will detract from the taste of wine served with them. Do not serve your best full-bodied or mellow wines with such dishes, but rather serve rosé or Beaujolais types.

FORTIFIED WINES

Fortified wines have had their fermentation stopped by addition of a certain amount of brandy or other spirit. Their alcoholic content varies between 19 and 22 percent. The best-known are port, sherry and Madeira. In cooking, fortified wines may be allowed to reduce, or they may be added in small amounts without boiling to finished brown sauces or soups. The situation in acquiring fortified wines is opposite to table wines; it is to your advantage to buy imported fortified wines.

Fortified wines come in several degrees of sweetness.

For drinking and cooking	*For drinking, desserts, cakes*
MADEIRA (Portugal)	MADEIRA
Sercial, extra dry	Boal or Bual, sweet
Verdelho	Malmsey, very sweet
Rainwater	
SHERRY (Spain)	SHERRY
Manzanilla	Oloroso
Fino, bone dry	Cream Sherry
Amontillado, medium dry	Brown Sherry
	Sweet Sherry
PORT (Portugal)	PORT
White Port, medium dry	Ruby Port, medium sweet,
Tawny Port, medium dry	rich

Vintage port, the port of a single great year, and crusted port, so called because a heavy sediment is formed in the bottle, should be reserved for drinking.

SPIRITS

A brandy or *eau-de-vie* (*aqua vitae*), or Akvavit in Scandinavia, is a transparent liquid resulting from the distillation of wine, fruit or grain. By cooking or "distilling" 10 bottles of wine, 1 bottle of clear brandy is obtained. Young brandy is colorless, but as it ages in casks, the wood slowly gives it a brown color. The most famous brandies distilled from wine are Cognac, made of white wines grown in the area around the French city of Cognac, and Armagnac, distilled from wine of the Gers Département.

Brandies distilled from fruits are aged in crocks and remain white or colorless. Other fruit liqueurs such as cordials are compounded rather than distilled and they are sweetened and usually strongly colored.

Marc is a brandy distilled from the pressings of the grapes after the wine or juice has been extracted. The wine made from the grapes gives its name to the marc, as *marc de Champagne, marc de la Romanée-Conti.*

Akvavit is an example of a spirit distilled from grain (or grain and potatoes).

Various brandies made from fruits are imported to the United States; here is a partial list:

Grapes (wine)	Cognac (France)
	Armagnac (France)
Grapes (pressings from wine making)	Marc (France)
Apples (cider)	Calvados (France)
	Applejack (United States)
Prune-plums	Quetsch (France)
	Slivovitz (Czechoslovakia)
Raspberries	Framboise (France)
	Himbeere (Switzerland, Germany)
Strawberries	Fraise (France)
	Erdbeere (Switzerland, Germany)
Cherries	Kirsch (Germany, Switzerland, France)
Pears	Poire (France)
	Birnengeist (Switzerland and Germany)

In cooking, domestic brandies may replace imported brandies, and applejack can replace Calvados. Brandies and applejack are used to flambé meats and to flavor pâtés, while fruit brandies are used to flavor desserts, especially pastries and creams.

Liqueurs are sweetened and flavored spirits. They are used for drinking, of course, but also to flavor desserts. These imported liqueurs have the predominant flavors listed. There is a domestic liqueur with the same flavor in each case. Either may be used.

Liqueur	Flavor
Apry	apricot
Cherry Marnier	cherry
Cherry Heering	cherry
Cherry Rocher	cherry
Cointreau	orange
Curaçao	orange
Crème de Cacao	chocolate
Noyau de Poissy	almond

Certain other imported liqueurs have no domestic substitute and you must use the original to get the exact flavor.

Liqueur	Flavor
Grand Marnier	orange and brandy
Tia Maria (Jamaica)	coffee
Kahlúa (Mexico)	coffee
Kona (Hawaii)	coffee
Chartreuse Verte (green)	over 100 mountain herbs
Chartreuse Jaune (yellow)	sweeter, less alcoholic
Bénédictine	herbs
B & B	Bénédictine and Brandy

Rum, the pastry spirit *par excellence,* can be chosen according to your own taste, but with almond-flavored desserts light rum is better and lime-flavored desserts are enhanced by dark rum.

A FEW LAST WORDS

Avoid processed, precooked, prebaked, fancy frozen foods. They cost a great deal without bringing much enjoyment to the dinner table. Of course we welcome the convenience of many frozen foods and those processed in other ways, but nothing can fully replace fresh produce freshly cooked. Only butter tastes like butter, and only cream tastes like cream. If you use unprocessed foods, every dish you prepare will have an individual character.

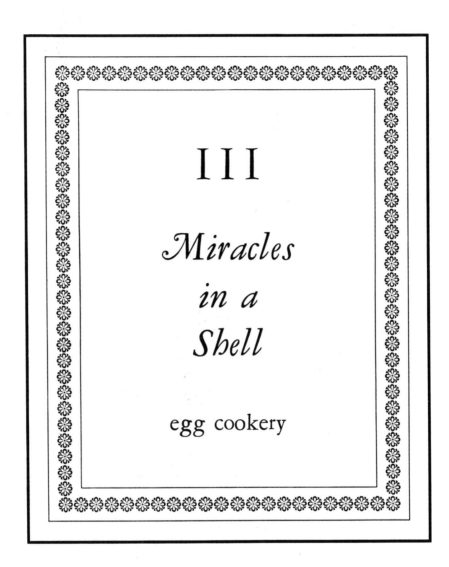

III

Miracles in a Shell

egg cookery

THE SHELL, of course, is that of an egg, quasi-miraculous food and most fun-bringing ingredient ever to enter a kitchen.

It is not conventional to write about eggs so early in a cookbook, but if you have an early knowledge of the culinary possibilities of eggs, you will better understand the making of sauces.

Egg yolk contains all the vitamins except vitamin C; the deeper the color of the yolk, the higher its content in carotene, which is converted to vitamin A in the human body. Of the multiple minerals present in the yolk, iron and phosphorus are the most abundant, but calcium is totally absent. In some underdeveloped countries, the pounded shells of eggs are often incorporated in the diet as a source of calcium. Egg yolk contains also, besides a large amount of proteins, 33 percent fat and about 50 percent water.

Egg white contains over ten different proteins, each of them with a very important role in the future development of the chicken. A globulin known as lysozyme even has an antibiotic power to protect the chicken embryo against infection; the still active lysozyme allows refrigerated egg whites to keep for a relatively long time without spoiling. Of all the vitamins contained in the white, the B-complex riboflavin is the most valuable; it gives the egg white its yellow-greenish tinge. Egg white contains as much as 87 percent water; this large amount of water is most useful in bakery.

Lucky the farmer who raises chickens and has day-old eggs! In large cities, fresh eggs are more of a rarity nowadays than is ever realized. The freshest grade to be found on the market is Grade AA, Fresh Fancy Quality; if at all possible, these should be used for feeding infants and young children and for poaching. The chances are that these eggs are not more than 10 to 12 days old. Plain Grade AA is easier to locate; these eggs are between 12 and 18 days old. Grade A may be as old as 3 weeks. I do not recommend using Grade B eggs, even in making a dish in which the egg is mixed with other ingredients.

A fresh egg is easily recognizable. A whole fresh egg in its shell falls to the bottom of a pan of water immediately, because its content is dense, compact, heavy. The egg has not been in contact with the surrounding atmosphere long enough to allow air to penetrate the porous shell and accumulate in the air pocket. Conversely an older egg, full of air, bobs to the surface of the water or even floats.

When broken, a fresh egg from 8 to 10 days old shows an air pocket the size of a dime. The size of the air pocket increases to that of a penny from 2 weeks on. Break a Grade B egg and try to figure out how old the poor thing is! Also, a fresh egg has a brightly colored and plump-looking yolk, as well as a compact white that barely spreads in a hot pan.

To preserve their freshness, you should store eggs in the refrigerator, but never on the open shelf built by refrigerator makers for the purpose. Keep the eggs in the carton in which they are sold. Keep them as they are sold, that is to say blunt end up. The United States Department of Agriculture states that this keeps the yolk centered. If you pay no attention to the centering of the yolk, you may be interested to know that some old-fashioned French farmers do just the contrary; they maintain that when the eggs are stored pointed end up, the weight of the egg presses on the air pocket, thus keeping it as small as possible. Eggs must be kept away from foods with strong smells, for these odors can be absorbed through the porous shells and thus modify the taste of the eggs.

Eggs cook better when they are removed from the refrigerator about 4 hours before being used. In case of forgetfulness, a stay of 30 minutes in lukewarm water will do. Eggs must always reach room temperature in their shells; if they are broken, the yolks dehydrate and harden.

Use preferably large eggs rather than jumbo or medium-size ones, but if large eggs are not available use these measurements to compensate adequately. One 8-ounce measuring cup contains:

> 5 large eggs
> 4 extra-large eggs
> 6 medium-size eggs
> 7 small eggs

Sometimes recipes will call for ½ egg. To divide an egg into halves, break it into a cup and beat just to mix. Measure the table-spoons of beaten egg in the cup and use half of the amount.

Eggs are considered part of the liquid ingredients of a recipe.

CHEMICAL AND PHYSICAL PROPERTIES OF EGGS

If you are aware of the elementary chemical and physical proper-ties of eggs, you will be more efficient in egg cookery.

That taste of semispoiled, semistale eggs, too often present in cooked eggs, is caused by hydrogen sulfide, which is released from the sulfur contained in the white if the egg is cooked at too high a temperature. That discouraging-looking gray ring around the yolk of a hard-cooked egg and the unpleasant smell it has would not be there if the egg had not been overcooked, giving time for the iron in the yolk to combine with the sulfur in the white and produce iron sulfide.

Cookery utilizes the capability of egg protein to coagulate and foam. Viscous in the raw state, egg proteins coagulate when sub-mitted to heat.

> Egg white becomes firm between 145° and 150°F.
> Egg yolk coagulates between 144° and 150°F.
> A whole egg coagulates around 180°F.

When egg yolks are mixed with a liquid, the protein in the yolk is precipitated. It coagulates and falls to the bottom of the pot if the liquid is heated too much. Sauces or creams made with a mixture of egg yolks and a liquid are said to curdle when the temperature of the mixture rises above 190°F. When the temperature of the mixture stays between 160° and 180°F., the egg coagulates just enough to thicken the liquid, and a sauce, custard or cream results. A slightly different situation exists when the sauce or cream or custard contains a starch (flour, cornstarch, etc.); then the temperature not only can, but *must* then be raised to the boiling point, 212°F. An attempted explanation for this fact is given in Chapter V; see Liaison, page 111.

The foaming capacity of egg protein is used in making soufflés, sauces (hollandaise and sabayon types), and cakes (spongecake, but-ter cake, *génoise*). Both egg yolk and egg white foam when submitted to the mechanical action of a hand beater, whip or electric mixer. Air bubbles are trapped within the walls of protein, which keep expanding. The more prolonged the whipping, the more numerous the bubbles and the firmer the foam. Excessive beating of egg proteins, however, can result in problems; see page 58. In later chapters you will read more about this.

Acids (lemon juice, vinegar, cream of tartar) have a stabilizing effect on egg-white foam and retard its disintegration when the beating has stopped. Both egg-yolk and egg-white foam disintegrate if left to stand, but deflated yolks may be whipped again while deflated whites cannot. Acids also have a bleaching effect on flavones, some of the pigments contained in the white, and turn them from yellow to white.

The expression "she does not even know how to cook an egg," generally applied to brides with no kitchen experience, is, to say the least, unfair. All methods of cooking eggs are tricky and require attention.

CODDLED EGGS

There are at least five different ways of coddling, or soft-cooking, an egg. This is the easiest.

Use at least 1½ cups water per egg, and bring the water to a boil. Immerse the eggs, still in shells, in violently boiling water. Remove the pot from the heat. Cover it and keep it tightly closed for 4 to 6 minutes, depending on the doneness you desire. Then immerse the eggs in cold water to stop the cooking.

Coddled eggs are to be enjoyed without garnish, just with bread and butter; they make a royal meal.

SHIRRED EGGS

Shirred eggs are usually baked in individual round shallow dishes just large enough to contain 1 or 2 eggs. Shirred eggs also taste better without garnish, but they may be sprinkled with grated cheese; or 1 or 2 tablespoons heavy cream may be spooned over them before cooking. A very aromatic shirred egg is obtained when the dish is first rubbed with a garlic clove.

Shirring eggs is easy, but watch that timer! Heat 1 teaspoon butter in the shirred-egg dish; break the egg into it. Set the "shirrers" on a cookie sheet. Bake in the upper third of a 500°F. oven for 1½ minutes. Baste each yolk with another teaspoon of melted butter, and bake for another minute. The intensity of the heat is such that the albumen is coagulated immediately without having time to harden.

Eggs in ramekins or cocottes are another version of shirred eggs. A custard cup or a deep round ramekin is used instead of a shirrer. The thickness of the layer of egg white requires slower cooking for even penetration of the heat. Set the buttered custard cups in a hot-water bath, and bake at 375°F. for 12 to 14 minutes.

FRIED EGGS

Fried eggs may be panfried or deep-fried. Deep-fried eggs, a garnish of some stews in the old French cuisine, are seldom used nowadays. This is no great loss, since a deep-fried egg is surrounded by a golden but tough layer of overcooked egg white, very unattractive to the tastebuds.

The fried eggs we are familiar with are those cooked in fat in a frying pan. Taste intervenes here; some people like them sizzled, some not. To obtain sizzled eggs, fry in the fat of your choice over medium heat. Cover the pan during the last few minutes of cooking to solidify the upper layers of white. To obtain unsizzled fried eggs —the healthiest—cook them in butter over very low heat. Also, cover during the last 2 minutes of cooking to finish cooking the top; when eggs are fried this way, they are very close to shirred eggs.

SCRAMBLED EGGS

Scrambled eggs are *mis*-scrambled by the millions every morning in America. "I can't eat wet eggs" is the culprit most of the time. Mother made dry scrambled eggs, and isn't Mother's cooking still the best? Please give yourself and your family the chance to taste a truly scrambled egg once. Your pan should be thick; cast aluminum or enameled cast iron are best. Plain cast iron is not a good choice for the taste of scrambled eggs.

Use 1 tablespoon butter per egg. Beat the eggs well, but do not liquefy them. If you desire, add ½ tablespoon heavy cream per egg. Use very little salt, for it hardens the egg proteins. Heat the butter, add the eggs and, stirring *constantly* with a whisk or large fork, cook over *very low heat*. The eggs soon form a slightly granular custard. Keep breaking the curds; the smaller the curd, the softer and creamier the eggs. As soon as the eggs are two-thirds solidified, remove the pan from the heat. The heat retained in the pan is sufficient to finish cooking the eggs. If you leave them over heat longer, they start drying up.

The higher the heat you use, the drier the eggs. The steadier and the faster the whisking, the smaller the curd and the creamier the eggs. If you still prefer dry scrambled eggs with large curds, all you have to do is whisk slowly. Scrambled eggs at their best still have a shiny appearance. Scrambled eggs have a tendency to lose their creamy custardlike consistency when milk, water or any water-producing food is added to them before scrambling; any vegetable addition (tomatoes, mushrooms) should be presautéed. Some acid cheeses (Parmesan) also have a liquefying effect and should be added during the last stage of cooking after the pan has been removed from the heat. Cold scrambled eggs are considered a delicacy by some, but rather unattractive by others.

POACHED EGGS

Poaching eggs can be fun if the eggs are not more than 3 days old, but who can be sure except the farmer? With older eggs, poaching is not that much fun any more. The older the egg is, the more difficult it is to poach, since the fluid white produces stragglers in the water.

To make things easier, butter a frying pan and add about 2 quarts water; the water should be 2 inches deep. Bring the water to a boil and add 2 tablespoons vinegar and 2 teaspoons salt; they will help coagulate the egg faster. Reduce the heat to have the water barely simmering. Break an egg into a buttered teacup. Tilt the cup and lower it into the water; count slowly to fifteen, then let the egg gently slide down in the water. If stragglers appear, bunch them on top of the egg with a slotted spoon. Cook the egg for 4 minutes, then remove from the water with a slotted spoon. Immerse the egg in a bowl of cold water immediately to stop the cooking and remove the vinegar taste.

Poached eggs may be cooked ahead of time and kept immersed in cold water; reheat them in that same water before using them. Drain the eggs on a clean thick towel before saucing and garnishing.

Should you find it difficult to poach eggs—and the age of your eggs will be responsible more than your skill—break them into buttered custard cups of the smallest size; set the custard cups in a larger vessel filled with hot water and bake in a 375°F. oven for 12 to 14 minutes. When unmolded, the eggs will look unnaturally regular in shape, but they will fit neatly on a buttered crouton.

OEUFS MOLLETS AND HARD-COOKED EGGS

Another kind of egg cooked in the shell is the 6-minute egg or *oeuf mollet*. *Oeufs mollets* can replace poached eggs in various dishes such as eggs in aspic. So that the eggs all cook for the same length of time, place them in a frying basket and lower them into the boiling water all together. Simmer for exactly 6 minutes. Remove the basket from the hot water to immerse it immediately in cold water. The contact with the cold water produces a layer of steam between egg and shell, which makes peeling easy.

The very same method is used for hard-cooked eggs. They should be left to simmer for 10 minutes, not more, to avoid the formation of the iron sulfide mentioned earlier.

To peel a *mollet* or hard-cooked egg, roll it at the center against the sharp angle of a table or counter; remove the soft cracked shell belt first. The top and bottom of the shell will come off with just a little pull, and the egg will show no scar.

CROUSTADE

Poached, *mollet* and scrambled eggs are often served in a croustade, which may be a pastry shell, but more often is made out of white bread. To use the French method, cut a slice 1½ inches thick out of an unsliced loaf of white bread. Remove the crust. Trace a square on top of the slice, leaving an edge ⅓ inch wide all around. Empty the crumb from the center with a teaspoon, leaving a bottom layer also ⅓ inch thick. Brush the croustade with melted butter and bake at 350°F. until golden.

The American-style croustade is easier and faster to make, and also tastes better. Remove the crust of a regular slice of white bread. Butter on both sides and gently bend to fit into a muffin tin. Bake in a 350°F. oven until golden.

OMELETS

How was the first omelet born? Who knows? If we believe Prosper Montagné in the *Larousse Gastronomique,* many people are involved, from the Romans to a mythical king of Spain. The truth is probably that an involuntary breakage and scrambling became along the centuries a technique to be mastered. Making a good omelet requires correct ingredients and mastery of a few simple techniques.

PAN FOR OMELETS

It is by no means a fable that having a pan for omelets only is a guarantee of success, although after omelet making has become second nature to the cook, an omelet can be made in any kind of pan, especially conditioned or not. The recommended pans are slightly porous and retain a certain amount of fat on their surface.

The best omelet pan is the French professional omelet pan made of black cast iron. This is reasonably porous, conditions fast and well, and allows the cook to make all types of omelets. The pan bears no brand, only numbers stamped on the handle. Buy number 20 for 2 eggs, number 22 for 3 to 5 eggs. This pan, imported from France, is difficult to find, but it is an inexpensive lifetime investment. The true omelet pan is molded cast iron; numerous French imitations are embossed steel.

The French pan can be replaced adequately by some American brands, which are easier to find. Among these are an 8- or 9-inch aluminum frying pan from the Wearever restaurant supply line; chef's omelet pan of Wagnerware Magnalite; thick omelet pan from the Boston Pot Shop; Rudolf Stanish omelet pan. The last two are especially devised for beautiful scrambled omelets. You can also use an old-fashioned 8- or 9-inch skillet made of thick cast iron.

CONDITIONING AN OMELET PAN

Mix 2 tablespoons cooking oil with 1 tablespoon kosher salt. Scrub the new pan with the mixture, using sturdy paper towels. Repeat the scrubbing until no more industrial grime appears on the paper. Fry 2 sliced onions in about 3 tablespoons oil in the pan. Discard the onions, which will have acquired the industrial taste of the pan. Pour off the oil and dry the pan with a paper towel. Fill the pan with cooking oil to within ½ inch of the brim. Heat the oil to the smoking point. Turn off the heat and let the pan stand, with the oil still in it, for 24 hours. Pour out the oil (it may be reused for deep-frying). Wipe the pan dry with a paper towel. The pan is now ready to use.

From now on, keep the pan in a place of its own so that it is not absent-mindedly used for other purposes. Do not use it to cook anything else than omelets. Do not wash it at any time; just wipe it dry with a paper towel after making omelets. Keep it hidden from baby-sitters, who will instinctively elect it to fry and burn hot dogs! If the pan starts to stick at any time, give it another salt and oil treatment.

Butter in Omelets

Clarified butter helps beginners (see p. 17). Experienced omelet makers may use unsalted or salted regular butter to taste. Do not use whipped butter. If using margarine is a must, use the regular stick margarine; the soft tub margarine will burn.

Preparations for Omelet Making

It is better to make a 1-egg, or 2-egg, or 3-egg omelet per person than to make a 6-egg or 7-egg omelet for 2 or 3 persons. Have the eggs at room temperature. Brush the pan with 1 teaspoon clarified butter or oil before heating it so it does not stand empty and need reconditioning in a hurry. Preheat the pan, preferably over an asbestos pad, for a minimum of 10 minutes, or the omelet will stick.

Have a bowl, a fork or rotary hand beater, and a long metal spatula on hand. Proceed in the following order: Break the egg into a bowl; add 1 teaspoon heavy cream, 2 turns of the pepper mill, and just a few grains of salt sprinkled over the heavy cream, so it does not start hardening the egg protein.

Remove the asbestos pad from under the pan. Test the pan with a tiny piece of butter; if the butter sizzles, the pan is ready. Wipe the pan clean with a paper towel. Put the butter in which the omelet will be cooked into the pan (2 tablespoons for a 2- to 3-egg omelet). Let the butter get hot over low heat while you beat the eggs.

Beat the eggs with 30 strokes of a fork or 10 rapid turns of a rotary hand beater. *Do not overbeat;* liquefied egg protein loses its ability to develop volume and gives hard flat omelets.

Raise the heat under the pan very high. Electric stove users must have 2 burners on: one set at low heat for preheating, the other set at high heat for cooking. This high heat is important, for hot butter is a must; it forms a film that insulates the egg mixture from the bottom of the pan. If the butter is only warm, it mixes with the eggs, hence the omelet sticks and becomes badly scrambled eggs.

As soon as the butter has finished foaming, add the omelet mixture to the pan. From this point on, the key word is *speed*—the faster, the better. An omelet is the result of a combination of speed and high heat affecting an egg mixture that scrambles in large curds. The curds coagulate in the shortest possible amount of time and, as a result, stay soft. The bottom layer of the omelet is exposed a bit longer to the heat and hardens just enough to form a casing for the bulk of the eggs.

THE THREE METHODS OF MAKING AN OMELET

SCRAMBLED OMELET

This method is mostly used in England and the United States. With the left hand, shake the pan back and forth on the burner while the right hand stirs the eggs in a circular motion. Work with lightning speed (my French friends and I call this omelet the "agitation" omelet) and try not to scrape the bottom of the pan. Within 15 seconds, the eggs are scrambled. Tilt the pan at a 45° angle, bunch the eggs at the lower end of the pan, and invert them on a plate.

BEATEN OMELET

This is the French home method, and is also taught at the Cordon Bleu in Paris. Pour the omelet mixture into the pan. Let it set for 5 seconds, counting 1 when the mixture hits the pan. Then beat with a fork, introducing as much air as possible into the eggs until they are scrambled. Shake the pan back and forth three times to make sure that the omelet slides easily in the pan. Let it slide forward almost out of the pan. With a spatula, fold the flap hanging out of the pan back upon itself; slide the spatula under the portion of egg still on the bottom of the pan and fold it over the first flap. Invert on a plate.

SHAKEN OMELET

Pour the omelet mixture into the pan; let it set for 8 seconds, counting 1 when the mixture hits the pan. Grab the handle of the pan with *both* hands and raise the pan so it forms a 45° angle with the burner. Shake the pan back and forth so that the egg mixture is thrown against the front lip of the pan and coagulates there. Very soon the batter forms a dam enclosing still liquid egg; quickly give a circular motion to the pan to let the liquid portion pour out into the pan. Continue both shaking and circular motions until the eggs are scrambled; the whole operation requires 15 seconds. The lower portion of the omelet will fold upon itself, forming the first flap. Raise the pan a little higher and fold the second flap over the first with a spatula; or do it by hitting the pan handle with the right fist. Invert the omelet on a serving plate.

TO INVERT AN OMELET

Open your hand palm up, close it on the pan handle, and turn the pan upside down on a plate. What was the bottom of the omelet in the pan becomes its top on the plate. Rub the top of the omelet with a piece of cold butter stuck on the tines of a fork; this will make it glisten and look attractive.

FILLINGS FOR OMELETS

A plain omelet becomes an elegant dish when filled. However, any filling containing either protein or water should not touch the pan or the mixture will start to stick to the pan and a mush of egg and filling will result.

Fillings that can be added to the omelet mixture before cooking are chopped herbs and diced potatoes or croutons sautéed in butter (those may even be sautéed in the omelet pan itself). Meats or any combination of sauce and meats should be laid on the flat unfolded omelet and encased between the two flaps. Grated cheese added to the omelet mixture before cooking makes the pan stick; instead sprinkle cheese on top of the cooked omelet before folding. The omelet is hot enough to melt the cheese, and a spool of tasty strings will be found at the center as one cuts through. Fillings will not escape from an omelet if they are set at its very center before folding.

BASIC OMELET

An omelet for 1 person should be made with 2 tablespoons butter, 2 eggs, 2 teaspoons heavy cream, and salt and pepper to taste.

BROWN BUTTER SCRAMBLED EGGS
3 SERVINGS

6 tablespoons butter	Pepper
6 eggs	3 tablespoons grated cheese,
3 tablespoons heavy cream	preferably Gruyère
⅛ teaspoon salt	

Heat the butter until it turns brown and smells very nutty; let it cool slightly. Add the eggs beaten with the cream and seasonings; scramble. Serve on toast, and sprinkle with grated cheese. The brown butter adds a little "zing" to the bland eggs.

DUXELLES SCRAMBLED EGGS
3 SERVINGS

3 slices of bread	3 tablespoons heavy cream
8 tablespoons butter	⅛ teaspoon salt
½ cup mushroom duxelles	Pepper
(p. 340)	Chopped parsley
6 eggs	

Remove crusts from bread slices and sauté the slices in 2 tablespoons of the butter, or toast them. Spread the croutons with half of the *duxelles*. Keep warm. Heat the rest of the butter and add the eggs beaten with the cream and seasonings. Scramble the eggs; add remaining *duxelles* during the last stage of cooking. Serve the eggs on the prepared croutons, and sprinkle with chopped parsley.

AVOCADO SCRAMBLED EGGS

3 SERVINGS

1 large potato	*Salt and pepper*
Clarified butter, or half butter	*6 eggs*
and half oil	*3 tablespoons heavy cream*
1 pea-size piece of garlic	*Chopped cilantro or Italian*
1 large avocado	*parsley*
1 teaspoon lemon juice	

Shred the potato, and shape the shreds into 3 small flat cakes; brown in clarified butter or oil until golden on both sides. Mash the garlic and half of the avocado together. Add lemon juice and salt and pepper to taste. Spread the mixture on the potato cakes. Dice the other half avocado.

Heat 6 tablespoons butter and add the eggs beaten with the cream, ⅛ teaspoon salt and pepper to taste. Scramble the eggs; add the diced avocado during the last stage of cooking. Serve the eggs on the potato cakes, and sprinkle with *cilantro* or parsley.

BUTTERED ALMOND AND PISTACHIO SCRAMBLED EGGS

3 SERVINGS

3 croustades	*4 tablespoons chopped blanched*
3 tiny soft-shell crabs	*pistachios*
9 tablespoons clarified butter	*6 eggs*
Salt and pepper	*3 tablespoons heavy cream*
2 tablespoons slivered blanched	
almonds	

Make croustades according to the preferred method (see p. 43). Sauté the crabs in 3 tablespoons of the butter for about 2 minutes on each side. Sprinkle them with salt and pepper and keep warm. Heat the rest of the butter and sauté the slivered almonds and half of the pistachios in it until lightly browned. Reduce heat; add the eggs beaten with the cream, ⅛ teaspoon salt and pepper to taste; scramble. Pile eggs in prepared croustades; top each with a sautéed soft-shell crab and sprinkle with the rest of the pistachios.

SCRAMBLED EGGS SUPER
6 SERVINGS

To Doctor Seuss, with my gratitude, for many quiet hours with two children around!

Basic savory crêpe batter	*1 teaspoon salt*
(p. 506), flavored with	*Pepper*
1 tablespoon chopped	*3 wedges of processed Swiss*
chives	*cheese*
12 tablespoons butter	*12 slices of bacon, cooked until*
12 eggs	*crisp*
½ cup heavy cream	

Make 6 large crêpes with the batter. Heat the butter. Beat the eggs with the cream and salt, and scramble until very soft and creamy. Season highly with pepper. Cut cheese into very small dice. Sprinkle half of each crêpe with 2 teaspoons diced cheese; top with scrambled eggs and 2 bacon slices. Fold the other half of the crêpe on top of the filling, and serve.

BEEFSTEAK À CHEVAL
6 SERVINGS

This is my version; the original recipe calls for a fried egg and has no sauce. This makes an excellent company brunch.

6 large croutons	*6 small tenderloin steaks, free of*
5 tablespoons clarified butter	*fat or gristle*
¼ pound mushrooms, minced	*3 tablespoons oil*
6 poached eggs (p. 42)	*Chopped parsley*
1 cup classic brown sauce	
(p. 114)	

Sauté the croutons in 3 tablespoons of the butter. Sauté the mushrooms in 2 tablespoons butter until brown and dry. Use eggs poached ahead of time; reheat them in water while you prepare the mushrooms. Add mushrooms to the brown sauce; reheat well.

Sauté the steaks in the oil to preferred doneness. Spoon 1 teaspoon sauce over each crouton and top with a steak. Top each steak with a poached egg, spoon sauce over the top, and sprinkle with chopped parsley.

POACHED EGGS BUDAPEST
6 SERVINGS

This dish did not originate at Gundel's in Budapest, but the ingredients of the sauce are those of a bona fide Hungarian *gulyás*.

2 tomatoes	*1 tablespoon Hungarian paprika*
1 green pepper	*Salt and pepper*
3 large onions	*6 poached eggs (p. 42)*
6 tablespoons butter	*6 large croutons*
½ teaspoon caraway seeds	*½ cup sour cream*
¾ cup heavy cream	

Immerse tomatoes in hot water for 1 minute, then peel. Immerse the pepper in hot water for 12 minutes, then peel. Squeeze the tomatoes to remove as many seeds as possible. Dice tomatoes, pepper and onions; sauté in 3 tablespoons of the butter for a few minutes. Add caraway seeds, cover, and let cook until tender. Add heavy cream, paprika and salt and pepper to taste. Let everything simmer until the cream coats the vegetables. This may be done ahead of time. Poach the eggs ahead of time also.

Sauté the croutons in 3 tablespoons butter. Gently reheat the sauce and poached eggs. Add the sour cream to the sauce. Reheat the sauce, but *do not boil* after adding the sour cream. Correct seasoning. Set a poached egg on each crouton, spoon the sauce over them, and sprinkle with more paprika.

ALAN'S POACHED EGGS
6 SERVINGS

My husband's birthday breakfast.

6 large croutons	*6 poached eggs (p. 42)*
6 tablespoons cream cheese	*2 cups mousseline sauce*
2 tablespoons heavy cream	*(p. 129)*
Salt and pepper	*1 garlic clove*
6 slices of smoked Nova Scotia	*2 tablespoons chopped parsley*
salmon	

Toast the croutons. Whip the cream cheese while adding cream little by little to lighten the texture. Season to taste. Spread cream cheese on croutons. Top each with a slice of smoked salmon. Set on a cookie sheet and warm in a 275°F. oven.

Poach eggs or reheat already poached eggs. Make the mousseline sauce and strain it into a bowl rubbed with the garlic. Add the parsley and mix well. Set poached eggs on the warmed salmon. Top with some of the sauce and serve the rest in a sauceboat.

SUCCOTASH RAMEKINS
6 SERVINGS

1 package (10 ounces) frozen	*Pinch of sugar*
succotash	*Salt and pepper*
1¼ cups heavy cream	*6 eggs*

Boil the succotash until the beans in it are half tender. Drain well, and mix with ⅔ cup heavy cream. Season with the sugar and salt and pepper to taste. Simmer until cream coats the vegetables. Place 2 tablespoons of the succotash in each of 6 buttered ramekins or custard cups. Break an egg into each ramekin, then top each egg with 2 tablespoons heavy cream. Set the ramekins in a larger vessel of hot water, and bake in a 375°F. oven for 12 to 14 minutes.

FRIED EGGS SAINT VINCENT
6 SERVINGS

From Northern Italy.

1 large eggplant	Clarified butter (6 to 8
2 large tomatoes	tablespoons)
1 large or 2 small zucchini	½ small garlic clove, minced
Flour	1 tablespoon minced parsley
Olive oil	2 tablespoons grated Parmesan
Salt and pepper	cheese
1 cup fresh bread crumbs	6 eggs

Cut the eggplant, tomatoes and zucchini to make 6 large slices of each kind of vegetable. Coat them with flour and sauté in olive oil. Season with salt and pepper. Meanwhile, sauté bread crumbs in as much clarified butter as you like. Mix the buttered crumbs with the minced garlic and parsley and grated Parmesan.

Fry the eggs, keeping them runny on the top. In each of 6 individual fireproof dishes, put 1 slice of sautéed eggplant, then 1 slice of tomato, then 1 fried egg. Top with 1 slice of zucchini, and add some of the bread crumb mixture last. Fill the rest of the dishes in the same way. Broil for 1 minute. Serve piping hot with a bottle of Bardolino.

POTATO OMELET
1 SERVING

As elementary as this may be, try it on any man, and he will love you for life.

1 small potato, diced	Basic omelet for 1 person
4 tablespoons butter	(p. 48)

Sauté potato dice in 3 tablespoons butter until golden. Beat eggs with cream and seasonings and add to the pan. Cook the omelet, fold, and rub the top with remaining butter. Serve immediately.

OMELETTE CHAMONIX

I SERVING

A memory from the Refuge du Couvercle in the Mont-Blanc massif in July 1949. The omelet was made by a retired Guide to restore our mountain-worn energy.

Basic omelet for 1 person   *1 tablespoon diced ham*
   (p. 48)   *1 tablespoon minced parsley*
2 teaspoons chopped walnuts   *1 tablespoon butter*
1 tablespoon fine-diced Gruyère
   cheese

Beat omelet mixture and add the chopped walnuts. Cook the omelet; before folding sprinkle cheese, ham and parsley on the center of the omelet. Fold, rub with the butter, and serve.

THE DEVIL'S OMELET

I SERVING

I'll be the devil anytime; the name comes from my great-grandmother, who mixed *le diable* with *diablotins,* tiny croutons spread with mustard.

1 slice of white bread   *Basic omelet for 1 person*
2 tablespoons butter   *(p. 48)*
Prepared Dijon-style mustard
   (about 2 teaspoons)

Remove crust from the bread. Sauté the bread in 1 tablespoon butter until golden on both sides; let cool. Spread the cooled bread on both sides with a very thin film of mustard, then cut the bread into small dice. Beat the omelet mixture and just before cooking add the mustard croutons. Cook the omelet. Mix 1 tablespoon butter with ½ teaspoon mustard and spread over the finished and folded omelet.

OMELETTE LYONNAISE
1 SERVING

1 large onion, sliced thin
2 tablespoons butter
¼ teaspoon vinegar
1 tablespoon melted meat glaze,
or ⅛ teaspoon commercial
meat extract

1 teaspoon chopped parsley
Salt and pepper
Basic omelet for 1 person
(p. 48)

Sauté onion slices in the butter until soft and translucent; *do not brown.* Add vinegar, meat glaze, parsley, and salt and pepper to taste; mix well. Beat the omelet mixture and cook. Fill with the onion mixture, fold, and serve.

OMELETTE CAGOUILLARDE
1 SERVING

For snail lovers.

Marinade for snails (see Lo
Cagaraulo, p. 285)
6 snails
1 tablespoon chopped parsley

1 tablespoon chopped hazelnuts
Basic omelet for 1 person
(p. 48)
1 tablespoon butter

Make the snail marinade and marinate the snails overnight. Reheat the snails in the marinade. Drain the snails and mix them with the parsley and hazelnuts. Beat the omelet mixture, and cook the omelet. Fill with snails and rub with the butter. Serve without delay.

A MILLIONAIRE'S OMELET
2 SERVINGS

Look what happened to our humble little omelet! This version is very expensive but worth the effort.

½ cup Madeira sauce (p. 118)	1½ ounces goose liver pâté
3 tablespoons heavy cream,	(foie gras)
whipped	1 small sweetbread, sautéed
1 tablespoon Cognac	Basic omelet for 2 persons
2 small truffles, peeled	(p. 48)

Bring sauce to a boil and reduce to ¼ cup. Add whipped cream and Cognac. Cut truffles, *foie gras* and sweetbread into fine dice and mix into sauce. Beat omelet mixture, cook the omelet, fill, and fold. This omelet deserves an excellent French Bordeaux wine.

The Madeira sauce may be replaced by 3 tablespoons meat glaze mixed with 1 tablespoon Madeira. If no meat glaze is available, avoid commercial meat extract; instead simply deglaze with Madeira the pan in which you sautéed the sweetbread, and mix the deglazing with the cream.

CREAMED SALMON OMELET
2 SERVINGS

Inspired by a lovely brunch at the Beverly Hills Hotel.

⅔ cup heavy cream	Pepper
4 slices of smoked Nova Scotia	Basic omelet for 2 persons
salmon, chopped	(p. 48)
1 teaspoon Beluga caviar	
(optional)	

Reduce heavy cream over low heat to ¼ cup; let cool. Stir the chopped salmon and the caviar into the cream; these ingredients should not cook. Season the mixture with pepper to taste. Beat the omelet mixture and cook two omelets. Fill each with half of the prepared mixture and fold. Serve with a good glass of California Pinot Chardonnay or a French Meursault.

USING EGG FOAMS

Earlier in this chapter you read something about the foaming capacity of egg protein. Bringing the egg to a foaming state, stabilizing egg foams, and using egg foams call for special techniques.

SEPARATING EGGS
Egg yolks and whites are used separately to achieve different purposes. With your right hand crack the shell and quickly drop the whole egg into the hollow of your left hand. Let the white run out into a bowl. Pinch the ligaments on either side of the yolk between your fingers and drop the yolk into another bowl. Try not to break the yolks; any loss of yolk means loss of volume for the dish prepared.

This is not the only way to separate an egg, but when you get used to it you will find it the quickest and easiest way. The familiar method of passing the yolk from one half shell to the other can be used, but I do not recommend it. When the eggs are at room temperature (see p. 38), the shell can easily pierce the yolk, thus letting yolk and white mix. An egg separator can also be used.

As for the ligaments, the chalazas, it does not matter whether they are left in the white or not; they are pulverized by the electric mixer or by the hand beater.

RIBBON
In recipes you will often find the instruction to "beat yolks and sugar until thick and lemon-colored." This direction is misleading; it would be more specific to have: "beat the egg yolks and sugar until they form a ribbon."

To make a ribbon is to combine the capacity of the yolks to foam and trap air when submitted to mechanical action, with the capacity of sugar for attracting moisture. The beater introduces air into the egg protein at the same time that the sugar absorbs the moisture contained in the yolk, thus forming a syrup. The result is a light yellow, bulky, sticky mixture in which the air remains trapped within protein walls that keep expanding as the beating goes on. When the beating stops, the mixture falls from the beater(s) into the bowl in a long flat band that folds upon itself as a silk ribbon would if dropped onto a table. A "ribbon" is never straight.

Add the sugar slowly and in regular small additions if you mix by hand or rotary hand beater. If you use a modern electric mixer, you may add the total amount of sugar at once in one slow steady stream. The power of the motor will break down the mixture quickly and effortlessly.

If you ribbon too long and about half to two thirds of the sugar has turned to syrup, with no moisture left to dissolve the remainder of the sugar, the mixture turns granular. To prevent this happening, a recipe often directs to add 1 tablespoon water to the ribboning mixture.

Ribboning insures an even dispersion of the lightened yolks through the whole batter; the air enclosed in the yolk protein dilates as soon as reached by the oven heat. Without that air, the heavy yolk bears down on a batter and coagulates too fast. A cake made with a yolk mixture that has not been ribboned has a definite taste of hard-cooked egg yolk and does not rise as it should.

Use a ribboned mixture immediately, or the protein walls will collapse, the air will escape into the atmosphere, and only a deep yellow mixture of protein and water will be left. Although this will re-form a ribbon when beaten again, a considerable amount of air is lost.

Whole eggs and sugar can also be ribboned; see Génoise (pp. 444–45); read the instructions in that recipe very carefully.

If the recipe directs to "ribbon," do not beat longer than that or you will reach the "peak" stage and have a "cotton-textured" cake.

BEATING EGG WHITES

Egg whites will acquire a better volume if they have reached room temperature when you beat them, because their proteins will expand more rapidly. Make sure that the whites do not contain the slightest trace of egg yolk and that the beating bowl is free of fat and moisture. Fat emulsifies in the water contained in the egg whites, softens the proteins and weighs them down; as a result there is little foaming and no increase in volume. A film of water on the inside of a metal bowl prevents development of static electricity (a foam-furthering agent) between beaters and bowl. Add an acid (cream of tartar) to the whites to stabilize the foam and a pinch of salt to firm up the proteins.

BEATING WHITES WITH A COPPER BOWL AND WHISK

Beating egg whites by hand produces one third more volume of foam but is only worth the effort if the correct instruments are at hand: a 10-inch unlined copper bowl and an 18- to 20-inch-long whisk with a 3½- to 5-inch balloon wire.

Rub the inside of the bowl and the whisk with pure vinegar for more acidity. Dry them with paper towels exclusively. Start beating the whites the minute they are in contact with the bowl; if they must wait, let them do so in a china bowl. With your wrist or elbow, beat without interruption slowly for 45 seconds. It will break the albumen and produce large air pockets. Add the pinch of salt. You need no other acids than the vinegar already used to rub the bowl. Continue beating for 3½ minutes at 250 strokes per minute to break the air pockets and multiply the air bubbles. Add 1 tablespoon sugar for each 4 egg whites if needed (p. 61) and continue beating until the eggs are about seven times their original volume. Finally, give the whisk six good turns around the bowl, scraping well against the sides. This procedure, called *forcer* in French culinary jargon, homogenizes the foam by forcing out possible large pockets of air.

BEATING EGG WHITES WITH AN ELECTRIC MIXER

With a large standard mixer, run a spatula along the edges of the bowl to push the whites back into the mixer blades. This keeps the centrifugal force generated by the beaters from throwing too much air out of the whites and whipping them too hard at the center of the bowl and too soft around the edges.

With an electric hand mixer, turn the mixing bowl from left to right as you beat and keep moving the beaters up and down the sides of the bowl to make sure that the whole bulk of whites is constantly kept in movement. For each 4 egg whites, use ¼ teaspoon cream of tartar as acid, a pinch of salt before stage II, and 1 tablespoon sugar before stage III if needed (see p. 60).

Mixer Type	Add	Beat Stage I	Add	Beat Stage II	Add	Beat Stage III
Mixmaster	salt	1 minute, speed 2	acid	2½ minutes, speed 9	sugar	30 seconds, speed 11
Kitchen-Aid	salt	1 to 4 whites, 1 minute, speed 3	acid	3 minutes, speed 8	sugar	15 seconds, speed 8
		5 whites & more, 2 mintues, speed 3	acid	3 to 4 minutes, speed 6	sugar	15 seconds, speed 6
Electric hand mixers	salt	2 minutes, medium speed	acid	2 minutes, high speed	sugar	30 seconds, high speed

SUGAR WITH EGG WHITES

Add sugar before the last stage of beating, the time when the egg foam is most susceptible to separation, only if needed, that is, if any water starts exuding from the proteins. The sugar will mix with the water to form a syrup viscous enough to rehomogenize and restabilize the foam. Never use sugar for savory soufflés.

Whether beaten by hand or by mixer, the whites are firm enough when:

- ✤ an uncooked egg in its shell sinks only ¼ inch deep in the foam;
- ✤ the foam does not slide down when the bowl is turned upside down;
- ✤ the foam retains the trace of a knife or a spatula;
- ✤ the foam forms a *toupe,* a tuft, on the beaters when they are withdrawn from the bowl.

A foam is overbeaten if an egg sits on top of it without sinking.

FOLDING

Folding is the procedure used to incorporate egg foams into batters or dry ingredients into egg foams. When you fold, the heavier ingredient must be at the bottom of the bowl.

To incorporate a foam, mix first about one fourth to one third of the total volume of the foam into the heavier mixture—the batter— to lighten it and bring its consistency closer to that of the foam. Put the remainder of the egg whites on top of the batter. With a large spatula, cut through whites and batter at the center of the bowl and down to its bottom. Lift up the batter and turn your wrist to deposit it on top of the foam. Meanwhile turn the bowl from left to right with your left hand. Continue folding until no traces of foam are left. *Be fast.* The batter should remain pale yellow and light with no traces of large air bubbles. Never fold from one edge of the bowl to the other; the batter will liquefy, and the preparation will be heavy. Never turn the handle of the spatula in your hand, and never let the spatula rest on the batter; you will lose an appreciable amount of air.

To incorporate dry ingredients into an egg foam, divide their total volume into three or four equal parts. Sprinkle one part on top of the egg foam and fold until completely incorporated; repeat until all the dry ingredient has been incorporated.

FLOURLESS EGG SAUCES AND STIRRED CUSTARDS

These sauces are called "custards" and they are related to hollandaise in the sense that they make use of the coagulating and foaming capacities of egg yolks. They contain no butter, and the liquid used to make them is either milk, wine or a fruit juice. They can be used as thick dessert sauces, or they can be used as desserts, especially if they are stabilized with gelatin.

ENGLISH OR STIRRED CUSTARD (*Crème Anglaise*)

The principle of stirred custard is that of poaching egg yolks in scalded milk or cream. Here is the way to a perfect custard without trauma or trepidation. Have a wooden spoon and whisk at hand and, if you wish, a candy thermometer.

4 egg yolks	*1 cup scalded milk*
¼ cup sugar	*1 teaspoon vanilla extract*
¼ teaspoon salt	

In a saucepan mix egg yolks, sugar and salt well with a wire whisk, but *do not ribbon*. The reason for not ribboning is that you must avoid the development of a large amount of foam. If there is too much foam at the surface of the custard, the novice cook will be unable to control the cooking, for there is not time for the foam to be absorbed by the time the custard reaches 165°F. If the cooking is continued past this point, the mixture will curdle. By simply mixing the egg yolks and sugar, you will quickly obtain a silky mixture. Lift the wire whisk about 2 inches above the surface of the mixture and you will see that it forms a very short and breaking stream, not a smooth and continuous ribbon. The egg yolks and sugar are now mixed enough so that the yolks will not curdle on contact with the hot milk. Also the foam layer is thin enough so that it will be absorbed by the time the mixture reaches a temperature of 165° to 170°F. This could be called "ribboning lightly." Very slowly add the hot milk, stirring well. Insert the thermometer in the custard at the side of the pan. Notice the thick layer of foam. With a spoon, stir *without stopping* over medium-high heat. At 140°F. on the thermometer steam starts rising from the pan. At 155° F. the foam starts lightening, and gradually the millions of tiny air bubbles consolidate into larger ones. At 165°F. the surface of the custard is smooth, and the custard is ready. Remove the pan from the heat and only now whisk the custard as strongly as possible to cool it and stop the poaching. Add vanilla, or other chosen flavoring.

The custard may safely heat up to 180°F. but not above. The total cooking time is 3 to 4 minutes. Strain into a bowl and stir at regular intervals to prevent formation of a skin.

Remember, while cooking a stirred custard do not whisk the sauce violently or you will continue producing foam and you will have no control over the various stages of the cooking. Instead stir it with a wooden spoon.

Do not use cornstarch for stirred custard; it is only a useless crutch.

Stirred custard can be made in different thicknesses, by using only 2 or 3 egg yolks per cup of milk. Make it thin if you use it to soak a cake, and keep it thick and rich as the base of a Bavarian cream (p. 496). You may at any time replace the milk by light or heavy cream as in the gorgeous *crème brûlée* so well liked at Monticello.

The following variations can be used with the basic recipe:

Liqueurs　Add 2 tablespoons of the liqueur of your choice after cooking.

Citrus Fruits　Infuse 1 tablespoon fine-grated lemon, lime, orange, tangerine or grapefruit rind in the milk before making the cream; or use extracts.

Coffee　Add 1½ teaspoons, or more to taste, of a good instant coffee powder to the scalded milk before making the custard.

Chocolate　Mix 2½ tablespoons powdered cocoa with the sugar and stir with the egg yolks; make the custard as usual.

Praline　Replace half of the sugar by Praline Powder (p. 23).

Almond　Replace milk by Almond Milk (p. 22); make custard as usual.

Butterscotch　Replace sugar by dark brown sugar.

To Stabilize Stirred Custard

You will see recipes instructing you to add gelatin to a stirred custard. This is how to proceed. Use ½ envelope unflavored gelatin for the proportions of custard given above. Melt the gelatin in 2 tablespoons water in a double boiler. Add to the custard when you have removed it from the heat. As you whisk the mixture to cool it, the gelatin will be completely mixed with the custard. Stabilized stirred custard is known in culinary jargon as *crème anglaise collée*.

Here are two variations on the French *oeufs à la neige*. In these recipes an egg-white foam is used to make meringue "eggs," which float on a custard made from an egg-yolk foam.

EGGS TIA MARIA
6 SERVINGS

6 eggs	*1 ½ cups scalded milk*
9 tablespoons sugar	*1 to 3 tablespoons Tia Maria*
Salt	*(coffee liqueur)*
1 ½ teaspoons instant coffee	*1 teaspoon powdered cocoa*
powder	

Separate the eggs. Ribbon lightly (see p. 62) egg yolks, 6 tablespoons sugar, ¼ teaspoon salt and the instant coffee powder. Be sure to avoid formation of an excessive amount of foam. Add the scalded milk. Make the custard over medium heat; add Tia Maria to taste. Cool, strain into a crystal dish, and cool completely.

Bring 2 quarts water to boil in a 10-inch skillet. Beat the egg whites with a pinch of salt, adding the remaining 3 tablespoons sugar little by little while beating. Beat them until the egg-white foam can hold a raw egg in its shell. With 2 large serving spoons shape the meringue into 6 large "eggs." Drop the eggs into the simmering water and poach for 2 minutes on each side. If the skillet will not hold all the eggs, shape them a few at a time. Rebeat the egg whites lightly if necessary before shaping and cooking the next batch of "eggs." Drain the cooked eggs on a clean towel, then pile them in a pyramid on the custard. Chill thoroughly. Sprinkle with powdered cocoa and serve.

EGGS PRALINE
6 SERVINGS

6 eggs	7 tablespoons praline powder
4 tablespoons sugar	2 ½ tablespoons powdered cocoa
Salt	2 teaspoons vanilla extract
1 ¾ cups scalded milk	1 to 2 tablespoons rum

Separate the eggs. Ribbon lightly (see p. 62) egg yolks, sugar and ¼ teaspoon salt. Add the scalded milk, 3 tablespoons of the praline powder and 2 tablespoons of the powdered cocoa. Make the custard over medium heat. Remove from the heat and add the vanilla and rum to taste. Cool, and strain into a crystal dish.

Bring 2 quarts water to boil in a 10-inch skillet. Beat the egg whites with a pinch of salt, adding the remaining 4 tablespoons praline powder little by little while beating. Shape the meringue eggs and poach them as for eggs Tia Maria. Drain them, arrange on the custard, and sprinkle with the rest of the cocoa.

MOLDED SCARLET CUSTARD
6 SERVINGS

A favorite with the young fry.

1 tablespoon fine-grated lemon rind	¼ teaspoon salt
1 ½ cups scalded milk	2 teaspoons unflavored gelatin
6 egg yolks	Raspberry sauce (p. 384)
6 tablespoons sugar	

Infuse the lemon rind in the scalded milk. Make a custard with the egg yolks, sugar, salt and milk. Melt the gelatin and add to the custard.

Cool. Strain the custard into a buttered 4-cup Charlotte mold. Chill. Unmold on a plate and cover completely with raspberry sauce.

ZABAGLIONE OR WINE-BASED CUSTARD

Zabaglione is truly Italian, but it has been imitated the world over. The variations are multiple. *Zabaglione* can be a sauce or a custard dessert. In Italy it is always served warm—foamy, ethereal and flavored with the great Italian Marsala vergini (dry). But many a cook has brought his grain of salt to *zabaglione* so that now it comes in all flavors and is served either warm or cold. When prepared for chilling, it must be stabilized with gelatin (½ teaspoon for each 4 egg yolks) to avoid separation in the refrigerator. Some *zabaglione* recipes are so similar to recipes for mousses that it is difficult to see a difference.

It is not absolutely necessary to own one of those lovely Italian pans with a round bottom in which the whisk can turn and spin without encountering the angles it would in an ordinary pot. But if you are fortunate enough to own such a pan, use it over a bath of simmering water. The bottom of the pan must be 2 inches above the surface of the water; the pan is heated only by the steam. If you do not own a *zabaglione* pan, an enameled cast-iron pan will do very well, and with this you can work directly on a very low burner. The *zabaglione* will be slightly thicker.

CLASSIC ZABAGLIONE

8 egg yolks   *½ cup Marsala vergini or solera*
½ cup sugar   *(dry)*

Ribbon the yolks and sugar heavily. Place the pan over the source of heat (steam or low burner). While continuing to beat, slowly add Marsala. Continue beating until the mixture is thick, foamy, and spinning a fat ribbon. The temperature of the custard should be 165°F. Pour into sherbet glasses and serve immediately; it should be lukewarm.

VARIATIONS

These variations are all designed for the basic recipe based on 8 egg yolks. The technique is the same. Whip any liqueur into the finished sauce when it is off the heat to retain the alcohol.

Almond ½ cup sugar, ½ cup almond milk, 1 to 2 ounces almond liqueur to taste.

Coffee ⅔ cup sugar, ½ cup prepared coffee, 2 teaspoons good instant coffee powder, 1 to 2 ounces Tia Maria or Kahlúa to taste.

Chocolate 6 tablespoons powdered cocoa, ⅔ cup sugar, ⅔ cup scalded light cream, 1 to 2 ounces crème de cacao, rum or Grand Marnier to taste.

Citrus fruits For all citrus flavors, remove 1 tablespoon sugar from the total amount. Mash that sugar together with citrus rind until the sugar has acquired the color of the rind. Dissolve the sugar in a mixture of citrus juice and wine and let steep for 2 hours; strain. Make the *zabaglione* as usual with the egg yolks, remainder of the sugar and the flavored juice-wine mixture.

Orange and tangerine ⅔ cup sugar, 1 tablespoon fine-grated orange or tangerine rind, ¼ cup each of orange juice and sweet Madeira, 1 to 2 ounces Grand Marnier, Curaçao or Triple Sec to taste.

Lemon or lime 1 cup sugar, 1 tablespoon fine-grated rind, 6 tablespoons white wine, 2 to 3 tablespoons lemon or lime juice to taste, 1 to 2 ounces rum to taste.

Grapefruit Use pink grapefruit preferably. 4 teaspoons grated rind, ⅔ cup sugar, ¼ cup white wine, 6 tablespoons grapefruit juice, 1 ounce rum.

FRAU PELIZAEUS WEINSAUCE
6 SERVINGS

A recipe from a dear friend in Germany. Use preferably Spätlese Moselle or Rhine wine. Lemon juice and rinds as well are often used in Germany.

4 whole eggs	*¾ cup sugar*
4 egg yolks	*1½ cups Rhine or Moselle wine*

Ribbon whole eggs, egg yolks and sugar with an electric mixer. Place over low heat and gradually add the wine. Continue beating until the mixture is thick and feels warm to the finger (165°F.). Pour into sherbet glasses; serve warm or chilled.

MUSCATEL SABAYON

You may use any sweet white wine you like; the recipe was first made with a leftover Château d'Yquem 1962.

6 egg yolks	¾ teaspoon unflavored gelatin,
½ cup sugar	melted
1¼ cups Muscatel or other sweet	1 ounce Cognac or brandy
white wine	

Ribbon yolks and sugar; thicken over heat. Gradually add wine and continue beating until the mixture feels warm to the finger (165°F.). Add melted gelatin. Remove from the heat and add the liqueur. Transfer to a bowl placed over ice and beat until cold; turn into sherbet glasses and chill.

CREAM PORT SABAYON
6 SERVINGS

This is almost a mousse; compare with mousse recipes in Chapter XIV.

2 whole eggs	1 teaspoon unflavored gelatin,
5 egg yolks	melted
½ cup sugar	1 ounce Maraschino
1 cup ruby or cream port	¾ cup heavy cream, whipped

Ribbon whole eggs, egg yolks and sugar; gradually add the port and beat until the mixture feels warm to the finger (165°F.). Add melted gelatin, remove from the heat, and blend in the Maraschino.

Transfer to a bowl over ice and beat until cold. Fold in the whipped cream and turn into sherbet glasses. Chill.

Eggs are used for another type of custard, the baked custard. For an explanation of this, see Chapter XIV. Eggs are the critical ingredient in soufflés, and these too are dealt with in Chapter XIV.

IV

Happy Marriages

stocks and soups

SOMETHING TERRIBLE happened to onion soup after it crossed the ocean and came to America. Unless we cooks hurry and do something about it, the taste of this famous dish will be lost forever.

It is believed that this soup was created by Louis XV from a flat bottle of Champagne and a few onions on an occasion when he came back famished from a gay night in 18th-century Paris. Over the last century *la soupe à l'oignon* became the specialty of all the bistrots and cafés around les Halles, the old central markets of Paris. This is the recipe for the soup served nowadays at restaurants in the market complex, although now they have moved to the outskirts of Paris; it is easy, authentic, and well worth the valley of tears brought on by those onions.

SOUPE À L'OIGNON COMME AUX HALLES
6 SERVINGS

4 tablespoons butter *6 slices of French bread*
6 large onions, sliced *6 tablespoons grated Gruyère*
7 cups cold water *cheese*
Salt and pepper

Heat the butter and sauté the onions in it slowly until brown. Cover onions with the water, bring slowly to a boil, and simmer uncovered for 45 minutes, or until the liquid is reduced to 6 cups. Season to taste.

Pour an equal amount of soup into 6 fireproof casseroles, and set casseroles in a broiler pan. Float 1 slice of bread on top of the soup in each casserole and quickly sprinkle with cheese. Broil for 2 minutes and serve piping hot.

Try adding 3 or 4 bouillon cubes to your onion soup; it will taste better. Try making the soup with canned beef or chicken broth, or a combination of both instead of water, and it will still taste still better; but you will immediately notice that no additional salt is necessary, since the broth used was already strongly salted at the cannery.

By covering the onions with water and simmering both together, you have made a broth or stock. In *Le Guide Culinaire* (Flammarion, 1927), the great French master Auguste Escoffier says, "Stocks are the fundamental basis, the elements of first necessity without which nothing can be accomplished . . . the most skilled worker in the world cannot accomplish something with nothing. It would be arbitrary to exact from him accomplished work if he is given insufficient or low quality ingredients with which to perform. . . ." In other words, food is as good as the basic ingredients used to prepare it. Stocks are a basic ingredient for all sorts of other preparations, but especially for soups and sauces. They are in a sense the "base of the pyramid" of good cookery. They include such simple stocks or broths as the one you have made with water and onions and such complicated stocks as brown meat stock.

QUICK BROTH
Different types of packaged products can be used to make a quick broth.

I. Dry meat and vegetable extracts like *bouillon cubes* or *granules;* these are best dissolved according to the package directions.

II. Semisolid *meat extracts* sold in jars; these are commercially made stocks partially dried and concentrated by slow cooking or by vacuum processing. They contain concentrated proteins of meats and vegetables and are highly salted for preservation. They can be a boon in household kitchens. When carefully diluted with water, they can replace freshly made stock for the cook-in-a-hurry. How much extract should be used is entirely up to the cook's taste; some cooks use as much as 1 teaspoon extract per 1 cup liquid; I use barely ½ teaspoon. A typical example of overgenerous use of meat extract can be found in almost any average American restaurant, where the onion soup is oversalted and burns the throat. Whatever the commercial product chosen, great care must be taken that the pungent taste of the extract cannot be detected in the finished dish. This requires a bit of personal experimentation.

III. Although they contain too much salt, celery and monosodium glutamate, *canned stocks* are not bad for certain dishes. For onion soup, for example, canned stock serves well because the characteristic taste of the onions takes over that of the stock. *Crème sénégalaise,* curried pea soup, may also be made successfully with canned broth, for what other spice could hold its own against curry? But when a subtle white sauce is involved, canned broth gives results that are truly short of perfection. To be used in fine sauces, brown or white, canned stocks have to be upgraded by being mixed with unsalted vegetable broth in the proportions of 1½ cups vegetable broth for each 10½-ounce can of condensed stock.

The following vegetable broth recipe may be multiplied by two, four, six, etc. It is the famous *bouillon de légumes,* French nectar of health, cure for all the French overwined and overdined livers.

VEGETABLE BROTH

2 QUARTS

2 *carrots*	2 *tablespoons butter*
2 *onions*	10 *cups cold water*
4 *scallions, green and white parts*	*Small* bouquet garni
4 *leeks, green and white parts*	NO SALT
1 *celery rib*	NO PEPPER

Peel and slice all vegetables. Sauté them in the butter until soft. Cover them with the water, bring slowly to a boil, skim well, and add the *bouquet garni.* Simmer for 2 hours, or until the volume of liquid is reduced to 8 cups. Strain through a conical strainer lined with cheese-cloth.

Store in refrigerator, or freeze in 1½-cup Mason jars.

Vegetable broth is considerably easier to prepare than a meat stock. However, in the well-equipped American kitchen, it is to the advantage of the serious cook to make his own stock. Since making fresh stock every week would be extremely time-consuming, consider in-stead three stock-making sessions a year at four-month intervals, which will concentrate time and work. Pull out your soup kettle, make your stocks, and freeze them in Mason jars. The jars should be labeled with freezer tape showing the date at which the contents have been frozen (brown stock, January 1970). In a reliable freezer, stocks frozen in properly sealed containers will keep for 4 to 6 months with-out losing too much flavor.

Stocks are made with nutritive elements: the meats; with season-ings: salt and pepper; with aromatic elements: the vegetables and herbs; and water. The most important elements are, of course, the meats.

Meats are made of muscle fibers surrounded and held together by connective tissues. Two different types of connective tissues exist. The most important for the cook is *collagen,* which is white, mostly thin, but thicker when surrounding a' muscle. Collagen has the capacity of hydrolizing, *i.e.,* liquefying, when submitted to heat. When collagen hydrolizes, gelatin is released. The second connective tissue, called *elastin,* has very little interest for the cook, since it has no hydrolizing capacity and remains rubberlike even after long cooking. When meats are immersed in water, various products are released in the water and form the stock. A few proteins and enzymes are freed by the cold water. As the water is slowly brought to a boil and a long simmering follows, a larger amount of protein is released together with vitamins, fats, the gelatin produced by the liquefied collagen, mineral salts and a few substances called extractives (lactic and amino acids).

Similarly, while cooking, vegetables and spices release such ele-ments as pectin, starches, acids (citric, tartaric and oxalic) and sulfur compounds, which help to give the stock taste, flavor and aroma.

WHITE STOCK
5 QUARTS

White stock is made exclusively with unbrowned white meats. It looks white and opaque and is used in soups, white stews and white sauces. For the veal used in stock, you may purchase cheaper, less tender cuts.

For the giblets, use only gizzards and hearts—no livers, for they muddy the stock. This is an all-purpose white stock. Pure chicken stock may be made with a stewing hen and pure veal stock with exclusively veal meat.

5 *pounds veal*	4 *scallions*
4 *pounds chicken carcasses*	1 *very small white turnip*
1 *large veal knuckle, sawed into*	6 *large leeks*
4 *pieces*	2 *celery ribs*
A *few giblets*	1 *tablespoon salt*
6 *quarts cold water*	*Large* bouquet garni
6 *carrots*	6 *white peppercorns*
3 *large onions*	

Barely cover meats and bones with lukewarm water. Quickly bring to a boil and discard the water. This "blanching" cleans the meats and reduces the amount of scum. Rinse meats and bones well.

Return the meats to the stock pot and cover with the cold water. Bring slowly to a boil, and skim carefully. Add vegetables, salt and *bouquet garni,* and skim again. Simmer for 6 to 8 hours. As evaporation brings down the level of the stock, add more boiling water. During the last hour of cooking, add the peppercorns. Line a strainer with cheesecloth and strain the stock into large bowls. Cool at room temperature; refrigerate overnight.

The vegetables and meats other than the veal knuckle will be soft and mushy and should be discarded. However, since it takes at least 12 hours for the gelatin contained in cartilages and bones to dissolve completely in a simmering stock, do not discard the veal knuckle. These pieces can be reused; freeze them unless you plan to use them again at once.

The next day, lift off and discard the layer of hardened fat on the surface of the stock. Store the stock in Mason jars and freeze. *Immediate reboiling after defrosting is a must.*

BROWN STOCK
5 QUARTS

Brown stock is made with red meats roasted in the oven before being immersed in water. The sapid meat juices, which have caramelized and browned around the pieces of meat, dissolve in the cold water and give the stock its characteristic brown color.

6 pounds beef shin with bones	*1 ham rind, well scraped of all*
5 pounds veal shank or other	*fat (optional)*
low-priced cuts	*6 quarts cold water*
6 carrots	*4 scallions*
3 large onions	*1 very small white turnip*
6 cloves (2 stuck in each onion)	*6 large leeks*
1 veal knuckle, sawed into 4	*2 celery ribs*
pieces	*1 tablespoon salt*
	Large bouquet garni

Preheat oven to 400°F. Roast the beef and veal meats and the carrots and onions for about 40 minutes. Blanch the veal knuckle if used for the first time. Put bones, meats and ham rind if used in a stock kettle. Cover with the water and bring to a boil. Dissolve all the meat juices caramelized at the bottom of the roasting pan with hot water and add to the kettle. Skim. Add the vegetables and skim again. Add the salt and *bouquet garni.* Simmer for 6 to 8 hours. As evaporation brings down the level of the stock, add more boiling water. Strain the stock into bowls. If the stock is not brown enough, the meat was not browned enough. Correct the situation by coloring artificially with a small amount of commercial coloring. Refrigerate overnight, defatten, and freeze. *Immediate reboiling after defrosting is a must.*

STOCK IN A HURRY

1 QUART

Suppose you would like to make stock, but for one reason or another, it is just too time-consuming for you. Here is a recipe for stock in a hurry—1½ hours from start to finish!

3 cups chopped or ground lean meat (chicken or veal for white stock, beef for brown stock)	2 large onions
	2 cloves
	2 large leeks
	Small bouquet garni
5 cups cold water	1 teaspoon salt
2 carrots	3 peppercorns

Cover the meat with the water. Bring to a boil very slowly, and add the vegetables and seasonings. Skim, and simmer for 1 hour. Strain carefully. The stock is ready to use. Color beef stock artificially.

Stocks may be made with all kinds of meats such as the giblets of ducks, game birds and venison, but pork should never be used except for pork rinds, which are used for the gelatin content. Lamb must never be used in an all-purpose stock; its strong flavor would dominate that of the other ingredients.

MEAT GLAZE

What if you make stock, a lot of it, and have no freezer to store it? Defatten the stock carefully and boil it down until it becomes very sticky and heavily coats the back of a spoon. The end product is *glace de viande,* or meat glaze, which can be stored in 4-ounce baby-food jars in the refrigerator.

To make 4 ounces of meat glaze, 1 full quart of stock is needed. You may boil rapidly at the beginning and must skim often, but remember to slow down the heat toward the end of the cooking when the glaze becomes thicker and very prone to burn. Canned stocks are not rich enough in gelatin and are too salty to produce good meat glaze.

Meat glaze is used to reinforce the taste of sauces or as a base for butter sauces. Reconstituted in the proportions of 4 ounces (½ cup) glaze to 3½ cups water, it becomes stock again. As a reinforcement agent, it may be replaced by commercial semisolid meat extracts (p. 74). For each 2 tablespoons of homemade meat glaze, ¼ teaspoon of commercial extract should be used. No, my hand is not light; more extract results in a salty and pungent sauce lacking finesse.

Meat glaze need not be frozen; should it mold superficially, lift the mold spots with a spoon and reboil the glaze for 5 minutes. The glaze will be as good as new.

Jus

If you find it all too complicated to have to make both white and brown stocks and are tempted to use canned products, try another type of stock called *jus*. *Jus* can be made with any type of meat—fowl, veal, beef—or a mixture of all. The most useful of all is the *jus de veau,* or brown veal stock. Its flavor is such that used alone, it tastes frankly like veal. Used with chicken, it acquires a definite chicken flavor; used with beef, it becomes very rich and beefy. If I had to recommend making one type of stock, *jus* is the one I would choose. If packers of canned soup should one day market a concentrated pure veal stock with a solid list of instructions on how to use it, the level of taste of most dishes produced in the United States would improve considerably.

BROWN VEAL STOCK (*jus de veau*)
5 QUARTS

For this stock, keep all bones and pieces of veal trimmed from roasts or chops. The stock freezes well. Use a thick braising pot.

5 pounds veal shank	*4 carrots*
2 to 3 pounds veal trimmings and bones	*3 large onions*
	1 large leek

2 tablespoons butter	*1 tablespoon salt*
2 cups white wine	*1 large* bouquet garni
6 quarts warm water	

Brown the meats in the oven, and brown the vegetables in butter on top of the stove. Put vegetables and meats in a braising pot. Cover the pot and place over very low heat without disturbing for 20 to 25 minutes. Remove the lid and add ⅔ cup of the wine. Raise the heat very high and let the stock evaporate until the meat juices at the bottom of the pot brown and caramelize. Perform the same operation, each time using ⅔ cup of the wine, twice more. Cover the meats with the *warm* water and bring to a boil. Add the salt and *bouquet garni.* Simmer for 5 to 6 hours. Strain and let cool at room temperature. Refrigerate, defatten, and freeze.

Notice how different the technique of making *jus* is from that of making stock. When the pot is covered and slowly heated, steam rises from the meats, condenses on the lid, and falls back on them; the moist and warm atmosphere causes a shrinkage of their outside layers and the opening of large canals between the fibers, through which considerable amounts of melted collagen escape to the bottom of the pot. Adding the wine helps precipitate the juices still surrounding the meats and also reinforces the flavor of the stock. The successive evaporations and caramelizations deepen the color of the stock. This procedure of browning, called "pinching" in culinary jargon, should not be pushed to the point where the onions start burning or the stock will turn bitter. The caramelization happens faster in a thick pot.

Reduced brown veal stock produces a very rich thick meat glaze with the same keeping qualities as any other meat glaze. Each quart of veal stock produces 1 cup of meat glaze. Inversely, 1 cup veal meat glaze mixed with 3 cups water will give 1 quart stock ready to use.

Fish Fumet

A *fumet* is a very concentrated stock that may be made with poultry, game, or fish. It is interesting to note that *fumet* in French also means the strong, pleasant, characteristic smell of a particular food.

When you first make fish *fumet,* you will understand why the name *fumet* is given to fish stock; the smell is robust and, contrary to what could be expected, quite pleasant. Fish *fumet* is made with either white or red wine. A dish often bears the name of the wine used in making the *fumet,* for example, *sole au Chablis.*

The best *fumet* is made with flounder, fluke, sole and whiting heads and bones. Skins give a gray tinge to the stock. Celery and bay leaf may be used only in limited amounts due to their pungency. Only top-quality wine should be used, or the *fumet* will look grayish. New York State Labrusca wines and vermouth are not recommended for *fumet*; *fumet* tastes better when made only with water than it does when prepared with cheap wine. To cook *fumet,* use only an enamel-ware or stainless-steel pot. Do not use aluminum, for the relatively large amount of acid contained in the wine combines with aluminum to produce a dark stock.

Fish is high in water, collagen, gelatin, calcium and phosphorus. With the help of the acid in the wine, the collagen, contrary to that of meats, dissolves very rapidly in liquid, so that compared to other stocks fish *fumet* is very quickly done.

Once fish *fumet* has reached the boiling point, do not let it boil too violently, or it will look muddy; do not let it cook beyond 30 to 35 minutes, or it will acquire a pronounced taste of fish bones; 35 minutes of well-regulated simmering over medium heat are sufficient to extract all the flavor out of the fish. If the *fumet* is too thin, strain it and reduce it to the strength you desire. Do not skimp on the amount of bones used, since the quality of the *fumet* depends on it.

Fish *fumet* should not be stored for more than 3 days without re-boiling. It freezes very well; since only 2 cups are needed to make a dish for 6 persons, freeze any excess in Mason jars. *Immediate reboiling after defrosting is a must.*

Fish *fumet* may be replaced by bottled clam juice, but the sauce obtained is not as rich and the salting of the dish is more delicate to judge. If you are tempted to use too much clam juice, remember that it costs the same amount as 1 cup of decent California wine. However, clam juice remains a boon in areas where fish bones are nowhere to be found.

WHITE-WINE FISH FUMET
1½ TO 2 QUARTS

1 large onion, sliced
½ very small carrot, sliced
1 tablespoon butter
½ cup mushroom stems and
  pieces
4 pounds fish heads and bones

2 cups good dry white wine
8 cups water
Very small bouquet garni
½ teaspoon salt
6 white peppercorns

Sauté onion and carrot in the butter, then add mushrooms and fish bones. Cover the pot and let cook over very low heat for 15 minutes, or until fish bones fall apart. Add wine and water and bring briskly to a boil. Add *bouquet garni* and salt. Cook over medium heat for 30 to 35 minutes. Add peppercorns during the last 10 minutes of cooking. Strain.

RED-WINE FISH FUMET
2 QUARTS

Red wine is less acid than white wine, so that a larger amount of red wine is needed to give an equivalent taste to the stock. Proceed exactly as for white-wine fish *fumet.*

2 small onions, sliced
½ small carrot, sliced
1 small garlic clove
2 tablespoons butter
¼ cup mushroom stems and
  pieces
4 pounds fish bones and heads

4 cups dry red wine
8 cups water
Large bunch of parsley
Pinch of dried thyme
½ bay leaf
½ teaspoon salt

FISH GLAZE
Fish glaze can be made following the same method as for meat glaze. Fish glaze, however, is highly perishable and must be reboiled twice a week.

While in our practical America a soup is a soup—sometimes a bisque or a chowder—I can offhand think of fifteen different words for soup in French. They all make sense for Frenchmen, since I have yet to meet one, wealthy or not, who has not been "raised" on soup.

A soup was originally a broth or a *coulis* (broth plus purée of meat or vegetable), thickened by pouring the liquid part of the concoction on slices of bread. The onion soup at the beginning of this chapter is the classic example. Nowadays, all denominations have become more fluid, and the name "soup" is widely used for preparations with or without bread slices.

Soup is not as ancient a nourishment as roasted or grilled meats, but it can be easily related to the discovery of pottery-making. It may even have been made before, when early man boiled water in stone-lined holes in which the water was kept boiling by immersing other stones that had been heated directly over the fire. Soups and *coulis* reached their peak of glory in the late Middle Ages; it is said that Joan of Arc subsisted on them while her companions at arms feasted on much more terrifying fare (instances of cannibalism were not rare up to the middle of the 15th century). From way back, soups have come to us from all over the world and all civilizations.

Soups are divided roughly into four categories: vegetable soups, clear or so-called clear soups, chowders and fish soups, and cream soups, all of them marriages of basic sauces and stocks with meat, fish and vegetables.

Vegetable Soups

Vegetable soups all have a more or less country origin, and it is easy to see the relationship of our American vegetable soup with the Italian *minestrone* and the French *potage paysanne*. Vegetable soups may contain anything—meat, potatoes or no potatoes, any type of vegetable; they are all made according to the age-old principle: bring water to a boil, add vegetables, and simmer for as long as you like. That's all.

The soup becomes more refined when broth or flavorful stock is used instead of water and when, just before eating, a large chunk of butter is stirred into each cup or bowl. Try it; it works, even with canned condensed soups.

CLEAR SOUPS

Truly clear or so-called clear soups are made with the stocks described in the early part of this chapter. Such soups may be served plain or with a garnish. The old favorite consommé in its original form has, during the last twenty-five years, positively vanished from home and restaurant table, to be replaced by canned and processed products. For a change from the uniform taste of the can, try making your own consommé. It does not involve as much work as you may expect.

CHOWDERS AND FISH SOUPS

There is nothing more gorgeous, more delicious and heartwarming than that lovely New England clam chowder, but I see no reason for degrading the Manhattan-type chowder. If you cross the Atlantic and find yourself in one of those small Brittany ports, you will observe that they prepare both types and call both *chaudrée*. Try to pronounce the word without trying to show off your best French accent, and you immediately find the origin of the American word "chowder."

A chowder always contains potatoes, while a fish soup is always served with slices of bread. Let imagination take over and use whatever fish or shellfish is at hand. The best base is a strong fish *fumet,* but clam juice cut with water and a little white wine will do very well. Add tomatoes or tomato sauce if you like them, and use cream to your heart's content.

Just remember that a chowder cannot go on boiling forever once the fish has been added or, evidently, the fish will fall apart. If the fish is in large chunks, give it a wild boil for 5 to 10 minutes, depending on its texture; test its doneness to be sure. If the fish is in small pieces, add it to the boiling liquid and turn off the heat; the fish will poach in the hot liquid. Add shellfish last if it is already steamed. Whenever a recipe calls for mussels or mussel juice, use the same amount of clams or clam juice if mussels cannot be located.

CREAM SOUPS

Before you start reading this section on making cream soups, read Chapter V, pages 103 to 112.

Cream soups can be purées, veloutés and creams; all of them contain a large amount of cream and are made following the same methods but with a different thickener.

PURÉE

Purées are thickened with a purée of vegetable or meat. If the vegetable is very starchy (potato, lima bean, chestnut, peas), it will adequately thicken the soup. If the vegetable starch is not strong enough to produce a good binding, another starch is used as a thickener; it may be cornstarch in modern style or rice in the old-fashioned style or even a *roux,* but it is not rare even today to find a purée thickened with bread crumbs.

For 6 servings of 6 ounces each, basic proportions are generally 1½ cups purée plus starch if necessary, 2 cups liquid, usually stock, and 1 cup or slightly more enrichment. The enrichment is cream, or cream and egg yolks.

BISQUE

A bisque used to be a purée of shellfish thickened with rice or cream of rice. It has now become more often the equivalent of a fish or shellfish cream soup.

VELOUTÉ AND CREAM

The veloutés, as their name indicates, are made with a base of velouté sauce, while the creams are made with béchamel or plain white sauce. In both cases, the proportions for 6 servings of 6 ounces each are 2½ to 3 cups velouté or béchamel sauce, 1 to 1½ cups purée, and 1 cup heavy cream. You may either use any velouté or béchamel stored in the freezer, or you may make the sauce on the spot *without skimming,* using the proportions for a thin sauce (1 tablespoon flour plus 1 tablespoon butter per cup of milk). If the consistency of your frozen sauce is medium, make the soup with 1½ cups frozen sauce, 1 cup stock, 1 to 1½ cups purée, and 1 cup heavy cream.

It is never possible to give the exact amount of stock or sauce in a purée, velouté or cream, since the vegetables of one preparation may have very different textures and consistencies from those of another. It is up to the cook to judge whether, for his taste, the soup needs additional stock to make a thinner consistency. Based on the proportions given above, the soups are rarely too thin.

The use of canned stocks for cream soups is, unless otherwise indicated, perfectly acceptable; the taste of the vegetable usually overcomes the "canned" taste. No unreasonably long simmering is necessary, and the salt concentration is diluted by the large addition of cream.

PURÉEING AND STRAINING SOUPS

For plain vegetable soups the use of a food mill is perfectly acceptable and the presence of relatively coarse pieces of vegetable is normal and, even more, pleasant to the palate, but it should be avoided for all types of cream soups. A fine cream soup should contain no trace of vegetable skins or fibers, and the purée should be very smooth.

Cream soups should be strained through a large drumlike sieve, a *tamis,* with the help of a large wooden pestle. Push the pestle from the farside rim of the *tamis* toward yourself, without going back and forth; keep repeating the back-to-front motion, lifting the pestle from the surface of the *tamis* at each and every stroke. Since a *tamis* may not be easy to come by, the same result can be obtained in a conical strainer with a large wooden spatula: apply one clean stroke from the bottom of the strainer to the rim, pushing the vegetable against the side of the strainer closest to you. The procedure is not time-consuming if small amounts at a time are strained and the skins and fibers of the vegetables are discarded every time.

What about the blender? It can be used to purée vegetables containing no starch or a negligible amount of it, but very starchy vegetables, especially potatoes, must not be put in a blender. The mechanical action of the blades on the potato pulp forms "gluten," a tough filmy protein that makes soups gummy. The skins of peas and beans may be broken by a quick passage in the blender on slow speed to make straining easier.

ENRICHING SOUPS

Soups are enriched with butter, plain cream, or a liaison of egg yolks and cream.

BUTTER

Add a pat of raw butter to each cup of soup and give your guests the pleasure of stirring it in themselves.

CREAM AND LIAISON

If the soup is thickened with cornstarch, make a "slurry" with the starch, cream and egg yolks if applicable, and enrich and thicken at once.

If the soup is a velouté or cream, make a liaison with egg yolks and cream and enrich with the same precautions you would use with a white sauce (p. 111).

Bear in mind that egg yolks mixed with a starch must be given one short boil, or the soup will stay thin. If the soup contains no starch or flour, enrich it and reheat just below the boiling point, but *do not boil* or the yolks will curdle. Remember, in any case, to heat those yolks very slowly. It takes just a few minutes to enrich a soup; *do it just before serving.*

SERVING SOUP

If the main course of a meal is to be sauced with a rich white or emulsified sauce, the best soup is a clear consommé; if, on the contrary, the main course is a lean piece of broiled fish or red meat, or a simple roasted chicken, any type of cream soup is acceptable. No wine is usually served with soup, but in England one sometimes meets with the most pleasant custom of serving a glass of Madeira.

A chowder is a meal in itself, so make plenty of it and serve a crisp salad and an attractive dessert afterwards. A chowder is great informal party fare; thick with fish and shellfish, it will be most tasty with a glass of dry white wine.

FREEZING SOUP

All soups generally freeze well, unless otherwise directed in the recipe. However, always add enrichments and liaisons *after defrosting.*

SIMPLE CONSOMMÉ
6 SERVINGS

Ingredients for stock	*1 egg shell*
in a hurry (*p.* 79)	*1 egg white*

Mix together the raw meat and vegetables in a large pot. Add the seasonings. Beat the egg white very lightly and add to the pot. Crumble the egg shell over the other ingredients. Cover with the water and, *stirring constantly,* bring to a boil. Simmer for 1 hour. Strain through a cheesecloth. The egg white and shell will attract all particles that would make a cloudy stock. This process is called "clarifying."

The egg white in this recipe is the culprit that forces the cook to stay at the stove and stir until the consommé comes to a boil; should the stirring be omitted, the egg white, which does the clarifying work, would fall to the bottom of the pan, burn there, and spoil the taste of the consommé.

If you cannot spare the time for this clarifying, omit the egg white and garnish the finished soup with a good tablespoon of seasoned whipped cream; no one short of an expert wise to the trick will know that under the cream your soup is cloudy rather than clear.

DOUBLE CONSOMMÉ
6 SERVINGS

Use brown stock (p. 78) and beef meat for beef consommé, white stock (p. 76) and half veal, half chicken meat for white consommé.

2 cups ground fat-free meat	*3 peppercorns*
2 carrots, minced	*1 egg white*
2 leeks, white part only, minced	*1 egg shell*
1 onion, minced	*5 cups cold stock*

Mix meat, vegetables, peppercorns, slightly beaten egg white and the egg shell. Cover with cold stock, bring to a boil, stirring constantly, and simmer over very low heat for 1 hour. Strain through cheesecloth.

SOUP GARNISHES

In the days when soup and consommé were still an all-important part of a meal, elaborate garnishes were prepared. Nowadays, the following light garnishes are preferably used: julienne of vegetables or crêpes (p. 506), soup noodles, instant tapioca, minced truffles or sautéed mushrooms, blanched julienne of Boston lettuce, blanched watercress, minced herbs, whipped sweet or sour cream.

KAMMAN'S ONION SOUP
6 SERVINGS

This is a more delicate soup than the bistrot type.

6 large onions, sliced	3 tablespoons Madeira
4 tablespoons butter	12 very thin slices of French
3½ cups homemade chicken	bread, dried in the oven
stock, cold	¾ cup grated Gruyère cheese
3½ cups homemade beef stock,	
cold	

Brown the onions well in the butter. Cover with the cold stocks, bring to a boil, and simmer for 40 to 45 minutes. Add Madeira. Put 1 slice of bread in each of 6 fireproof casseroles, top with ½ tablespoon cheese and fill with soup. The bread will come floating to the surface; immediately top it with another slice and another 1½ tablespoons cheese. Put under the broiler and brown for 2 to 3 minutes.

SORREL SOUP
6 SERVINGS

We had sorrel in our garden; this recipe is a combination of the formulas of two great cooks in the family.

4 tablespoons butter
3 cups sorrel, cleaned and cut into chiffonnade, or 3 cups fresh spinach and 2 tablespoons lemon juice
4½ cups white stock (p. 76) or water

2 eggs, separated
¼ cup heavy cream
6 slices of French bread, sautéed in butter

Heat the butter, add sorrel or spinach, and toss over medium heat until the greens are wilted. Cover with the stock and simmer for 10 minutes. Strain the unbeaten egg whites through a conical strainer directly into the soup, stirring constantly. Mix egg yolks and cream and make the liaison (p. 111) without boiling. Serve each portion over a slice of sautéed bread.

RADISH-GREEN SOUP
6 SERVINGS

A product of the war when there was no watercress. We replaced it by the greens of the radishes in our garden. Now I buy the radishes just for the greens.

3 cups chopped radish greens (from 2 bunches of radishes)
4 tablespoons butter
4 cups cold chicken stock or water

2 large Idaho potatoes, peeled and diced
1 cup heavy cream
1 tablespoon chopped chives
Salt and freshly ground pepper

Toss radish greens in hot butter, cover with the stock or water, and bring to a boil. Add the potatoes and simmer for 20 minutes. Strain through a food mill. Add cream, chives, and salt and pepper to taste. Serve piping hot.

FIVE ONIONS SOUP
6 SERVINGS

A great favorite of "my three men" after a cold hike or a wild basketball game.

¼ pound slab bacon	3 cups beef stock
6 leeks, white part only, sliced fine	2 large Idaho potatoes, peeled and sliced
6 scallions, white part only, sliced fine	Salt and pepper
	¾ cup heavy cream
2 large onions, sliced fine	½ cup sour cream
3 shallots, minced	3 egg yolks
3 cups chicken stock	1 tablespoon chopped chives

Blanch the bacon: cover with cold water, slowly bring to a boil, and simmer for 3 to 4 minutes. Drain, blot dry, and cut into ⅓-inch dice. Cook over very low heat until golden. Add the leeks, scallions, onions and shallots and toss in bacon fat until soft. Add stocks and bring slowly to a boil. Add potatoes, and salt and pepper to taste. Simmer for 30 to 35 minutes. Strain through a food mill.

Mix both creams and the egg yolks and make a liaison (p. 111). Reheat the soup to just below the boiling point; add chives. Serve piping hot.

GREEN FISH POT
6 HEARTY SERVINGS

On one of my visits to Paris, M. Barnagaud, owner of Prunier, the best seafood restaurant in the world, gave me Prunier's recipe for *Marmite Dieppoise;* it inspired this recipe.

2 *dozen small clams*
2 *dozen black mussels*
4 *tablespoons butter*
2 *onions, minced*
1 *carrot, minced*
3 *leeks, white part only, minced*
2 *cups chiffonnade of Boston
   lettuce*
1 *cup chiffonnade of sorrel, or 1
   cup chiffonnade of spinach
   plus 2 tablespoons lemon juice*
1 *tablespoon chopped parsley*
Pinch of dried thyme

¼ *bay leaf, crushed*
3 *cups white-wine fish* fumet
   (*p. 83*), *cold*
½ *cup white wine*
6 *fillets of sole, flounder, small
   brill, or large dab*
2 *dozen small raw shrimps,
   shelled*
Salt
Freshly ground pepper
1 *cup salted whipped cream*
*Basket of small dried slices of
   French bread*

Steam the clams and mussels until they open. Discard the shells, set aside the shellfish, and strain and reserve the juices. There should be 1 cup clam juice and 1 cup mussel juice. Heat the butter and sauté onions, carrot and leeks until soft. Add the greens and toss until wilted. Add the herbs, *fumet,* wine, and the reserved clam and mussel juices; simmer for 15 minutes. Bring the soup to a violent boil. Add the fish fillets cut into ⅓-inch-wide strips and the raw shrimps. Turn off the heat and let stand for 10 minutes. Add salt if needed and pepper to taste. Reheat well but do not boil. Add the cooked clams and mussels. Serve piping hot, with the whipped cream in a serving dish for each person to add as he pleases, and the basket of bread.

BAR HARBOR CHOWDER
6 SERVINGS

On the beach at Bar Harbor in Maine, the author with a large kettle, picking mussels. A Yankee comes running: "We don't eat those!" Author (belligerently): "They are better than clams." Yankee: "Never tasted them, but it can't be true!"

2 *dozen black mussels*
2 *dozen steamer clams*
½ *cup white wine*
2 *onions, chopped*

2 *tablespoons chopped parsley*
3 *live lobsters, 1½ pounds each*
8 *tablespoons butter*
1 *ounce brandy, Scotch or*

bourbon	*¾ cup heavy cream*
2 cups water	*2 egg yolks*
2 potatoes, cut into ⅓-inch dice	*Pepper*

Steam mussels and clams open with the wine, 1 chopped onion and the parsley. Discard shells, set aside the shellfish, and strain and reserve the cooking juices; there should be about 2½ cups shellfish juice. Split lobsters into halves. Mix tomalley and coral, if any, with 2 tablespoons butter, and reserve. Sauté lobsters in 5 tablespoons hot butter until the shells are bright red; flambé with the spirit. Remove lobster meat from shells and dice; reserve.

Add whatever juice is in the pan to the shellfish juice; deglaze the pan if necessary with a little of the water. Sauté the second onion in the remaining 1 tablespoon butter until golden. Add reserved shellfish juice and the water; bring to a boil, add diced potatoes, and simmer for 20 minutes. Make a liaison (p. 111) with cream and egg yolks and add to the soup. Add reserved shellfish and lobster; reheat well but do not boil. Add the mixture of tomalley, coral and butter; mix well. Season with pepper to taste; there will be enough salt in the shellfish juices. Serve with a glass of California Fumé Blanc.

This chowder does not freeze well.

PURÉE OF CAULIFLOWER
6 SERVINGS

Do not blanch the watercress; the heat of the soup will do it.

1 very large white head of cauliflower	*2 tablespoons cornstarch*
4½ cups chicken stock	*½ cup fine-chopped watercress*
1 cup heavy cream	*Salt and pepper*

Clean cauliflower; blanch (p. 315) for 2 minutes. Bring chicken stock to a boil, add cauliflower, and simmer until it falls apart. Purée through a strainer or with an electric blender. Reheat well. Make a slurry with cream and cornstarch and thicken the soup. Add chopped watercress, season to taste, and serve.

The puréed cauliflower freezes well, but complete the soup only just before serving.

INDIAN PURÉE
6 SERVINGS

Corn and beans, an American classic as succotash, make a delicious combination in this puréed soup.

7½ cups chicken stock	*¾ teaspoon sugar*
3 packages (10 ounces each)	*1½ cups shoepeg corn*
frozen large lima beans	*Salt and pepper*
1½ cups heavy cream	

Bring chicken stock to a boil. Add lima beans and simmer, uncovered, until they are very tender and discolored. Break the bean skins in an electric blender and then strain through a *tamis* or conical strainer. Add heavy cream and sugar. Reheat to just below the boiling point. Add shoepeg corn and poach for 2 minutes. Add seasoning to taste and serve.

This freezes, but there is a loss of flavor.

PURÉE GLORIA
6 SERVINGS

A variation by my friend Gloria Einbender on my recipe for *crème sénégalaise.* Replace the pineapple by diced white chicken meat, and the soup may be served hot.

1 large onion, minced	*3 egg yolks*
5 tablespoons butter	*1 cup heavy cream*
1 head of Boston lettuce, chopped	*Salt and pepper*
1½ teaspoons fresh curry powder	*1 cup unsweetened pineapple*
5 cups chicken stock	*tidbits*
1 bag (24 ounces) frozen large	
peas	

Sauté onion in 4 tablespoons of the butter until soft. Add chopped lettuce and toss until softened. Add curry powder and cook for 3 to 4 minutes. Add chicken stock and bring to a boil. Add peas and simmer until very tender and discolored (a must to develop the starches completely). Break the pea skins in an electric blender and strain through a *tamis* or conical strainer. Enrich with a liaison (p. 111) made with egg yolks and cream. Reheat very well but do not boil. Add seasoning to taste and deep chill. Just before serving, sauté the pineapple tidbits in the last tablespoon of butter and add them to the soup.

This soup may be frozen after the mixture has been puréed. Then, defrost on the day you are serving it, make the liaison early in the day, and deep chill again.

PURÉE OF CARROT
6 SERVINGS

Make this nice and peppery or it will be a bit too feminine for the gentlemen. Do not use an electric blender; if the rice is allowed to cool even a little, blending makes it gummy and the soup will be filmy.

1 large onion, chopped	*1 teaspoon dried chervil, or 1*
4 tablespoons butter	*tablespoon fresh parsley*
1 pound carrots, shredded	*Salt and pepper*
5 cups chicken stock	*¾ cup heavy cream*
⅓ cup uncooked rice	*¼ cup sour cream*
3 shallots, minced	*¼ teaspoon grated nutmeg*

Sauté onion in butter until soft. Add carrots and toss over medium heat for 3 to 4 minutes. Add chicken stock and bring to a boil. Add rice, shallots, chervil or parsley, and salt and pepper to taste. Simmer for 30 minutes, until the carrots fall apart and the rice is overcooked. Purée through a *tamis* or conical strainer. Bring back to a boil and blend in the creams. Reheat until very warm but do not boil because boiling would alter the taste of the cream. Correct seasoning, add nutmeg, and serve.

PURÉE OF CHESTNUT SOUP
6 SERVINGS

In the holiday mood for Christmas and Thanksgiving.

3 cups shelled chestnuts	*Salt and pepper*
3 cups white stock (p. 76)	*¼ cup Madeira*
3 cups brown stock (p. 78)	*¾ cup heavy cream*
3-inch piece of celery rib	*3 tablespoons butter*
½ teaspoon coriander seeds	*Minced celery leaves*

Cover shelled chestnuts with both stocks. Bring to a boil and add the celery rib in one piece and the coriander seeds. Simmer until nuts crumble. Remove celery rib and purée the soup. Add seasoning to taste. Add Madeira and cream. Add more cream or stock if too thick. Reheat well but do not boil. Whisk in the butter, and correct seasoning. Sprinkle with minced celery leaves and serve.

MUSHROOM VELOUTÉ
6 SERVINGS

The velouté must be thick, since the mushrooms are added raw and render a lot of moisture. The truffle is optional, but makes a great deal of difference in the final taste.

3 cups thick velouté (p. 108)	*1 large truffle, shredded*
1½ pounds firm fresh	*(optional)*
mushrooms	*3 egg yolks*
Salt and pepper	*1 cup heavy cream*
1 tablespoon minced shallots	*2 tablespoons dry sherry*

Bring velouté to a boil. Shred mushrooms directly into the velouté. Add salt and pepper to taste, the shallots and shredded truffle. Simmer for 15 minutes. Make a liaison (p. 111) with egg yolks and cream and enrich the soup. Correct seasoning, add sherry, and serve.

AVOCADO VELOUTÉ
6 SERVINGS

This soup is good warm or chilled, but make it only with very ripe avocados.

2 ½ cups thin velouté (p. 108)	1 ½ tablespoons minced cilantro
1 ½ cups mashed avocado	(fresh coriander leaves) or
2 tablespoons lime juice	Italian parsley
Salt and pepper	2 slices of white bread
1 cup heavy cream	1 garlic clove
	2 tablespoons butter

Bring velouté to a boil. Mix avocado with lime juice and salt and pepper to taste, and push through a strainer into a mixing bowl. Slowly whisk in the warm velouté. Blend in the cream and reheat just below the boiling point. Add the minced *cilantro* or parsley.

Remove crusts from bread and toast slices very lightly. Rub toast as much as desired with garlic; sauté in the butter and cut into small croutons. Serve the soup topped with croutons.

CREAM OF CALIFORNIA WHEAT
6 SERVINGS

The spices give this soup a faint medieval flavor. Use the driest sherry with a "nutty" flavor.

¾ cup California hulled wheat	2 ½ cups thin béchamel (p. 109)
5 ½ cups cold chicken stock	or cream sauce
½ teaspoon salt	1 ½ cups heavy cream
⅛ teaspoon pepper	2 to 3 tablespoons dry sherry
⅛ teaspoon each of ground	¼ cup pine nuts
cardamom and coriander	2 tablespoons butter
⅛ teaspoon grated nutmeg	

Cover wheat with chicken stock and bring to a boil. Add salt, pepper and spices, and simmer until all but ½ cup of the stock has been absorbed. Mix wheat and hot béchamel or cream sauce. Add heavy cream and reheat well. Correct seasoning and add sherry to taste. Sauté pine nuts in butter and sprinkle some on the top of each serving.

Note: California hulled wheat is unpolished whole grains of wheat. It is not cracked wheat or bulgur. If you cannot find the whole grains, this soup can be made with cracked wheat, but the texture and character of the soup will be different.

ALAN'S OXTAIL
6 SERVINGS

6 tablespoons butter
6 tablespoons flour
3 cups strong oxtail broth or beef stock
1 large truffle, peeled and diced

1 cup heavy cream
¼ cup melted meat glaze, or
½ teaspoon commercial meat extract

Make a brown *roux* with butter and flour. Whisk in broth or stock and bring to a boil. Add truffle and simmer for 5 to 6 minutes. Add cream and meat glaze or extract. Reheat well and serve piping hot.

CREAM OF LEEKS
6 SERVINGS

12 large leeks, white part only
6 tablespoons butter
¼ cup flour
4½ cups scalded milk
¼ teaspoon grated nutmeg
½ teaspoon salt

⅛ teaspoon ground white pepper
3 egg yolks
2 cups light cream
1 tablespoon chopped chives
Croutons, browned in butter

Slice leeks paper-thin. Sauté in the butter until very soft, then cover the pot and let them soften completely without coloring. Sprinkle with flour, whisk in the scalded milk, and bring to a boil, stirring. Add nutmeg, salt and pepper. Simmer for 30 minutes. Push through a *tamis* or conical strainer. Make a liaison (p. 111) with egg yolks and cream, and reheat slowly, giving the mixture one small boil (there is flour). Correct seasoning and add the chives. Serve with small croutons browned in butter.

SPANISH BISQUE OF TOMATO
6 SERVINGS

2½ cups béchamel sauce (p. 110)	¼ teaspoon ground saffron
3 large onions, minced	½ bay leaf
6 tablespoons butter	Pinch of dried thyme
2 cups tomato essence (p. 120), or 1 cup tomato paste plus 1 cup water	1 tablespoon chopped parsley
	1 cup heavy cream
	Salt and pepper
	1 tablespoon dry sherry
1 large garlic clove, minced	1 large green pepper

Have béchamel ready. Sauté onions in 4 tablespoons butter until golden. Add tomato essence, garlic, saffron, bay leaf, thyme and parsley. Simmer until 1½ cups of tomato essence are left. Blend this mixture into the béchamel bit by bit, and reheat well together. Strain. Add heavy cream and season to taste. Add sherry.

Immerse the green pepper in boiling water for 12 minutes; peel, and cut into very fine julienne. Sauté the strips in remaining butter, keeping them slightly crisp. Add the julienne to the soup and reheat well together.

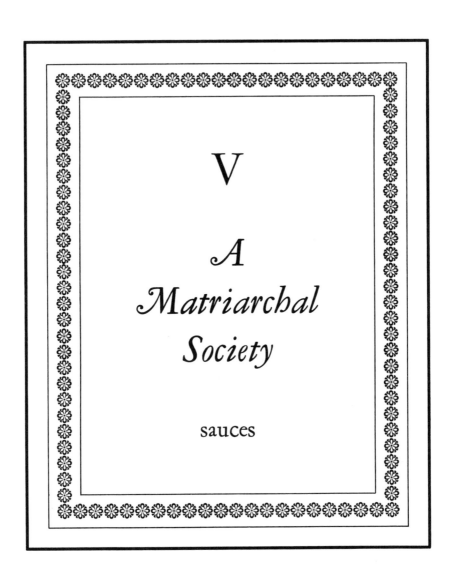

V

A

Matriarchal Society

sauces

LIKE THE OWNER of any new cookbook, you will skip around this book and see many strange sauce names and a number of other mysterious expressions. They will make sense if you read this chapter first. It is designed to give the reader an overall view of the "sauce jungle."

A sauce—not to be confused with a gravy that is made from the drippings of a meat—is a flavored liquid that has been thickened and garnishes a piece of meat or a vegetable. Depending on the cook's skills, it can be a joy or a bitter disappointment to the palate. The better the liquid used to make a sauce and the tastier the flavorings added to it, the richer and the more flavorful the sauce will be.

Sauces are thickened or, in culinary language, *bound* in several ways: with starches such as potato starch, cornstarch, arrowroot, flour; with a mixture of flour and fat; with a protein (egg yolk); with emulsified butter. Each of these thickening elements results in a different consistency and appearance. There is a typical sauce for each of these thickening methods. In French culinary terminology this typical or basic sauce, which is a pattern for others, is called a *sauce mère,* a "mother sauce," and a variation on the basic pattern is called a "small sauce." In the pages that follow the description of each type of sauce will begin with a basic or "mother" sauce.

Another kind of sauce is a "neutral sauce," one which contains no meat or meat stock.

STARCH-BOUND SAUCES

Starch can be used to bind sauces because it gelatinizes when mixed with a liquid and submitted to heat.

Mix 2 tablespoons of any starch with 1 cup of cold water. The starch sinks to the bottom of the container. If the liquid is kept cold, the starch absorbs some of the water, but no further change occurs. If the liquid is stirred and heated, the swelling of the starch granules continues; a starch may absorb as much as 300 percent of its own weight in water by the time the temperature of the liquid reaches 60°F. The swelling continues and reaches the ratio of 2500 percent water absorption by the time the temperature reaches between 190° and 212°F. When the liquid reaches the boiling point, the starch granules reach their maximum swelling capacity; they burst open and spill the totality of their starches into the surrounding liquid. The viscosity of the mixture, which has kept increasing during the heating process, reaches a maximum when the rupture of the granules occurs and a *gel* is obtained.

Some gels are more stable than others. A cornstarch or potato-starch gel may, if heated too long, liquefy again; the mixture is then said to have *hydrolyzed.* A flour gel may also hydrolyze easily in the presence of strong acid (tomato) or uncooked egg yolk. A gel hydrolyzes when the starches are broken by the heat into chemically simpler starches and sugars, which take up the elements of the water present in the pot.

BINDING A SAUCE WITH A SLURRY

Cornstarch, potato starch and arrowroot are fine starches containing very little protein. To thicken a sauce with any of them, you must prepare a *slurry,* a watery mixture of the starch with a liquid. In modern cuisine, starch slurries are very often used to thicken sauces because they are fast and require a minimum amount of work.

Mix the starch well with some cold liquid, preferably the same liquid used to make the sauce. Add a few tablespoons of the hot sauce base to the slurry; the slurry will gradually warm up and hydrolization of the starch by a sudden contact with the hot liquid in the pot will be avoided. *Stirring gently and constantly with a wooden spoon,* add the warmed slurry to the hot liquid in the pot; you will see the gel form almost immediately. Bring the sauce to a boil.

Whisking violently with a wire whisk is not recommended for this type of sauce since some starch gels are easily liquefied by fast mechanical action. A gel liquefied by mechanical action will form again on standing, but one liquefied by hydrolysis will not.

Starch-bound sauces, due to their varying stabilities, should be thickened just before serving to avoid hydrolysis; they present no major timing problem for the cook since they thicken within seconds.

Cornstarch produces more stable sauces than arrowroot or potato starch. For thickening white sauces, use the following proportions of cornstarch and arrowroot for 1 cup liquid:

Sauce Consistency	Cornstarch	Arrowroot
Thin	2 teaspoons	1 teaspoon
Medium	1½ tablespoons	2 teaspoons
Thick	2½ tablespoons	3 teaspoons

Cooked cornstarch produces a thick opaque gel, easily recognizable to anyone who has ever eaten pudding; arrowroot gel is filmy, not always of a pleasant appearance when thick. Potato starch contains so little protein that it produces a very clear gel, ideal for thickening brown sauces; potato-starch gel is smooth, light, not too filmy.

FLOUR-BOUND SAUCES

THICKENING WITH A ROUX

The best sauces are those made with a *roux,* a cooked mixture of fat and flour. Depending on how long the *roux* cooks, it takes on more or less coloration and is known as a white, golden, or brown *roux.* White sauces are made with a white or golden *roux* combined with a white stock, milk or cream; brown sauces with a brown *roux* combined with a brown stock.

The opaque appearance of a flour-bound sauce is due to the coagulation by the heat of the proteins contained in the flour. Different flours give different types of thickening, depending on their ratio of starches and proteins. Cake flour (the richest in starch) thickens more than pastry flour, and pastry flour more than all-purpose flour. Bread flour (the richest in proteins) should never be used for thickening a sauce; it contains a high amount of the proteins forming gluten (a most important element in bakery, about which more will be said later); the sauces made with bread flour are gummy and unpleasant. The differences between cake, pastry or all-purpose flours are not significant enough for the lay cook to worry about, so that all-purpose flour, the easiest to buy, can be used without hesitation.

Making a *roux* has a double purpose. Taste a bit of raw flour and notice how sour and almost bitter your palate becomes. The precooking of the flour in a fat removes that unpleasant taste and also initiates the swelling of the starch granules.

Cooking a *roux* is more delicate than is often realized. It should be done over medium and very even heat. If the fat is too hot, instead of swelling, the starch granules shrink. The tiny cellulose envelope enclosing the starch hardens and loses its ability to absorb water. A sauce made with an overcooked *roux* thickens half as much as was expected or even not at all; a white sauce in these conditions simply remains thin and still looks palatable, but a brown sauce does not bind at all, and the burned granules can be seen accumulating at the bottom of the container as the sauce stands.

COOKING A WHITE OR GOLDEN ROUX

Use a thick pot that carries heat evenly (copper, enameled cast iron). If you have only a thin pot, you *must* use an asbestos or metal pad to control the heat.

Heat the fat, preferably butter—either raw or clarified, until the foam recedes. Take the pot from the heat. Add the flour, mix well, return the pot to medium-low heat and cook, stirring occasionally, for a suitable length of time, according to the chart. A white *roux* looks straw yellow, a golden *roux* golden yellow.

| *Amounts* | | *Cooking Time* | |
| | | WHITE | GOLDEN |
BUTTER	FLOUR	ROUX	ROUX
2 tablespoons	2 tablespoons	2 minutes	4 minutes
3 tablespoons	3 tablespoons	3 minutes	6 minutes
4 tablespoons	4 tablespoons	4 minutes	8 minutes
½ cup	½ cup	8 minutes	12 minutes

COOKING A BROWN ROUX

A thick pot is a must. Even an asbestos or metal pad cannot prevent the flour burning in a thin pot. A black cast-iron pot gives the best results. For larger quantities, start the cooking on the stove and

finish it in a 275 °F. oven; stir often during the last stages of cooking.
Use preferably clarified butter (p. 17).

BUTTER	FLOUR	COOKING TIME
4 tablespoons	3 tablespoons	8 minutes
7 tablespoons	6 tablespoons	12 to 14 minutes
⅓ cup	½ cup	20 minutes, the last 6 in the oven

ADDING LIQUID TO A ROUX

Have the liquid very hot. As soon as the *roux* is cooked, remove the
pot from the heat and whisk half of the hot liquid into the hot *roux*
until the mixture is homogenous. It will be thick. Whisk in the rest of
the liquid until smooth. Whisking *hot* liquid into *hot roux* insures
constant temperature for the starch granules and less chances of hy-
drolyzing, which flour can do as well as starch. Return the mixture to
the heat and, stirring constantly, bring to a boil. Stirring avoids the
formation of lumps in the gel and cools it by introducing air into it, so
that the starch granules are submitted to the last gradual increase of
temperature without risking hydrolysis.

SKIMMING A FLOUR-BOUND SAUCE

As soon as a flour-bound sauce boils, a skin forms at its surface; the
skin thickens as the sauce simmers and becomes scum. This scum is
made of proteins, mostly cellulose, contained in the flour. Below the
scum is a layer of liquid fat; it is the butter used to make the *roux* that
was in emulsion—or suspended in millions of droplets—in the sauce
before the boiling point was reached but now accumulates in a large
puddle as simmering breaks the emulsion. Flour-bound sauces made
with stocks must be skimmed as much as possible of both scum and
liquid fat, or they will be heavy and gummy. Flour-bound sauces
made with either milk or cream not only need not be skimmed, but
cannot be skimmed, because scum and fat are trapped in the very
viscous milk proteins and cannot be disassociated from them.

FREEZING COOKED ROUX

Roux may, if desired, be prepared in bulk and frozen, although the
practice does not save that much time. If you find it useful, make it

with 1 cup liquid clarified butter and 1 cup flour, and cook to the degree of coloration desired. Pour the finished *roux* into a flat 8-inch-square cake pan. Cool and freeze in a perfectly horizontal position to obtain even thickness through the pan. When solid, cut into 16 equal-size squares, and store these in a polyethylene bag in the freezer. Each square has the thickening power of 1 tablespoon of flour. Before using frozen *roux,* let it defrost completely and reheat it very gently.

FREEZING FLOUR-BOUND SAUCES

Flour-bound sauces may be frozen. As they defrost at room temperature, *syneresis,* or weeping of water out of the starch gel occurs, and the sauce looks curdled. Empty the sauce into a pan and reheat it slowly to the boiling point while whisking to restore the sauce to its normal consistency. Too fast heating will cause hydrolysis.

BASIC FLOUR-BOUND WHITE SAUCES

These basic or "mother" sauces are *velouté* and *béchamel.*

A sauce made with a white *roux* plus white stock (chicken or veal) or fish *fumet* is called a *velouté* (velvet sauce). Velouté may be made with different consistencies.

Consistency	*Amounts*
Thin (for cream soups)	1 tablespoon flour per 1 cup liquid
Medium (for sauces)	1 ½ tablespoons flour per 1 cup liquid
Thick (for soufflés)	3 tablespoons flour per 1 cup liquid

Velouté may be made in larger quantities and frozen, or it may be made on the spot. The skimming of a velouté is not an absolute necessity, but it is highly recommended for better taste and appearance. To make velouté in bulk with the proper consistency for sauces, follow the recipe below.

VELOUTÉ

2 QUARTS

1 cup butter	*1 cup chopped mushroom stems*
1 cup sifted flour	*or pieces*
3 ½ quarts white stock	*Small* bouquet garni
	4 white peppercorns

Make a *roux* with the butter and flour and cook for 10 to 12 minutes. Add 3 quarts hot stock and bring to a boil over medium heat. Add mushrooms and *bouquet garni.* Let simmer for 30 minutes. Skim as much as possible. Add remaining ½ quart cold stock and bring to a boil again. Let simmer and reduce to 2 quarts, skimming at regular intervals, until fat free. Strain into 1½-cup Mason jars. Let cool at room temperature; seal well and freeze if desired.

To relax from those technical details and before we pass on to yet another "mother," let me tell you its story.

Louis de Béchamel, steward to Louis XIV of France, had a genial cook who apparently first thought of adding cream to a basic velouté. The modest chef gave his master's name to his creation and *la sauce Béchamel* was born. The Duc d'Escars, man of the world, up in years and irritated at the *parvenu* gourmet, could not restrain himself and exclaimed: "How lucky that little Béchamel. I was making minced chicken in cream sauce twenty years before he was born, but never was lucky enough to give my name to any sauce . . ." Both Béchamel and the Duke went down in posterity through the sauce. The Italians even translated the name to *besciamella!*

Nowadays the sauce is similar to an American cream sauce and made with plain milk; only the presence of flavorings distinguishes it from its American cousin. Up to thirty years ago, béchamel was flavored with veal and a *mirepoix* (p. 12); in modern cookery books these have been replaced by a lonely little onion. Some even call béchamel a white or cream sauce flavored only with nutmeg. Béchamel freezes well and may be prepared in bulk and frozen in Mason jars.

Considering how widely used it is in modern cuisine (because it requires no skimming), it must be flavorful. Like the velouté, béchamel may be made in different thicknesses.

Consistency	*Amounts*
Thin (for cream soups, creamed vegetables)	1 tablespoon flour per 1 cup milk
Medium (for sauces)	2 tablespoons flour per 1 cup milk
Thick (for soufflés)	3 tablespoons flour per 1 cup milk

BÉCHAMEL

FOR 1 QUART	FOR 5 QUARTS
1 small onion	*2 large onions*
1 small carrot	*2 large carrots*
½ celery rib	*1½ celery ribs*
½ cup butter	*2½ cups butter*
½ cup flour	*2½ cups flour*
4½ cups scalded milk	*6 quarts scalded milk*
Salt	*Salt and pepper*
Pepper	*½ teaspoon grated nutmeg*
Nutmeg	*Large bunch of parsley stems*
Small bouquet garni	*½ teaspoon dried thyme*
	2 small bay leaves

Cut vegetables into large *mirepoix* (p. 12) and sauté in butter until onion is translucent. Add flour and cook for 4 to 5 minutes (10 to 12 for large recipe), stirring occasionally. Whisk in scalded milk. Bring back to a boil; add salt, pepper and nutmeg to taste, and the *bouquet garni* (or all the herbs for the large recipe). Simmer for 45 minutes. Strain; use, store, or freeze after cooling.

SMALL WHITE SAUCES

The "mother" white sauces become "small" white sauces when different ingredients are added to them. For example, a chicken velouté reduced to a very thick consistency and thinned again with cream becomes a *suprême sauce,* while a fish velouté simmered with a mixture of reduced white wine and shallots becomes a *bercy sauce.* Tomato sauce or purée added to a béchamel sauce makes it an *aurore sauce,* while a mixture of grated Gruyère and Parmesan cheeses makes it a *Mornay sauce.*

ENRICHING AND FINISHING A WHITE SAUCE

A small amount of fortified wine, plain or flavored butter, cream, or a mixture of cream and egg yolks called *liaison,* can be added to a basic white sauce to enrich it and make it taste better. The sauce is then said to be "finished" with whatever element has been used. Follow these directions:

FORTIFIED WINE

Add 1 to 2 tablespoons port, sherry or Madeira per cup of sauce when it is ready to serve.

BUTTER, PLAIN OR FLAVORED

Whisk the *raw unmelted butter* into the ready-to-serve sauce. As you whisk, the butter emulsifies in the sauce, which thickens further and looks shiny and velvety. You may reheat the sauce but *never reboil* it or the emulsion of butter will break.

CREAM

Choose any of these methods:

❀ Reduce the sauce until very thick; thin to desired consistency with the required amount of cream.

❀ Bring the sauce to a high boil. Stirring constantly with a wooden spatula, add the cream, 3 tablespoons at a time. Continue stirring over high heat even after the cream has been added until the sauce coats the spatula. This is a *haute cuisine* method called "reduction on high flame." If you choose this method—the best—be sure to stir constantly or the bottom of the pot will scorch.

❀ Mix sauce and cream, bring to a boil, and simmer gently until coating consistency has been reached.

LIAISON

Put yolks and cream in a large cup or bowl; mix well. Whisk half of the hot sauce *bit by bit* into the liaison to heat the yolks *very slowly*. Reverse the process and very slowly whisk the warm liaison into the rest of the hot sauce. Reheat the sauce slowly until you can see one or two boils bubble at the surface of the sauce; then remove it from the heat. These two boils are *a must*. Without them, the sauce hydrolizes and stays liquid. The reason remains mysterious; an enzyme in the egg yolk possibly hydrolizes the starch in the same manner as the amylase of saliva liquefies a sauce when the cook tastes it and puts the spoon back into the saucepan instead of into the sink. Those two boils insure that the overall temperature in the pot is at least 190°F., the temperature at which most enzymes become inactive. Remember that a flour-bound sauce not only *can* but *must* boil if it contains egg yolks. The important step is to heat the enriched sauce *very slowly* so that the yolks have no chance to curdle under a sudden burst of heat.

Auguste Escoffier in *Le Guide Culinaire* (Flammarion, 1927) is very explicit on this point. In the recipe for allemande sauce (p. 15), the master directs his readers to "... mix velouté, egg yolks, stock and a few other ingredients, bring to a boil, and reduce by one third on full flame, stirring constantly with a spatula. ..."

SEPARATION

Very rich sauces heavy in cream, egg yolks and butter may, if they stand, separate. Tiny puddles of fat appear at the surface of the sauce while the thickened proteins form blocks. It is evaporation that causes the sauce to separate. Avoid this possibility by never letting a finished egg-enriched sauce stand at a temperature higher than 140°F. If, in spite of this precaution, the sauce starts separating, quickly whisk into it a few tablespoons of stock to replace the moisture lost while the sauce was waiting.

BROWN SAUCE

A brown sauce must not be thick. Its consistency should be somewhere between those of light cream and heavy cream. Brown sauce can be served with a meat roasted at high temperature which, consequently, has no natural gravy (p. 160), or it can be used in small quantities as a binder for the pan juices of panfried or braised meats.

The average serving of a brown sauce is 2 to 3 tablespoons per person. Therefore, 1 cup will serve 6 to 8 persons, 2 cups will serve 12 to 16 persons, 3 cups will serve 18 to 24 persons.

There are four methods of making brown sauce.

LAZY COOK'S BROWN SAUCE
1 CUP

Make a slurry with 1⅓ teaspoons potato starch and ¼ cup cold beef bouillon or stock. Heat well ¾ cup beef bouillon; blend the slurry into the hot sauce and thicken.

This concoction does not taste any better than it looks; rather than use it, you might as well open a can of beef gravy.

SHORT-CUT BROWN SAUCE
1⅓ CUPS

This version tastes better than canned beef gravy but is not worth being made in bulk or frozen.

1 large piece of veal shank	*3 tablespoons flour*
4 chicken wings	*4 cups hot water*
1 large onion	*½ cup dry white wine*
1 small carrot	Bouquet garni
1 large leek	*1 tablespoon tomato paste*
⅓ celery rib	*Meat extract*
4 tablespoons butter or fat	*Food coloring*

Brown meats in a 400°F. oven. Cut vegetables into *mirepoix* and brown *mirepoix* well in butter or fat. Add flour to pot, and cook until light brown. Whisk in the hot water, and bring the sauce to a boil. Add wine, *bouquet garni,* browned meats and tomato paste. Simmer until reduced to 1½ cups. Then strain into a glass measuring cup, and let stand until sauce and fat have completely separated.

Remove fat-free sauce with a meat baster. Correct the taste and color by adding commercial meat extract to your taste and food coloring if needed.

This basic short-cut brown sauce can be adapted to use with various meats, poultry and game.

Beef: Add commercial beef extract to your taste to finished sauce.

Veal: Leave sauce just as it is.

Duck: Replace chicken wings with browned duck giblets (no livers).

Squab: Use browned squab giblets (no livers).

Game birds: Use browned giblets (no livers) of the game birds you are saucing.

Venison: Replace chicken wings with venison bones; use as many as you can obtain.

CLASSIC BROWN SAUCE (HOME METHOD)
1⅓ CUPS

The basic components of the sauce remain the same, but stock is used instead of water.

1 small onion	*4 cups hot stock*
1 small carrot	*Small* bouquet garni
1 small leek, white part only	*1 tablespoon tomato paste*
4 tablespoons butter	*½ cup dry white wine*
3 tablespoons flour	*1⅓ tablespoons Madeira*

Cut vegetables into *mirepoix.* Brown well in butter. Add flour and cook until the *roux* is light brown. Whisk the hot stock into the hot *roux,* and bring to a boil, stirring constantly. Add *bouquet garni,* tomato paste and white wine. Simmer, regularly skimming off the fat and cellulose, until the sauce is reduced to about 1⅓ cups. Strain into a container and add the Madeira. Cool, and store or freeze. No correction of color should be necessary.

This classic brown sauce also can be adapted to use with various meats, poultry and game.

Beef: For the stock use homemade beef stock or canned beef broth properly diluted with unsalted vegetable broth.

Veal: Use white veal stock artificially colored or brown veal stock.

Duck, squab, game birds: Use stock made with browned giblets (no livers) of any of those birds.

Venison: Use stock made with browned venison meat scraps and bones.

When good stock is used, this sauce is worth being made in bulk and frozen in Mason jars. Use the following proportions:

STOCK	BUTTER	FLOUR	FINISHED SAUCE
4 cups	4 tablespoons	3 tablespoons	1⅓ cups
2 quarts	½ cup	6 tablespoons	2⅔ cups
3 quarts	¾ cup	9 tablespoons	4 cups
4 quarts	1 cup	¾ cup	5⅓ cups

Increase the other ingredients in proportion. Add 1 tablespoon Madeira for each cup of finished sauce.

CLASSIC BROWN SAUCE (CHEF'S METHOD)

The classic brown *espagnole* and *demi-glace* sauces are quite a production. They are by far the best of all, and any dish they adorn will be a joy to behold and taste, but time is involved in preparing them, and the cook must follow scrupulously the instructions given here. For both these sauces good brown stock is bound with brown *roux* and reduced and skimmed until the liquid has been reduced to the stage where it is half as thick as meat glaze, hence the name *demi-glace,* or semiglaze.

Use only the strongest flavored homemade perfectly defatted stock. Brown veal stock is the best because the sauce obtained is versatile and adapts to the taste of all meats. *Do not in any case use commercial stocks,* for if you do, the sauce will be oversalted and you will have a total loss of time and money.

When such a good stock is involved, and especially if it is your first try, do not hesitate to *underbrown* the *roux* rather than burn it. The difference in the final taste will be minimal, and the final color can be modified artificially.

Skim, skim, skim; the more you do, the better the sauce. Make the sauce on a stay-home day. Leave it over very low heat and skim it as you happen to pass by.

Use only *clarified butter* for the *roux.*

If the sauce captures your fancy, make it twice a year. Keep some on hand frozen; it freezes very well. Serve it only to those of your friends whose palates will know the difference.

ESPAGNOLE SAUCE
1½ QUARTS

2 carrots	5½ quarts stock
2 onions	2 tablespoons tomato paste
½ cup diced veal meat	Bouquet garni
3 tablespoons raw butter	1 cup dry white wine
¾ cup clarified butter	⅓ cup Madeira
1¼ cups flour	

Stage I: Brown the *mirepoix* (carrots, onions, diced veal) in the raw butter until onions are golden brown. Meanwhile, cook the *roux* (clarified butter and flour). Whisk 4 quarts *very warm* stock into the hot *roux;* bring to a boil. Add the browned *mirepoix,* the tomato paste, *bouquet garni* and white wine. Simmer for 2½ hours, skimming as much as possible. Strain the sauce into a large mixing bowl; cool at room temperature and refrigerate overnight.

Stage II: Remove the layer of butter solidified on the surface of the sauce; it may be reused for vegetables. Return the sauce to a large pot, mix with remaining 1½ quarts *cold* stock, and bring to a boil again, stirring. The cold stock replaces the moisture lost the day before and allows further skimming. Let simmer until reduced to about 6 cups, skimming faithfully at regular intervals. The finished sauce is fat free, and you could use it as a mirror; it coats the back of a spoon like a thick sticky syrup. No correction of color should be necessary, but should it be, caramelize 1 teaspoon sugar in a heavy pan until it starts smoking. Cool the pan and dissolve the dark caramel with some of the sauce; stir into the balance of the sauce. Add the Madeira and strain into 1-cup Mason jars. Cool, and store or freeze.

DEMI-GLACE SAUCE
1 QUART

Mix 1 quart finished *espagnole* sauce with 1 quart brown veal stock. Simmer together and skim again (what else is there to do?). Reduce to 3¾ cups. Add ¼ cup sherry or Madeira.

Did you get there? Congratulations! You are a great cook.

MODERN REPLACEMENT FOR DEMI-GLACE SAUCE

When made with very thick, flavorful brown veal stock that becomes a very firm jelly if refrigerated, the following "small sauce" can replace *demi-glace*.

	For 1 Cup	*For 1 Quart*
SLURRY	*3 tablespoons cold stock*	*¾ cup cold stock*
	1⅓ teaspoons potato starch	*5¼ teaspoons potato starch*
STOCK	*¾ cup*	*3 cups*
FLAVORING	*1 tablespoon Madeira, sherry or port*	*¼ cup Madeira, sherry or port*

Make the slurry and blend, stirring, into the hot stock. Cook over low heat until thickened. Add wine.

ENRICHMENT OF BROWN SAUCES

Brown sauces are rarely enriched with anything else than butter. It should be whisked raw and unmelted into the ready-to-serve sauce. Do not reboil. Occasionally a brown sauce will be enriched with heavy cream, plain or whipped. Reduce the sauce to a thick consistency and bring it back to its original consistency by adding the required amount of cream.

SMALL BROWN SAUCES

A "mother brown sauce" becomes a "small brown sauce" when different ingredients are added to it. A reduction of claret and shallots added to a basic brown sauce makes it a *bordelaise sauce,* while a reduction of white wine and shallots and an addition of mustard transforms it into a *Robert sauce.* Any recipe in this book containing a basic brown sauce mixed with other ingredients is a "small brown sauce."

CLASSIC MADEIRA SAUCE
1½ CUPS

1¼ cups classic brown sauce	*2 tablespoons dry Madeira*
(p. 114) or demi-glace sauce	*2 tablespoons butter*
(p. 117)	*Salt and pepper*

This tastes better made with demi-glace sauce. Blend in Madeira and fluff in butter. Add seasoning if necessary. Strain into a sauceboat.

ANCHOVY AND OLIVE SAUCE
1½ CUPS

2 tablespoons chopped onion	*6 green olives, blanched and*
2 tablespoons butter	*chopped*
¼ cup dry vermouth	*1 teaspoon anchovy paste*
1¼ cups classic brown sauce	*Dash of freshly grated pepper*
(p. 114)	*Salt*
6 black olives, chopped	

Sauté the onion in the butter until tender and add vermouth. Reduce to ¼ cup. Add the brown sauce and simmer together for 10 minutes; strain. Add black and green olives and blend in anchovy paste; pepper vigorously. Add salt if needed. Fluff in as much additional butter as you like.

PARSLEY AND GARLIC SAUCE
1½ CUPS

3 whole garlic cloves, peeled	*Salt and pepper*
1 shallot, minced	*¼ cup fine-chopped parsley*
⅓ cup dry white wine	*3 tablespoons butter*
1¼ cups classic brown sauce	
(p. 114)	

Crush the garlic cloves, and put in a saucepan with the shallot and white wine. Reduce to 2 tablespoons. Add the brown sauce and simmer together for 10 minutes. Add seasoning to taste and strain into a serving bowl. Blend in parsley and fluff in butter.

THICKENING WITH KNEADED BUTTER (BEURRE MANIÉ)

Kneaded butter (*beurre manié*) is a mixture of equal parts of flour and butter mixed together with a fork until a smooth paste is obtained. This paste is used to thicken quickly fish or meat sauces resulting from poaching or braising. It could also be called the great redeemer of cooks who burn *roux* and find themselves with liquid sauces, since some kneaded butter added to such a failed sauce will bring it back to the proper consistency. The proportions used are:

Thin sauce   1 tablespoon flour and 1 tablespoon butter per 1 cup liquid

Medium sauce   2 tablespoons flour and 2 tablespoons butter per 1 cup liquid

To make *beurre manié,* the butter must be at room temperature, or the mixture will be uneven and lumps will adorn the finished sauce. To thicken the sauce, whisk the kneaded butter very fast into the boiling sauce; the heat immediately dilates the granules of starch. *Stop the boiling and/or simmering as soon as the sauce has thickened.* Otherwise, since the flour has not been cooked before being incorporated into the sauce, the sour or bitter taste of raw flour will permeate the sauce. A flour-bound sauce can only simmer a long time after thickening if the flour has been precooked in a *roux*. *Beurre manié* is the ideal thickening agent for cooks in a hurry.

TOMATO SAUCES

Making a bad tomato sauce is easy. Unripe tomatoes, insufficient cooking, too many seasonings and herbs are the main offenders. For a good tomato sauce, first, use only sun-ripened garden tomatoes; the hot-house vegetable is lifeless; second, cook the sauce long enough; it takes hours to break down completely the natural acidity of the fruit. Well-cooked tomato sauce is slightly orange rather than bright red.

I follow here a method recommended by Prosper Montagné; I make an all-purpose tomato essence that can be used as an additive and as well easily transformed into a tomato sauce. This tomato essence freezes well but should be thickened only *after defrosting* since the acidity of the tomatoes helps hydrolize the thickening starch.

ESSENCE OF TOMATOES I
(all-purpose essence made with tomatoes)
ABOUT 5 CUPS

8 to 10 pounds fresh ripe	*2 teaspoons sugar*
tomatoes	*1 teaspoon salt*
¼ cup oil	*Dash of pepper*
2 small onions, chopped	*Potato starch*

Wash and halve the tomatoes, but do not peel; squeeze out all traces of seeds and water. Chop, and measure; you will need 12 packed cups. Heat the oil, add onions, and sauté until onions are translucent. Add tomatoes, sugar, salt and pepper; mix well. Cook, covered, over medium heat for 1 hour. Uncover the pot and continue cooking in a 300°F. oven for 3 hours, stirring at regular intervals. Strain into a large saucepan. (At this point the tomato essence can be frozen.) Thicken with 1 teaspoon potato starch per cup of sauce.

ESSENCE OF TOMATOES II
(all-purpose essence made with canned tomato sauce)
2 CUPS

Canned tomato sauce is still too acid and needs to be recooked a little. Before buying the canned product, *read the label.* Citric acid is always there and should be. If onions are mentioned, recook the sauce without any further addition of onions. Beware of green pepper; it has no place in a basic tomato sauce, but it is often present; the taste can ruin hours of work, unless the sauce prepared is intended to be a pepper sauce. The word "spices" on the label more often than not indicates the presence of cayenne pepper. Taste the sauce; if the back of your tongue burns, omit pepper in your essence.

> *2 large onions, chopped* *¼ teaspoon salt*
> *¼ cup oil* *Dash of pepper (if needed)*
> *3 cups canned tomato sauce* *Potato starch*
> *1 teaspoon sugar*

Sauté the onions (if used) in the hot oil until translucent. Add tomato sauce, sugar, salt and pepper, and bring to a boil. Let simmer, uncovered, in a 300°F. oven for 1½ hours. Strain. Thicken with 1 teaspoon potato starch per cup of sauce.

SPICED TOMATO SAUCE

Use the recipe for Essence of Tomatoes II. As soon as the sauce boils, add all the desired herbs and garlic and let them simmer with the sauce.

WARM EMULSIFIED SAUCES

An emulsion is the suspension in each other of two liquids which *cannot be mixed.* An oil and vinegar dressing is a *temporary emulsion,* which breaks into a layer of oil and a layer of vinegar when left to stand. Hollandaise sauce is the "mother sauce" of the warm emulsified sauces. Emulsified sauces are *permanent emulsions,* in which a large amount of liquid butter is emulsified in thickened egg yolk. The egg-yolk molecules coat the droplets of liquid butter and keep them from fusing together again; the emulsion of the butter in the yolks is helped by a small amount of acid (citrus fruit, juice, vinegar, etc.). The emulsion will remain permanent as long as the sauce is kept at a temperature lower than 180° F.

INFUSION

An emulsified sauce acquires its particular taste from an "infusion," or simmered mixture of flavorings in an acid liquid. The base of hollandaise is a mixture of water, salt and lemon juice, while that of béarnaise is a mixture of vinegar and herbs cooked and reduced together. The herbs have been "infused," or steeped, in the vinegar and have flavored it with their rendered juices. The infusion always contains the necessary salt and pepper to season the sauce. Once cooked, the sauce is too fat for additional salt to dissolve properly in it; therefore, salt must be dissolved in a little warm water before being added to a finished sauce.

EMULSION

By whisking both infusion and egg yolks together very fast over very low heat, you will obtain a very thick custardlike mixture. Very slow heating of the yolks over very low heat is a must; too much heat and/or too fast heating will invariably bring on their curdling, and curdled yolks cannot retain the emulsified butter.

The emulsion of the butter in the poached yolks will become stable only if the butter is *warm, not hot.* The molecules of fat in the butter have a tendency, at first, to slide against the protein molecules of the yolks; a good emulsion can only be obtained by adding the butter *drop by drop* until the sauce shows signs of thickening. Only then can it be added in progressively larger amounts (½ teaspoon, then, 1 teaspoon, then 1 tablespoon, and so on) without any separation or a too liquid consistency resulting. One properly poached egg yolk can absorb as much as 6 tablespoons of melted butter.

INGREDIENTS FOR EMULSIFIED SAUCES

The eggs for hollandaise should be of extreme freshness (Grade AA preferably). The butter should be *unsalted*. The vinegar used in emulsified sauces should be of first quality. If you have difficulty finding good wine vinegar, make your infusion with half white wine and half vinegar. The amount of lemon juice used in a hollandaise is a question of personal taste; use as much as you like. Dried herbs added to an emulsified sauce as a finishing touch must be revived with hot water.

SAUCEPAN FOR MAKING EMULSIFIED SAUCES

Use a very thick pot capable of holding the heat evenly. A 1-quart pot of porcelain enamel over cast iron is excellent, but as with anything else, an emulsified sauce can be made in any pot by the cook who uses her head and does not panic.

THE FOUR METHODS OF MAKING HOLLANDAISE SAUCE

BLENDER METHOD

The blender makes a very stiff and compact sauce because the centrifugal movement of the blades homogenizes butter and yolks, but at the same time chases the air out of the sauce toward the sides of the container. After you beat egg yolks, lemon juice, salt, pepper and some hot water until foamy, add the very warm butter to the mixture in a *steady not too slow stream;* the faster the addition of the butter, the more liquid the sauce. If the finished sauce is still too compact, add a few tablespoons of warm water.

COLD BUTTER METHOD

Mix well the infusion and the egg yolks. Stick 4 tablespoons of cold butter in a solid chunk at the end of a wooden spoon. Put the pot directly over very low heat and stir in the butter so that the chunk constantly scrapes along the bottom of the pot. The butter melts slowly, with a cooling effect on the yolks; thickening of the sauce is usually simultaneous with complete emulsification of the butter. The consistency of the sauce is medium, and it can be lightened to taste by adding lukewarm water to the sauce.

This is an excellent method to give the beginner cook confidence, but it is time-consuming when more than 3 egg yolks are involved.

DOUBLE-BOILER METHOD

This method is the most commonly used and is responsible for more disasters and frustrated cooks than any other. While the cook concentrates on the sauce to the point of mesmerization,,the water in the lower container of the double boiler starts surreptitiously boiling. The result is a gorgeous mess of lemon-flavored hard-boiled egg yolks in the upper container. But why? says the poor cook.

Under ideal circumstances, yolks and infusion must be beaten in a container placed at least 2 inches above *very hot* water. The heat should be turned on and off regularly to make sure that the water *never comes to a boil.* Once the yolk mixture is foamy white, the melted butter is trickled down into the sauce to make the emulsion.

PROFESSIONAL METHOD

This method is used by all chefs and taught at the Cordon Bleu in Paris. I urge all beginner cooks to use it without hesitation.

Mix infusion and egg yolks. Place the pot over direct very low heat; if the pot is thin, use an asbestos or metal pad to control the heat. Start whisking very fast and introduce as much air as possible into the yolks while they poach. In about 3 or 4 minutes, the mixture is almost white and frothy, as if it had been beaten with an electric mixer.

Remove the pot from the heat before the eggs are too thick and dry; as soon as it is off the heat, start dribbling in the melted *warm,* but *not hot,* butter while you continue whisking with gusto. Behold, the lovely foamy bulk of butter sauce, promising and mouth-watering!

SEPARATION

Once the sauce is finished, it may happen that the sauce becomes too warm (above 140°F.) and separates on standing. Small islands of liquid butter appear at the edges of the pot, and what is still bound in the center of the pot is deep yellow and compact. This separation is due to complete evaporation of the little bit of liquid contained in the original infusion; adding 1 or 2 tablespoons of lukewarm liquid (water or stock) and giving the mixture a good whisking will bring the sauce back to its normal consistency.

CURDLING

If the sauce heats beyond separation (above 185°F.), the egg will continue cooking and start to curdle. At this point, the emulsion will be completely broken, and you will see bits of hard egg yolk swimming in clarified butter. Redeem the sauce by making a slurry with 1 teaspoon cornstarch or potato starch dissolved in 3 tablespoons water. Add the slurry to the sauce, whisk well, and thicken, but keep that sauce for family use. It is not fit for company, it looks pitty, and has a definite taste of hard-boiled egg yolk.

SERVING AN EMULSIFIED SAUCE

Strain the sauce through a course strainer into a sauceboat rinsed with boiling water and carefully dried. A too fine strainer will separate the emulsion.

Make emulsified sauces ahead of time and keep them warm over water heated to 140°F., but no hotter, to avoid last-minute scrambling while guests are in the living room. If the sauce thickens while standing, lighten it with 1 or 2 tablespoons water.

Beware of hollandaise that stands a long time; the lemon taste intensifies and the sauce becomes very acid. Use a minimum of lemon to make the sauce and add more, if necessary, just before serving.

STABILIZING A SAUCE

Should a sauce have to be cooked a rather long time before serving it, stabilize it with a starch slurry. In restaurants, a tablespoon of béchamel or cream sauce is added to the *finished* sauce to accomplish this stabilization. If you have no béchamel, prepare a slurry with ½ teaspoon cornstarch, ⅓ cup water or milk, and a little salt and pepper. Thicken the slurry and add it to your sauce in the proportion of 1 tablespoon slurry to 3 egg yolks. The sauce will neither separate nor curdle.

Do not add raw cornstarch to the infusion *before* making the sauce; since a true hollandaise thickens without boiling, the cornstarch will not produce a gel and the raw starch will be felt very easily on the tongue.

BLENDER HOLLANDAISE
ABOUT 2 CUPS

4 egg yolks	¾ cup melted unsalted butter
½ teaspoon salt	2 tablespoons warm water
1 tablespoon lemon juice	Dash of white pepper
1 tablespoon hot water	

Blend egg yolks, salt, lemon juice and hot water on medium high speed until eggs are foamy. Melt the butter, let it bubble, and cool for 1 minute. Turn blender on high speed; add half of the butter in a steady stream. Add 1 teaspoon warm water and the rest of the butter; blend again. Add the pepper. Taste the sauce; if more salt is needed, dissolve it in the rest of the water and add to the sauce. Blend for 15 more seconds. Strain into a warmed bowl.

COLD BUTTER HOLLANDAISE
ABOUT 2 CUPS

⅓ cup water	¼ teaspoon ground white pepper
1 tablespoon lemon juice	3 egg yolks
½ teaspoon salt	¾ cup unsalted cold butter

Mix water, lemon juice, salt and pepper; boil together until only 2 tablespoons liquid are left. Add egg yolks and mix well. Add the cold butter, 4 tablespoons at a time, as indicated on page 123. Add more lemon juice to the finished sauce if desired. Strain into a warmed bowl.

PROFESSIONAL HOLLANDAISE
ABOUT 2 CUPS

For mothers: throw those kids out of the kitchen when you try it for the first time; they won't even bother you next time.

⅓ cup plus 2 tablespoons water	*¼ teaspoon ground white pepper*
1 tablespoon lemon juice	*3 egg yolks*
⅔ teaspoon salt	*½ pound* unsalted *butter, melted*

Mix the ⅓ cup water, the lemon juice, salt and pepper, and reduce to 2 tablespoons. Add the egg yolks. Whisk over very low heat until the mixture is very thick and white. Remove from the heat and dribble in the warm melted butter; add the remaining 2 tablespoons water by teaspoons at regular intervals. When butter and water have been incorporated, strain into a warmed bowl.

HORSERADISH HOLLANDAISE
ABOUT 2 CUPS

For poached strong fish (rockfish, mackerel); poached or boiled meats (beef, chicken, tongue); poached eggs.

½ cup water	*3 egg yolks*
2 teaspoons vinegar	*½ pound* unsalted *butter, melted*
1 tablespoon fine-grated	*1 to 2 tablespoons water*
horseradish	*1 teaspoon Dijon-style prepared*
⅓ teaspoon salt	*mustard*
¼ teaspoon white pepper	

Prepare the infusion with water, vinegar, horseradish, salt and pepper; reduce to 2 tablespoons. Proceed then as for hollandaise. Blend the mustard into the finished sauce.

ANCHOVY HOLLANDAISE
ABOUT 2 CUPS

For all poached fish, especially salmon. The anchovy paste alone will salt the sauce so no additional salt is necessary.

2 tablespoons water	*1 teaspoon vinegar*
1 tablespoon anchovy paste	*3 egg yolks*
1/4 teaspoon ground white pepper	*1/2 pound* unsalted *butter, melted*

Mix 2 tablespoons water, the anchovy paste, pepper, vinegar and egg yolks, and whisk together over low heat until foamy. Proceed then as for hollandaise, adding 1 or 2 more tablespoons water if necessary. Strain into a warmed bowl.

CAPER HOLLANDAISE
ABOUT 2 CUPS

For cauliflower; poached fish, especially salmon; poached white meats; poached lamb.

1 jar (2 ounces) capers in	*1/4 teaspoon ground white pepper*
vinegar	*3 egg yolks*
1/3 teaspoon salt	*3/4 cup melted* unsalted *butter*

Drain the preserving juice of the capers into the saucepan. Add salt and pepper and stir until the salt is dissolved. Make the hollandaise in the usual way and stir the capers into the finished sauce.

GARLIC HOLLANDAISE
ABOUT 2 CUPS

I have developed this sauce to use with a good piece of grilled or roasted lamb or as a topping for a dish of snails.

½ *cup white wine*

2 *tablespoons fine-chopped shallots*

2 *tablespoons fine-chopped leek*

¼ *teaspoon dried rosemary*

¼ *teaspoon dried thyme*

¼ *bay leaf*

1 *tablespoon chopped fresh* parsley stems

3 *egg yolks*

¾ *cup melted* unsalted *butter*

1 *tiny garlic clove*

1 *tablespoon chopped fresh* parsley leaves

Make an infusion with the wine, shallots, leek, rosemary, thyme, bay leaf and parsley *stems*. Reduce the infusion to 2 tablespoons and proceed as for hollandaise. When the butter is all incorporated, mash the garlic clove in the serving bowl, add the chopped parsley *leaves*, and strain the sauce on top. Mix well.

MUSTARD HOLLANDAISE

For all poached or boiled white meats; all fish, especially deep-fried, panfried or breaded fish; grilled chicken; poached eggs.

Make hollandaise following the professional method. Blend in 1 tablespoon, or more to taste, prepared Dijon-style mustard.

MOUSSELINE SAUCE

The prettiest daughter of hollandaise; for asparagus, cauliflower, broccoli; all poached fish; poached eggs.

Make hollandaise. For each recipe, whip ¼ cup heavy cream until it barely mounds. Season the cream with salt to taste and fold in the hollandaise.

ROQUEFORT MOUSSELINE

For braised lettuce or escarole.

Make mousseline sauce with very little lemon juice. For each recipe break enough Roquefort or blue cheese into fine crumbs to make 1½ tablespoons. Add crumbled cheese to finished sauce.

CAVIAR MOUSSELINE

For poached or grilled salmon and other firm-fleshed fish; poached eggs and topping for omelettes.

Make mousseline sauce with very little salt. For each recipe, blend 1 tablespoon caviar of the best available grade into the finished sauce.

CURRY MOUSSELINE

For poached eggs; poached fish.

Make a basic mousseline sauce, adding 1½ teaspoons curry powder and 1 teaspoon tomato paste to the infusion at the beginning of the recipe.

IRISH SAUCE

Excellent on poached leg of lamb.

Make a basic mousseline sauce, adding 1 to 1½ teaspoons minced fresh mint to the infusion at the beginning of the recipe.

MALTAISE AND MIKADO SAUCES
1½ TO 2 CUPS

For asparagus exclusively. Maltaise is made with sour orange juice. Mikado is made with tangerine juice. The method is the same as for hollandaise.

2 tablespoons water	½ teaspoon salt
1 teaspoon lemon juice	Pinch of pepper
¼ cup plus 2 tablespoons orange or tangerine juice	3 egg yolks
2 teaspoons fine-grated orange or tangerine rind	½ pound unsalted butter, melted

Make an infusion with the water, lemon juice, ¼ cup orange or tangerine juice, the orange or tangerine rind, the salt and pepper. Proceed then as for hollandaise. Incorporate the remaining 2 tablespoons orange or tangerine juice, a teaspoon at a time, to lighten the sauce. Strain into a warmed bowl.

KEY LIME SAUCE
1½ TO 2 CUPS

For grilled pompano and shrimps.

¼ cup water	*½ teaspoon salt*
1½ tablespoons plus 2 tablespoons lime juice	*¼ teaspoon ground white pepper*
	3 egg yolks
½ teaspoon fine-grated lime rind	*½ pound unsalted butter, melted*

Make an infusion with water, 1½ tablespoons lime juice, the lime rind, salt and pepper. Proceed then as for hollandaise. At the end, lighten the sauce with the rest of the lime juice, or use water if you prefer, adding it a teaspoon at a time.

WHITE-WINE FISH SAUCE
ABOUT 2 CUPS

A gorgeous robe for all poached fish, especially sole. The *fumet* may be mixed with part mussel or mushroom juice.

⅔ cup white-wine fish fumet *(p. 83)*	*⅔ teaspoon salt*
	¼ teaspoon ground white pepper
5 egg yolks	*¾ pound unsalted butter, melted*
Few drops of lemon juice (optional)	

Reduce the *fumet* to ¼ cup. Add the egg yolks, drops of lemon juice, and salt and pepper. Fluff up the eggs; then proceed as for hollandaise. The sauce does not thicken very much because of the low acid content. The lemon juice helps, but do not use too much, for it would change the flavor.

BÉARNAISE
ABOUT 2 CUPS

This is the best of all French sauces. It is nearly always miscooked and misseasoned. When correctly prepared, it is the loveliest of concoctions to use for grilled red meats, chicken or fish; also excellent for poached eggs.

This recipe is entirely based on dried herbs; if fresh herbs can be found, use 1 tablespoon fresh herb in place of each teaspoon of dried herb.

½ cup white wine	¼ bay leaf
⅓ cup wine or cider vinegar	⅓ teaspoon salt
2 tablespoons minced shallots	½ teaspoon cracked white pepper
2½ teaspoons dried tarragon	3 egg yolks
2 teaspoons dried chervil	½ pound unsalted butter, melted
4 teaspoons fine-chopped fresh parsley	1 tablespoon boiling water
	Cayenne pepper

Make an infusion with the wine, the vinegar, shallots, 1½ teaspoons of the tarragon, 1 teaspoon of the chervil, 3 teaspoons of the fresh parsley, the bay leaf, salt and white pepper. Cook until only 5 teaspoons of liquid are left when the herbs are pressed with the back of a spoon. Add the egg yolks and whisk over heat until the mixture is thick, just as with hollandaise. Then remove from the heat and dribble in the warm melted butter. When the butter is incorporated, strain into a warmed bowl.

Meanwhile revive the remaining 1 teaspoon tarragon and 1 teaspoon chervil in the tablespoon of boiling water. Add the remaining teaspoon of fresh parsley and as much cayenne pepper as you can pick up on the tip of a paring knife (a good pinch). Add this revived-herb mixture and the liquid to the strained sauce; the herbs and their liquid are used as a lightener for the sauce.

For those cooks who like béarnaise sauce and would like to make it often, the base or infusion can be made in bulk and kept refrigerated. The ingredients given here may be multiplied any number of times, and the infusion may be stored in a jar. Use 1 teaspoon of infusion (herbs and all) per egg yolk to give a superb sauce. The vinegar infusion ages and mellows with time.

CHORON SAUCE

This is a béarnaise finished with 1½ tablespoons tomato paste mixed with 1½ tablespoons heavy cream instead of the revived herbs. Its uses are the same as those of béarnaise.

BÉARNAISE SAUCE BRAZIER

This variation is served at the Restaurant de la Mère Brazier in Lyon with *poularde pochée demi-deuil*. To 1 recipe of strained basic béarnaise, add 1 generous teaspoon of prepared creamed horseradish.

VALOIS SAUCE

Add 3 tablespoons melted meat glaze (p. 79)—sorry, homemade only—to 1 recipe of béarnaise sauce. For all grilled meats, especially lamb chops.

COLD EMULSIFIED SAUCES

Our much-used mayonnaise is the "mother" of the cold emulsified sauces. Was it really first made at Fort Mahon and first called *mahonnaise* and from that *mayonnaise?* Or does it get its name from *moyeux,* an old French word for egg yolks, still in use in some of the French provinces? Authorities are still discussing, and we shall let them.

Although it is so easy to reach for a jar of mayonnaise in the supermarket, every cook should once try for that most satisfying achievement: making a mayonnaise by hand.

True mayonnaise does not contain any mustard. The emulsion of cold oil in the raw egg yolks occurs with the help of a very small amount of vinegar or lemon juice. The principles are exactly those of hollandaise, but since the yolks are not poached, the sauce is easier to make.

In the electric blender, no difficulty exists. The sauce may be made either with 3 egg yolks or 1 whole egg. By hand, it is preferable to use a small bowl that is as cylindrical as possible. Rinse the bowl with hot water and dry it before starting. Use a whisk; it is more efficient than a wooden spoon. Mix the yolks with salt, pepper and lemon juice, but *no sugar.* Add the oil drop by drop at the beginning, then accelerate as soon as the sauce thickens. All ingredients should be *at room temperature,* for cold oil makes a broken mayonnaise.

The choice of oil is important but is truly a question of taste. I prefer the clean taste of corn oil and would definitely avoid safflower oil or olive oil. A mayonnaise made with olive oil only is obnoxiously strong; if you like the taste of olive oil, use half corn, half olive oil; the sauce will be more subtle. Olive oil alone should be used only for the garlic *aioli.* The more experienced you become, the more oil your yolks will be able to absorb; if the mayonnaise must wait before using, do not use more than 1/2 cup oil per yolk.

Mayonnaise is finished with a good tablespoon of boiling water. This stabilizes it, so that on standing the sauce will not "bleed" droplets of oil. The consistency of the sauce thins considerably after the addition of water, but thickens again and piles beautifully after a 2-hour stay in the refrigerator. Taste your mayonnaise before adding the boiling water; if more salt is needed, dissolve some in the water before adding it to the sauce.

SEPARATION

If a handmade mayonnaise separates, blender mayonnaise will not. Let the separated sauce stand for 30 minutes. The egg yolk will precipitate at the bottom of the bowl. Spoon off the oil almost completely. Whisk the sauce in the bowl well until it thickens. Then proceed with the oil you have spooned off just as you would with new ingredients. If the emulsion obstinately refuses to form, add 1 fresh egg yolk; your troubles will end.

BLENDER MAYONNAISE
ABOUT 1¼ CUPS

1 egg
1½ teaspoons vinegar
⅓ teaspoon salt
¼ teaspoon ground white pepper
1 teaspoon English or prepared mustard

1 cup oil
1 to 2 tablespoons lemon juice
1 tablespoon boiling water

Put all ingredients except ¾ cup oil, the lemon juice and water in the blender container. Blend on medium speed. Add remainder of oil in a steady stream. Add lemon juice to taste and the water last. Remove to a bowl and refrigerate for at least 2 hours.

HANDMADE MAYONNAISE
ABOUT 1½ CUPS

3 egg yolks
⅓ teaspoon salt
¼ teaspoon ground white pepper
2 teaspoons vinegar

1¼ to 1½ cups oil
1 to 2 tablespoons lemon juice
1½ tablespoons boiling water

With a whisk, mix egg yolks, salt, pepper and vinegar. Add the oil drop by drop, stirring vigorously. As the sauce thickens, add progressively more oil and the amount of lemon juice desired. Add the boiling water, whisking well. Refrigerate for 2 hours.

WATERCRESS OR DILL MAYONNAISE
ABOUT 1½ CUPS

For cold salmon especially. For full taste, do not blanch the herbs; they have more bite and character.

1¼ cups mayonnaise
⅓ cup fine-chopped watercress
*   or fresh dill*

2 teaspoons fine-chopped scallions

Mix all ingredients together.

AÏOLI THE AMERICAN WAY
ABOUT 2 CUPS

For boiled fish or shellfish. Use excellent olive oil exclusively, and lemon juice, not vinegar. The blender takes care of the difficulty of binding the sauce at the beginning; good-bye to my grandmother's slice of bread to "help it start." For a more or less "angry" *aïoli,* use more or less garlic to taste.

3 egg yolks
3 to 6 large garlic cloves, chopped
1 tablespoon lemon juice
⅓ teaspoon salt

¼ teaspoon ground black pepper
1 cup olive oil
3 tablespoons boiling water

Mix egg yolks, garlic, lemon juice, salt and pepper in the blender container. Blend on medium speed for 30 seconds. Turn off the blender. Repeat twice. Dribble ⅓ cup oil into the container, blending on medium speed until the sauce thickens. Add the remainder of the oil in three additions; the sauce will be very thick. Lighten it with the boiling water and blend well. Refrigerate for 2 hours.

HARD-COOKED-EGG-YOLK MAYONNAISE
ABOUT 2 CUPS

This tastes better made in the blender.

3 hard-cooked egg yolks
1 uncooked egg white
2 teaspoons prepared Dijon-style
mustard

⅓ teaspoon salt
¼ teaspoon ground white pepper
1 to 1½ cups oil
Lemon juice

Mash the egg yolks and push through a strainer into the blender container. Add egg white, mustard, salt, pepper and 3 tablespoons of the oil; blend on medium speed. Gradually add the remainder of the oil on medium speed. Add lemon juice to taste.

GRIBICHE SAUCE
ABOUT 1½ CUPS

This may be made with regular mayonnaise or with hard-cooked-egg-yolk mayonnaise. It is excellent for poached fish.

1¼ cups mayonnaise
2 tablespoons minced dill pickles
2 tablespoons minced capers
1 tablespoon minced fresh parsley

1 tablespoon minced fresh
tarragon
1 tablespoon minced fresh chives

Blend seasonings into the finished mayonnaise.

MOUSQUETAIRE SAUCE
ABOUT 1 CUP

Excellent for cold roast beef, cold chicken and pork.

⅓ cup dry white wine
1 tablespoon fine-chopped
shallots

⅛ teaspoon commercial meat
extract
1 cup mayonnaise

Make an infusion with wine, shallots and meat extract; reduce to 1 tablespoon; cool. Blend into mayonnaise.

CAVIAR AND LOBSTER MAYONNAISE
ABOUT 1½ CUPS

For cold fish or shellfish; cold eggs.

1 can (2 ounces) lobster spread　　*1½ tablespoons caviar, the best*
1¼ cups mayonnaise　　　　　　　　*available*

With a whisk or electric mixer, cream together the lobster spread and 3 tablespoons of the mayonnaise. Strain through a conical strainer. Blend the strained mixture and the caviar into the bulk of the mayonnaise.

AVOCADO MAYONNAISE
ABOUT 1⅔ CUPS

For cold salmon, Pacific or Atlantic, red snappers, sand dabs, shellfish, salads, cold eggs.

1¼ cups mayonnaise　　　　　　　*½ cup mashed and strained*
½ teaspoon fine-grated lime rind　　*avocado*
　　　　　　　　　　　　　　　　1 tablespoon lime juice, or more

Put all ingredients in the blender and mix until smooth. Refrigerate for 2 hours before serving.

SWEDISH APPLE MAYONNAISE
ABOUT 1½ CUPS

For cold roast pork, cold chicken, turkey and goose.

2 tart apples　　　　　　　*1¼ cups mayonnaise*
1 tablespoon lemon juice

Grate the apples and mix with lemon juice. Cook until only 2 tablespoons are left. Put in the blender container, add mayonnaise, and blend together. Chill.

BUTTER SAUCES

The finest sauces are those made with no other thickener than butter emulsified in a very small amount of liquid. A plain, thin, alkaline liquid will not bring on a very good emulsion, but a very acid one—vinegar or wine infusion—or a viscous one—meat or fish glaze, reduced stock—will.

EMULSIFIED BUTTER SAUCES ON AN ACID BASE

The "mother" sauce is the French *beurre blanc,* or white butter. The basic principle lies in emulsifying the butter in a very concentrated reduction of vinegar and shallots. This is done over very low heat, and a small whisk is used. It is *imperative* that the temperature of the butter not rise above 130°F. Use a small-power burner on an electric stove and the burner with a thermostat (if you have one) on a gas stove. The resulting sauce is surprisingly thick and creamy white.

The white butter in France always raises gastronomic storms; every one has "the formula." I have developed a few variations on it, which appear in the next pages, and I beg the pardon of all my French ancestry for having dared the undareable—variations on the Divine White Butter.

EMULSIFIED BUTTER SAUCES ON A GLAZE BASE

There is no "mother" in this category. When meats are sautéed or panfried, they leave a deposit of caramelized proteins on the bottom of the skillet. After removing the fat which covers them, you can add some stock, or even water, to the pan. With this stock, dissolve the caramelized proteins by scraping well with a wooden spatula. Add a little wine if you desire. This procedure is called "deglazing." Reduce the deglazing mixture to about 3 tablespoons. Turn down the heat; let the temperature of the glaze drop to very medium; in all cases, the temperature should never exceed 130°F. Whisk in, tablespoon by tablespoon, as much unmelted raw butter as you desire. You may either use a whisk or shake the pan back and forth. And behold the gorgeous, shiny, delicious sauce, thick enough to coat a piece of meat! The same result is achieved with reduced fish juices.

CLASSIC FRENCH WHITE BUTTER
(beurre blanc angevin)
ABOUT 1 CUP

This recipe is, in my opinion, the best! It was taught to me by my Aunt Claire Robert. A Brittany *beurre blanc* would be made with vinegar only.

For pike and shad, but excellent also on saltwater fish.

⅓ cup white-wine or cider vinegar	2 tablespoons fine-chopped shallots
⅓ cup dry white wine (preferably Muscadet or California Folle Blanche)	½ teaspoon salt
	¼ teaspoon ground white pepper
	½ pound unsalted butter

Make an infusion with the vinegar, wine, shallots, salt and pepper. Reduce until 3 tablespoons are left, solids and liquids together. Cool the pot, place over very low heat, and whisk in the butter, tablespoon by tablespoon. Strain into a warmed sauceboat.

VIRGIN BUTTER (A CLASSIC SAUCE)
ABOUT 1 CUP

For vegetables and poached fish.

⅓ cup water	½ cup unsalted butter
2½ tablespoons lemon juice	⅓ cup unsweetened whipped cream
⅓ teaspoon salt	
⅛ teaspoon ground white pepper	

Reduce water, lemon juice, salt and pepper to 2 tablespoons. Whisk in the butter, tablespoon by tablespoon. Fold in the whipped cream.

GENEVA BUTTER
ABOUT 1 CUP

I developed this butter as a replacement for the time-consuming genevoise sauce. For all poached or broiled fish, especially salmon.

4 shallots, chopped fine	*1 tablespoon minced fresh parsley*
2 tablespoons vinegar	*1 tablespoon anchovy paste*
½ cup water	*Dash of pepper*
½ cup full-bodied red wine	*¾ cup unsalted butter*
½ teaspoon each of dried	
tarragon, sweet basil, chervil	

Mix all ingredients except butter and reduce to 3 tablespoons. Fluff in the butter, tablespoon by tablespoon. Strain into a warmed sauce-boat.

MUSTARD BUTTER
ABOUT 1 CUP

For poached and broiled fish, broiled chicken, poached chicken breasts.

½ cup white wine	*¼ teaspoon ground white pepper*
¼ cup chopped Italian parsley	*1 tablespoon prepared Dijon-style*
1 tablespoon minced onion	*mustard*
1 tablespoon minced shallots	*¾ cup unsalted butter*
⅛ teaspoon dried thyme	*2 tablespoons unsweetened*
⅓ teaspoon salt	*whipped cream*

Mix all ingredients except mustard, butter and cream. Reduce to 3 tablespoons. Add mustard and fluff in the butter, tablespoon by tablespoon. Add whipped cream. Strain the sauce into a warmed bowl.

MUSHROOM BUTTER
ABOUT 1 CUP

For poached fish, poached chicken breasts, braised lettuce.

½ cup minced raw mushrooms
½ cup white wine
2 tablespoons minced scallions
1 tablespoon lemon juice
½ teaspoon salt

4 white peppercorns
¾ cup unsalted butter
2 tablespoons heavy cream,
   whipped

Measure ⅓ cup of the mushrooms and set aside. Make an infusion with the rest of the mushrooms and the other ingredients except butter and cream. Reduce so that only 3 tablespoons liquid are left. Fluff in the butter, tablespoon by tablespoon, and strain the sauce into a warmed bowl. Blend in the whipped cream and the reserved raw mushrooms.

PROVENÇAL BUTTER
ABOUT 1 CUP

For broiled and barbecued steaks; also for broiled fish.

⅔ cup dry vermouth
¼ teaspoon meat extract
2 garlic cloves, chopped fine
2 tablespoons chopped fresh
   parsley
1 tablespoon chopped shallots

1½ teaspoons anchovy paste
2 tablespoons tomato paste
Dash of pepper
No salt
¾ cup unsalted butter

Make an infusion with all the ingredients except the butter. Reduce to 3 tablespoons, fluff in the butter, and strain into a warmed bowl.

GREEN BUTTER
ABOUT 1 CUP

For trout, but also good with all grilled and poached fish.

⅔ cup dry vermouth
2 tablespoons each of chopped
spinach, escarole, chicory,
watercress, parsley
½ teaspoon each of dried
tarragon and basil

¼ teaspoon fine-grated orange
rind
1 very small garlic clove, minced
1½ teaspoons anchovy paste
¾ cup unsalted *butter*
2 tablespoons fine-chopped
walnuts

Make an infusion with all the ingredients except butter and walnuts. Reduce until 3 tablespoons liquid are left. Fluff in the butter, tablespoon by tablespoon. Strain into a sauce bowl, pushing on the herbs with a wooden spatula to extract their essence. Add the walnuts.

CAPER BUTTER
ABOUT 1 CUP

For all poached fish; for broccoli and cauliflower.

2 tablespoons small capers
2 tablespoons caper vinegar
⅓ teaspoon salt
¼ teaspoon ground white pepper

¾ cup unsalted *butter*
2 tablespoons unsweetened
cream, whipped

Heat capers, vinegar, salt and pepper until the salt has melted. Add butter, tablespoon by tablespoon, and finish the sauce with cream.

KEEPING AND FREEZING BUTTER SAUCES
Once finished, a butter sauce will keep over a hot-water bath but only if the water never goes over 100°F. This rule must be observed

scrupulously to avoid the disappointment of seeing the sauce separate into two layers, one of the acid infusion and another of clarified butter. If this happens, cool the sauce in the refrigerator until the butter is thick. Put the sauce in the small bowl of an electric mixer, and cream the mixture. The emulsion will re-form. Serve it cool; it will melt on the hot food anyhow.

Another way is to melt a bit of the butter and start again the whole process of fluffing the butter into this small amount of melted butter. Keep an almost nonexistent heat under the pan.

Butter sauces freeze well. Let them defrost at room temperature, and reheat over the lowest possible heat.

CUSTARD SAUCES: A GENERALIZATION

In these sauces, which have no "mother," the same deglazing principle as in the pure butter sauces is applied; but this time instead of being thickened with emulsified butter, the deglazing is bound with a liaison. The deglazing is always a meat or a fish glaze containing some wine.

After deglazing and reducing the liquids, return whatever meat or fish you are cooking to the pan. Mix egg yolks and cream, usually 4 eggs yolks for each 1 cup cream, and add them to the pan. Shake the pan back and forth over medium-high heat. Within 2 or 3 minutes, you will see the sauce coat the food. Remove the pan from the heat, still shaking it to cool off the sauce, and serve immediately.

Pure butter sauces and custard sauces are one part of *haute cuisine* readily accessible to the modern housewife. They are quickly prepared, exquisitely delicate, and widely used nowadays by those professionals who know and love their profession enough to gain time without reaching for that downfall of our modern palates—the can.

FLAVORED BUTTERS

Flavored or compound butters (*beurres composés*) are a remnant of the old classic cuisine. They were added to a finished sauce to give it a proper flavor. They have been, so to speak, banished from modern cuisine by hectic chefs and housewives. They make very simple but delicious sauces. Use for poached fish, seafood, meats, and blanched vegetables.

All herbs must be chopped very fine. Fresh or dried herbs will serve. Use half as much dried herbs as fresh. If you use salted butter to make compound butters, do not add any additional salt. If you use unsalted butter, salt to taste. Always cream the butter, then add the herbs. Let the completed butter stand for a few hours before using. Strain only if mentioned in the recipe.

Usually the butters are used at room temperature, but another way is to serve them cold on a hot dish. The heat of the dish will melt the butter and release the flavor of the herbs. Shape the completed butter into a roll or stick, and chill or freeze it. Then at serving time cut slices from the roll.

NOISETTE BUTTER

This is clarified butter cooked until it turns a golden-brown color. Use with lemon juice to flavor breaded or floured panfried meats and fish.

RAVIGOTE BUTTER
ABOUT ½ CUP

Use on carrots, green beans, peas, cauliflower, potatoes, rice, grilled meats, fish, poached chicken cutlets. This butter can be frozen.

½ cup butter
1 tablespoon each of shallots, parsley, tarragon, chives, chervil

Salt and pepper

MAÎTRE D'HÔTEL BUTTER
ABOUT ½ CUP

Use on carrots, green beans, rice, all grilled meats and fish, poached chicken cutlets. This butter can be frozen.

½ cup butter
1 tablespoon chopped parsley
Salt and pepper
Lemon juice (1 to 3 tablespoons)

COLBERT BUTTER
ABOUT ½ CUP

Use on carrots, beans, cauliflower, potatoes, grilled meats and fish. This butter can be frozen.

½ cup butter
1 tablespoon chopped parsley
2 teaspoons lemon juice
2 tablespoons melted meat glaze,
or ¼ teaspoon meat extract
dissolved in 1 tablespoon water
Salt and pepper

SNAIL BUTTER
ABOUT ½ CUP

Use on green beans, rice, potatoes, snails, shellfish, grilled or sautéed meats, fish. This butter can be frozen.

½ cup butter
½ teaspoon minced shallot
½ teaspoon minced garlic
2 tablespoons minced parsley
Dash of grated nutmeg
Salt and pepper

Strain this butter before serving; you want to retain the garlic juice but not the little pieces of garlic.

MUSTARD BUTTER
ABOUT ½ CUP

Use on green beans, cauliflower, potatoes, rice, all grilled meats and fish. This butter can be frozen.

     ½ cup butter   *Salt and pepper*
     1 tablespoon prepared Dijon-style
       mustard

TARRAGON BUTTER
ABOUT ½ CUP

Use on carrots, cucumbers, rice, grilled meats, poached chicken, veal chops, veal *scaloppine*. A similar butter may be made with any herb. This butter can be frozen.

     ½ cup butter   *Salt and pepper*
     1 tablespoon minced fresh
       tarragon

BASIL BUTTER
ABOUT ⅓ CUP

     1 garlic clove, split   *Salt and pepper*
     6 tablespoons butter   *1 teaspoon crumbled dried basil*

Rub a bowl with the cut sides of the garlic clove. Add the butter to the bowl and cream it. Add salt and pepper to taste and the finely crumbled basil; mix well. This butter can be frozen.

TOMATO-BASIL BUTTER
ABOUT ½ CUP

Use on green beans, boiled potatoes, zucchini, grilled steak. This butter can be frozen.

½ cup butter
3 tablespoons tomato paste

1 teaspoon crumbled dried basil
Salt and pepper

TABASCO BUTTER
ABOUT ½ CUP

Special for boiled corn. If you freeze this butter, add the green pepper after defrosting.

½ cup butter
2 teaspoons Tabasco

2 tablespoons fine-diced raw
green pepper
Salt and pepper

MINT BUTTER
ABOUT ½ CUP

Special for boiled peas. This butter can be frozen. Be generous with the pepper to make this taste lively.

½ cup butter
1 teaspoon finely crumbled dried
mint

¼ teaspoon sugar
Salt
White pepper

CARAWAY BUTTER
ABOUT ½ CUP

Use on turnips, parsnips, kohlrabi, cauliflower. This butter can be frozen.

½ cup butter   *Salt and pepper*
2 teaspoons caraway seeds

POLISH BUTTER

Special for cauliflower and broccoli. This mixture is sometimes called polonaise sauce. This is a butter that cannot be frozen.

½ cup butter   *1 hard-cooked egg, chopped fine*
⅓ cup fresh bread crumbs *1 tablespoon minced parsley*

Melt the butter, add the bread crumbs, and toss over medium heat until the crumbs are golden. Mix with remaining ingredients.

Even though this chapter has concerned itself with many sauces of different kinds, this does not cover all the possible sauces. You will find many examples of emulsified sauces on a glaze base in the chapters on meat and fish cookery (Chapters VI and VII). Cream sauce for vegetables is discussed in Chapter IX. Dessert sauces are few, but these few have many variations; you will find custard sauces (stirred or English custard) in Chapter III and fruit sauces in Chapter X. Those creams that are used chiefly for filling and icing cakes and pastries will be found in Chapter XIII. You may even find here and there a sauce designed for a particular dish. If you have mastered the techniques described in this chapter, none of the other sauces will present any problems.

VI

The True Way
to
That Man's Heart

meat cookery

THERE IS NO DOUBT in the minds of most American housewives that dinner for the man of the house means "meat and potatoes"; whatever comes before or after is the feminine part of the meal.

Besides a 75 percent content of water, meat contains iron, phosphorus and copper, and a large amount of vitamins, especially those of the B complex. Meat proteins contain all the amino acids necessary for the body tissues to grow and constantly maintain themselves in a state of pleasant repair.

In this chapter, the recipes are grouped by techniques of meat cookery rather than by category of meats. Consult the index for all the meat recipes contained in the book.

To understand the techniques of meat cookery, keep in mind the information on meats in the chapter on stocks and soups (Happy Marriages). Muscle fibers of meats are held together by *connective tissues;* the only connective tissue valuable to the cook is *collagen,* because while cooking it undergoes changes that turn it into liquid gelatin.

BUYING MEATS

The chances of buying ungraded meats are unlikely in our modern markets; nevertheless, be sure to look for the stamps on the fat side of the meat.

The round stamp tells you that the meat has been "inspected and passed," i.e., that it has been processed under the best sanitary conditions and comes from a perfectly healthy animal. The round stamp is applied by Federal Law.

The shield-shaped stamp tells you which grade of meat you are buying, whether PRIME, CHOICE, or GOOD. Only a few markets sell meats graded below CHOICE.

All other grades of meats come from healthy but older animals and are sold to process luncheon meats. Grading is done voluntarily by the meat packers; however, *the stamp must correspond to the quality of the meat sold.*

As for poultry, these gradings appear on tags attached to the wing and are too often removed by the supermarkets.

When buying meats and poultry look for the following conditions:

The proportion of meat should be large compared to that of bone and fat.

The fat should be white and firm; yellow fat reveals an old animal.

The muscle fibers should have a fine grain and be well marbled.

The bird you are buying should show no accumulation of fat under the skin except over the backbone; the color of the meat must be clearly visible through the skin; watch for feathers and holes in the skin—birds with these should be avoided; the giblets should be wrapped.

TENDER MEATS, AGED MEATS

When animals are slaughtered, a stiffening of the muscles follows the hardening of the proteins. Letting the meat hang allows that stiffness to disappear. The chemical reactions involved cover pages of chemistry manuals and are not yet completely understood. Meats cooked immediately after slaughtering are extremely tough, because they contain a relatively large amount of acids (lactic acid and others).

As the meat hangs it becomes more pliable, more tender, juicier, and more capable of developing good flavor and aroma while cooking. Meat usually hangs for a minimum of 2 weeks, but it tastes better when hanging lasts 4 weeks or longer. Western Europe prefers well-aged meats; America does not.

Aged meats look dark because their red pigments (myoglobin and hemoglobin) oxidize in the presence of oxygen to form new darker and browner compounds (metmyoglobin and methemoglobin). Aging brings on a chemical reaction called *autolysis* in which large protein molecules are split and the formation of amino acids results. Autolysis is possible only through the presence of enzymes, and it is responsible for the progressive tenderization of the meat.

Only joints of meat protected by large layers of fat can age properly. Aging meats is a very expensive proposition; a second trimming is necessary after aging to remove the bacterial "whiskers" developing on the surface of the joints. Aging meats lose weight as they lose moisture. The prices requested by butchers are justified by the work, time and additional storage expenses involved.

Although small pieces of meat do not age as well as large joints, a very good experiment can be made at home. A large rib roast purchased in a supermarket can be aged quite well in the refrigerator. Place the unwrapped cut on a cake rack on the lowest shelf of the refrigerator; protect it with a tent of paper opened at both ends for proper ventilation. Let it age close to a week. The outside of the cut will turn dark brown from oxidation and superficial dehydration. Check the meat every day. Meat starts spoiling when its surface becomes moist and slippery. Should it happen—it is very unlikely—rub it with vinegar, dry it well, and use it immediately.

I strongly urge housewives *not* to use meat tenderizers containing an enzyme extracted from papaya; when such tenderizers are sprinkled on the meat, they break down the proteins from large molecules into smaller ones. These tenderizers do not penetrate into the deeper layers of the meat; while they work on the outer layers with supreme efficiency and render them mushy, the core of the joint remains as tough as ever. Nothing short of the proper cooking method will tenderize a tough piece of meat.

Marinating and Curing Meats

Meats are *marinated,* or steeped in an acid liquid, for several reasons:

- tenderizing; however, except in thin cuts, the tenderizing remains superficial and minor;
- flavoring; the surface of the meat acquires a definite taste from the liquid and its seasonings;
- retarding bacterial growth if the meat must wait longer than expected to be cooked.

Meats are cured by salting or smoking. Both insure preservation by respectively suppressing and slowing bacterial development. Salted and cured meats remain a bright red *even after cooking* because of the action of sodium nitrate on their myoglobin.

Storing, Freezing and Defrosting Meats

For short-range storing in the refrigerator, meats must be loosely wrapped so that the air can reach the meat. Poultry and veal are more susceptible to spoiling than red meats and should be prepared as soon as possible after purchase, or frozen.

The ideal would be not to freeze meats, but since it must be done, prepare the meat for cooking—pare, trim, and tie it—before freezing. Wrap it in plastic bags surrounded by foil. *Keep the temperature of the freezer as steady as possible;* you may lower it but never raise it.

Veal, beef and lamb will keep frozen from 3 months to 1 year; pork and all types of poultry for 3 to 6 months only. Do not freeze uncooked ground meats; if you find a bargain in ground meats, prepare and cook several ground-meat dishes and freeze them cooked.

About 30 minutes before freezing meats, turn the refrigerator or freezer to its coldest setting, so that the water inside the meat will freeze to small crystals; large crystals break through tissues and provoke a large loss of juices when defrosting.

Thaw meat as slowly as possible. Remove a cut from the freezer to the refrigerator at least 4 days before cooking it. Wrap it in kitchen towels and place it on the lowest rack of the refrigerator. About 4 hours before cooking, remove the roast from the refrigerator. About 2 hours before cooking, remove all the wrappings and rub the meat with oil; let it stand at room temperature until cooking time. A minimum of juices will be lost. Even with this care, the meat will not taste as good as a piece that has not been frozen.

Cutting and Boning Meats

To cut slices or steaks, use your large chopping knife. To bone, use a sharp paring knife; slide the blade between bone and meat and separate them neatly; never tear the meat off the bone.

TO BONE A LEG OF LAMB

Do not cut the leg open. Cut the meat around the thigh bone with a narrow sharp knife and pull out the bone until you reach the articulation; cut the tough ligament attaching the thigh bone to the shank. Do not remove the shank bone; the roast will look better.

TO BONE A WHOLE CHICKEN, TURKEY,
DUCK OR SQUAB

Remove wingtips. Put the bird breast down, the tail facing you. With a sharp paring knife make a cut along the backbone. Neatly separate skin and meat from bone, wrapping the skin backward around your left hand as you go along. Sever the thigh and wing articulations as soon as exposed. Slide the knife blade between breast meat and breastbone until you reach the cartilage.

Turn the bird around. Starting from the tail, repeat the same steps on the other side. Cut along the breastbone cartilage without making a hole in the skin. Remove both wing and thigh bones. Keep the drumsticks in for appearance unless otherwise directed in the recipe.

TO BONE CHICKEN BREASTS TO MAKE CUTLETS

A chicken breast consists of two cutlets, each attached to one side of the breastbone. Use your chopping knife to bone this.

Slide two fingers under the skin; pull off the skin and discard it. Lay the breast on its side with the ribcage opening on your left. With the palm of the left hand, press down as hard as possible on the upper fillet; with the right hand slide the knife blade between fillet and bone and cut 1½ inches deep.

Turn the breast by 90 degrees so that the cut you just made is now facing you. Slide the knife blade with the point straight ahead into the cut between bone and fillet. Push ahead so that the tip of the blade comes out at the center of the line marking the end of the fillet along the rib cage.

Pass your left thumb between blade and meat; hold the cutlet firmly between thumb and index finger; give one stroke of the blade to the right, then one to the left. You will have cut the meat from the ribs, and you will be holding a chicken cutlet. Repeat on the other side to sever the second cutlet.

Each cutlet is made of a small fillet attached to a larger one. Should they be separated, put them back together, they will fuse while cooking. Remove the white tendon visible on the small fillet.

To cut a pocket in a cutlet, lay the boned cutlet on the board, small fillet down. Cut the pocket in the thickest part of the large fillet, two thirds of its thickness down and 1 ½ inches deep. The thin part of the large fillet combines with the small fillet to make the second flap of the pocket.

CUTTING A CHICKEN FOR SAUTÉING

Remove wingtips. To remove legs: Pull each leg away from the body and cut through the skin around the thigh joint. Pull the leg backwards until the joint cracks and the leg lies flat on the board. Cut through the articulation at the thigh joint.

To remove the wings and obtain a boneless cutlet attached to the shoulder: Cut along the breastbone to free the cutlet, then cut through the shoulder articulation.

To remove the oysters: Cut the tail off. Bend the lower back backward, it will break off easily; cut through the skin.

FLAMBÉING MEATS

Meats are flambéed to remove all harsh alcohol from the spirits used for cooking; also, while burning, the spirit leaves its flavor and aroma on their surface. All spirits must be well heated before flambéing.

Home flambéing method: Pour the required amount of spirit into a small pot. Light the spirit with a match and pour it ablaze on the hot meat. Shake the pan back and forth until the flame dies out.

Chef's flambéing method: Pour the required amount of alcohol directly into the sautéing or frying pan. Tilt the pan toward the flame of the stove; the alcohol will immediately catch on fire. Shake the pan as mentioned above. Electric stove owners cannot use this method.

ROASTING—DRY-HEAT PROCEDURE

Roasting is the most ancient meat cookery procedure; it was used by early man to cook his catch over an open fire. In roasting, heat seals the outside layers of a cut of meat so that its juices concentrate inside a coating of caramelized proteins and cannot escape. The best roasting is done on a spit because any steam rising from the joint escapes into the air. In an oven, steam always condenses and produces a small but appreciable amount of moisture detrimental to the sealing of the roast.

As the coagulation of the outside proteins progresses and moisture evaporates, shrinkage can be observed. Inside the roast, some collagen melts and mixes with the water contained in the tissues. The fat that was marbling the uncooked meat breaks down; the fat cells split open and the liquid fat is dispersed all through the roast by the collagen acting as emulsifier. Melted collagen and emulsified fat make the meat juicy and tender.

Very soon after roasting has started, you will notice on the bottom of the pan a deposit of "drippings." They will continue cooking and become caramelized, and can be used to make gravy.

About halfway through the roasting time the meat will give off its particular aroma, very special to each type of meat. This is the result of the formation of volatile compounds as the heat breaks down the amino acids.

Rare meat stays rich in vitamins. Well-done meat, although it may be harder to chew, is easier to digest since all the bacteria it may have contained have been thoroughly destroyed by the heat; but a large portion of the vitamin content has also been destroyed.

The tenderness of a piece of roasted meat depends on many factors such as the animal's feed and age, the amount of collagen and fat the joint contains, and last but not least the skill of the cook. The longer a roast cooks, the deeper the protein coagulation is and the harder the meat becomes to chew. In a well-done roast most of the collagen has escaped into the roasting pan and mostly dry fibers are left.

You may roast to obtain a succulent meat, or to obtain a good meat and a good gravy. Both methods are efficient; choose that best adapted to your personal taste.

If a roast needs tying, use white $\frac{1}{10}$-inch-thick kitchen string. Space the ties $\frac{1}{2}$ inch apart. Do not squeeze the knot too tight or the meat will show "string scars."

Do not brush the roast with anything other than melted fat; basting with any liquid produces steam and delays caramelization and concentration of the juices. If the cut has some natural suet, put the fat side up in the roasting pan.

Roast meat on a rack, not on the bottom of the roasting pan where the bottom of the cut will panfry and overcook. Use a smaller roasting pan where the fat can drip in a thick layer and not burn. To keep the caramelized meat drippings from burning on the bottom of the pan, a very small amount of liquid may be added to the pan, but only *after* the outside of the meat is well sealed. If too much liquid fat accumulates for the pan to be handled safely, remove it with a baster.

Bones conduct the heat of the oven to the center of the meat; as a result boned meats do not roast as fast as pieces with the bone in.

ROASTING AT MEDIUM-HIGH TEMPERATURE (400°F.)

If you roast in a well-preheated oven at a high temperature, the concentration of the juices will be quick. Concentration will be further accentuated if any surface of the cut not covered by a natural layer of suet is brushed with oil and if the meat is *not salted before cooking,* but only when the cut is two thirds done.

In meats cooked this way the shrinkage is relatively large, the flavor highly concentrated, and the contrast between the "brown flavor" of the outer layers with the juiciness of the center is a delight for the palate. Such a roast looses no more than 1 or 2 tablespoons of very concentrated drippings out of which no gravy can be made. It must be enjoyed for its own juiciness or with a separately made sauce.

ROASTING AT MEDIUM TEMPERATURE (325°F.)

If you roast in a medium oven, the meat will obviously not seal as fast and there will be time for some juices to escape. If the meat is sprinkled with salt before the roasting starts, the salt will shrink the bundles of muscular fibers of the outside cut, leaving gaps between them for more juices to escape and drip into the roasting pan. The caramelization will be slightly delayed by the moisture produced by the melting salt, but the dripping will stop as soon as enough caramelization has been completed.

The results are a less noticeable shrinkage, less juiciness, a good "brown flavor," and a large amount of drippings to prepare a delicious natural gravy.

DEGLAZING

Dissolving the pan juices of a roast with a liquid is called deglazing. Deglaze beef with beef stock or water. Leave 1 or 2 tablespoons of fat in the gravy for flavor. Deglaze lamb with veal stock, water, or vermouth; for turkey and chicken use veal or chicken stock; for ducks and game birds use veal stock or a stock made with their bones, either of them laced with a dash of lemon juice or brandy; for pork use water or white wine.

The gravy obtained by deglazing may be thickened, if desired, with *beurre manié* (2 tablespoons butter and 1 tablespoon flour per cup of gravy), or with a slurry made with 1 ⅓ teaspoons potato starch per cup of gravy.

The gravy may be enriched with butter for the brown meats or with cream for the white meats. Whenever a gravy is made with natural (unfortified) table wine, the gravy should be boiled to evaporate the alcohol of the wine. Or adding already reduced wine to the pan juices is acceptable, although slightly more complicated for the cook.

RESTING A ROAST

Let a roast or a roasted bird stand at room temperature for 15 to 20 minutes before carving it, to allow the pressure on the internal juices to diminish slowly; this will allow most of the juices to remain between the fibers instead of rushing out of the meat as soon as a slice is removed. Carving too soon is the downfall of the most skillfully roasted meat.

ROASTING BEEF

Roast only the rib, the loin (strip and tenderloin), the sirloin, the rump and the true eye of the round, of PRIME or CHOICE beef. Even in lesser grades, the rib, tenderloin and strip will make very good roasts even if not as tender as butter.

ROASTING TIME PER POUND FOR OVEN ROASTING AT 400°F.

Cut of Meat	Rare	Medium Rare
Tenderloin	12 minutes	14 minutes
Strip	13 minutes	15 minutes
Rib, bone in	15 minutes	18 minutes
Rib, rolled	16 minutes	20 minutes
Eye round	15 minutes	18 minutes

ROASTING TIME PER POUND FOR OVEN ROASTING AT 325°F.

Cut of Meat	Rare	Medium Rare
Rib, bone in	23 minutes	27 minutes
Rib, rolled	26 minutes	30 minutes
Rump	23 minutes	27 minutes
Eye round	23 minutes	27 minutes

The internal temperatures on the meat thermometer should read:
Tenderloin, rare: 130°F.; Strip, medium rare: 140°F.;
Rib, rare: 140°F.; medium rare: 150°F.;
Rump, rare: 140°F.; medium rare: 150°F.

Spit-roast meats from 20 to 30 minutes more than the total oven roasting time, or spit-roast for two thirds of the total roasting time and allow the meat to finish cooking in a 250°F. oven.

ROASTING VEAL AND CALF

Veal is—or should be—baby beef from 3 to 15 weeks old. If the animal has been 100 percent milk fed, the meat should be barely pink and the fat scarce and absolutely white. Veal is difficult to locate; more often stores offer 4- to 12-months-old calf, the color of which varies from pink to light red. The darker the meat the older the animal and the more solids it has been fed before being marketed. Veal is extremely tender and sometimes flavorless, while calf, although less tender, has a much more pronounced flavor.

Veal or calf are too dry to be spit-roasted. Only a rolled loin of veal can be oven-roasted successfully. All other cuts taste better when casserole roasted (p. 207).

Because of its total absence of marbling, roast veal at 325°F. for about 23 minutes per pound. During the last 10 minutes of roasting, raise the temperature of the oven to 400°F. to allow the piece to brown.

ROASTING LAMB

Lamb is always less than a year old while mutton is over that venerable age. The lamb usually sold in markets is over 5 months old and its age can be roughly determined by the weight of a leg. An early-season leg does not weigh more than 5 pounds while a fall leg will easily climb to 6½ pounds. The darker the color of the meat and the thicker the fat, the older the animal.

Roast the rib (rack or crown), loin (must be especially requested from the butcher), leg and shoulder. Lamb, more than any other meat, is tough if too "fresh" and must be aged to reach its peak of flavor. Do not hesitate to let any cut of lamb age a bit in a tent of foil. A rack can wait almost a week and a leg *must* wait the full week. Nothing adverse can happen to the meat since lamb sold in butcher shops and supermarkets is never aged.

Colorado and Iowa produce some of the finest lamb in the world, which is dutifully overcooked by millions of American housewives every day. Lamb tastes better, it is not "lamby," and it is more appetizing if served *pink*. May I suggest a progressive "rarification"?

Although I personally like a rare leg of lamb, I recommend not to serve it to a person used to well-done lamb roast; the shock will be provoking. Start with chops; panfry them to keep them juicy; graduate then to a rack on the pinkish side; and finally try for a medium-rare leg of lamb; it is a treat. And please, leave that old mint jelly for pear salad!

You may cook lamb in a 400°F. oven to obtain well-done or medium-rare meat. The higher heat will give more succulent meat when you are cooking it medium-rare. If you prefer cooking at a lower temperature, use that for well-done meat only.

ROASTING TIME PER POUND FOR LAMB AT 400°F.

Cut of Meat	Medium Rare
Rack, bone in	total time 45 to 50 minutes
Loin, bone in	12 minutes
Leg, bone in	12 minutes
Shoulder, bone in	total time 50 to 55 minutes
Loin, boned	15 minutes
Leg, boned	20 minutes
Shoulder, boned	20 minutes

TIMETABLE FOR WELL-DONE LAMB AT 325°F.

Cut of Meat	Time Per Pound
Rack or crown	30 minutes
Leg, bone in	30 minutes
Leg, boned	40 minutes
Shoulder, bone in	30 minutes
Shoulder, rolled	40 minutes

The internal temperature of lamb on the meat thermometer should read for medium-rare: 145°F.; for well-done: 160° to 170°F.

ROASTING PORK

Pork is marketed between the ages of 5 months and 1 year, and great care is taken not to keep the animal longer than necessary to avoid excessive fat. The best pork available is light pink; the rosier the meat, the older the animal. Extensive marbling is not desirable, as the meat does not contain the large amounts of collagen necessary to emulsify streaks of fat.

Roast the loin, the rib (crown), the shoulder and the ham. Pork can be delicious and juicy, but the complaint of dryness is heard all over the land for no other reason than overcooking to avoid infection by the parasite *Trichinella spiralis* or trichinae; but trichinae are destroyed at 132°F. and, according to the Bureau of Animal Industry, cooking a piece of pork to an internal temperature of 137°F. will dispose of all trichinae it may contain. So why always cook pork until all its goodness has dribbled into the gravy pan? However, that internal temperature of 132°F. may dispose of the trichinae but it is not enough for a properly cooked piece of meat. Roasted pork is ready to eat when its internal temperature reaches 170°F.

The tightly woven fibers of pork are tastier when roasting is done at 325°F., so that the heat penetrates the piece slowly and regularly. Roast for 35 to 40 minutes per pound. Pork tastes better marinated or heavily spiced because almost all its flavor is concentrated in its fat rather than in its meat.

As for cured pork, such as smoked hams or precooked hams, the cooking methods vary according to the way the meat has been processed. Follow the instructions given by the packers.

ROASTING CHICKENS AND TURKEYS

Like the old gray mare, chicken "ain't what it used to be." There is no doubt that "hothouse" meal-fed chickens will never have the flavor so particular to wheat- or corn-fed birds.

A good roaster is 3 to 5 months old and weighs from 3½ to 4½ pounds; it still has a flexible breastbone; capons are usually 6 to 8 months old; their tender meat is less flavorful than that of chicken. A good turkey may be of any size, but those around 12 pounds seem to be the most flavorful. Can I urge you to celebrate your holidays with freshly killed birds, rather than frozen ones?

Nothing is more delicious than poultry roasted on the spit, and it is a pity that most of us have to use an oven. Remove both pads of fat from the cavity. Sprinkle the seasoning *in the cavity* rather than on the skin, and add a good pad of butter to keep the inside of the breast moist and tender. Truss the bird.

Whole birds should be trussed

❊ for better appearance of the finished dish;

❊ to allow more even penetration of the heat;

❊ to prevent loss of juices from the cavity of the bird.

To Truss a Whole Chicken, Duck, Turkey, Goose or Squab

ENGLISH METHOD

Measure 2½ feet of string. Tie the middle of the string around the tail so as to have the same length of string on each side, and make a knot. Cross the string over and around the ends of the drumsticks; tie. Bring each piece of string alongside the breast and on each side thread the end of the string through the hole made by the wing folded akimbo. Turn the chicken over and tie both ends of the string over the back of the bird.

FRENCH METHOD

Step I. Thread a long trussing needle with about 3 feet of kitchen thread. Put the chicken on its back with the neck to your left. With the left hand raise the legs as high as possible and hold them. Thrust the needle into the middle of the thigh on the right side of the bone; the needle will come out at exactly the same spot on the other side. Pull the string through, leaving about 6 inches of string hanging out. Turn the chicken on its side, breastbone facing you. Pass the needle through one wing at the shoulder, through the gathered neck skin, then through the second wing at the shoulder. Pull the string through and tightly tie the free end of the string to the 6-inch piece you left at the thigh. With your paring knife, cut both ends of the string ½ inch above the knot.

Step II. Thread the needle again. Pierce the leg a second time in front of the thigh and drumstick articulation; pass the needle through to the other side, leaving about 6 inches of string hanging out. Coming back toward yourself, pass the needle through the skin under the tip end of the first drumstick, through the tip end of the breastbone in line with it, and then through the skin under the end of the second drumstick. Pull the string through and tightly tie the free end to the 6-inch piece you left at the articulation. Knot a third piece of string around the tail and the drumstick ends and tie.

While roasting poultry, brush often with melted butter, oil or rendered chicken fat. A chicken may be roasted in either a hot or a medium oven. A large turkey will be better in a medium oven to insure progressive penetration of the heat to its center. A hot oven would result in an underdone center and an overdone skin.

All vegetables and sausage fillings should be precooked and the bird stuffed as close as possible to roasting time to avoid bacterial development.

Roast chicken and turkey for one third of the roasting time lying on its right side, one third of the roasting time on its left side, the last third breast up. The neck should face the back of the oven where the heat is slightly more intense.

ROASTING DUCKS AND GEESE

Ducks and geese are considered red meats. Roast them with either medium or high heat. I recommend using a 325°F. oven.

Do not brush with any oil or fat; set the bird breast side up on the rack; roast for 20 minutes, then prick the sides of the bird below the breast to allow the already melted fat to run out. Remove the fat from the baking dish with a baster at regular intervals. Discard duck fat, but keep goose fat in jars (it can be used to fry delicious potatoes).

Do not stuff ducks. Stuff geese only with a nonabsorbent filling, for any kind of starchy material will soak up fat and be indigestible.

POULTRY ROASTING TIMETABLE

	Temperature	Time Per Pound in Oven	Time Per Pound For Spit-Roasting
Chicken, Rock Cornish Game hen	400°F.	18 minutes	25 minutes
Chicken, Rock Cornish Game hen, turkey	325°F.	25 minutes	35 minutes
Duck	400°F.	15 minutes	25 minutes
	325°F.	25 minutes	25 minutes
Goose	400°F.	18 minutes	25 minutes
	325°F.	25 minutes	

CÔTE DE BOEUF PARIS-LONDRES

The most succulent rib of beef you will ever have tasted. Use a piece with at least 3 ribs, and have it weighed without the short ribs. Preheat the oven to 400°F., and roast for 15 minutes per pound. Salt the roast when three quarters done. Pepper it 5 minutes before removing it from the oven. Let it stand for a good 20 minutes before carving. There will be no gravy. Serve with Anchovy and Olive Sauce (p. 118), Parsley and Garlic Sauce (p. 119), or Madeira Sauce (p. 118).

Wine: California Cabernet-Sauvignon or *French Côte de Nuits*

STANDING RIBS OF BEEF WITH GRAVY

Sprinkle the meat with salt and pepper all around. Preheat oven to 325°F., and roast for 25 minutes per pound. Let stand for 20 minutes before carving. To make the gravy, spoon out all the fat except 1½ tablespoons. Add 1¼ cups water or beef broth and scrape the bottom of the roasting pan well. Thicken the gravy with potato starch or *beurre manié*. Enrich the gravy with as much butter as you like.

Wine: California Cabernet-Sauvignon or *French Côte de Nuits*

VEAL LOIN TANTE CLAIRE
6 SERVINGS

1 onion, chopped fine	*4 tablespoons Madeira*
5 tablespoons butter	*1 cup fresh bread crumbs*
½ pound mushrooms, chopped	*1 boneless loin of veal, 3 pounds*
1 tablespoon fine-chopped shallots	*Clarified butter*
1 teaspoon dried tarragon	*1 veal kidney*
Salt and pepper	*1 cup heavy cream*

Sauté the onion in 3 tablespoons of the butter until soft. Add mushrooms, shallots, tarragon, and salt and pepper to taste. Sauté over high heat until dry. Add half of the Madeira and the bread crumbs. Let the mixture cool.

Spread the mixture inside the cut of veal; roll the meat and tie with kitchen string. Wrap the roast in a large piece of buttered parchment paper. Roast in a preheated 325°F. oven for 1¼ hours. Remove the paper, brush the roast with clarified butter, and roast for another 15 to 20 minutes at 400°F. to brown.

Dice the kidney into ⅓-inch cubes. Sauté very fast in remaining butter (see p. 229) and drain in a colander. When the veal loin is cooked, deglaze the roasting pan with the heavy cream and remaining 2 tablespoons Madeira; simmer together for a few minutes. Add the drained kidney, reheat without boiling, and serve as a sauce for the roast.

Note: This same recipe may be used for casserole roasting (see p. 207).

Wine: California Riesling or *French Pouilly Fumé*

RACK OF LAMB PERSILLADE
6 SERVINGS

1 whole rack of lamb, about 3 pounds	*¼ cup minced parsley*
2 tablespoons olive oil	*1 small garlic clove, minced (optional)*
2 tablespoons prepared Dijon-style mustard	*½ teaspoon salt*
1 cup fresh bread crumbs	*⅛ teaspoon pepper*
	Clarified butter

Have the butcher split the rack and remove the backbone. With a sharp knife remove the fell yourself and discard all fat until you reach the bare muscle.

Brush olive oil on each half rack. Roast in a 400°F. oven for 15 minutes. Brush mustard on the meat, then with the hand apply a mixture of the crumbs, parsley, garlic, salt and pepper. Baste with clarified butter and continue roasting for 35 minutes. Serve with Garlic Hollandaise (p. 128).

Wine: California Gamay Beaujolais or *French Bourgueil*

ROAST LOIN OR SHOULDER OF PORK IN CRUMB COAT

6 SERVINGS

3 garlic cloves
1 boneless loin of pork, 3 pounds
*⅛ teaspoon each of ground
    cinnamon, cardamom, allspice,
    coriander*
⅛ teaspoon grated nutmeg
*¼ teaspoon each dried tarragon
    and marjoram*

Pinch of ground cloves
½ teaspoon salt
Oil
1½ cups fresh bread crumbs
½ teaspoon rubbed sage
Prepared Dijon-style mustard
Clarified butter
⅓ cup dry white wine

Insert the garlic cloves inside the meat at regular intervals. Mix all the spices and herbs (except sage) and the salt and rub over the surface of the roast. Let the meat stand in the refrigerator for 24 hours.

Rub the roast with a little oil and roast in a 325°F. oven for 1 hour. Mix bread crumbs and sage. Remove the roast from oven, brush with mustard as thickly as you like, and roll in the crumb mixture. Apply more crumbs to the top if necessary. Return the meat to the roasting pan and baste liberally with clarified butter. Continue roasting for another hour, or until golden brown. Dissolve pan juices with the wine and boil together for a few minutes. Adjust seasoning if necessary. Add a little butter to the gravy if desired, but serve unthickened.

Wine: California Mountain Chablis or *French Sancerre*

ROAST CHICKEN TARRAGON

4 TO 6 SERVINGS

Although tarragon is the most pleasant herb with chicken, it may be replaced by other herbs such as basil or rosemary or even ordinary poultry seasoning.

4 tablespoons butter
2 tablespoons chopped fresh
    tarragon, or 2 teaspoons dried
    herb
Salt and pepper

1 roasting chicken, 3½ to 4
    pounds
Melted butter or oil
Chicken broth or water
    (⅓ to ½ cup)

Cream the butter with the tarragon and add salt and pepper to taste. Put half of the butter in the cavity of the chicken. Divide the rest of the butter into 2 equal parts and slide them under the skin over the breasts. Truss the bird and brush with melted butter or oil. Roast in preheated oven at the desired temperature (see chart, p. 167) and baste at regular intervals with the butter in the roasting pan.

When the chicken is done, dissolve the juices with chicken broth or water. Defatten the liquid completely and serve unthickened.

Wine: California Semillon or French White Graves

TANTE ELSE'S GANS
8 SERVINGS

This dish brings back memories of Christmas 1948 in Germany. I dedicate it to Mel Gordon, Pennsylvania's first vintner and a great gourmet.

½ cup butter
12 red Delicious apples, peeled
    and cored, each cut into 6
    wedges
4 tablespoons (2 ounces) akvavit
1 goose, 8 to 10 pounds
Salt and pepper
6 white potatoes

1 cup chicken or veal stock or
    water
½ teaspoon caraway seeds
Beurre manié *or starch slurry*
    (optional)
Butter for sauce enrichment
    (optional)

Heat the butter and sauté the apples in it until they are very brown but still crisp inside. Turn off the heat and add 2 tablespoons akvavit; mix well with the apples. Let cool completely.

Remove all fat from the goose cavity. Salt and pepper inside, and rub with about 4 teaspoons of akvavit. Stuff with the cooled apples. Truss the bird and roast, breast up, in a 325°F. oven (see chart, p. 167). Prick the skin for the fat to escape, and remove the fat as the bird cooks.

Peel and trim potatoes, cut into pieces, and parboil. Panfry them very slowly in goose fat until nice and golden; it will take a good 40 minutes.

Defatten completely the juices of the cooked bird; dissolve or mix them with chicken or veal stock. Add the caraway seeds and simmer together for about 10 minutes. Thicken the sauce, if desired, with a starch slurry or *beurre manié* (1 tablespoon butter and 1 tablespoon flour per cup of liquid). Add remaining 2 teaspoons akvavit and butter to taste. Serve. Merry Christmas!

Wine: California Cabernet Sauvignon or French Pomerol

ROAST DUCK CITRUS
6 SERVINGS

I have tried, from childhood memories, to re-create the taste of the bigarrade orange.

1 cup classic brown sauce (p. 114), made with veal or duck stock	2 tablespoons white grapefruit juice
2 tablespoons julienne of orange rind	2 ducks, 4 to 5 pounds each
½ teaspoon julienne of lime rind	2 teaspoons Grand Marnier or Triple Sec
½ teaspoon julienne of lemon rind	4 teaspoons brandy or Cognac
1 teaspoon julienne of grapefruit rind	Salt and pepper
⅓ cup Florida orange juice	¼ cup dry white wine
2 teaspoons lime juice	2 teaspoons sugar
1 teaspoon lemon juice	1 teaspoon vinegar
	Butter for sauce enrichment (optional)
	Orange and grapefruit sections

Make the brown sauce. Prepare the julienne of rinds and blanch in boiling water. Drain and keep ready to use. Squeeze the juices, mix them, and keep ready to use.

Rub each duck with Grand Marnier and brandy and let stand at room temperature for 2 hours. Season the cavities. Roast the ducks in a 400°F. oven for 20 minutes, then prick the skins to allow the fat to escape. Reduce oven heat to 325°F. and continue roasting for another 1½ hours. When the birds are done, remove all the fat from the roasting pan and deglaze the pan juices with the white wine.

Cook sugar in a small pan to the smoking caramel stage, cool, and dissolve with vinegar. Mix pan juices, caramel and brown sauce, and simmer together for 15 minutes. Strain into a gravy boat and add the fruit juices and blanched rinds. Butter the sauce to taste, and correct the seasoning if necessary.

Serve the ducks decorated with orange and grapefruit sections.
Wine: California Cabernet Sauvignon or *French Saint-Émilion*

BROILING—DRY-HEAT PROCEDURE

A cut of meat is broiled when it is cooked under radiant heat, a gas or electric broiler, or over glowing white-hot charcoal.

PREPARING MEAT FOR BROILING

Beef, lamb and chicken are excellent for broiling; veal is too dry; pork can be broiled if the cut is thin.

Broil only well-marbled cuts from ¾ inch to 2½ inches thick. To avoid spattering, remove all fat except ¼ inch all around the piece of meat. Score through the connective tissues surrounding steaks and chops at ½- to 1-inch intervals so that they will not buckle and cook irregularly. Brush the surface of the meat very generously with clarified butter or oil. To broil small pieces slightly less than 1 inch thick, brush them with butter and sprinkle them with bread crumbs; the crumbs will partially insulate the meat and keep it juicy.

THE TECHNIQUE OF BROILING

Put the piece or pieces to broil on a *cold* rack over a broiler pan where the melted fat will be able to accumulate. Brush the meat lavishly with fat, but *do not salt or pepper.* Exposed to the heat, the salt would melt, produce unwanted moisture, shrink the outer bundles of muscular fibers, and draw the juices from the meat; the pepper would burn and turn bitter.

The goal is to cook the piece of meat to the desired degree of doneness inside without burning the outside. As in a roast, the juices will be concentrated at the center of the cut and the juiciness will be the result of the marbling fat melted and emulsified in whatever small amount of collagen will have time to hydrolyze during the short cooking period.

For thin pieces (less than 1 inch) place the meat between 4 and 5 inches from the source of heat. Broil until brown (5 minutes). Salt and pepper the browned side, turn over, and broil until brown on the second side (3 minutes). Salt and pepper the second side before serving.

For thick pieces (2 to 2½ inches), the technique is a bit more difficult. Expose the first side to the heat for 5 minutes, then turn down the heat if the broiler is thermostatically controlled and cook for another 4 minutes. If the broiler is not so controlled, move the cut 9 to 10 inches away from the source of heat and cook for another 4 minutes. Season the cooked side with salt and pepper. Turn the piece over and repeat on the other side. Keep brushing the meat with oil or clarified butter.

Since no two stoves are identical, read the maker's instruction booklet carefully. Only one feature is common to all stoves. You broil with the door closed in a gas oven and with the door ajar in an electric oven. Over charcoal, control the heat by moving the barbecuing rack up and down over the charcoal.

To check the doneness of a broiled piece of meat, press it with your finger. A rare meat will give under finger pressure, a medium-rare piece will give half as much, a well-done piece will be firm. Droplets of red juices appear at the surface of a steak when it reaches the rare stage. Broiled chicken is ready to eat when the tip of a knife penetrates the thigh and comes out without resistance, releasing colorless juices.

CHATEAUBRIAND
2 SERVINGS

This dish was created by Montmireil, chef to the romantic French writer, François René Vicomte de Chateaubriand. Traditionally the Chateaubriand is a thick steak cut from the center part of the beef tenderloin; it is usually prepared for two and served with béarnaise sauce. For a change try the Provençal Butter on page 142.

1 piece (3 inches long)	*Clarified butter exclusively*
tenderloin (center cut), or 1	*Salt and pepper*
slice (2 inches thick) rib or	
sirloin strip	

Trim meat of *all traces of fat and gristle*. Brush with clarified butter and broil according to general instructions for thick pieces of meat on page 173. Cut into ⅓-inch-thick slices and serve with the sauce of your choice.

Wine: This will vary with the sauce, but it should always be a full-bodied red.

BROILED LAMB NUGGETS AND BASIL BUTTER
6 SERVINGS

Basil butter (p. 147)	*2 cups fresh bread crumbs*
12 medium-thick loin lamb chops	*Salt and pepper*
Clarified butter	

Make the basil butter, shape it into a stick, and freeze it.

Bone the chops, and secure tenderloin and strip with a wooden food pick. Brush with clarified butter. Sprinkle generously with bread crumbs. Broil over high heat for 5 minutes; sprinkle with salt and pepper. Turn over. Brush the second side with clarified butter and sprinkle with crumbs. Broil for 3 to 5 minutes; sprinkle with salt and pepper.

Cut the frozen roll of basil butter into 12 slices and top each chop with a slice.

Wine: California Grenache Rosé or French Tavel

BROILED CHICKEN AUX AROMATES
6 SERVINGS

This makes a succulent little bird that tastes best when the charcoal adds its flavor to the crisp skin. Vary the herbs to taste.

1 teaspoon each of dried tarragon, marjoram, basil	*1 tablespoon chopped fennel, or ½ teaspoon fennel seeds*
1 tablespoon chopped fresh or frozen chives	*6 tablespoons raw butter*
1 tablespoon chopped fresh parsley	*3 broilers, 2½ pounds each, split into halves*
	Clarified butter

Mix all herbs and crush well. Cream the butter, add herbs, and let the mixture mellow in the refrigerator for a few hours.

Let the butter soften again and divide it into 12 parts. Brush some on the insides of the chicken halves, and slide the rest under the skin covering the breast and the thigh meats. Broil for 15 minutes on each side, starting with the meaty side: 5 minutes with high heat and 10 minutes with lower heat, basting often with the melted butter escaping into the broiler pan, or with additional clarified butter. Total broiling time should be 30 to 35 minutes.

Wine: California Semillon Blanc or French Cassis

PANBROILING AND PANFRYING—
DRY-HEAT PROCEDURE

Panbroiling and panfrying should be done in a thick frying pan (iron, thick aluminum or enameled cast iron). Avoid thin aluminum or stainless steel, for they do not conduct the heat evenly.

If you panbroil, brush only a thin film of fat over the whole surface of the pan. If you panfry, the bottom of the pan must be covered by a ¹⁄₁₀- to ⅛-inch layer of melted fat. The fat may be oil (better for red meats) or clarified butter (better for white meats).

PREPARING A MEAT FOR PANFRYING

You may panfry beef steaks, lamb chops, veal (not calf) scaloppine, thin pork chops, chicken cutlets. Steaks and chops must be defattened and their connective tissues scored at regular intervals, as explained on page 173.

PANFRYING RED MEATS

Use tenderloin, sirloin and rib steak of beef, rib and loin chops of lamb. Do not add flour, salt or pepper. Sear one side until brown. The meat juices will appear on the unseared side. Turn over and salt the seared side. The salt will shrink the outside bundles of muscle fibers, leaving gaps between them, while the heat of the pan sealing the second side of the meat will cause the juices to travel upward. When the juices appear at the surface of the meat, the steaks or chops will be done *rare*. Continue cooking to the desired degree. Remember that a well-done steak is a ruined steak; try those lamb chops on the pink side for a juicy surprise.

PANFRYING WHITE MEATS

Sprinkle white meats with flour, salt and pepper. They need seasoning because of their blander flavor, and the coating of flour is there to trap the juices that would otherwise be lost in the pan. Floured panfried meats have a thin, delicious, flavorful outside crust. Panfried white meats are done when the tip of a knife penetrates them and comes out easily.

For both red and white meats, the initial amount of heat must be high to bring on an efficient sealing, but the heat must be reduced to finish cooking the meat to the center. High heat maintained throughout the cooking time will cause the cut to be overdone on both sides while the center will stay raw and the fat in the pan will burn.

CHICKEN CUTLETS

Reread the instructions given on page 157 for boning. Flatten the cutlets a little, using the side of your hand, and flour them. Panfry them in clarified butter exclusively. They will cook in a total time of 6 to 8 minutes, depending on their thickness, and will need no additional cooking or simmering in a sauce; in fact they will become tough if you cook them further. The initial heat should not exceed 375°F. or the delicate fibers will toughen beyond repair. If the cutlet is filled with a meat filling that may swell under the influence of the heat, sew it closed and pull out the thread after cooking; if the filling is cheese or nuts, just press the pocket closed; the collagen will keep it sealed.

PANFRYING BREADED MEATS

Do not bread pieces of meat for panfrying if they are thicker than ¾ inch. Well-breaded meats are succulent because the hermetic sealing of the egg protein prevents any escaping of juices; also the cook can judge the cooking by the color of the breading and can thus avoid overcooking.

Make fresh bread crumbs in the blender and strain them so they are of even size. The egg coating for breaded meats is called an *anglaise* and is made according to the following recipe:

ANGLAISE AND BREADING
FOR 12 CHICKEN CUTLETS OR 6 CHOPS

1 egg	*Pinch of pepper*
1 teaspoon oil	*1 cup fine fresh or dry bread*
1 teaspoon water	*crumbs*
½ teaspoon salt	

Mix egg, oil, water, salt and pepper until the mixture is emulsified. That is the *anglaise*.

Have flour on a sheet of wax paper, *anglaise* in its container, and bread crumbs on a second sheet of wax paper, all lined up on the table or counter.

Flour the meat; pat it between your hands to discard excess flour. Brush the *anglaise* on the meat with a pastry brush; use very little. Invert the brushed side on the bread crumbs, brush the second side with *anglaise,* and sprinkle that side evenly with crumbs shaken through a conical strainer.

Fold a piece of wax paper over the breaded meat and apply a little pressure to secure the crumbs. Shake the piece of meat to discard excess crumbs. Breaded meats may wait in the refrigerator or be frozen. They taste best when panfried in clarified butter.

In the recipes that follow, notice that an emulsified sauce on a glaze base is the finishing touch for some, a butter sauce for others, and that brown sauces are used in many different combinations.

ONION STEAKS
6 SERVINGS

6 *large onions, sliced thin*	2 *tablespoons meat glaze, or* ¼
9 *tablespoons unsalted butter*	*teaspoon commercial meat*
6 *tablespoons oil*	*extract*
6 *strip steaks, 1 inch thick*	*Salt and pepper*
⅓ *cup white wine*	*Chopped parsley*
1 *teaspoon vinegar*	

Sauté sliced onions in 3 tablespoons butter until soft, cover, and let simmer for a few minutes. Uncover and toss again until moisture free. Keep ready to use.

Heat the oil and panfry steaks to preferred doneness. Remove steaks to a warm platter. Discard cooking oil completely. Add to the steak pan the white wine, vinegar, meat glaze or extract, and the prepared onions. Cook quickly until only 2 tablespoons moisture are left in the pan. Turn off the heat and fluff in 6 tablespoons soft unsalted butter. Add salt and pepper to taste. Spoon the onion sauce over the steaks, sprinkle them with chopped parsley, and serve piping hot.
Wine: California Pinot Noir or *French Moulin-à-Vent*

THE ANCESTOR OF STEAK DIANE
6 SERVINGS

This is how Steak Diane should taste; it is well worth the time involved in making the classic brown sauce.

6 tenderloin steaks, ¾ to 1 inch thick	2 peppercorns
	1 cup dry white wine
7 tablespoons Cognac or brandy	2 tablespoons vinegar
1 small onion, chopped fine	1 cup classic brown sauce
1 shallot, chopped fine	(p. 114)
2 tablespoons fine-diced celery	3 tablespoons oil
1 tablespoon minced parsley stems	3 tablespoons unsweetened whipped cream
1 garlic clove, mashed	Salt and pepper

Marinate the steaks in 3 tablespoons Cognac for 1 hour. Lift out steaks and pat dry.

Mix onion, shallot, celery, parsley stems, garlic, peppercorns, white wine and vinegar, and reduce to ⅓ cup. Mix with the brown sauce and simmer together for 10 minutes. Keep ready to use.

Panfry steaks in the oil to desired doneness; discard cooking oil. Heat remaining 4 tablespoons Cognac and flambé the steaks; remove them to a warm platter. Blend the prepared sauce with the juices in the frying pan. Turn off the heat and blend in the whipped cream. Correct seasoning of the sauce and spoon it over the steaks.
Wine: California Pinot Noir or French Côte de Beaune

MODERN PEPPERED STEAK
6 SERVINGS

The *chemise* (crêpe) is the idea of André Soltner, Executive Chef at Lutèce Restaurant; the sauce is my concoction.

6 *large crêpes (p. 506),*
  flavored with chopped parsley
  and chives (optional)
Cracked black pepper
6 *tenderloin steaks, ¾ to 1*
  inch thick
3 *tablespoons oil*
¼ *cup marc or brandy*
¼ *cup orange juice*

2 *tablespoons meat glaze, or ¼*
  teaspoon commercial meat
  extract
1 *tablespoon Worcestershire*
  sauce
Dash of lemon juice
½ *cup unsalted butter*
Salt and pepper

Make the crêpes. Spread cracked pepper on a sheet of wax paper and coat each side of the steaks with pepper. Panfry steaks in the oil to desired doneness. Discard cooking oil and flambé steaks with marc or brandy. Remove steaks to a serving platter to keep warm.

Add orange juice, meat glaze or extract, and Worcestershire sauce to the frying pan. Quickly reduce to 3 tablespoons; add lemon juice, reduce heat, and fluff in the butter, tablespoon by tablespoon. Correct seasoning of the sauce.

Put each steak on one edge of a crêpe, spoon some sauce over, and fold the crêpe to enclose the steak.

Wine: California Grenache Rosé or *French Cabernet Rosé d'Anjou*

MARINATED LAMB CHOPS
6 SERVINGS

A recipe for venison lovers who cannot find venison.

2 *cups dry vermouth*
1 *onion, chopped*
1 *shallot, chopped*
1 *bay leaf, crushed*
½ *teaspoon cracked pepper*
½ *teaspoon dried basil*
¼ *teaspoon dried thyme*
¼ *teaspoon dried rosemary*
5 *tablespoons olive oil*

12 *rib or loin lamb chops,*
  ¾ inch thick
1 *cup classic brown sauce*
  (p. 114)
1 *ounce gin*
1 *teaspoon dried sweet basil,*
  revived
2 *tablespoons unsalted butter*
Salt and pepper

Mix vermouth, onion, shallot, bay leaf, cracked pepper, dried basil, thyme, rosemary and 2 tablespoons olive oil. Place the chops in a large glass baking dish and cover them with the mixture. Marinate in the refrigerator from 1 to 3 days, depending on how strong you like the venison taste.

Drain the chops and pat them dry. Cook the marinade until only ¼ cup is left. Stir into the brown sauce and blend. Keep ready to use.

Panfry chops in remaining 3 tablespoons oil to the desired doneness. Discard the frying fat and flambé with heated gin. Blend sauce and pan juices and strain into a sauceboat. Add revived basil and the butter. Add salt and pepper to taste. Serve over the chops.

Wine: California Zinfandel or French Hermitage

TSCHUDI'S SCALOPPINE
6 TO 8 SERVINGS

Tschudi is Viennese and married to smashing Roman Aldo. This is her version of *scaloppine à la Naturschnitzel mit Sardellenbutter.* Buy a piece of veal rump and cut the *scaloppine* yourself.

2 *pounds veal* scaloppine, ⅛ *inch thick*	⅔ *cup thickened brown veal stock (p. 117) or chicken stock (p. 77)*
Flour	*1 tablespoon anchovy paste*
2 *tablespoons oil*	*1 tablespoon lemon juice*
½ *cup plus 2 tablespoons unsalted butter*	*12 pitted black olives, sliced*
⅓ *cup dry white wine*	*Very little salt*
	Pepper

Flatten the *scaloppine,* flour them, and shake them to remove excess flour. Sauté quickly in the oil and 2 tablespoons butter until brown. Discard cooking oil. Remove meat to a platter.

Add white wine, stock, anchovy paste and lemon juice to the pan; scrape well to deglaze all the caramelized juices. Reduce to ¼ cup. Turn down the heat and fluff in ½ cup butter, tablespoon by table-

spoon. Correct seasoning if necessary. Strain the sauce over the *scaloppine* and sprinkle with sliced olives.
Wine: Austrian Gumpoldskirchner

ZÜRCHER CORDON BLEU
6 SERVINGS

The recipe is Swiss, not French, as is often believed. Use clarified butter for taste or lard for authenticity. The recipe comes from Mrs. Walter Frei of Oerlikon, a small town now part of Zurich.

6 veal scallops, ⅓ inch thick,	*Flour*
from top round or round	*Anglaise (p. 178)*
6 slices of boiled ham, 2½ inches	*½ cup fresh bread crumbs*
long, 1½ inches wide	*½ cup clarified butter or lard*
6 slices of Gruyère or	*Salt and pepper*
Emmenthal cheese, 2½ inches	*6 lemon slices*
long, 1½ inches wide	*Chopped parsley*

Cut a pocket in each veal scallop; stuff with ham and cheese slices; sew or press closed. Flour, brush with *anglaise,* and coat with bread crumbs. Fry on both sides in clarified butter or lard until golden. Season with salt and pepper to taste. Serve topped with a slice of lemon and sprinkled with chopped parsley.
Wine: Swiss Fendant du Valais or *Neuchâtel*

CHICKEN CUTLETS IN HAZELNUT CREAM
6 SERVINGS

A recipe from the village of La Balme de Thuy, high in the French Alps. Oregon cooks, use your own *fresh* hazelnuts for a special treat.

12 small chicken cutlets	*6 tablespoons clarified butter*
Salt and pepper	*1 cup heavy cream*
Flour	*2 tablespoons meat glaze, or ¼*
6 ounces hazelnuts, shelled but	*teaspoon commercial meat*
unpeeled	*extract*

Pinch each of ground cardamom   Beurre manié (*p. 118*)
and cinnamon   *1 tablespoon dry sherry*

Bone the chicken cutlets. Sprinkle them with salt and pepper and coat with flour. Keep ready to use. Preheat oven to 350°F. Set unpeeled hazelnuts on a cookie sheet; roast for 5 to 6 minutes. Rub nuts in a towel to remove the peels. Chop enough nuts to make ⅓ cup. Sauté in clarified butter until golden. Remove from the butter. In the same butter, panfry the chicken cutlets for 4 to 5 minutes on each side. Remove to a serving platter.

Add to the butter and juices in the pan, if any, the cream, meat glaze, cardamom and cinnamon. Bring quickly to a boil and thicken with the *beurre manié* (1 ½ tablespoons each of butter and flour per cup of liquid). Add the nuts and sherry. Correct seasoning if necessary and spoon the sauce over the chicken cutlets.

Wine: California Wente Grey Riesling or *Alsatian Riesling*

CHICKEN CUTLETS WITH GREEN ONIONS
6 SERVINGS

⅓ cup dry white wine
½ cup brown veal stock (p. 80)
or chicken stock (p. 76)
½ cup fine-chopped green onions
2 fresh basil leaves, snipped with
scissors, or ⅓ teaspoon dried
basil

2 tablespoons meat glaze, or ¼
teaspoon commercial meat
extract
12 small chicken cutlets
Salt and pepper
Flour
4 tablespoons clarified butter
½ cup unsalted butter
1 tablespoon chopped parsley

Make an infusion with wine, stock, green onions and basil, and reduce to 3 tablespoons. (If you are serving this for a company meal, be sure to make the infusion ahead of time because it is aromatic.) Add meat glaze or extract. Pound cutlets to flatten, sprinkle with salt and pepper, and flour lightly. Panfry in clarified butter for 4 to 5 minutes on each side. Remove cutlets to a serving platter. Add the infusion to the frying pan and fluff in the unsalted butter, tablespoon by table-spoon. Strain the sauce onto the chicken cutlets, and sprinkle them with chopped parsley.

Wine: California Mountain White or *French Chablis* or *Loire Valley*

POJARSKI AND BITOQUES
6 SERVINGS

A dish from the cookery of Imperial Russia. Use only tender cuts of meat. This is expensive, but different for a company meal. *Pojarski* are made with white meat, *bitoques* with beef.

1 ¾ *pounds veal (rib eye, loin or round) or chicken (cutlets)* for pojarski, *or beef (tenderloin only) for* bitoques, *or 2 ½ cups of packed 1-inch cubes*	1 *teaspoon salt*
	¼ *teaspoon ground white pepper*
	Flour
	Anglaise (*p. 178*)
	1 ½ *cups fresh bread crumbs*
10 *thin slices of ordinary white bread, crusts removed*	¾ *cup clarified butter*
½ *cup heavy cream*	⅓ *cup noisette butter* (*p. 145*)
¾ *cup unsalted butter*	*Lemon juice (for white meats only)*

Cut the meat into very small pieces and chop it by hand to a fine paste; grinding is acceptable but juices are lost. Shred the bread and soak it in the cream. Cream the butter in a large mixer bowl. With the mixer still on creaming speed, add the meat, 2 or 3 tablespoons at a time. Add the soaked bread, bit by bit, and last the salt and pepper. Continue beating until the mixture is homogenous.

By hand, shape 12 cutlets ⅓ inch thick and 2 inches long. Flour the cutlets, brush with *anglaise,* and coat with bread crumbs. Sauté the cutlets in clarified butter until golden on both sides. Season with salt and pepper to taste. Serve basted with noisette butter, and with lemon juice if you have made *pojarski.*

Wine: for pojarski, *Puilly-Fuissé; for* bitoques, *Hermitage*

OLD GIOVANNI'S RABBIT CUTLETS
6 SERVINGS

This recipe comes from the Italian Alps, but we can use California farm rabbit. Use only the loins for this recipe, and make a stew with the legs (p. 204).

Loins of 3 rabbits, cut into   Anglaise (*p. 178*)
  cutlets ¼ inch thick   *½ cup fresh bread crumbs*
1 cup milk   *½ cup clarified butter*
Flour   *⅓ cup hazelnuts, peeled*
Salt and pepper

Pound cutlets very thin and soak in milk for 2 hours. Pat dry. Flour, sprinkle with salt and pepper, brush with *anglaise,* and coat with bread crumbs. Sauté in clarified butter until golden on both sides. Remove to a platter. Toss the hazelnuts in the cooking butter. Sprinkle them over the rabbit.
Wine: Soave

HICKORY CHICKEN CUTLETS
6 SERVINGS

An American variation on the Cordon Bleu (p. 183).

6 large chicken cutlets   *½ cup fresh bread crumbs*
6 slices of hickory-smoked bacon   *1 tablespoon fine-ground black*
3 wedges of processed Swiss   *walnuts*
  cheese   *½ cup clarified butter*
¼ cup flour   *¼ cup noisette butter (p. 145)*
Salt and pepper   *Chopped parsley*
Anglaise (*p. 178*)

Cut a pocket in each cutlet. Cook the bacon until fat is rendered but not until the slices are crisp. Cut cheese wedges into halves. Fill each cutlet with half a wedge of cheese rolled in a slice of bacon; seal. Sprinkle the cutlets with flour, salt and pepper; brush with *anglaise* and coat with bread crumbs mixed with black walnuts. Sauté the cutlets in clarified butter until golden on both sides. Serve immediately, basted with noisette butter and sprinkled with chopped parsley.

Wine: California Zinfandel or *French Beaujolais*

LIEDERKRANZ CHICKEN CUTLETS
6 SERVINGS

6 large chicken cutlets	*½ cup fresh bread crumbs*
1 Liederkranz cheese (4 ounces)	*¼ cup ground almonds*
¼ cup flour	*½ cup clarified butter*
Salt and pepper	*¼ cup noisette butter (p. 145)*
Anglaise *(p. 178)*	

Cut a pocket in each cutlet. Scrape the cheese only if it is very ripe. Cut it into 6 slices and stuff each cutlet with 1 slice. Sew the cutlets to close because this cheese is more liquid when melted than Gruyère types. Flour the cutlets, sprinkle with salt and pepper, brush with *anglaise,* and coat with a mixture of bread crumbs and ground almonds. Panfry in clarified butter until golden on both sides. Serve basted with noisette butter.

Wine: California Zinfandel

DEEP FRYING—DRY-HEAT PROCEDURE

Safety first! Do not start deep frying without a box of baking soda on hand to smother a possible fire. Never sprinkle a burning oil bath with water, for the oil will splatter, dispersing flames all over the kitchen.

Deep-fried foods have become almost anathema in our lean modern world, although we are fed more deep-fried chicken, fish, clams and fritters than any other nation in the world.

A properly deep-fried golden piece of food is a pleasure to behold and a treat for the palate. In former times, deep frying was done in animal fats, usually rendered beef or veal kidney suet. Nowadays, vegetable oils are almost exclusively used; they are less saturated and require no rendering. The most commonly used are corn and peanut oils, followed closely by the hydrogenated vegetable shortenings. I recommend that you use oil because it reaches 400°F. without burning; the shortenings are more susceptible to heat. Never use olive oil for its taste is too pungent.

Whatever the frying medium used, heat it to 370°F. and fry a small piece of bread in it before using it for the first time. This step will help to remove any off-taste in the frying fat. You may eliminate this step if you know your oil is highly refined.

Render and use animal suet if you like. Cut the raw fat into small pieces and mix it with 2 cups of water for each 5 pounds of suet. The water softens the connective tissues in the fat until they break and let the liquid fat spill out. The fat is ready to use when the connective tissues are deep fried. Filter the liquid fat through a damp cheesecloth into heatproof glass containers.

Do not store frying fat at room temperature. As soon as it has cooled, strain it back into its glass container to discard all the particles fallen from the fried food. If left in the fat, these particles would burn when the fat is reheated, or they would become rancid on standing. Cover the glass jars with airtight seals and keep them refrigerated.

Do not use the oil bath more than twice without adding some fresh oil to it; this lengthens its life. When the bath has become too dark for meats or vegetables, use it for frying fish. Once a bath has been used for fish, it may not be used for any other food; a potato fried in a bath can remove partly the taste of onions, but never that of fish.

Fry in a deep kettle with straight sides. Do not fill the fryer more than half full, and handle it gently with quiet motions to avoid spilling. Do not deep fry in a frying pan with a handle that can be misplaced or catch on something and cause spilling. The best fryer is an electric one controlled by thermostat, but a large kettle with side handles is perfectly acceptable if a thermometer is used so that you can check and control the temperature of the bath.

If you have no thermometer, the degree of heat of the oil can be recognized easily by using a crust of bread. If the oil shivers around the bread, the temperature is between 365° and 370°F.; if the oil foams, the temperature ranges between 375° and 380°F.; if the bread turns brown almost instantly and the fat smokes, the temperature is between 385° and 390°F.

Small pieces of meat must be fried so that they cook fast but are done to the center. Immerse the meat when the bath reaches the temperature of 360°F.; the addition of cold food will make it drop to the required 350°F. The heat of the oil bath has the same concentrating effect on the meat juices as that of the oven heat in roasting.

Do not fry too much food at a time or the oil will cool off too much and not sear properly; the food will be saturated with fat and become soggy; this will also happen if the bath is not hot enough.

Dip a frying basket into hot oil, deposit the food in it, and immerse. If the food is coated with a fritter batter, lift each piece *on* the two prongs of a long-handled kitchen fork and immerse; do not pierce the coated food. Remove the fried food from the bath either with the basket or with a slotted spoon; let it drain on several layers of crumpled paper towels. Serve fried foods on a white napkin folded on a serving platter. If the food must wait, store it, unsalted, in a 225°F. oven. Salt just before serving.

To coat meats for frying, dip into flour, brush with *anglaise,* then coat with bread crumbs (see p. 178); or dip them into a fritter batter. Here is a recipe for an all-purpose fritter batter for meats and savories.

SAVORY FRITTER BATTER

1 cup sifted flour	*1 cup water*
1 teaspoon salt	*2 egg whites*
2 tablespoons oil or melted butter	

Mix flour, salt, oil or butter, and water without beating. Let stand for 20 minutes. Whip the egg whites and fold into the flour mixture.

BREAKFAST STEAKS
6 SERVINGS

6 *small steaks, tenderloin or strip,*	*Oil for deep frying*
¾ inch thick	*Salt and pepper*
Flour	*6 eggs, fried*
Anglaise (*p. 178*)	*Maître d'hôtel butter (p. 146)*
1 cup fine fresh bread crumbs	

Flour the steaks, brush with *anglaise,* and coat with bread crumbs. Immerse in an oil bath heated to 360°F., and let fry until golden. Sprinkle with salt and pepper. Serve each steak with a fried egg and a little maître d'hôtel butter.

✴ CHICKEN-LIVER FRITTERS
6 SERVINGS

½ pound chicken livers	*Flour*
¼ cup port or Madeira	*Savory fritter batter (p. 189)*
Salt and pepper	*Lemon juice*

Cut raw livers into bite-size pieces. Marinate in port or Madeira for about 2 hours. Sprinkle with salt and pepper, roll in flour, and dip into fritter batter. Deep fry at 360°F. until golden. Serve sprinkled with lemon juice.

DEEP-FRIED CHICKEN CUTLETS

Any of the recipes given in the section on panfrying may be used. Deep fry the cutlets instead of panfrying them in butter. You will notice the difference in taste.

BRAISING—MOIST-HEAT PROCEDURE

Braising, from the French word *braise,* which means smoldering coals, is a process of cooking with a small amount of liquid in a tightly covered pot called a *braisière*. In centuries past and as recently as the 1900's, braising was done by cooking with fire under and on top of the pot. The pot was set on a bed of embers and more embers were put on the lid, which was slightly concave for this purpose. While cooking, the piece of meat rested on several layers of aromatics and raw ham and veal slices called *fonds de braise*.

Nowadays, the procedure has been oversimplified and is more often than not misunderstood. A short study of the elements and principles of braising will forever banish watery sauces and washed-out meats.

When a piece of meat is seared and acquires a brown crust, its juices —hydrolyzed collagen and emulsified fats—concentrate at its center. After the meat is put to braise in the oven, the heat around the piece becomes more and more intense, penetrates deeper toward the center of the piece, and causes the collagen to break down into protein concentrates and steam.

When the temperature has reached its maximum at the center of the meat, the pressure of the steam is such that it bears on the meat fibers and slowly pries them open; the juices now slowly make their way from the center of the piece toward the outside, break through the seared outside layer, and mix with the pan juices.

This can only happen if the piece of meat is held in such a tight space that the steam has nowhere to go and no place to condense. Therefore using the right pot is very important. The pot should be thick (copper, enameled cast iron) and just big enough to contain the piece of meat; there should be no wide space between meat and lid. Since this is often difficult to realize, cover the meat first with a large piece of aluminum foil resting flush over the meat and shaped so as to form an inverted lid. Then cover with the pot lid. The foil is used as an inverted second lid to catch the steam condensing on the pot lid. If the condensation is allowed to fall back into the cooking juices, there will be no concentration of the juices and the result is a boiled piece of meat instead of a braisé.

LARDING

If a cut is not covered by a layer of fat, or well marbled, lard it. For this use a long larding needle, a *lardoir*. Push long strips of pork fat, lardoons, through the piece. The lardoons should be ⅓ inch wide. Before using them, marinate them in Cognac or brandy, and season them with salt, pepper and grated nutmeg. Use fresh pork fatback preferably; if it cannot be located use salt pork and in that case do not salt the lardoons. Larding is not a necessity, but it is useful to add flavor and juiciness to the meat, if you can spare the time to do it.

MARINATING

Meats for braising, especially red meats, are often marinated in wine, a mixture of wine and vinegar, or a mixture of vinegar and water, but never vinegar alone for it is too pungent and corrosive. Beside making the meat more flavorful, the acid marinade tenderizes its outer layers.

Salt and pepper the meat. Prepare 1 cup liquid marinade per pound of meat. Divide the aromatics for the prepared marinade—the vegetables and herbs—into 2 parts; put one at the bottom of the vessel, the other on top of the piece of meat to be marinated. Arrange the aromatics, the meat, and the marinating liquid in a stainless-steel, enameled cast-iron or heatproof glass vessel. Turn the meat at regular intervals. Let the meat marinate as long as the particular recipe specifies. Before cooking, drain the meat on a cake rack and dry it completely with kitchen towels (cloth or paper).

WHITE-WINE MARINADE
2 QUARTS

1 small bay leaf	*¼ celery rib, sliced*
⅛ teaspoon dried thyme	*1 tablespoon chopped parsley*
6 white peppercorns	*stems*
2 whole cloves	*6 cups white wine*
2 shallots, sliced	*1 cup white-wine vinegar*
1 large carrot, sliced	*1 cup oil*
2 onions, sliced	

The herbs, spices and vegetables are the "aromatics" of the marinade. For an uncooked marinade simply mix all the ingredients together.

For a cooked marinade, sauté the vegetables in the oil, and crush the spices. Add liquids and spices to the vegetables and simmer for 30 minutes. Cooking reinforces the strength of a marinade.

RED-WINE MARINADE

Use the same ingredients as in white-wine marinade, but replace the white wine with good-quality red wine. The vinegar may be omitted if desired and replaced with an additional cup of wine. Other spices such as rosemary and juniper berries may be used, especially for lamb and venison.

FONDS DE BRAISE

As *fonds de braise* use 1 large piece of blanched pork rind, well scraped of its fat; put it on the bottom of the pot, fat side down. On top, add carrots and onions sautéed in fat or butter. The rind will contribute its gelatin to the sauce, and the vegetables will add their flavor. Do not add fresh bones to the braising pot; they have no time to gelatinize enough to influence the richness of the cooking juices. The pork rind is much more useful to that effect.

BRAISING RED MEATS

Beef and lamb for braising need not be the tenderest cuts. Tougher pieces such as all cuts of chuck, round and shoulder are used with great success, but the grade of the meat must remain U. S. CHOICE or GOOD. Below that grade the meat will be stringy.

Sear the red meats in lard on top of the stove or in a very hot oven (450°F.) until a brown crust of caramelized juices has formed. Searing is *essential* for a large piece of red meat and highly recommended for cubes of meat; it is not essential for white meats. The larger the piece of meat, the longer the browning.

Set the browned meat on its bed of aromatics, the *fonds de braise* and the vegetables and herbs from the marinade. Add the liquid of the marinade and reduce it over high heat to a few syrupy tablespoons. This completely burns off the alcohol and concentrates the flavor. Add enough stock to half cover the piece of meat. Bring the stock to a boil and add the *bouquet garni* and other condiments. Cover the meat with the inverted piece of aluminum foil and then with the pot lid. Cook in a 325°F. oven until a skewer inserted in the meat comes out freely.

With red meats the braising time is relatively long so that when the juices of the meat have mixed with the pan juices, all the canals left gaping between the meat fibers start acting as capillaries and slowly suck back the mixture of meat and pan juices. At this point the pan juices, which had been quite abundant, have reduced at least by half; sometimes they have almost disappeared. Test the doneness of the meat, it should be almost ready; if the skewer does not yet come out freely, add small quantities of stock at regular intervals, if needed, to make sure that the pan juices do not burn, and turn the meat to keep it constantly moistened by the pan juices.

The stock is the most important ingredient for braising. The better the stock, the better the meat and juices. Use in order of preference:

brown veal stock
brown stock
white stock plus commercial meat extract
water plus commercial meat extract

Bear in mind that commercial canned stocks are highly salted; if you use them, thin them with wine, water, tomato sauce or juice. Whatever the stock, salt little before cooking. The concentration of the juices is such that more salt is rarely needed when the dish is ready.

Strain the cooked juices into a measuring cup. Let the fat rise to the surface and remove the fat-free juices with a baster. Carefully measure the volume of the juices and thicken with a *beurre manié* or a slurry of potato starch (p. 104).

When brown veal stock has been used, usually no thickening is necessary; the stock reduces to a glaze while cooking. Should it remain somewhat thin, reduce it quickly in a small pot until it reaches coating consistency.

BRAISING WHITE MEATS

The elements of the braising are the same. Here too the pork rind is most useful. The vegetables for the *fonds de braise* are quickly sautéed in butter without coloring. The meat (veal roast or bird) may be quickly seared in a 375°F. oven to tighten its outside layers or the skin, but it is not a necessity.

The stock used is exclusively white. The best is veal stock, but chicken stock or broth and even water plus commercial chicken extract are acceptable. The stickier the stock the better; therefore, if you cannot find a pork rind, add a teaspoon or so of commercial gelatin per cup of broth used.

Set the white meat on the vegetable bed, and add about ½ cup of stock. Let it reduce to 1 tablespoon. This operation is called in French culinary jargon *tombage à glace;* repeat it a second time for good concentration of the juices at the bottom of the pan. Add the braising stock to cover about half of the piece of meat. Cover with foil and pot lid and braise in a 325°F. oven. Baste the piece every 10 minutes with the braising juices so that their gelatin forms a coating which will help the meat retain its own juices. The braising time is short compared to that of red meats. A 4-pound chicken is ready in 45 minutes, a 6-pound capon in 1¼ hours, from the time they start braising in the oven. A veal roast weighing about 3 pounds will be done in about 2 hours.

For white meats, the second phase, the exchange of juices, does not and should not occur or the delicate flesh would fall apart. As a consequence, a piece of braised white meat always has more pan juices than a piece of braised red meat.

A braise of white meat is not truly a braise, but rather a half-breed between roasting and braising. Braised white meats look pale and must be glazed for better appearance. Brush the finished piece with some of the gelatinous juices and put it, uncovered, in a hot oven (400° to 425°F.) for a few minutes; it will take on a lovely brown color.

REHEATING AND FREEZING BRAISES

The more a braise reheats, the better it tastes. Do not hesitate to prepare braised meats ahead of time. Freeze if possible in the braising pot itself, and reheat slowly in a 325°F. oven.

HORSERADISH BRAISED BEEF
6 TO 8 SERVINGS

This is what you get by crossing a French *boeuf à la mode* with a German *Sauerbraten.*

½ recipe white-wine marinade (p. 192)	1 onion, sliced
	1 pork rind (if available)
½ teaspoon dried marjoram	Best available stock
1 teaspoon ground ginger	½ cup sour cream
1 bay leaf, crushed	2 tablespoons cream-style
3 to 4 pounds beef rump or round, in one piece	horseradish
	Salt and pepper
Lard	2 tablespoons butter
1 carrot, sliced	

Assemble marinade ingredients, adding the marjoram, ginger and crushed bay leaf. Cook the marinade. Cool. Marinate the meat in the refrigerator overnight, turning twice during marination.

Drain the meat and pat dry. Reserve the marinade. Brush meat with lard and sear in a 450°F. oven. Meanwhile, sauté carrot and onion in lard.

Put the ingredients in the pot in the following order; pork rind, sautéed vegetables, meat. Add the marinade, bring to a boil, and reduce the liquid to ⅓ cup. Add hot stock and bring to a boil. Cover the meat with foil and pot lid, and braise in a 325°F. oven for 3 to 3½ hours. Turn meat 3 times during cooking.

Remove cooked meat to a serving platter. Strain and defatten the cooking juices and thicken as desired. Blend in sour cream and horseradish. Correct seasoning if necessary and butter the sauce.

Wine: California Pinot Noir or *French Côte de Beaune*

BRAISED VEAL LOIN OR TOP ROUND
6 SERVINGS

½ *pound fresh pork fatback*
2 *tablespoons Cognac or brandy*
½ *teaspoon salt*
⅛ *teaspoon pepper*
¼ *teaspoon grated nutmeg*
1 *veal loin or top round, 3 to*
   4 *pounds*
Pork or veal suet (*for top*
   round)

1 *large pork rind*
2 *onions, sliced*
1 *carrot, sliced*
Butter or lard
½ *cup white wine*
Brown veal stock (*p.* 80)
Jardinière of vegetables (*p.* 322)

Cut fatback into strips and marinate the strips in the Cognac, salt, pepper and nutmeg for 2 hours. Lard the meat with the strips. If you use the top round, wrap it in pork or veal suet. Blanch the pork rind. Sauté onions and carrot in butter or lard until soft but not colored. Sear the meat in a 375°F. oven for 15 minutes.

Set the ingredients in the braising pot in the following order: pork rind, sautéed vegetables, meat. Add the wine and reduce over high heat to 2 teaspoons. Add ¼ cup stock and reduce again to 2 teaspoons. Add enough stock to half cover the meat and bring to a boil. Cover the meat with foil and pot lid, and braise for 1½ hours. Continue braising the meat for another 45 minutes, basting the meat with the juices every 10 minutes. Uncover the pot to let the meat color during the last 10 minutes.

Strain and defatten cooking juices. (If canned stock has resulted in an oversalted sauce, mix it with some heavy cream to rebalance the taste.) Serve with the jardinière of vegetables.
Wine: California Wente Grey Riesling or *Alsatian Riesling*

SHOULDER OF LAMB MOUNTAIN STYLE
6 SERVINGS

A good dish for a winter day. If you are a knowledgeable mushroom collector, add any late autumn wild mushrooms you may be able to locate in your woods.

½ recipe red-wine marinade
 (p. 193), made with Zinfandel
2 garlic cloves, mashed
8 juniper berries, crushed
½ teaspoon dried rosemary
¾ teaspoon dried sweet basil
1 boned shoulder of lamb,
 3 pounds
2 slices of white bread, shredded
¼ cup Zinfandel
½ pound pork sausage
1 onion, grated
4 tablespoons fine-chopped
 parsley
¼ teaspoon rubbed sage

1 whole egg
1 teaspoon salt
⅛ teaspoon pepper
3 garlic cloves, whole
¼ pound slab bacon
2 tablespoons (1 ounce) gin
Best available brown or white
 stock
1 teaspoon tomato paste
1 teaspoon meat extract
½ cup dried mushrooms, soaked
 in ½ cup water
3 large red potatoes, peeled,
 trimmed and halved
12 white onions, blanched

Make the uncooked marinade, adding the mashed garlic, the juniper berries, ¼ teaspoon of the rosemary and ½ teaspoon of the basil. Marinate the boned shoulder in the refrigerator overnight.

Drain the meat and dry well in kitchen towels. Reserve the marinade. Soak the bread in the Zinfandel. Mix sausage, grated onion, half of the chopped parsley, the sage, remaining rosemary and basil, soaked bread, egg, and salt and pepper in a bowl; mix well to make a forcemeat. Put the whole garlic cloves on the inside of the boned lamb, then stuff it with the forcemeat. Roll and tie the meat.

Cut the bacon into ½-inch pieces and render the pieces in the braising pot until golden. Remove bacon pieces to a plate. Brown the tied shoulder well on all sides in the bacon fat. Discard the fat and flambé the meat with the heated gin. Add the marinade and reduce by two thirds over high heat. Add enough stock to half cover the meat and bring to a boil. Add tomato paste, meat extract and soaked mushrooms with the soaking liquid. Cover with foil and pot lid and braise in a 325°F. oven for 1½ hours.

Strain and defatten cooking juices completely and return them to the pot. Add potatoes, bacon pieces and onions and continue baking for another 30 minutes. Serve in the braising pot, sprinkled with the rest of the parsley.

Wine: California Zinfandel or French Côtes-du-Rhône

LOIN OF PORK BRAISED IN MILK
6 SERVINGS

This recipe from the Alps makes the pork very soft and tender.

3 cups milk	*Pinch of cayenne*
¼ teaspoon dried rosemary	*2 onions*
⅛ teaspoon each of dried thyme and sage	*1 carrot*
1 bay leaf	*3 tablespoons butter*
1 tablespoon chopped parsley stems	*1 teaspoon arrowroot*
	3 tablespoons sour cream
1 boneless loin of pork, 3 pounds	*1 teaspoon dry mustard*
½ teaspoon salt	*1 tablespoon chopped chives*

Bring milk to a boil, add all the herbs, and simmer down to 2 cups. Sear the pork in a 400°F. oven for 20 minutes. Sprinkle with salt and pepper. Sauté onions and carrot lightly in butter in the braising pot. Add the pork, cover with the milk, and bring to a boil. Cover tightly with foil and pot lid. Bake in a 325°F. oven for 1½ to 2 hours. Remove the cooked meat to a serving platter.

Strain the cooking juices into a measuring cup and defatten them. The juices will be clear as the straining will discard the milk solids. Bring the meat juices to a boil again. Make a slurry with the arrowroot and a little water and stir in to thicken the juices. Blend in sour cream and mustard. Reheat but do not reboil. Add chives and correct seasoning.

Wine: California Semillon or Sauvignon Blanc or French Sancerre

BALLOTTINE OF BRAISED DUCK
OLD ENGLISH STYLE
8 OR MORE SERVINGS

This recipe may be prepared as much as 3 days ahead of time, and will result in compliments!

2 ducks, 4 to 5 pounds each
1 cup white or tawny port
2 slices of bread, crusts removed
3 tablespoons milk
1 cup packed cubes of lean pork
    meat
1 cup cubes of pork fat,
    preferably fresh (salt pork
    will not do as well)
2 medium-size eggs
2 teaspoons salt
1/4 teaspoon pepper

2 tablespoons each of oil and
    clarified butter
1 onion, sliced
1 carrot, sliced
1/4 cup orange juice
1 1/2 teaspoons julienne of
    orange rind
1/8 teaspoon each of ground
    allspice and cinnamon
1 cup drained, canned dark sweet
    cherries

At least a day ahead bone both ducks or have the butcher do it. The duck breasts should be removed as 4 boneless fillets or cutlets. Be sure that one skin is left absolutely whole without the smallest tear. Marinate the 4 duck fillets and 1 duck liver in 1/2 cup of the port for 4 hours. Brown all the duck bones and use them and the duck giblets except the livers to make a good stock. Reserve 1 cup of stock, and with the rest make 1 1/2 cups brown sauce (p. 114).

Soak the bread in the milk. Grind twice the pork meat, pork fat, the second duck liver, and all the duck meat except the already marinating fillets. Add the soaked bread, the eggs and salt and pepper. Whip with an electric mixer at medium speed to obtain a homogenous mixture.

Just before cooking form the *ballottine*. Cut the marinated fillets and liver into strips. Spread out the duck skin, outside down. Alternate layers of stuffing and strips of duck on the inside of the skin, starting and ending with the stuffing. Roll and tie with soft butcher's string.

Rub the *ballottine* with oil and clarified butter and sear in a 400°F. oven for 30 minutes. Meanwhile, sauté onion and carrot in remaining oil and butter for *fonds de braise* until brown. Set *ballottine* on top of the vegetables in the braising pot, add the reserved 1 cup duck stock and the brown sauce, and bring to a boil. Cover with foil and pot lid, and braise in a 325°F. oven for 1 1/2 hours.

While the *ballottine* braises, prepare the following infusion: mix remaining 1/2 cup tawny port, the orange juice, julienne of orange rind, allspice and cinnamon, and reduce to 1/3 cup. Add the well-drained sweet cherries.

Strain the juices of the cooked *ballottine*, defatten them, and mix them with the infusion. Glaze the *ballottine* in the oven for a few minutes, if desired, and serve.

Wine: California Pinot Noir or *French Côte de Beaune*

CONFIT DE PIGEONS
6 SERVINGS

This dish was created for the Philadelphia Chapter of the Wine and Food Society. This expensive but supremely elegant dish is for sophisticated cooks only—a true challenge with guaranteed reward.

6 squabs, ¾ pound each	*Brown veal stock (p. 80) or*
½ cup duxelles *(p. 340)*	*squab stock*
6 tablespoons foie gras *(p. 29)*	*1 cup classic brown sauce*
3 large truffles	*(p. 114), made with veal stock*
3 tablespoons clarified butter	*3 tablespoons raw butter*
5 tablespoons Cognac or brandy	*2 tablespoons tawny or white port*
1 onion, sliced	*6 large croutons, butter-fried*
1 carrot, sliced	*6 large mushrooms, poached*
Salt and pepper	

Bone the squabs, leaving only the drumsticks. Make stock with the bones if you wish, or make brown veal stock. Stuff each bird with 1½ tablespoons *duxelles,* 1 tablespoon *foie gras* and one third of a peeled truffle. Sew closed, using a fine needle and white thread. Brown squabs on all sides in clarified butter. Flambé with 4 tablespoons of the Cognac. Remove to a plate.

Brown onion and carrot slices in the same butter, and transfer to a braising pot. Set the squabs on the vegetable bed, sprinkle with salt and pepper, and half cover with stock. Bring to a boil and cover with foil and pot lid. Braise in a 325°F. oven for 1 hour to 1¼ hours. If the squabs weigh more than ¾ pound, allow the longer time.

While the squabs cook, peel the remaining truffle and add all the peels to the brown sauce; simmer together for 15 minutes. Defatten completely the cooking juices from the braising pot; add them to the sauce. Whisk in the raw butter. Strain the sauce and add remaining tablespoon of Cognac, the port, and the last truffle, diced. Reheat without boiling.

Serve each squab on a fried crouton, topped with a mushroom. Spoon the sauce over.

Wine: Pomerol Petits Villages

STEWING—MOIST-HEAT PROCEDURE

There are two types of stews—brown stews made with beef, veal, chicken or rabbit, and white stews made with veal and chicken.

BROWN STEWS

Brown stews are nothing else than true braises. While in a true braise a *large piece of meat* is half covered with stock, in a stew *cubes of meat* are, according to the consecrated expression, "barely covered" with the stock. Occasionally, a brown poultry stew (*coq au vin*) will be called a "brown fricassee." The cooking procedure and the physical principles governing brown stews are identical to those for braises.

The cook has two choices, either brown the meat without flouring it and obtain a strong sauce that may be thickened after completion of the cooking, or sprinkle the browned meat with flour before adding the stock. The sauce obtained with the second procedure is thickened by the time the cooking is finished, but it is not quite as strong and flavorful.

You may have run across the name *daube* applied to a beef stew. A *daube* is a stew made with marinated, floured but unbrowned beef cubes or slices. The meat is barely covered with stock and is stewed in a pot hermetically sealed with a paste of water and flour. The best implement for this type of stew is a bean pot. You can prepare 3 to 4 pounds of meat in 3 to 3½ hours in a 325°F. oven, but leaving the pot overnight in a 250°F. oven gives undescribably delicious results (p. 241).

WHITE STEWS

White stews are known as *blanquettes* or *fricassees*. In a *blanquette*, the meat is immersed in cold water or stock and allowed to simmer until tender. In a *fricassee,* the meat is first lightly seared in hot butter, floured if desired, and then covered with water or stock and allowed to simmer until tender.

In both cases, the resulting sauce is a *velouté,* which is usually enriched before serving with cream or a liaison of yolks and cream.

GUINNESS BEEF STEW
6 TO 8 SERVINGS

A variation on the Belgian *carbonnades de boeuf.* In Belgium, they use Lambic, a slightly sour light beer; the present variation started with a leftover of Guinness—you know, Guinness is so good for you! The sauce is pleasantly bitter.

4 pounds rump or round of beef	*1 bottle (12 ounces) Guinness*
Lard or oil	*Stout*
2 tablespoons flour	*2 to 3 cups classic brown stock*
12 large onions, sliced	*(p. 78)*
Salt and pepper	*Small bouquet garni*
½ teaspoon ground ginger	*1 dime-size piece of lemon rind*
2 garlic cloves, mashed	*2 tablespoons butter*
2 tablespoons blackstrap molasses	

Cut the beef into ⅓-inch slices. Brown in lard on both sides. Sprinkle with flour and let cook for a few minutes. Sauté onions in lard until brown. Transfer meat and onions to the braising pot, arranging them in alternate layers. Salt and pepper each layer. Mix ginger, garlic, molasses and stout; pour over the meat. Cook down over high heat until the liquid is reduced by half. Add stock to barely cover the meat and bring to a boil; add *bouquet garni* and lemon rind. Cover the pot with foil and the pot lid. Braise in a 325°F. oven for 1½ to 2 hours.

Uncover the pot, taste the sauce, and correct the seasoning; spoon off any trace of fat from the top of the pot. Replace by small dots of butter. Serve from the pot, with a dish of buttered noodles, rice or gnocchi.

Beverage: no wine please, but Guinness Stout

KAMMAN'S VEAL STEW
6 SERVINGS

A family concoction. As an additional vegetable, try glazed turnips, buttered zucchini or cucumbers.

3 pounds stewing veal, cut into 1-inch cubes
6 tablespoons butter, or 3 tablespoons butter and 3 tablespoons lard
2 to 3 cups brown veal stock (p. 80)
1 carrot, sliced
1 onion, sliced
Bouquet garni
1 garlic clove, mashed
1 large bunch of fresh dill, or 2 tablespoons dried dillweed
Gnocchi (p. 521), flavored with 2 tablespoons chopped fresh dill, or 1 tablespoon dried dillweed
Beurre manié (*p. 119*)

Brown the veal cubes in half of the butter or in the lard. Discard browning fat and deglaze the pan with some stock. Brown carrot and onion in 3 tablespoons butter in the braising pot. Add the veal cubes, the deglazing juices and enough stock to barely cover the veal. Bring to a boil, and add *bouquet garni*, garlic and dill. Cover with foil and the pot lid, and bake in a 325°F. oven for 1½ hours.

Make gnocchi paste; keep ready to use. Strain the braising juices of the meat, defatten them, and use them to poach the gnocchi. Thicken the juices with *beurre manié* (1 tablespoon flour and 1 tablespoon fat per cup of liquid) and strain over the meat and gnocchi. Reheat well.
Wine: California Gamay Beaujolais or French Fleurie

CALIFORNIA RABBIT FRICASSEE
6 SERVINGS

Be a sport! They raise beautiful farm rabbits in California, and they can be found in the supermarket freezer. Rabbit is delicious; I always serve it without giving it a name and everybody loves it!

1 frozen rabbit, about 3 pounds
½ recipe for red-wine marinade
    (p. 193)
2 garlic cloves
½ pound large prunes
Lard
1 ounce Cognac or brandy
2½ cups white stock (p. 76)

1 teaspoon tomato paste
¼ teaspoon commercial meat
    extract
Beurre manié (p. 119)
Salt and pepper
Chopped parsley
2 tablespoons butter
12 small croutons, butter-fried

Defrost the rabbit. Make the marinade with California Grenache Rosé and add the garlic cloves. Marinate the rabbit in the refrigerator overnight. Soak the prunes in water overnight.

Drain the rabbit well, and reserve the marinade. Pat the meat dry and brown well in lard in a braising pot. Discard the lard and flambé the meat with the Cognac. Add 1 cup of the marinade, bring to a boil, and reduce to ⅓ cup. Add stock, tomato paste and meat extract, and bring to a boil. Cover with foil and the pot lid, and bake in a 325°F. oven for 15 minutes. Add the prunes and continue baking for another 30 minutes.

Remove rabbit and prunes to a serving casserole. Strain and defatten the cooking juices and thicken with *beurre manié*; use 1½ tablespoons butter and 1½ tablespoons flour per cup of liquid. Correct seasoning. Strain the sauce on top of the meat. Sprinkle with chopped parsley and dot with small pieces of butter. Surround with the butter-fried croutons.

Wine: California Grenache Rosé or *French Rosé d'Anjou*

FRICASSEE OF CHICKEN AND ARTICHOKES
6 SERVINGS

To Ellen Simon, who tested the recipe.

6 whole chicken legs
6 tablespoons butter
Salt and pepper
1¾ teaspoons dried tarragon

2 packages (10 ounces each)
    frozen artichoke hearts
1 dime-size piece of lemon rind
2 tablespoons flour

3 cups white stock (p. 76) or	*¾ cup heavy cream*
water	*2 tablespoons chopped fresh*
1 small carrot	*parsley*
2 onions	*12 croutons, butter-fried*
3 whole cloves	

Skin the chicken legs and cut apart to obtain 6 drumsticks and 6 thighs. Heat 4 tablespoons of the butter and lightly sear the pieces. Sprinkle with salt and pepper and add 1 teaspoon of the tarragon. Cover with lukewarm white stock or water. Slowly bring to a boil; skim if necessary. Add carrot, onions and cloves. Simmer for 40 minutes.

While the meat cooks, add ½ cup stock or water to the artichokes and bring to a boil. Add lemon rind and ¼ teaspoon dried tarragon, and let cook slowly until all the liquid has been absorbed. Keep ready to use. Revive the remaining ½ teaspoon dried tarragon with boiling water.

Transfer the cooked chicken and artichokes to a serving casserole. Strain the cooking juices into a quart-size measuring bowl. Make a white *roux* with the remaining 2 tablespoons of butter and the flour, and add 2 cups of the strained cooking liquid to make a velouté. Bring to a boil and skim. Add the heavy cream very slowly, stirring constantly. Continue stirring until the sauce coats the spatula. Add the revived tarragon. Correct the seasoning. Strain the sauce on top of the meat and vegetables, and sprinkle with chopped fresh parsley. Decorate with the croutons.

Wine: California Grey Riesling or *French Vouvray Moelleux*

ABBACCHIO E FINOCCHI
6 SERVINGS

3 pounds spring lamb, cubed	*2 onions*
8 tablespoons butter	*2 whole cloves*
Salt and pepper	*1 carrot, halved*
3½ cups white stock (p. 76)	*½ teaspoon dried rosemary*
or water	*Bouquet garni*

6 small heads of fennel   *¾ cup grated Gruyère cheese*
2½ tablespoons flour   *¼ cup grated Parmesan cheese*
¾ cup heavy cream

Choose the lamb as young and tender as possible. Sauté the cubed meat in half of the butter in a braising pot without browning. Sprinkle with salt and pepper. Cover meat with 3 cups of the cold stock or water and slowly bring to a boil. Add the onions stuck with the cloves, the carrot, rosemary and *bouquet garni,* and simmer for 1 hour.

While the meat cooks, trim the fennel heads and cut them across in 1-inch-thick slices. Chop and set aside 1 tablespoon of the fennel greens. Immerse the fennel slices in boiling water and simmer for 4 minutes; drain. Melt 1 tablespoon butter in a pot; add the fennel slices and remaining ½ cup stock; season with salt and pepper. Cook slowly, covered, for 20 to 25 minutes.

Remove cooked meat and cooked fennel to a serving casserole. Strain the meat cooking stock into a 4-cup measuring bowl. With remaining 3 tablespoons butter, the flour and 2 cups of the strained cooking stock, make a velouté; bring it to a boil and skim a little. Slowly add the heavy cream, stirring constantly with a wooden spatula until the sauce coats the spatula. Strain the sauce on top of the meat and vegetables. Mix both cheeses, sprinkle on top of the casserole, and slide under the broiler for 2 minutes. Serve sprinkled with the chopped fennel greens.

Wine: Soave

POT-ROASTING—DRY- AND MOIST-HEAT PROCEDURE

POT-ROASTING I (*French casserole roasting*)

This is an excellent procedure for smaller roasts, birds and large chops. Birds and small roasts will be best cooked in an enameled oval braising pot, and chops in a round copper or thick aluminum pan called a *sauteuse.*

Brown the meat first so as to concentrate the juices. Add very little stock or none at all, in any case, never more than ½ cup, cover the pan, and complete the cooking in a 325°F. oven. The meat juices will break down into protein concentrates and steam and travel back from the center of the piece to the pot where they will make a lovely gravy. Baste the meat once in a while with the melted butter in the pot.

Make sure that birds are evenly browned; if the skin seems very thin and you fear that it may break, start the searing in a hot oven. Defatten the cooking juices before serving in the same pot in which the meat or poultry has been cooked. If there is not enough gravy, add a little brown veal stock or the best stock at hand.

Pot-Roasting II (French *poêlage*)

Whenever you see a recipe for "poêled" meat, this procedure will be applied, although often the method described above is also used.

Use a thick braising pot, just large enough to contain the piece to be "poêled." Salt and pepper the meat and roll it in melted butter. *Do not sear it.* Put it on a *mirepoix* (p. 12) of sautéed vegetables and cover the pot. Bake in a 325°F. oven, basting the meat with melted butter every 15 minutes. The meat is cooked when a skewer penetrates it easily and comes out freely. Since the meat will be rather pale, uncover the pan and let it brown during the last 15 to 20 minutes of cooking, turning the piece to obtain even coloration on all sides. Vegetables may be added to the cooking pot. There will be some gravy; if more is desired, add a little veal stock.

In this procedure, approximately the same amount of meat juices escape into the pot and remain in the meat. It is an ideal cooking method for any small roast not surrounded by too much fat and not too well marbled.

French Sautéed Chicken

This French way of cooking chickens can lead to multiple combinations of vegetable garnishes and a large choice of flavoring for the pan gravy. Auguste Escoffier in *Le Guide Culinaire* lists 64 different recipes in 10 pages.

In the recipes included in this section, I have purposely included truly American garnishes to encourage the cook to use whatever she pleases as a garnish. Any fresh vegetable from the garden is welcome to this type of "chicken pot."

To cut the chicken, refer to the instructions given on page 158. Use a *sauteuse* or a skillet with a heatproof handle. Brown the chicken well in butter on all sides. Salt and pepper it, then cover the pot, and bake in a 325 °F. oven for 30 to 35 minutes. Or, if you prefer, add ½ cup stock or wine to the *sauteuse* and cook over very moderate heat on top of the stove. The liquid is necessary on top of the stove to compensate for greater evaporation. Add the vegetable garnish in time to allow it to be cooked when the chicken is. This procedure is nothing else than pot-roasting.

Serve the chicken with its own plain defattened gravy, or add stock, wine or cream to the pan gravy to make a sauce. When the sauce is made with cream, the chicken is usually not allowed to color very deeply and it is just sautéed very quickly in hot butter to stiffen the skin.

You will notice that most of the examples are recipes for chicken legs. If you plan to use a whole chicken, do not overcook the breasts. Sear them, transfer them to a plate, and finish cooking them during the last 5 minutes of the total cooking time; the breasts will be done. Do not ever allow the white meat to simmer in the sauce at any time or it will toughen. A chicken breast with the shoulder bone attached, but otherwise boneless, cooks in 10 minutes; beyond that it becomes stringy.

KREBSBUTTERHÜHNER (*CASSEROLE METHOD*)
6 SERVINGS

This recipe was adapted from a mid-19th-century German cookbook.

1 small double chicken breast	*Pinch of four spices (p. 27)*
2 slices of white bread, crusts removed	*½ teaspoon salt*
	Pepper
¾ cup plus 2 tablespoons heavy cream	*3 Rock Cornish Game hens*
	Clarified butter (about 6 tablespoons)
3 tablespoons unsalted butter	
1 can (2 ounces) lobster spread	*½ cup fine-diced cooked lobster or crabmeat*
1 egg	
Pinch of cayenne	*2 tablespoons Cognac or brandy*

¼ cup veal or chicken stock　　　*1 teaspoon arrowroot*
　(p. 76)　　　　　　　　　　*6 large croutons, fried*

Skin and bone the chicken breast and chop the raw chicken meat with a chopping knife; measure ½ cup chopped meat. Soak the bread in 2 tablespoons of the heavy cream. Put the ½ cup chicken and the moistened bread in a mixer bowl. Gradually add the unsalted butter and half of the can of lobster spread. Add egg, spices, salt, and pepper to taste. Beat well to homogenize.

The game hens may be boned or not. To bone them, see page 157. Stuff each bird with one third of the filling. Brown in a 475°F. oven for 20 minutes. Transfer to a braising pot, and add 2 tablespoons clarified butter. Reduce oven heat to 325°F. and bake the birds, covered, for 45 minutes, basting every 15 minutes with clarified butter. While the birds cook, reheat the lobster or crab in clarified butter. Then flambé with Cognac.

When the birds are cooked, defatten the cooking juices and deglaze the pot with ¾ cup heavy cream. Make a slurry with stock and arrowroot and thicken the sauce. Whisk in the remainder of the lobster spread and strain the sauce over the warm lobster dice. Correct seasoning. Cut each bird into halves, and set each half on a fried crouton. Spoon the sauce over.

Wine: New York State Vinifera Riesling or *German Naturwein Mosel*

CHICKEN AND APPLES (SAUTÉ)
6 SERVINGS

An American version of the famous but often disparaged Vallée d'Auge chicken. This dish should contain only apple products. You may add an onion if you desire, but positively no herbs. Only Red Delicious or Grimes Delicious apples will remain whole.

1 chicken, 3 pounds, cut up, or　　*2 ounces applejack*
　6 chicken legs　　　　　　　*6 Delicious (Red or Grimes)*
6 tablespoons clarified butter　　*apples, peeled, each cut into*
Salt and pepper　　　　　　　*6 slices*

¼ *cup apple cider*
¼ *cup 20% apple wine or*
  hard cider
1½ *teaspoons cider vinegar*

¾ *cup heavy cream*
Beurre manié (*p. 119*)
Fried croutons
Watercress

Sauté the chicken in clarified butter in a braising pot until just stiffened; do not let it color. Sprinkle with salt and pepper. Remove the butter to another pot. Flambé the chicken with 1 ounce of the applejack. Cover the pot with foil and pot lid and bake in a 325°F. oven for 25 minutes.

Meanwhile, sauté apple slices in the reserved butter. Add apples to the chicken pot and bake together for another 12 to 15 minutes. Remove chicken and apples to a serving casserole.

Add cider, apple wine and vinegar to the braising pot. Reduce to 3 tablespoons; add heavy cream and remaining applejack. Immediately thicken with *beurre manié;* use 1 tablespoon butter and 1 tablespoon flour per cup of liquid. Correct seasoning, and strain the sauce over chicken and apples. Decorate with fried croutons and watercress.
Beverage: apple cider or *hard cider* or *apple wine*

CHICKEN SUCCOTASH (SAUTÉ)
6 SERVINGS

It took me no time to discover succotash. I added this formula to the family's repertoire a week after "landing" in New York!

¼ *pound salt pork*
6 *whole chicken legs*
Salt and pepper
½ *cup chicken stock*
2 *packages* (*10 ounces each*)
  frozen succotash, thawed

⅓ *teaspoon rubbed sage*
1 *cup heavy cream*
1 *tablespoon fine-chopped*
  scallions

Cut salt pork into dice and render. Brown the chicken legs in the fat. Season with salt and pepper, and discard the fat completely. Add the chicken stock to the pot, cover with foil and pot lid, and cook on top of the stove for 15 minutes. Add succotash and let cook for another 15 to 20 minutes. Remove chicken to a serving casserole.

Add sage and cream to the pot and shake the pot back and forth over the burner until the cream coats the vegetables. Correct seasoning. Mix succotash and chicken and sprinkle with chopped scallions.
Wine: any New York State Labrusca white

JACK CHICKEN (SAUTÉ)
6 SERVINGS

½ pound slab bacon	*1 pound white onions*
6 whole chicken legs	*(silverskins), peeled*
Salt and pepper	*3 tablespoons butter*
1 garlic clove, minced	*½ pound Monterey Jack or*
Bouquet garni	*Vermont Jack cheese, grated*

Cut bacon into chunks 1 inch by ⅓ inch. In a large skillet or a braising pot render the bacon until slices are crisp, then remove them to a plate. Brown the chicken in the rendered bacon fat. Sprinkle with salt and pepper. Drain off most of the browning fat. Sprinkle chicken with minced garlic and add the *bouquet garni*. Cover with foil and lid and cook over low heat for 15 minutes.

Meanwhile, sauté the onions in the butter until brown. Remove to the same plate as bacon. Add both to chicken pot and continue cooking for 20 more minutes. Remove cover, tilt the pot, and remove any excess fat. Sprinkle the chicken with grated cheese and put under the broiler for 2 to 3 minutes. Serve immediately.
Wine: California Mountain Chablis or California Sauterne

CALIFORNIA MUSCAT CHICKEN (SAUTÉ)
6 SERVINGS

If no California Muscatel is available, use Greek Samos or French Frontignan. No bottled red grape juice, please, for the Labrusca taste would overpower the dish and you would fail to recognize its charm.

6 chicken legs
3 tablespoons clarified butter
1 ½ cups seedless or Muscat
　grapes
Salt and pepper
⅓ cup brown veal stock (p. 80)
　or chicken stock (p. 76)

¼ cup Muscatel wine
¾ teaspoon potato starch
2 tablespoons raw butter
Croutons, butter-fried

Brown the chicken in clarified butter. Meanwhile, blend ½ cup unpeeled grapes in the blender and strain to obtain the juice. Discard the browning butter, and replace it with this strained grape juice. Sprinkle the chicken with salt and pepper, cover with foil and pot lid, and bake in a 325°F. oven for 30 minutes. Add remaining 1 cup grapes, peeled if desired, and bake for 5 more minutes. Remove chicken and grapes to a serving casserole. Keep warm.

Deglaze the pan with stock and wine. Boil together for 2 to 3 minutes. Make a slurry with a little cold stock and the potato starch and add to the sauce, stirring until blended and thickened. Turn off the heat and whisk in the raw butter. Strain the sauce over the chicken and decorate with the croutons.

Wine: California Muscatel followed by a glass of sparkling water to clear the palate

POT-ROASTED SQUABS (CASEROLE METHOD)
6 SERVINGS

6 squabs, ¾ pound each, or
　Rock Cornish Game hens
Salt and pepper
Sweet basil, fresh or dried
Oil or clarified butter
2 ounces gin
¼ cup dry vermouth

1 teaspoon dried basil
½ teaspoon arrowroot
2 tablespoons chicken stock
　(p. 76) or water
½ cup sour cream
6 croutons, fried

Sprinkle the cavity of each bird with salt and pepper. Add a good sprig of fresh basil or a large pinch of dried herb. Truss the birds

Brown in oil or clarified butter in a braising pot slowly and on all sides. Remove browning fat. Add gin and flambé. Cover the pot and bake in a 325°F. oven for 15 to 20 minutes for rare (the French taste), or for 45 to 60 minutes for well done (it also tastes good). Remove squabs to a platter.

Discard all fat from the pot. Add vermouth and basil to the cooking juices, and reduce to about ¼ cup. Make a slurry with arrowroot and the cold stock or water; thicken the sauce. Blend in sour cream. Correct seasoning, and reheat without boiling. Spoon the sauce over the birds and garnish with the croutons.

Wine: California Zinfandel or French Pomerol

LE LAPIN DE MÉMÈRE (POÊLÉ METHOD)
6 SERVINGS

My grandmother's recipe. If you have never tried rabbit, now is the time to start. You will need a 6- to 8-quart roaster.

3 pounds onions	*Salt and pepper*
¾ cup butter	*½ teaspoon four spices (p. 27)*
1 whole rabbit, skinned and cleaned but uncut	*½ cup veal stock, if necessary*

Peel the onions and cut into ¼-inch slices. Sauté onions in the butter in the roasting pan until they are soft and translucent. Set the whole rabbit on the onions. Sprinkle with salt and pepper and the four spices. Cover with foil and pot lid and bake in a 325°F. oven for 40 minutes. Uncover the pot. Raise the oven temperature to 375°F. and let the rabbit brown for 15 to 20 minutes on each side, basting with the butter in the pot. If there is not enough liquid in the pot, add from 2 to 4 tablespoons veal stock.

Serve the rabbit surrounded by the onions. The portions are 2 legs, 2 loins, 2 shoulders and 2 bonuses—the kidneys; don't fight over them, although I always did.

Wine: California Folle Blanche or French Quincy

SHOULDER OF LAMB OR VEAL POÊLÉD
WITH HERBS (POÊLÉ METHOD)
6 SERVINGS

This recipe can be used not only for shoulders but for all small pieces (flanken, brisket) that may be rolled.

¼ teaspoon dried basil	*1 rolled shoulder of lamb, 3*
½ teaspoon dried tarragon	*pounds*
1 teaspoon chopped fresh or	*Salt and freshly ground black*
frozen chives	*pepper*
1 tablespoon chopped fresh	*Clarified butter*
parsley	*½ cup veal or chicken stock*
Pinch each of dried rosemary	
and savory	

Mix all the herbs. Sprinkle on the inside of the meat, then sprinkle with salt and pepper, roll and tie. Roll in clarified butter. Place in a braising pot, cover, and bake in 325°F. oven for 1¼ hours. Baste with more clarified butter at regular intervals. Raise the oven heat to 375°F. Uncover the pot and brown the meat for 15 to 20 minutes, still basting with butter. Transfer meat to a serving platter.

Completely defatten the cooking juices. Add stock to the juices and boil together for 3 to 4 minutes. Serve the unthickened gravy in a sauceboat.

Wine: California Gamay Beaujolais or *French Hermitage*

PORK AND SPROUTS (POÊLÉ METHOD)
6 SERVINGS

This is an excellent way to obtain moist pork. The recipe may be used for loin, rolled shoulder, tenderloin and other cuts.

3 tablespoons clarified butter　*2 packages (10 ounces each)*
1 pork loin, 3 pounds　　　　*frozen baby Brussels sprouts,*
Salt and pepper　　　　　　　*thawed*
Pinch each of ground allspice,　*⅓ cup white wine*
　cinnamon and cloves

Melt the butter in a large braising pot. Sprinkle the meat with salt and pepper and with the spices, and roll in the butter. Cover the pot and bake in a 325°F. oven for 1½ hours. Add the thawed sprouts and continue cooking for 15 more minutes.

Remove sprouts to a serving casserole and keep warm. Uncover the meat, raise oven heat to 375°F., and let the meat brown all around for 20 to 25 minutes. Transfer meat to the serving casserole. Defatten pan juices, add the wine, and reduce by half. Correct seasoning. Serve the gravy unthickened.

Wine: California Gamay Beaujolais or *French Moulin-à-Vent*

POACHING—MOIST-HEAT PROCEDURE

As confusing as it may sound, "poaching" means to boil without boiling. A poached meat is cooked by immersion in a boiling liquid, but once a second boil has been reached, the temperature of the liquid must remain between 200° and 205°F.

Use only tender cuts or birds. A meat can be poached only if it is tender enough to be roasted. A rump of beef, a roasting chicken, a Rock Cornish Game hen, a leg of a young lamb (about 5 pounds)—these can be poached very successfully.

COOKING LIQUID

Poach good pieces of meat in as good a stock as possible, especially if a sauce is to be made afterwards. The stock flavors the outside of the cut, but the cooking time is too short to allow any exchange of flavors between meat and stock. Fine dishes like *poularde demi-deuil* or *piemontaise* deserve a strong fragrant homemade stock. However, you may use canned stock cut with vegetable broth (p. 75) and flavored with a few additional vegetables. Poach lamb in water and save the water to make a good bean soup.

STARTING THE POACHING

Clean red meats of all fat and gristle and tie loosely to obtain a regular shape. Immerse the meat in the boiling stock, so that the heat of the stock immediately coagulates the outer layers of the meat. As in roasting, the meat juices are trapped inside of the meat and concentrate at its center. About 15 minutes per pound of meat gives a very juicy and rare piece of beef.

As with a roast, allow the cooked meat to stand for 15 minutes before serving. Poached red meats are succulent but obviously blander than roasted meats since no brown flavor is present. A jar of good strong mustard or a pleasantly seasoned sauce are recommended. Sprinkle salt and pepper over the meat after carving.

White meats other than poultry are generally not poached, although the veal meat in a *blanquette de veau* is more poached than stewed.

Season chicken, game hens and baby turkeys in the cavity and immerse in *lukewarm* stock. Bring slowly to a boil and poach for 14 to 15 minutes per pound. The bird is done when the juices from the cavity run clear. To check the doneness, slide the handle of a long wooden spoon into the cavity and hold up the bird to let the juice run into a dish. If you are in a hurry, the immersion can be done in boiling stock, but notice that the leg tendons of a bird so treated will pull away from the drumstick bones, thus spoiling the appearance of the finished dish. Take care not to let the stock boil at any time or the skin will burst open.

To protect the tender meat of the breast, the custom is to wrap it in a sheet of fresh fatback. If fatback is difficult for you to locate, slide a thin layer of butter between skin and meat and wrap the bird in a sheet of parchment paper; this works just as well as the fatback.

SAUCES WITH POACHED MEATS

Make a sauce with the cooking stock, using the methods that apply to white or brown sauces. To obtain fat-free stock out of a boiling pot, dip in your ladle at the center of the boil.

POACHING CHICKEN CUTLETS IN BUTTER

Since chicken cutlets will not boil or simmer without becoming stringy, they must be poached with a different method.

Pound the cutlets with the side of the hand. With your finger feel the soft spongelike texture. Roll the cutlets in melted, cooled, *unclarified* butter. Very lightly season them and sprinkle them with lemon juice. Melt a little more butter in a *sauteuse* or large frying pan, add the cutlets, and cover with a buttered parchment paper and the pot lid. Put the pan in a 450° to 500°F. oven. The cutlets will cook so quickly that they will have no time to toughen. After 6 to 8 minutes, depending on their size, they will be cooked. If you feel the meat now, you will notice that it has become resistant and elastic to the finger. Cut into one and notice the pale pink, solid and compact meat; should you continue the cooking longer, more and more liquid collagen would leach to the bottom of the pan, and the dried and hard bundles of muscle fibers could be distinctly seen.

BOEUF À LA FICELLE
6 TO 8 SERVINGS

A *ficelle* is a kitchen string.

5 quarts beef stock (p. 78)	6 leeks, white part only
4 pounds rump or sirloin tip, in one piece	6 small celery ribs
	6 small potatoes, peeled
6 carrots, scraped	Düsseldorf- or Dijon-style
6 small white turnips, peeled	mustard

Bring 4 quarts of the stock to a boil. Tie the meat with kitchen string, and fasten the end of the string to the pot handle so as to suspend the meat in the pot. The meat should float in the stock, rather than rest on the bottom of the pot. Immerse the meat in the boiling stock, bring the stock back to a boil, and barely simmer for 1 hour, so as to keep the meat rare.

Bring the remaining quart of stock to a boil in a second pot, and use this to cook the vegetables. Add carrots to the pot first, then turnips. Add leeks, celery and potatoes about 20 minutes before the other vegetables are cooked. Arrange beef on a serving platter and surround with the vegetables. Serve piping hot, with mustard.

Wine: California Zinfandel or *French Pomerol*

ENGLISH POACHED LEG OF LAMB
6 SERVINGS

1 *shortened leg of lamb* (*shank* *end, without the saddle*)	4 *quarts vegetable broth* (*p. 75*)
Flour (*about 6 tablespoons*)	½ *cup plus 3 tablespoons butter*
Salt and pepper	2 *tablespoons capers*

Remove, or have the butcher remove, the part of the loin still attached to the leg. Rub the meat all around with a good amount of seasoned flour. Wrap the meat in a large damp cheesecloth and tie it at both ends. Bring the vegetable broth to a boil. Immerse the meat in the broth, bring back to a boil, and barely simmer for 15 minutes per pound.

Make a velouté with 3 tablespoons of the butter, 3 tablespoons of the flour and 1½ cups of the cooking broth. As soon as the sauce has thickened, add the capers; then whisk in ½ cup butter. Correct seasoning of the sauce, but do not reboil. Serve the sauce separately, and accompany the meat with a dish of garlic-flavored green beans.

Wine: California Folle Blanche or *French Sancerre*

POULARDE DEMI-DEUIL
8 SERVINGS

A classic of the Lyonnaise cuisine. The name means "chicken in half-mourning," which derives from its appearance, the creamy bird with the black spots of the truffles showing through the skin.

With a thought to Joan Bauer, who liked the bird so much in cooking class that she took the carcass home.

3 large truffles	*6 carrots, scraped*
1 ounce (2 tablespoons) Cognac	*6 turnips, peeled*
or brandy	*6 leeks, white part only*
Salt and pepper	*6 potatoes, peeled*
2 roasting chickens, 4 pounds	*3 tablespoons butter*
each	*3 tablespoons flour*
1 lemon, halved	*¾ cup heavy cream*
6 quarts chicken stock (p. 76)	

Peel all the truffles. Chop the peelings and mix them with 1 table-spoon Cognac; season with a little salt and pepper. Divide into 3 parts, and stuff one third into the cavity of each bird; set aside the third portion. Shave 2 truffles into very thin slices. Cut remaining truffle into dice or very thin slivers and set aside. Using half for each bird, slide the slices under the skin of the chicken over the breasts and thighs. Truss the birds. Rub each chicken with lemon, wrap in parchment paper, tie, and immerse in 5 quarts lukewarm stock. Bring slowly to a boil and simmer for 40 to 45 minutes.

Heat the remaining quart of stock and cook the vegetables in it. Start with carrots, then turnips, then add leeks and potatoes about 20 minutes before carrots are done.

When the chickens are ready, remove them to a platter and remove trussing strings. Make a velouté with the butter, flour and 1½ cups of cooking stock. Reduce the sauce over high heat gradually adding the heavy cream; add the remaining truffle peels. Strain the sauce into a boat and add the diced or slivered truffle. Arrange the vegetables around the chickens.

Wine: New York State Vinifera Pinot Chardonnay or *French Meursault*

POULARDE PIEMONTAISE

8 SERVINGS

A dish from the kitchen of a friend in Saint Vincent d'Aosta. Her garden yielded dreamy white truffles and fat yellow peaches.

2 cups shell pasta

11 tablespoons butter

10 tablespoons grated Fontina
cheese

2 white truffles

Salt and white pepper

2 roasting chickens, 4 pounds
each

1 lemon, halved

5 quarts chicken stock (p. 76)

1 teaspoon olive oil

3 tablespoons flour

6 toasts, buttered

Cook pasta in a large amount of water until cooked *al dente.* Drain well. While still warm, add 4 tablespoons butter and 4 tablespoons cheese. Peel the truffles; reserve the peelings. Chop 1 truffle into tiny bits and mix with the buttered pasta. Correct seasoning; let the pasta cool.

Salt and pepper the cavities of the chickens. Fill with the pasta mixture and truss well. Rub the skin with the lemon halves, tie a piece of parchment around the breasts, and immerse in lukewarm stock. Bring slowly to a boil and poach for 45 minutes.

With the olive oil, 3 tablespoons of the butter, the flour and 2 cups of the cooking stock, make a velouté (p. 108). Add the reserved truffle peelings and any juice remaining in the lemon, and simmer for a few minutes, skimming a bit. Correct seasoning, turn off the heat, and whisk in remaining 4 tablespoons butter. Slice the second truffle very thin or dice very small, place the bits in a sauceboat, and strain the sauce over it.

Sprinkle the rest of the cheese over the buttered toasts. Quickly slide under the broiler until the cheese is just melted. Serve each portion of chicken on a toast, with sauce spooned over.

Wine: Soave or *Frascati*

POACHED ROCK CORNISH GAME HENS
6 SERVINGS

This method of preparation makes a fine change of pace for this little bird.

12 tablespoons butter	*3 Rock Cornish Game hens*
3 teaspoons dried tarragon	*1 lemon, halved*
3 tablespoons fine-chopped fresh parsley	*5 quarts chicken stock*
	¼ cup vinegar
Salt and pepper	*2 shallots, chopped fine*
6 tablespoons fine fresh bread crumbs	*3 tablespoons flour*

Start this preparation several hours before you plan to cook the birds. Cream 6 tablespoons of the butter and add 1½ teaspoons of the dried tarragon, 1 tablespoon chopped parsley, 1 teaspoon salt and ¼ teaspoon pepper. Blend in the bread crumbs. Divide the mixture into 6 portions. Stuff each portion under the breast skin of a bird, one on each side; pat flat over each breast. Let the birds rest for several hours to absorb as much flavor as possible from the stuffing.

Salt and pepper the cavity of each bird. Rub the hens with lemon, truss, and wrap in parchment paper. Tie. Immerse in lukewarm stock, bring to a boil, and barely simmer for 30 to 35 minutes.

Make an infusion with the vinegar, chopped shallots and remaining 1½ teaspoons of tarragon. Cook until all but 1 tablespoon liquid has evaporated. Make a velouté (p. 108) with 3 tablespoons butter, the flour and 1½ cups of the cooking stock. Mix with vinegar infusion and simmer together for 5 minutes. Strain into a sauceboat; blend in remaining chopped parsley and remaining butter. Serve half of a bird to each person.

Wine: California Semillon

CHICKEN CUTLETS QUATTROCENTO
6 SERVINGS

12 small chicken cutlets	*2 tablespoons meat glaze, or ¼*
½ cup milk	*teaspoon commercial meat*
10 tablespoons chopped pistachios	*extract*
	¼ teaspoon pepper
3 tablespoons chopped prosciutto	*Salt*
3 tablespoons fresh bread crumbs	*Lemon juice*

4 tablespoons melted butter
1⅔ cups chicken velouté
  (*p. 108*)

3 tablespoons butter
¼ cup plus ⅓ cup heavy cream

Soak the cutlets in the milk for 2 hours. Mix 6 tablespoons of the pistachios, the prosciutto, the bread crumbs, the butter, ¼ cup cream and the pepper until homogenous. Add salt if needed. Remove chicken from milk and pat dry. Discard the milk. Cut a pocket in each cutlet and fill with an equal amount of stuffing. Sprinkle the cutlets with lemon juice, then roll them in melted butter and poach as indicated on page 218.

Mix velouté and remaining ⅓ cup heavy cream. Simmer for 5 minutes. Add the cooking juices of the chicken and the meat glaze, and mix well. Blend in remaining pistachios, and spoon the sauce over the cutlets.

Wine: Italian Soave or French Pouilly Fumé

CHICKEN CUTLETS JUDY
6 SERVINGS

To Judy Obermayer, who grows all sorts of herbs in her garden.

3 limes
12 small chicken cutlets
Salt and pepper
3 tablespoons melted butter

2 cups chicken velouté (*p. 108*)
1½ teaspoons fine-chopped fresh
  mint
⅔ cup sour cream

Grate the rind of 2 limes. Cut the remaining lime into 6 paper-thin slices and extract the juice from the others. Sprinkle the cutlets with salt and pepper and with 1 tablespoon lime juice. Roll them in the melted butter and poach as indicated on page 218, topping each cutlet with ½ slice of lime.

Simmer chicken velouté with ½ teaspoon of the grated lime rind and the chopped mint for a few minutes. Add the cooking juices of the cutlets. Blend in the sour cream and reheat without boiling. Correct seasoning, add more lime juice to taste, and spoon the sauce over the chicken cutlets.

Wine: California Emerald Riesling

VARIETY MEATS

Variety meats, also known as offal, are not always popular among consumers in the United States, and for this reason they remain relatively inexpensive. A plentiful source of proteins, vitamins of the B complex, vitamin A, phosphorus and iron, they also bring to the table an enjoyable change from the expensive cuts of meat designed for roasting or broiling.

Brains

The brains of beef, veal and lamb are the kinds chiefly used for cooking. Some preparations of brains are extremely delicate dishes. Brains are easy to digest, so they are often given to children and invalids. They bring good amounts of protein and phosphorus to the diet.

Brains may look rather discouraging or even shocking to the inexperienced cook. They will look better after soaking in cold salted water for at least 2 hours. Soaking is essential; not only does it clean the brains of all traces of blood, but it also softens the membrane, which adheres so snugly to the meat that otherwise it could not be removed. If at all possible, try to grasp some of that membrane between the thumb and index fingers of your left hand while you slide the tip of the index finger of your right hand between the meat and membrane and gently separate them from each other. You will discover that where beef and veal are concerned the membrane can be removed relatively easily; lamb brains will require more of your patience as the membrane tears easily and adheres so snugly to the meat.

Brains are highly perishable and must be prepared on the day they are purchased, and preferably eaten then also. If they must wait, soak them as described, then cook them in a *court-bouillon,* let them cool, and keep them refrigerated in the *court-bouillon.* The next day reheat them slowly until warm enough to be sauced or used in a dish. Brains are very bland in flavor, therefore the *court-bouillon* used for them should be strongly flavored. Precook the *court-bouillon* to obtain a maximum amount of flavor.

Because of the delicate texture, brains must be *poached,* not boiled in the *court-bouillon.*

Brains are usually served with a rather acid sauce. The French use brown butter and capers; the Italians use their tangy lemons to season them. In the recipe for Brains in Green Butter I use lime juice for the acid.

Poached brains, cooled, sliced and breaded, are very good sautéed in clarified butter. When breaded and deep-fried, they make a very different appetizer. Guests who taste them for the first time invariably declare them "heavenly." Those brain fritters will disappear very quickly if sophisticated guests discover them.

You can expect about 1½ pounds of brains (2 beef brains, 3 calves' brains, or 6 lamb brains) to serve 6 persons.

COURT-BOUILLON FOR BRAINS
1½ QUARTS

1½ quarts water	2 fresh parsley sprigs
½ small bay leaf	2 whole small onions
⅛ teaspoon dried thyme	1½ teaspoons salt
3 tablespoons wine vinegar	5 white peppercorns

Bring the water to a boil. Add bay leaf, thyme, vinegar, parsley, onions and salt, and simmer for 15 minutes. Add the peppercorns and simmer for another 5 minutes. Let steep from 2 to 24 hours.

TO POACH BRAINS
Immerse the brains in the barely lukewarm *court-bouillon*. Slowly bring to a boil. Barely simmer for 25 minutes for beef and veal brains and 20 minutes for lamb brains.

BRAINS IN GREEN BUTTER
6 SERVINGS

1½ pounds brains	2 tablespoons lime juice
Court-bouillon *for brains*	Pinch of grated lime rind
(*see above*)	½ to ⅔ cup unsalted butter
⅓ cup water	2 tablespoons chopped flat-leafed
½ teaspoon salt	Italian parsley
¼ teaspoon ground white pepper	

Poach the brains in *court-bouillon;* keep them warm. Mix water, salt, pepper, lime juice and rind, and boil down to 2 tablespoons. Over very low heat (130°F.), whisk in the butter, tablespoon by tablespoon, making sure that it stays creamy and white (see White Butter, p. 140). Add the chopped parsley, spoon over the brains, and serve.
Wine: California Grenache Rosé or French Tavel

Note: Because of the acid in the dish, do not plan to serve an expensive or too mellow wine with it!

The amount of butter whipped into the infusion depends on the acidity of the limes used; for average-tasting limes, the smaller amount of butter should be enough.

Heart

A beef heart weighs an average of 4 pounds, sometimes as much as 5 pounds, and will easily serve 6 to 8 persons. It is best prepared by braising. To make it a complete dinner dish, stuff it with 1½ to 2 cups of cooked rice pilaf (see p. 365) made with beef broth, or about 2 cups of old-fashioned bread stuffing, or ¾ pound of your favorite meat loaf. Use any herb you like to flavor it, but remember that basil and rosemary are best adapted to its natural taste. Braise in the usual manner: first brown the heart, then cook it, covered, in a 325°F. oven, using a little beef broth and a generous bed of onions and carrots (see braising, p. 190).

Veal and lamb hearts are tender enough to be cut into very thin slivers, which can be quickly sautéed in butter or oil like *scaloppine.* Since a veal heart does not weigh more than 1 pound, you will need 2 hearts to serve 6 persons. The most delicious heart is that of a lamb, which usually is not heavier than ⅓ pound; use 3 or 4 hearts for 6 persons.

Before cooking heart in any manner, remove all traces of blood vessels and of the powerful ligaments that make the organ function in the live animal; they are tough and even long cooking does not soften them completely.

Preferably do not poach heart as you will be disappointed by the rather flat taste. When you braise a beef heart, the long cooking time allows the meat to absorb some of the flavor of the *fonds de braise;* as the meat softens, the taste and flavor improve. Quickly sautéed slivers of veal or lamb heart are best seasoned with some of the stronger members of the onion family.

SAUTÉED HEART SCALOPPINE
6 SERVINGS

2 veal hearts, or 4 or 5 lamb hearts

3 tablespoons oil of your choice

¼ cup butter

1 tablespoon fine-chopped shallots

2 tablespoons meat glaze, or 2 tablespoons water and 1 pea-size piece of meat extract

1 ½ teaspoons fine-chopped garlic

2 tablespoons fine-chopped parsley

Salt and pepper

Remove the vessels and ligaments from the hearts and cut them into ⅛-inch-thick slivers. Heat the oil well, add the heart slivers, and sauté over high heat for 2 to 3 minutes. Remove the meat to a platter; keep warm. Discard the oil, replace it with the butter, and quickly sauté the shallots for not more than 1 minute. Off the heat, add the meat glaze, or water and meat extract, the garlic and parsley. Return the meat to the pan, salt and pepper it, and toss all ingredients over medium heat to blend for 2 minutes. Serve piping hot.

Wine: California Gamay Beaujolais or *French Beaujolais*

Kidneys

The kidneys of lamb, veal, beef and pork may all be used and prepared successfully. When buying kidneys, do not hesitate to smell them, as it is the only way to recognize a fresh kidney from a day-old one, in which the ammoniacal smell is already pronounced. Cook kidneys the day you buy them; they are too perishable to wait.

Lamb and veal kidneys have no unpleasant strong smell or aftertaste when cooked, and for this reason they are best cooked in a matter of minutes. Beef kidneys are cooked either quickly or slowly. Pork kidneys are very strong in taste, and also they can be a source of trichinae, so they must be cooked slowly and thoroughly.

Kidneys can be frozen successfully provided they are cooked as soon as defrosted. A lamb kidney defrosts in 2 hours, a veal kidney in 3 hours, and a beef kidney in about 5 hours, in the lower part of the refrigerator.

LAMB KIDNEYS

A lamb kidney is a great delicacy; it is the finest in taste of the various kinds. It may weigh from 2 to 3 ounces, and 2 or 3 kidneys will be needed for each serving.

Lamb kidneys are at their peak of flavor when broiled. The easiest way to prepare them is to skewer them first. Remove the outer membrane completely and cut off as much of the fat pad as possible with tiny manicure scissors. The kidney looks exactly like a huge bean. Cut it lengthwise into halves, starting on the concave side, but leave about ⅓ inch uncut on the convex side to serve as a hinge. Open the kidney flat; the opened kidney will be almost 3 inches wide. With your skewer, take a large butterfly-fashion stitch about ¾ inch wide at the center of each half. As the kidney cooks, the edges will curl up slightly, forming a small natural container in which a seasoning butter of your choice can be deposited just before serving.

Lamb kidneys can also be sautéed very successfully. Follow the method given for sautéed veal kidneys (p. 229). With lamb kidneys it is not necessary to drain the natural juices after sautéing.

Although lamb kidneys are rarely braised, the English like to use them in their beef and kidney pie. In this case they are cubed and mixed with beef after being sautéed; then they are stewed with the beef for 1 hour or so.

VEAL KIDNEYS

An excellent veal kidney is pink or very pale red rather than purplish. The average weight is ⅓ to ½ pound. One kidney will serve 1 person when cooked whole, possibly 2 persons when sautéed and mixed with a garnish such as mushrooms, but 4 veal kidneys are sure to serve 6 persons adequately.

Before cooking veal kidneys, remove the outer membrane and as much as possible of the central fat pad with tiny manicure scissors. You may leave a fat core not larger than a walnut at the center of the kidney without damage to the final taste of the dish.

TO BROIL VEAL KIDNEYS

Cut each kidney into halves. Sauté quickly in clarified butter or oil for 2 minutes on each side. Quickly skewer each kidney lengthwise, brush with clarified butter, and sprinkle with fresh bread crumbs if desired. Broil on each side for a maximum of 4 minutes. Serve with the butter sauce of your choice (see butter sauces, pp. 139 to 143).

TO POT-ROAST VEAL KIDNEYS

Method A   Keep some of the fat naturally surrounding the kidneys. Brown them lightly in unclarified butter. Cover them and bake in a preheated 325°F. oven for about 15 minutes. Remove to a platter when cooked. To make a sauce for 6 veal kidneys, add 2 tablespoons flour to the juices in the pan, cook for 3 minutes, and add 1½ cups hot veal or chicken stock. Cook until thickened, then add the seasoning of your choice (mustard, revived herbs, etc.). Off the heat whisk a good pat of butter into the obtained sauce. Slice the kidneys crosswise into ¼-inch slices and spoon the sauce over them.

Method B   Remove entirely the fat surrounding the kidneys. Roll the kidneys in melted unclarified butter; do not brown them. Season them lightly with salt, pepper and herbs of your choice, and bake in a preheated 325°F. oven for 25 minutes. Remove the cooked kidneys to a platter. Add 2 tablespoons meat glaze or ¼ teaspoon meat extract to the pan juices, reduce to 2 scant tablespoons, and whisk in 4 tablespoons butter. Slice the cooked kidneys into ¼-inch-thick slivers and spoon the sauce over them.

TO SAUTÉ VEAL KIDNEYS

This method is, in my opinion, that best adapted to veal kidneys. Remove all traces of outer skin and leave only a walnut-size core of fat. Cut the kidneys into ⅛-inch slivers or ½-inch cubes. Sauté quickly in hot clarified butter or oil until the meat turns grayish, at which point it is cooked. Put into a colander and drain; you can discard the juices that have run out of the meat, or if you like you can add those

juices to the sauce, but I recommend to any novice in kidneyland not
to do it. The sauce has a finer taste without these juices, for should the
kidney have the slightest strong taste, it is discarded with the juices.

A sauce can be made with stock and reduced wine, using any thickening method one desires, but one rule must be applied scrupulously:
if the sauce must boil, never add the kidney to it before it has boiled.
Boiled kidneys become as tough as rubber. Sautéed kidneys must always be reheated without boiling. Should they boil by accident, do not
serve them as sautéed kidneys, but let them stew for about 1 hour so
that the long cooking again softens the toughened tissues. Serve them
as stewed kidneys.

BEEF KIDNEYS

Buy beef kidneys weighing about 1 pound each. They may be sold
larger but the larger sizes will come from older animals and have such
a strong taste that even the best treatment will never completely free
them of this pungent flavor. One beef kidney will serve 2 to 3 persons.
Beef kidneys may be sautéed like veal kidneys, but there is no doubt
that they are best stewed as an ordinary beef stew.

TO SAUTÉ OR BRAISE BEEF KIDNEYS

Remove all traces of fat from the kidney, including the center core,
which does retain its pungency even when cooked. Dice the kidney
into ½-inch cubes; place the cubed meat in a colander. Blanch the
kidneys: Bring 3 quarts water to a boil. Count from 1 to 3; on the
count of 1, immerse the colander in the boiling water; on the count
of 2, leave it there; on the count of 3, remove it. Blot the meat completely dry in a towel. To sauté, follow the method described for sautéed veal kidneys. *Positively* discard the juices still running from the
meat after sautéing; the taste is so strong that it would completely
spoil the dish. To stew the kidneys, after sautéing proceed as for a
regular brown stew (see p. 202).

PORK KIDNEYS

A pork kidney weighs about ⅓ pound; 6 kidneys will be necessary
to serve 6 persons. The only way to prepare pork kidneys is by stewing
them as for beef kidneys. All the steps indicated for beef kidneys

should be strictly observed. Pork kidneys are very strong and not recommended if you are trying kidneys for the first time.

SKEWERED LAMB KIDNEYS
6 SERVINGS

12 large mushroom caps	*Salt and pepper*
Clarified butter (about ¼ cup)	*1 cup fine fresh bread crumbs*
12 lamb kidneys	*Provençal butter (p. 142)*

Sauté mushrooms in clarified butter until they have lost all their moisture. Cut kidneys open, but leave halves attached. Alternating mushrooms and kidneys, thread 2 mushrooms and 2 kidneys on each skewer. Brush with clarified butter, sprinkle with salt and pepper, and roll in bread crumbs. The kidneys need not absolutely be crumbed, but they retain more moisture if they are. Broil for 3 minutes on each side, starting with the cut side. Serve piping hot with Provençal butter.
Wine: California Zinfandel or *French Hermitage*

VEAL KIDNEYS TIO PEPE
6 SERVINGS

½ cup slivered blanched almonds	*2 tablespoons meat glaze, or ¼*
4 tablespoons clarified butter	*teaspoon commercial meat*
4 veal kidneys, sliced	*extract*
1½ ounces Cognac or brandy	*2 tablespoons heavy cream*
⅓ cup brown veal stock (p. 80)	*½ teaspoon arrowroot*
or chicken stock (p. 76)	*6 tablespoons unsalted butter*
½ cup extremely dry (Tio	*Salt and pepper*
Pepe) sherry	*6 croustades (p. 43)*

Sauté almonds in clarified butter until golden. Remove to a plate. In the same butter, sauté the kidneys until gray. Add 1 ounce of Cognac and flambé. Drain in a colander.

Add the stock, ⅓ cup of the sherry and the meat glaze to the pan.

Reduce to 3 tablespoons. Make a slurry with cream and arrowroot and thicken the sauce. Fluff the unsalted butter into the sauce. Correct seasoning. Add the remaining sherry and remaining Cognac to the sauce. Mix kidneys and almonds into the sauce, reheat slowly if necessary, spoon into the croustades, and serve.

Wine: dry sherry (Tio Pepe)

VEAL KIDNEYS IN MUSTARD SAUCE
6 SERVINGS

4 veal kidneys, slivered	2 tablespoons very strong
3 tablespoons clarified butter or	prepared mustard
oil	½ cup unsalted butter
2 ounces Cognac or brandy	Salt and pepper
⅔ cup brown veal stock	2 tablespoons chopped parsley
(p. 80) or chicken stock	6 croustades (p. 43)
(p. 76)	

Sauté slivered kidneys in hot clarified butter or oil. Flambé with 1 ounce of Cognac, and drain in a colander. Add stock and remaining Cognac to the pan and reduce to ½ cup. Add mustard and blend well. *Do not boil.* Return kidneys to the pan. While shaking the pan back and forth over the heat, fluff in the raw butter, tablespoon by tablespoon. Correct seasoning and add the parsley. Spoon into croustades.

Wine: California Fumé Blanc or French Sancerre

BEEF-KIDNEY AND MUSHROOM PIE
6 SERVINGS

½ cup dried imported	3 tablespoons butter
mushrooms	2 beef kidneys
English lard pastry (p. 392)	3 tablespoons oil
1 pound fresh mushrooms,	1 tablespoon flour
quartered	1½ to 2 cups hot beef stock or

    broth (*p. 78*)   *Small* bouquet garni
1 *garlic clove, chopped*   *Egg-yolk glaze* (*p. 421*)
1 *shallot, chopped*

Soak the dried mushrooms in ⅔ cup water for at least 4 hours. They will absorb all the water. Make the pastry and keep it well chilled. Sauté the fresh mushrooms in 2 tablespoons of the butter until their moisture has evaporated.

Trim the kidneys of all fat and cut into ½-inch cubes. Blanch in boiling water as described on page 230, and sauté in the oil. Drain into a colander and discard the escaping juices. With 1 tablespoon butter and the flour, make a brown *roux*. Add the stock, garlic, shallot and *bouquet garni;* bring to a boil. Add the kidneys and both types of mushrooms, and cook over medium heat for 1 hour. Cool completely. Put into a 1-quart 8-inch round baking dish.

Roll out the pastry. Cut a 9-inch lid from the pastry and fit it over the stew. Cut a vent at the center of the pie. Brush with egg-yolk glaze, and decorate if desired with pastry cutouts. Bake in a 375°F. oven for 25 to 30 minutes, or until golden.

Beverage: preferably beer, ale or *stout*

Liver

The livers of beef, calf, lamb, pork and all types of poultry are usable for human consumption. They can add to the diet relatively large amounts of vitamin A, B and C, as well as being the best known of all the foods rich in iron. Before cooking any type of liver except that of poultry, remove the surrounding membrane, which toughens during cooking.

CALF'S LIVER

By far the best of all livers is that of the calf. The color of calf's liver should never be reddish or purplish but very light. French chefs call calf's liver with a pale coloration *blond.* Calf's liver is very tender and has a fine flavor. It may be cut into ¼- to ⅓-inch-thick slices, simply floured, or if desired breaded with an *anglaise* (see p. 178), and panfried. Large whole pieces of calf's liver may be purchased in a butcher shop and braised or roasted after having been marinated, preferably in an acid marinade. For this type of preparation allow from 2½ to 3 pounds of liver for 6 persons. Various vegetables may be added to the braising pot; mushrooms, carrots and celery are the most popular.

Slices of calf's liver to be broiled must be from ⅓ to ½ inch thick and well brushed with clarified butter or oil. If the liver is to be skewered, have it cut into pieces of the same size, and presauté the pieces first in some oil; the liver will remain more tender and more moist inside.

BEEF LIVER

When buying beef liver make sure that its color is as pale as possible, since the redder it is the older the animal was and the less tender the liver will be once cooked. Young steer liver may be sautéed like calf's liver, but true beef liver is better braised even if sliced. Carrots, onions and celery may be used as *fonds de braise* (see p. 193). For 6 slices of liver use no more than ½ cup of stock. The seared slices of liver must simmer with the vegetables and stock for about 30 minutes.

LAMB LIVER

Handle lamb liver exactly as you would calf's liver.

PORK LIVER

It is unfortunate that pork liver has a rather strong taste, for of all the livers it contains the largest amount of iron. Pork liver may be panfried, but to make this preparation successful, it is essential that it be cut into slivers never thicker than ⅛ inch so that the cooking can be done fast enough to keep the liver tender but thoroughly cooked to destroy any possible trichinae.

Pork liver tastes best braised. Dice the meat into ½-inch cubes, brown it in fat, then barely cover it with stock or water, and braise for 15 to 20 minutes. Add prepared strong mustard and chopped parsley to taste to the reduced pan juices.

One of the best utilizations of pork liver is in pâtés. In the recipe given on page 306, chicken livers may be very successfully replaced by the same amount of pork liver.

CHICKEN OR OTHER POULTRY LIVERS

Chicken livers in recipes are generally interchangeable with other types of poultry livers. It is good to remember that a duck or goose liver added to a pâté gives it a better flavor.

Great care has to be taken to remove all traces of biliary ducts before using poultry livers since it is not rare to find some left on by the butcher. When sautéing small livers, do not overbrown them or their outside layers will be overcooked while the centers will remain, if not underdone, at least quite rare when they should be pink.

Poultry livers benefit from being flambéed with a little Cognac or brandy and seasoned with some port, Madeira or sherry.

FEGATO

6 SERVINGS

1 pound calf's liver, cut into	*½ teaspoon fennel seeds*
¼-inch-thick slices	*¼ cup chopped parsley*
Juice of 1 lemon	*Anglaise (p. 178)*
¼ cup flour	*1 small garlic clove, chopped*
Salt and pepper	*½ cup clarified butter*
1 cup fresh bread crumbs	*6 lemon slices*

Sprinkle liver slices with lemon juice. Let stand for 30 minutes. Pat dry, then sprinkle with flour and salt and pepper. Put the bread crumbs and fennel seeds in the blender and blend well to break the seeds into smaller pieces. Mix crumbs with the chopped parsley. Brush the liver with *anglaise* and coat with the bread-crumb mixture. Sauté the garlic in the clarified butter, then remove it completely with a slotted spoon. Sauté the liver slices in the same butter until golden on both sides. Serve piping hot, topped with the lemon slices and basted with the cooking butter.

Wine: Barolo or *Bardolino*

WALLISELLER SPIESSLI
6 SERVINGS

12 small breakfast sausages
¼ cup water
1 pound slab bacon
24 mushroom caps
2 tablespoons butter
6 slices of calf's liver, 3 by 4
  inches and ½ inch thick

⅓ cup oil of your choice
Salt and pepper
½ cup maître d'hôtel butter
  (p. 146)

Twist the sausages in their middles to make 2 midget sausages out of each breakfast sausage. Place all the sausages in the frying pan, add the water, and cook over medium heat until the sausages have rendered most of their fat. Discard the fat.

Cut the bacon into 24 chunks 1½ inches square and ⅓ inch thick. Place in a saucepan, cover with cold water, and bring to a boil; simmer for 5 minutes. Drain and blot dry in a paper towel.

Sauté mushroom caps in butter until all their moisture has evaporated. Cut each slice of liver into 4 equal pieces, and sauté in 3 tablespoons of the oil for 2 minutes on each side.

Using 4 pieces of each ingredient, skewer in the following order: sausage, liver, bacon, mushroom. Brush lightly with oil and sprinkle with salt and pepper. Broil for 3 minutes on each side. If the skewer does not look brown enough, broil for 1 more minute on each side, but do not overcook the liver. Serve with maître d'hôtel butter.

Note: In this recipe you may replace the calf's liver by 12 large chicken livers cut into halves.

Wine: California Zinfandel or Swiss Dole de Sion

SAUTÉED CHICKEN LIVERS
6 SERVINGS

1 cup heavy cream	*3 tablespoons butter*
2 tablespoons Madeira or sherry	*1 small onion, chopped very fine*
1 truffle, peeled and diced fine	*1½ pounds chicken livers*
(optional)	*1 ounce Cognac or brandy*
Salt and pepper	*6 croustades (p. 43)*

Mix cream, Madeira and diced truffle if used; add a pinch of salt and pepper and simmer together until reduced to ½ cup. Correct the seasoning and keep warm.

Heat the butter well, add the onion, and cook over low heat without allowing the onion to take on any color. Raise the heat, add the livers, and sauté, tossing often, until seared on all sides. Sprinkle with salt and pepper and flambé with heated Cognac or brandy. Cover and cook over low heat for 4 minutes. Uncover, and add the prepared cream mixture. Toss over medium heat until the livers are coated. Spoon into croustades.

Wine: French Barsac

Sweetbreads

The wildest guesses are made as to what sweetbreads really are. Every organ is cited except the true one, which is the thymus gland of lamb, veal and less than 1-year-old steer. In animals older than 1 year the gland shrinks and disappears. This is why one never finds "beef sweetbreads." Sweetbreads are a true delicacy as well as a good source of protein. They are so very perishable that they should be prepared without fail on the day they are purchased. Often they are frozen by butchers, who thus lengthen their period of availability.

Before attempting to prepare sweetbreads, soak them in a lot of cold water for at least 4 hours, changing the water every time it turns reddish. To defrost frozen sweetbreads immerse them, still frozen, in the cold water, and add 30 minutes more of soaking time. Sweetbreads have two parts, a small lobe called the throat sweetbread and a large lobe called the heart sweetbread. The long soaking of both lobes is an absolute must; it will bring to your plate sweetbreads perfectly white inside and outside, which is very important for the appetizing value of your dish as well as for its presentation.

Blanch the sweetbreads, starting in cold water and letting the temperature of the water in the pot increase very slowly. The heat will make the tissues swell so that any sudden burst of heat would cause the rupture of the much needed outside conjunctive membrane. Once the boiling point has been reached, let the sweetbreads poach for 2 minutes if you intend to braise them, and for 5 minutes if they are to be sliced and sautéed in butter or breaded for panfrying.

Drain the sweetbreads and rinse them thoroughly under running cold water. With a paring knife, remove all the sinews and blood vessels. Do not remove the conjunctive membrane that encases the tissues, which by now looks like a bloated balloon, or the sweetbread will fall apart in small pieces.

Do as the French do: place the sweetbreads between 2 plates or chopping boards and put a 4-pound weight on top. The sweetbreads will flatten to an even thickness of about ¾ inch. They will look better for presentation, and also it will be much easier to cook them as the heat will penetrate them evenly.

Sweetbreads may be braised with white or brown stock; they may be sliced and sautéed in butter. Mushrooms and sherry or Madeira are perfect companions for them. When you serve sweetbreads braised in brown veal stock as a main course or a first course and do not wish to enrich the cooking juices with cream or yolks to make a sauce, reduce those cooking juices to a glaze and roll the cooked sweetbreads in it; they will acquire a lustrous coat and look most appetizing. This procedure can replace the old-fashioned glazing done in a hot oven; in the oven glazing, the sweetbread is always in danger of glazing too long and drying out somewhat.

SWEETBREADS CARA MIA
6 SERVINGS

2 *large onions, chopped*	1 ½ *cups blanched fresh*
4 *tablespoons butter*	*artichoke hearts, or 1 package*
6 *sweetbreads, blanched and*	(10 *ounces*) *frozen hearts,*
flattened	*thawed*
1 *cup brown veal stock* (*p. 80*)	4 *egg yolks*
or chicken stock (*p. 76*)	1 *cup heavy cream*
Small bouquet garni	2 *tablespoons dry sherry*
1 *teaspoon salt*	*Lemon juice*
¼ *teaspoon pepper*	*Chopped parsley*

Sauté onions in butter in a braising pot (or a skillet with a heat-proof handle) until soft but not brown. Add the sweetbreads. Add stock and bring to a boil. Add *bouquet garni,* salt and pepper. Cover with buttered paper and pot lid. Bake in a 325°F. oven for 10 minutes. Add artichoke hearts and continue baking for another 20 minutes. Remove cooked artichokes to a platter and top with sweetbreads. Keep warm.

Reduce juices in the pan to ½ cup. Make a liaison with egg yolks and cream and thicken the sauce without boiling until it coats the spatula. Add the sherry, and lemon juice to taste. Spoon the sauce, onions and all, over the sweetbreads. Sprinkle with chopped parsley.
Wine: California Semillon or *French Meursault Charmes*

Tongue

Unfortunately, fresh tongues are becoming steadily more difficult to locate; in supermarkets smoked and pickled tongues are more generally available.

Soak fresh tongue in cold water for about 2 hours before poaching it. Tongue—fresh, smoked, or corned—is poached by immersing it in cold water to cover, bringing it to a boil, and simmering it a generous hour per pound. Add a lot of herbs, bayleaf, thyme, and dill if you like it. A beef tongue of 3½ pounds will make 6 servings, not more, since the upper part of the tongue is always very fat. Before serving, let the tongue cool a bit, slit the underside of the tongue, and slip off the tough glove of skin which encases it.

The best sauce for a poached fresh tongue is a vinaigrette (see p. 361), chock full of chopped fresh parsley, tarragon, chives and especially chervil.

Veal and lamb tongues are best braised. Use 1 veal tongue or 2 lamb tongues per person.

BRAISED VEAL TONGUES
6 SERVINGS

1 onion, sliced	*2 cups veal stock (p. 80)*
1 carrot, sliced	Bouquet garni
2 tablespoons butter	*3 cloves*
6 small veal tongues	*1 teaspoon arrowroot*
Salt and pepper	*⅓ cup heavy cream*
⅔ cup Madeira	*1 tablespoon chopped chives*

Sauté onion and carrot in butter. Set tongues on vegetables and sprinkle with salt and pepper. Cover pot and keep over very low heat until the tongues look steamed, 25 to 30 minutes. Add one third of the Madeira and reduce over high heat until 1 teaspoon liquid is left. Repeat the same operation twice with the remaining two thirds of the Madeira (a triple *tombage à glace*). Add stock, *bouquet garni* and cloves; bring to a boil. Cover with foil and pot lid and bake in a 325°F. oven for 1½ to 2 hours.

Strain and defatten the cooking juices. Skin the tongues and cut lengthwise into halves. Place on a serving platter. Bring the defattened juices to a boil and thicken with a slurry of arrowroot and cream. Add chives and spoon over the tongues.

Wine: California Mountain Chablis or French White Graves

Tripe
Tripe makes cheap and delicious eating and brings a large amount of protein to the diet. Tripe is the general name given to the stomach

lining of beef. Depending on which part of the animal's stomach it comes from, it bears different names. Honeycomb tripe, which comes from the largest part of the stomach, is easily recognizable by its thickness and its internal layer of tissues closely resembling that of a honeycomb. This is the best known and, as the meatiest of all, the most desirable of all kinds of tripe. Pocket tripe and smooth tripe, although their taste does not differ from that of honeycomb, are thinner.

Tripe is sold already cleaned and blanched, but it is a good security measure to blanch it again, starting the blanching in cold water. Tripe must cook for a very long time. Where the smooth tripe and the pocket tripe may sometimes be cooked through in 3 hours, honeycomb tripe will require a minimum of 5 hours to become thoroughly tender.

Tripe can be boiled in a *court-bouillon* until tender. The *court-bouillon* may contain some wine, but preferably no vinegar, and you may add to it all the vegetables used in a regular stock.

Once cooked, the tripe can be cooled, cut into strips, and breaded for panfrying, or brushed with melted butter and broiled. In either case serve it with a highly seasoned sauce containing a lot of pepper or mustard. Any leftover tripe can, with its own cooking broth, make an excellent soup such as the celebrated Philadelphia pepperpot. Strain the cooking broth to discard the vegetables which flavored the tripe, and replace them with freshly diced vegetables such as potatoes, carrots and corn. Some marjoram and pepper flakes added to a tripe soup enhance the taste considerably.

LES TRIPES EN AMÉRIQUE

12 SERVINGS

The best-known tripe dish (*à la mode de Caen*) comes from Normandy, but there are other places that provide the ingredients for a solid dish of tripe. This is an American version of the Normandy preparation. The cooking technique is that of a *daube,* which is the best way to cook tripe.

Make only a large amount since this requires overnight cooking to be truly delicious. Any amount of tripe not used can be chilled in the refrigerator, unmolded like a jelly, wrapped in 2 layers of aluminum foil, and frozen.

½ cup unsalted butter	1 large bay leaf
2 carrots	4 cloves
2 onions	6 peppercorns
2 leeks, white part only	½ cup applejack or Calvados
5 pounds cleaned and blanched tripe, cut into strips	1 cup 20% hard cider
	2 cups white wine
1 veal knuckle, cracked, or 1 pound veal shank	3 cups brown veal stock (p. 80)
	2 cups flour
2 teaspoons salt, approximately	1 cup water
⅓ teaspoon dried thyme	

Cream the butter. With the fingertips rub butter all over the inside surface of a 4-quart New England-style bean pot. Cut carrots and onions into thick slices. Cut the leeks into ¼-inch slices. Put a layer of part of the vegetables on the bottom of the bean pot and pack in half of the tripe. Press the veal knuckle or shank into the mixture. Sprinkle with half of the salt. Add all the herbs and spices. Add more vegetables, then the rest of the tripe. Sprinkle with the rest of the salt. Finish with a last layer of vegetables. Mix together applejack, hard cider, wine and 1 cup of the stock. Pour slowly over the contents of the pot. Add more stock if necessary to barely cover the contents of the pot. Close the pot and seal it with a paste made with the flour and water. Bake in a 275°F. oven overnight.

To serve, remove the veal knuckle or shank and spoon onto *very hot* plates.

Wine: any Chablis or hard cider, not too sweet

VII

Marine Treasures

fish cookery

GOOD FISH DISHES are too seldom prepared at home. Since fish takes a relatively short time to cook, home menus can be varied with fish dishes that are quick and easy to prepare.

Buy your fish at a fish store rather than at the fish counter of a supermarket. Fish is the business of a retailer whose pride it is always to offer first-quality merchandise. While many supermarkets, especially in coastal towns, do try to offer good quality, and mostly succeed, the best grade of seafood is still found in a specialized store.

A fish is fresh when the eyes are bright and transparent. The whiter the eyes, the older the fish, since the membranes become opaque through evaporation of their moisture. The smell should be slightly fishy, but never ammoniacal. At fisheries, fish fillets are often sprinkled with preservatives which make them look like mother-of-pearl; the preservatives delay fermentation considerably. In a whole fish, the inside of the gills is dark pink to bright red, never bluish or brownish. When a fresh fish is poked with the finger, the flesh is firm and resistant and does not become dented under pressure. Whole fish put on sale undressed has the best chance of being fresh, since it is highly perishable in this form.

If fresh fish cannot be located, the frozen fish counter is the department to visit. Frozen fish *must* form a solid block. Frozen fish coming from cold waters such as the Pacific Northwest, the coasts of New England, eastern and western Canada, Norway, Denmark and Japan is good. Flash-frozen seafood is best; the faster the freezing, the smaller the ice crystals formed between the fibers and the better the preservation of the original state of the flesh.

The defrosting of frozen fish should be done in the refrigerator and may take as long as 24 hours. If you are in a hurry, defrost fish under running cold water. Defrosting at room temperature results in loss of all the natural juices through fast melting of the ice crystals; the fish becomes dry and unpalatable. Slow defrosting at low temperature, on the contrary, allows the ice crystals to dissolve very slowly; thus moisture is retained between the fibers. One pound of fish defrosted in the refrigerator rarely releases more than 2 tablespoons of liquid.

Do not establish your menu on fish day before reaching the market. Be adaptable and see what looks good and what is the best buy. Although the famous Dover sole may be bought frozen at fantastic prices, it has usually been frozen too long and, being very delicate, is dried out before reaching your kitchen. Although its name is "Dover sole," the fish is not exclusively British; it can be found in the northeastern part of France, the coasts of Belgium and the Netherlands, all the Scandinavian countries and the coasts of Germany. If you visit in one of those countries, make it a point to taste the true sole where it has been freshly caught.

Meanwhile, if you live on the East Coast, flounder and lemon and gray soles are toothsome morsels to be enjoyed for themselves. The West Coast has sand dabs, brills and salmon unequaled anywhere in the World; and the Gulf Coast offers the lovely pompano. In the Central States, if one does not catch one's own trout, a fish market is an absolute necessity. Midwestern supermarkets are making an effort to keep their freezers well stocked with first-quality frozen products.

To Fillet a Flat Fish

If you wish to fillet a flat fish yourself, the use of a filleting knife is recommended, but an all-purpose 7-inch-blade chef's knife can do very well. Fillet first the tummy side where the white skin is tougher and the thickness of the whole fish makes it easier for you to cut through the skin faster. Lay the fish on its back on a board, with the head pointing away from you. Cut along the line marking the center of the body until both fillets are separated. Starting at the head, slide the blade between backbone and fillet and, scraping the bones, sever the left fillet. Two or three strokes of the blade will loosen it completely. Open the fillet as you would the pages of a book and cut along the fins. To remove the right fillet, turn the fish by 180 degrees, so that the head is now close to you. Sever the second fillet exactly as indicated above. To remove the other two fillets, turn the fish upside down and repeat the same operation.

To remove the skin from the fillets, slide the blade between fillet and skin. Pull the skin with the left hand while the right hand slides the blade forward.

Drop the fillets into a bowl of water acidulated with a few drops of lemon juice. Discard all the skins, but keep the head and bones to make fish *fumet* (p. 83). If the fish is dressed and filleted by the fish market, have the head and bones included in your package. If you buy fillets and still want to make *fumet,* ask the market for heads and bones; pounds of them are discarded every day.

To Bone a Long Fish (salmon, pike, etc.)

Cut along the backbone on both sides and follow the rib cage with your blade until you reach the abdominal cavity. Sever the backbone at the head and tail and pull gently, starting at the head. The whole bone structure will come out at once.

Fish Sauces

Although a fish velouté is better suited to sauce a fish dish, béchamel is often used instead. To serve with fish, béchamel should be blended with a certain amount of fish *fumet* or clam juice to give a characteristic fish flavor. A cardinal sauce, made with béchamel blended with fish *fumet* and enriched with lobster butter, is a good sauce, but a sauce containing only wine and milk or cream falls short of perfection, in my opinion.

The warm emulsified sauces are often used with fish, especially hollandaise, béarnaise or mousseline, and so are the butter sauces. The classic method of pounding lobster coral, tomalley and shells with butter to make lobster butter is time consuming. An acceptable but, of course, not as refined lobster butter can be obtained by blending a small can (2 ounces) of lobster spread with a few tablespoons of butter. The lobster taste is strong and the work limited. If you want a sauce with a deeper shade of red, add a few drops of red and yellow food coloring.

Serving Fish

Fish, more than any other food except perhaps lamb, needs to be served on hot plates. Given a choice between appearance and flavor, always sacrifice appearance. Remember that feeling in a restaurant when the taste—oh disaster—is not in harmony with the looks? Individual warm plates topped with a sautéed crouton or a mushroom cap will be more successful than an elaborately decorated dish.

If possible, serve fish as the first course of a meal, either by itself or garnished with fluffy rice or steamed potatoes. Served as a main course, the fish should here too be accompanied with rice or potatoes. In that case make the first course a vegetable soup, and present a good salad and cheese after the fish course. A substantial dessert is recommended.

Fish cooking procedures, like those for meat, are of two types— moist-heat and dry-heat methods.

POACHING—MOIST-HEAT PROCEDURE

POACHING FISH FILLETS AND SMALL STEAKS

Fish fillets and steaks are poached *à court-mouillement,* i.e., in a small amount of liquid. Large whole fish are poached in a *court-bouillon,* or a large amount of liquid.

In both cases, poaching fish means cooking the fish without boiling, so as to coagulate the proteins contained in and between the fibers. Under the influence of heat, collagen and fibers gel, and the fish can be considered cooked when the flesh looks milky white and feels firm to the touch. In fillets or steaks, the collagen can be seen forming pearllike white drops at their surface. If the cooking is prolonged, the fibers start shrinking and the collagen still liquid between the fibers escapes into the pan. What could have been a succulent piece of fish turns into dried-out fibers.

TO POACH SMALL PIECES OF FISH IN A SMALL AMOUNT OF LIQUID

Butter a baking dish generously. Line it with a bed of vegetables (carrots, onions, mushrooms, scallions, shallots, chopped herbs, or a combination of several), letting your taste and imagination be your guide. Presauté the vegetables if they are to be included in the sauce. Set the fish on the vegetables; salt and pepper lightly. Score fish fillets on the skin side to prevent bursting of the thin conjunctive membranes and breaking of the fillets under the influence of the heat. Fold all fillets no thicker than ⅓ inch, skin side in.

Pour a small amount of liquid on the fish. The best combination is half dry white wine with half fish *fumet* or clam juice. Do not poach in wine alone, or the fish will acquire a raw alcohol taste. If more than 4 tablespoons of wine are used, reduce the wine before using it to evaporate the alcohol. Butter a parchment or brown paper and place it, buttered side down, flush on the surface of the fish. It will keep the top from drying out in the oven.

Immediately put the dish to bake in a preheated oven. The temperature of the oven varies from 350°F. to 400°F. Decide on the temperature following these guidelines: Delicate fish with a loose fiber structure (halibut, warm-water flounder) requires 400°F. for fast cooking; solid firm sole that does not fall apart easily and haddock do best at 375°F.; the firm and rather dry swordfish tastes best poached at 350°F., so that the slow heat can penetrate the tight texture slowly without the outer layer drying out. Also, the larger the piece to poach, the slower the heat for the same reason. Use fillets of approximately the same size to avoid having small pieces drying while larger ones finish cooking.

Fish steaks will be cooked in 12 to 20 minutes, depending on the kind of fish and thickness of the cut. Fillets will cook even more quickly, in 8 to 10 minutes. Fish is done when the beads of collagen visible at its surface are set. If you cannot tell by the appearance, test the fish: if it can be flaked easily with a fork it is done. Do not overcook for that is the ruin of many a good fish preparation.

To make a sauce, blend the cooking juices with a basic velouté or béchamel, or thicken them with *beurre manié.* You can also reduce the juices to a glaze and fluff butter into them, or mix them with egg yolks and make an emulsified sauce.

FILLETS OF SOLE PROSPER MONTAGNÉ
6 SERVINGS

This is a simplification of the remarkable dish created by the great Prosper Montagné under the name *Sylvestre* or *Sylvette.* The truffle is optional in this home version, but mushrooms are a must. Amontillado, white port, or Madeira may be used for the sauce, but to be true to the Master's formula, no vermouth.

1 small carrot
1 large onion
1 large shallot
2-inch piece of celery rib
1 large black truffle
14 large mushrooms
Butter (about 1/3 cup)
Salt and pepper

1/2 cup sherry, Madeira or port
3 large gray sole, filleted, or 12 single fillets
1/3 cup medium-thick béchamel (p. 110)
1 cup heavy cream
12 ripe cherry tomatoes
Parsley for garnish

Cut the carrot, onion, shallot, celery, truffle and 2 mushrooms into fine dice. Sauté them in 3 tablespoons butter for a few minutes, season with salt and pepper, cover the pot, and cook slowly for 8 minutes. Add the chosen wine. Arrange the fillets in a buttered baking dish and pour the vegetable mixture on the fish. Poach for 8 to 10 minutes.

Remove cooked fillets to a warm platter. Blend the cooking juices and vegetables with béchamel; bring to a boil and reduce over high heat, slowly adding the heavy cream and stirring until the sauce coats the spoon or spatula.

Meanwhile roast the cherry tomatoes in 2 tablespoons butter in a 400°F. oven. Remove stems from remaining 12 mushrooms (save them for another use), and quickly cook the mushroom caps in a few tablespoons of acidulated water.

Put 2 fillets on each plate, spoon 3 to 4 tablespoons of the sauce over, and top with a mushroom cap. Add 2 tomatoes and a small bunch of parsley to each plate.

Wine: French Meursault Perrières

FISH STEAKS AU PERSIL
6 SERVINGS

This family-style dish can be made with swordfish, halibut or haddock.

1 tablespoon fine-chopped shallots
3 tablespoons fine-chopped Italian parsley
6 fish steaks

Salt and pepper
1/4 cup dry white wine
1 cup fish fumet (p. 83) or clam juice
1 cup thick béchamel (p. 109)

1 can (2½ ounces) tiny shrimps,   *⅓ cup salted whipped cream*
    drained   *2 egg yolks*

Sprinkle the bottom of a buttered baking dish with the shallots and 2 tablespoons of the parsley. Arrange the steaks in the dish and sprinkle with salt and pepper. Add wine and ¼ cup of the fish *fumet.* Cover with a buttered paper and put in an oven preheated to the best temperature for your fish (see p. 249). Bake for 15 to 20 minutes, depending on the kind of fish and thickness of the steaks.

Drain the cooking juices into a pot containing the béchamel. Add remaining ¾ cup of *fumet* or clam juice, bring to a boil, and simmer down to 1⅓ cups.

Skin and bone the steaks and transfer each to a small fireproof dish. Spread the shrimps on top. Mix one quarter of the finished sauce with the whipped cream and egg yolks. Strain an equal amount of the basic sauce onto each steak, then spoon 2 tablespoons of the whipped-cream mixture over the top of each dish. Glaze quickly under the broiler.

Wine: California Chenin or *Semillon*

FILLETS OF FISH MARTINI
6 SERVINGS

Another home presentation, quickly done, relatively not too rich.

Butter (about 7 tablespoons)   *1 tablespoon chopped fresh*
1 teaspoon salt   *parsley*
¼ teaspoon pepper   *12 single fillets of fish*
1 tablespoon minced fresh   *2 juniper berries, crushed*
    tarragon, or ½ teaspoon dried   *¼ cup dry vermouth*
1 tablespoon minced fresh   *¾ cup fish* fumet *(p. 83)* or
    chervil, or ½ teaspoon dried   *clam juice*
1 tablespoon minced fresh basil,   *1 tablespoon chopped shallots*
    or ½ teaspoon dried   Beurre manié
1 tablespoon minced fresh or   *2 tablespoons whipped cream*
    frozen chives   *Chopped parsley for garnish*

Cream 4 tablespoons of the butter. Add salt, pepper, tarragon, chervil, basil, chives and parsley. Let stand at room temperature for 1 hour. Spread 1 teaspoon herb butter on the scored skin side of each fillet. Fold each fillet in half and set them in a buttered baking dish. Add crushed juniper berries, vermouth and ¼ cup of the *fumet* or clam juice. Place in an oven preheated to the best temperature for your fish (see p. 249). Bake for 8 to 10 minutes. While the fish cooks, sauté the shallots in 2 tablespoons of the butter for 2 minutes. Press them with the back of a fork to extract juices.

Remove cooked fish to serving plates; keep warm. Mix the cooking juices with the remainder of the fish *fumet* or clam juice, and simmer together for 5 to 6 minutes. Thicken with *beurre manié;* use 2 tablespoons butter and 2 tablespoons flour per cup of liquid. Turn off heat and add shallots with their butter and the whipped cream. Strain the sauce on top of the fillets and sprinkle with more chopped parsley.
Wine: California Semillon or *French white Graves*

LEMON-LIME FISH STEAKS
6 SERVINGS

A very fresh combination, which will dress up any fish that may not be of the very first quality. If *cilantro* is not available, use Italian parsley with ⅛ teaspoon ground coriander. Keep the rinds in the sauce if you like their strong taste.

6 fish steaks or 12 fillets	*⅓ cup dry vermouth*
Salt and pepper	Beurre manié
½ cup fish fumet *(p. 83) or*	*½ cup sour cream*
clam juice	*1 teaspoon lime juice*
1½ teaspoons each of fine	*1 tablespoon chopped* cilantro
julienne of lemon and lime	*(Chinese parsley)*
rind	

Arrange fish in a buttered baking dish, salt and pepper lightly, and add the *fumet* or clam juice. Place in an oven preheated to the best temperature for your fish (see p. 249). Bake for 15 to 20 minutes for steaks or 10 to 12 minutes for fillets. Meanwhile, simmer the lemon and lime rinds in boiling water for 4 to 5 minutes; drain. Add vermouth to rinds and reduce to 2 ½ tablespoons.

Remove cooked fish to warm plates. Blend cooking juices with vermouth and rinds. Simmer together for 5 minutes. Thicken the sauce with *beurre manié;* use 2 tablespoons butter and 1 ½ tablespoons flour per cup of liquid. Blend in sour cream and reheat without boiling. Add lime juice and *cilantro.* Correct seasoning of the sauce and spoon over the fish.

Wine: California Chablis or French, but not a Grand Cru Chablis

SALMON STEAKS ZINFANDEL
6 SERVINGS

Red wine and salmon may be a shocker to uneducated palates, but it is a classic combination. The true blue American Zinfandel may be replaced by Cabernet Sauvignon or Pinot Noir if desired. If no red-wine fish *fumet* is available, make a quick one with one third each of clam juice, water and red wine and a couple of fish heads donated by your fishman. The recipe looks more complicated than it is, and it is worth the effort.

3 large onions	*⅓ bay leaf*
Butter (about ½ cup)	*1 teaspoon tomato paste*
¼ pound mushrooms, minced	*Commercial meat extract (about*
6 croutons (optional)	*½ teaspoon)*
Parsley	*¾ cup Zinfandel*
6 salmon steaks	*1 ¼ cups red-wine fish* fumet
1 tablespoon chopped parsley	*(p. 83)*
stems	*Salt and pepper*
Pinch of dried thyme	Beurre manié

Prepare the garnish first. Mince the onions and sauté two of them in 2 tablespoons butter over brisk heat for 5 to 6 minutes. Add the mushrooms and sauté until brown. Cover the pot and finish cooking over low heat; keep warm. Make croutons and sauté in 2 tablespoons butter until golden. Chop parsley fine. Keep all these ingredients ready to use.

Set fish steaks in a buttered baking dish. Mix remaining minced onion, the parsley stems, thyme, bay leaf, tomato paste and 1 pea-size lump of meat extract with the wine. Cook until reduced to ⅓ cup. Mix with ¼ cup fish *fumet* and pour onto fish; lightly salt and pepper. Bake in a 400°F. oven for 10 minutes. Remove cooked fish to a warm platter or plates.

Mix all the cooking juices with remaining cup of fish *fumet*. Add another pea-size lump of meat extract and simmer together for 5 minutes. Thicken with *beurre manié;* use 2 tablespoons butter and 2 tablespoons flour per cup of liquid. Enrich the sauce with 4 tablespoons butter. Correct seasoning. Serve each steak topped with a tablespoon of onion and mushroom garnish. Strain sauce over each portion, sprinkle with chopped parsley, and top with a crouton.

Wine: Zinfandel or other red wine used for the sauce

SALMON STEAKS IN MUSHROOM BUTTER
6 SERVINGS

In memory of the best King salmon I ever enjoyed. We bought it on a fishing sloop at Lapush on the Pacific and cooked it over a driftwood fire on a wild wind-blown beach.

½ pound mushrooms, cut into fine julienne	*6 salmon steaks, skinned and boned*
1 tablespoon lemon juice, or more to taste	*Salt and pepper*
	4 egg yolks
2 tablespoons dry vermouth	*1 cup unsalted butter*

Arrange mushrooms on the bottom of a buttered baking dish. Sprinkle with lemon juice and vermouth. Arrange salmon steaks on the mushrooms, season with salt and pepper, and cover with buttered paper. Bake at 400°F. for 12 to 15 minutes.

Remove cooked steaks to a flameproof serving platter. Remove mushrooms and cooking juices to a small saucepan; add more lemon juice, if desired, and salt and pepper to taste. Reduce to ½ cup. Add

egg yolks and fluff over low heat (see hollandaise sauce, p. 124).
When the mixture is thick, remove from the heat and slowly add
butter, little by little. Spoon the sauce over the steaks and slide under
the broiler for 2 minutes.

Wine: California Fumé Blanc or *French Pouilly Fumé*

CATFISH STEW
6 SERVINGS

There is more to catfish than frying. This recipe is for Claire and Warren Moses, who introduced me to Antoine's, and for Jimmy George,
the fishman of the Old New Orleans French Market who sold me
pompanos so gorgeous that I took them home in my wig case.

2 large onions, minced	*⅓ cup brandy or whiskey*
Butter (about 12 tablespoons)	*6 crayfish*
3 pounds catfish, cut into chunks	*4 shallots, minced*
1 teaspoon salt	*Small* bouquet garni
3½ cups Pinot Noir,	*12 croutons*
approximately	Beurre manié
4 garlic cloves, crushed	*Chopped parsley for garnish*
4 white peppercorns	

Sauté the onions in 4 tablespoons butter in a stew pot. Sprinkle the
fish with the salt and tuck the pieces on the bottom of the pot. Add
enough wine to barely cover the fish. Bring very slowly to a boil, and
add garlic and peppercorns. Heat brandy or whiskey, ignite with a
match, and pour flaming over the surface of the hot wine. Cover the
pot as soon as flames have died out. Barely simmer for 20 minutes.

Meanwhile, sauté the crayfish in 6 tablespoons butter until bright
red. Add shallots, *bouquet garni* and 1 cup of the wine. Barely simmer
for 10 minutes. Sauté croutons in butter. Keep ready to use.

Fish and crayfish will be ready to use at the same time. Remove
both to a serving casserole. Mix their cooking juices and reduce them
quickly to 2 cups. Whisk *beurre manié* into the simmering sauce; use

5 tablespoons butter and 2 tablespoons flour per cup of liquid. Strain over the fish; decorate with fried croutons and chopped parsley.

Wine: California Pinot Noir or *French Côte de Beaune*

POACHING WHOLE FISH OR LARGE PIECES OF FISH IN A COURT-BOUILLON

Poach whole fish, large or small, or larger pieces of fish in salted water, or in an infusion of herbs and vegetables flavored with wine or vinegar, which is called a *court-bouillon.* The principles of poaching in a *court-bouillon* are identical to those used in poaching poultry in stock. Always presimmer a *court-bouillon* and allow it to cool to let it acquire a maximum of flavor.

Preparing the fish: It will be difficult, unless you catch the fish yourself, to have it cleaned properly by the fish market. Ideally, the fish should not be scaled, and it should be cleaned in such a way that the water cannot reach the fish meat. The head should not be removed, and evisceration should be done through the gills and a small incision at the other end of the abdominal cavity. More often than not the head will be missing and the abdominal cavity completely opened; in such a case roll the fish in a cheesecloth and tie a double layer of parchment paper around the cut stomach end. Preferably use a fish poacher. If you do not have one, improvise with a long pan like a roaster that is fitted with a rack. Set the fish on the rack and lower the rack into the *cold court-bouillon.* Put the poacher over medium low heat and bring the liquid to a boil, relatively quickly if the fish is small, but slowly if the fish is large. The larger the fish, the slower should be the increase of temperature in the poacher, to insure a progressive and regular penetration of the heat to its center.

Never immerse a whole fish in a hot *court-bouillon* or the skin will rupture under the pressure of the dilating underlying tissues.

You may immerse fish in a *boiling court-bouillon* if the fish is cut into larger chunks, 2 pounds or more, so as to provide an immediate coagulation of the exposed meat tissues (the technique used for chowders).

If a whole fish is not extremely fresh, progressive heat would make the meat spoil completely. In this case, too, use a *boiling court-bouillon*; no skin rupture will occur since the tissues have already started dilating at room temperature.

As soon after immersion as the *court-bouillon* reaches the boiling point, reduce the heat. Use a thermometer to make sure that the temperature of the bath stays between 200° and 205°F. for the cooking time required in the recipe.

To serve a whole poached fish cold, first let it cool completely in the *court-bouillon*; then transfer it to a fish platter. Remove the upper skin. Lift the fillets carefully with a long spatula. If the fish is completely cold, they cannot break. Remove the backbone and replace the fillets to reshape the fish. Decorate with mayonnaise or fish aspic as desired (see Poached Trout in Aspic, p. 301).

MILK COURT-BOUILLON

2 quarts water	*½ teaspoon ground white pepper*
1 ½ cups milk	*2 lemon slices*
4 teaspoons salt	

This requires no advanced preparation. Just mix all ingredients together and use immediately.

WINE COURT-BOUILLON

Do not use cheap wine. For trout, pike, white-fleshed fish. For carp, use red wine.

3 quarts water	*Large bouquet garni*
2 bottles white or red wine	*3 tablespoons salt*
6 large onions, minced	*1 ½ teaspoons white peppercorns*

Mix cold water and wine and pour over onions, *bouquet garni* and salt. Bring slowly to a boil; simmer for 20 minutes. Add peppercorns, and simmer for another 10 minutes. Let cool and strain.

VINEGAR COURT-BOUILLON

For salmon, trout, lobster. If used for lobster and shrimps, increase the amount of salt to 3 teaspoons per quart of liquid and omit the vinegar.

4 quarts water	*5 onions, peeled and minced*
2½ cups wine or mild cider	*Very large bouquet garni*
vinegar	*2½ tablespoons salt*
3 carrots, peeled and minced	*1 teaspoon peppercorns*

Mix cold water and wine or vinegar and pour over vegetables, *bouquet garni* and salt. Bring slowly to a boil; simmer for 50 minutes. Add peppercorns, and simmer for another 20 minutes. Let cool and strain.

Wine and vinegar *court-bouillons* may be reused. Strain after using and freeze in large jars. Reboil, adding about ⅔ cup water per quart of liquid to compensate for loss of moisture during previous use. Use as a new mixture.

POACHED WHOLE SALMON

Poach salmon in vinegar *court-bouillon* for 8 minutes per pound. For warm sauces, use Geneva Butter (p. 140), Anchovy Hollandaise (p. 128), Mousseline Sauce (p. 129). For cold sauces, use any sauce in the mayonnaise family.

POACHED BASS

Poach in white-wine *court-bouillon* for 8 minutes per pound, or, better, in salted water; use 3 teaspoons salt per quart of water. For sauce, use Green Butter (p. 143).

POACHED COD OR HADDOCK

Poach in salted water (use 3 teaspoons salt per quart of water) for 8 minutes per pound. For sauces, use Caper Butter (p. 143) or Provençal Butter (p. 142).

POACHED RED SNAPPER

Poach only large fish of 8 to 10 pounds. Use white-wine *court-bouillon* and poach for 8 minutes per pound. Serve warm with Caper Butter (p. 143) or Key Lime Sauce (p. 131).

POACHED WESTERN BRILL

Cover with milk *court-bouillon.* Bring to a boil over medium heat. Skim. Poach for 8 minutes per pound, or for 9 minutes if the fish is smallish. Serve warm with Virgin Butter (p. 140), Caper Butter (p. 143), or Provençal Butter (p. 142).

FORELLE BLAU

This is the method used for the blue trout of Switzerland and the Black Forest of Germany. This is an ideal method for all cooks in the central states. If fresh trout are available, clean them through the gills; with a trussing needle pass a kitchen string through tail and gills and tie nose to tail, pulling the fish into a curve. Immerse in simmering wine *court-bouillon.* The skin will split—a sign, say the mountain people, that the fish is freshly caught! Poach for 8 to 9 minutes.

If only frozen trout are available, defrost them in the refrigerator. Do not wash them, but tie them as described above. Heat ½ cup red-wine vinegar; spoon 2 tablespoons on each fish. Immerse in barely lukewarm *court-bouillon,* bring to a boil, turn off the heat, and let stand for 10 minutes.

For sauce, use Virgin Butter (p. 140).

BRAISING—MOIST-HEAT PROCEDURE

Larger pieces of fish may be braised as well as smaller whole fish such as trout or small bass. The physical changes inside the fish during braising are similar to those that take place in braised white meats (see p. 195), but the technique is so closely related to that of poaching in a small amount of liquid that the procedures are very often confused with each other.

Always sauté the vegetables of the *fonds de braise*. You will see in the recipes that the liquid is rather abundant; always bring it to a boil on top of the stove before baking. Cover the dish with a buttered paper. Bake at 325°F. to allow regular penetration of the heat to the center of the fish, and baste several times with the cooking juices. Ideally, the juices should be reduced enough to form a sauce by themselves, but this does not always happen. Different fish within a single species have different juiciness and texture. If the juices are too liquid to form a sauce, don't worry, it happens also to professionals. Finish it with *beurre manié,* or reduce it and enrich it with butter or cream.

BRAISED WHITINGS
6 SERVINGS

Although whitings are not always easy to find undressed, they do taste best cooked with their heads on.

½ cup chopped scallions	*6 whitings, ⅓ pound each*
1 cup chopped mushrooms	*½ cup white wine*
2 tablespoons chopped parsley	*½ cup white-wine fish* fumet
2 tablespoons leeks, white parts	*(p. 83) or clam juice*
only	*Salt and pepper*
Butter (about ¾ cup)	

Sauté all the vegetables in 4 tablespoons butter until the moisture has evaporated; transfer to a baking dish. Set the whitings on the vegetables. Add wine and *fumet* or clam juice, and sprinkle with salt and pepper. Bring to a boil on top of the stove, then bake in 325°F. oven for 20 to 25 minutes. Baste several times while baking.

Transfer whitings to a serving platter. Reduce the cooking juices to 3 or 4 tablespoons and fluff in as much butter as you desire. Use as a sauce.

Wine: California Chablis or *French Petit Chablis* (*no Grand Cru*)

BRAISED COD OR HADDOCK RIVIERA
6 SERVINGS

A warm sauce for a cold-water fish. From a friend's kitchen on the Riviera.

6 tablespoons olive oil	½ cup white wine
2 tablespoons lime juice	1 teaspoon fennel seeds
2 tablespoons chopped Italian parsley	½ teaspoon dried basil
Salt and pepper	¼ teaspoon ground saffron
3 cod or haddock steaks, each 2 inches thick	1 cup essence of tomatoes II (p. 121) or canned tomato sauce
3 large tomatoes, seeded and peeled, or 2 cups canned whole tomatoes, without juice	½ cup bread crumbs
¼ teaspoon fine-grated orange rind	Butter

Mix olive oil, lime juice, parsley, ½ teaspoon salt and ⅛ teaspoon pepper. Brush the mixture on both sides of the fish steaks. Let them stand at room temperature for about 1 hour. Mix tomatoes, orange rind, white wine, fennel seeds, basil and saffron on the bottom of a baking dish. Place the fish steaks on this bed and pour tomato essence over them. Cover with buttered paper and bake in a 325°F. oven for 30 minutes, after bringing to a boil on top of the stove.

Transfer fish to an ovenproof serving dish. Strain all cooking juices to obtain a sauce. Spoon over the steaks. Sprinkle with bread crumbs, top with a good dot of butter, and slide under the broiler for 1 or 2 minutes.

Wine: California Grenache Rosé or *French Tavel*

LES TRUITES DE MONSIEUR POINT
6 SERVINGS

According to *Ma Gastronomie* by Fernand Point (Flammarion, 1969, p. 106), the original recipe was created by Paul Bocuse, who made the sauce with *beurre manié*. I reconstructed the recipe from memory in 1960.

6 small trout
Salt and pepper
¼ cup fine-shredded carrots
¼ cup fine-shredded mushrooms
2 teaspoons fine-shredded celery
1 large truffle, shredded
4 tablespoons butter
9½ tablespoons white port
1 cup heavy cream

1 tablespoon fresh bread crumbs
1 whole onion, minced
1 carrot, minced
1¼ cups excellent fish fumet
(p. 83). Do not use clam
juice!
4 egg yolks
Lemon juice

Cut along each side of the trout's backbone to expose the entire bone structure. Sever the backbone from the head and tail and pull gently. All the tummy bones will come out at once. Season lightly with salt and pepper.

Sauté all the shredded vegetables in 2 tablespoons butter until they have lost their moisture; add 2 tablespoons port and let it evaporate completely. Add salt and pepper to taste and ⅔ cup heavy cream; let cook gently until the cream coats the vegetables. Add bread crumbs, correct seasoning, and let cool completely. Spread an equal amount of cold filling into the bone cavity between the fillets of each trout.

Sauté minced onion and carrot in 2 tablespoons butter. Set the trout on the vegetable bed, sprinkle with salt and pepper, and add 6 tablespoons port and the fish *fumet*. Bring to a boil on top of the stove. Bake in a 325°F. oven for 15 minutes.

Transfer cooked trout to a warm plate. Skin them. If necessary, quickly reduce the cooking juices to ⅔ cup. Make a liaison with ⅓ cup cream and the egg yolks, add to the pan juices, and thicken the sauce without boiling. Add 1½ tablespoons raw port and a dash of lemon juice; correct seasoning. Strain over skinned trout.

Monsieur Point used to serve each trout decorated with a handsomely fluted mushroom and a lovely crayfish tail.

Wine: Hermitage Blanc or *Condrieu*

BROILING—DRY-HEAT PROCEDURE

Reread the instructions on broiling given in Chapter VI (p. 173). They remain valid; broil fish steaks and shellfish like small pieces of meat and whole larger fish like thick pieces of meat.

PREPARING FISH FOR BROILING

Steaks 1 inch thick Brush both sides with fat (salad oil, olive oil or clarified butter). Sprinkle with bread crumbs. Set the steaks on a cold cake rack placed over a jelly-roll pan. Broil 4 to 5 inches away from the source of heat for 5 minutes. Turn steaks over with a spatula. Repeat brushing with fat and crumbing. Baste crumbs with more fat and broil the second sides for another 5 to 6 minutes.

Whole fish The fish should weigh from 3 to 4 pounds. Remove the backbone or have it removed by the store, but keep the head on for better taste and presentation. Stuff flavorings into the bone cavity between the fillets of the fish. Flour and brush with oil on both sides. Set the fish on a cold cake rack placed over a jelly-roll pan. Broil 4 to 5 inches away from the source of heat for 8 minutes on the first side.

To turn the fish over, put a second cake rack over the broiled side. Grasp both racks together and turn over. Remove top rack to broil second side for another 10 minutes. Broiled this way, fish retains its moisture and absorbs some of the taste of the flavorings.

Serve broiled fish with simple sauces, or simply with melted butter and lemon juice.

If a fish is not stuffed with flavorings, cut slashes over its whole top to help the penetration of heat.

BROILED RED SNAPPERS WITH BASIL
6 SERVINGS

A recipe from a Turkish friend. Notice how closely the sauce is related to the Italian *pesto*.

2 red snappers, 3 pounds each	½ cup olive oil
Salt and pepper	½ small garlic clove
Fresh basil leaves, about 3 cups	2 tablespoons lime juice
Flour	

Remove the backbone of each fish. Season the cavity with salt and pepper and stuff with as many fresh basil leaves as you can fit in the cavity; use all but 1 cup of leaves. Flour the fish and brush with oil. Broil for about 10 minutes on each side.

Put ½ cup olive oil, the garlic, lime juice and 1 cup basil leaves in a blender container; add salt and pepper to taste. Blend until the sauce is thick and smooth. Serve over the fish.

Wine: California Folle Blanche or *Italian Soave*

BROILED WHOLE SHAD
6 SERVINGS

Shad and pike are the two companions to the true white butter. Enjoy yourselves with this recipe; it is food for the gods.

1 shad, 4 to 5 pounds	½ cup chopped parsley
4 tablespoons butter	Salt and pepper
1 cup chopped scallions	White butter (p. 140)

Have the fish market bone the fish; the bone structure is too difficult for a novice to try it. Whip the butter and mix with the scallions and parsley; add salt and pepper to taste. Spread between the fish fillets. Reshape the fish and broil 5 inches from the source of heat for about 8 minutes on each side. While fish is broiling, make the white butter.

Wine: French Muscadet

BROILED SEA BASS
6 SERVINGS

This is my personal interpretation of the famous *loup de mer grillé au fenouil*. A *loup* is a baby Mediterranean sea bass, and there is a whole ceremony about broiling the poor thing over dried fennel branches! This recipe is not worthy of a purist, but it does taste good.

2 sea bass, 3 pounds each	*Salt and pepper*
Fennel greens	*1 teaspoon lemon juice*
½ cup white wine	*½ cup unsalted butter*

Bone the fish. Chop enough fennel greens to make ¼ cup; set aside. Bruise the rest of the greens as much as possible with back of a knife, and insert these greens between the fillets of each fish. Let stand in the refrigerator for at least 4 hours.

Let the fish reach room temperature. Broil for 6 to 8 minutes on each side. Meanwhile, make the following sauce: Mix white wine and the chopped fennel greens. Add salt and pepper to taste and the lemon juice. Reduce to 3 tablespoons. Fluff in the butter and serve over the fish.

Wine: California Fumé Blanc or French Hermitage Blanc

BAKING—DRY-HEAT PROCEDURE

Baking a fish means *roasting* it in the dry heat of an oven without a trace of liquid. Keep the sauces very simple.

Fish Fillets Brush with melted or clarified butter or oil and sprinkle with fresh bread crumbs if desired. Bake at 375°F. to 400°F., depending on thickness.

Whole Fish Cut slashes 1 inch apart and ⅓ inch deep through the skin and the top fillet of the fish. (This is called *ciseler* in French.) Brush with oil or clarified butter and bake in a 350° to 375°F. oven, depending on size and weight, for 10 to 12 minutes per pound. The heavier the fish, the slower the heat. Cutting the slashes is not necessary if the fish is boned and stuffed, since the heat will penetrate through the cuts made for boning.

To test the doneness of both fillets and whole fish, spear the fish with a metal skewer for 30 seconds. Remove the skewer and touch the back of your hand with it. If it is hot, the fish is cooked. If it is only warm, continue baking. Also watch for the beads of collagen appearing through the slashes or crumbs. They are an indication that the fish will be ready within seconds.

BAKED MACKEREL À LA CROQUE AU SEL
6 SERVINGS

From my thrifty mother's kitchen. Mackerel is an inexpensive fish. Being fat, it roasts beautifully. The tartness of the lemon cuts through the fatty flavor.

6 mackerel, dressed	½ teaspoon salt
2 teaspoons kosher salt	⅛ teaspoon pepper
1½ tablespoons lemon juice	½ cup unsalted butter
¼ cup water	¼ cup chopped parsley

Cut slashes into the top of the fish (see p. 265). Butter a baking dish. Add mackerel, and sprinkle them with kosher salt. Bake in a preheated 375°F. oven for 25 minutes. Lift fish from the baking dish and remove the skins. Transfer fish to heated plates.

Boil the lemon juice, ¼ cup water, salt and pepper together till reduced to 2 tablespoons. Add unsalted butter and melt. Stir in parsley. Spoon some of the sauce on each fish.

Wine: California Mountain White or French white Graves

BAKED FILLETS OF PIKE FOR GOOD FRIDAY
6 TO 8 SERVINGS

4 pike, 2 pounds each	*2 cups fresh bread crumbs*
Salt and pepper	*Virgin butter (p. 140)*
1 cup clarified butter	*¼ cup chopped parsley*

Have the fish market fillet the pike, or do it yourself. Sprinkle the fillets with salt and pepper. Roll in clarified butter, then in bread crumbs. Sprinkle with more clarified butter. Bake in a 400°F. oven for 10 minutes. Serve with virgin butter mixed with parsley.
Wine: Swiss Dézaley

BAKED HADDOCK EMERGENCY
6 SERVINGS

This is my in-a-hurry recipe. The men in the family love it, and our Patriarch once stated, "I would not mind having this several times a week."

6 pieces of filleted haddock	*1 very small garlic clove, minced*
Melted butter	*½ teaspoon chopped chives*
1 cup fresh bread crumbs	*3 tablespoons chopped parsley*
½ cup unsalted butter	*Salt and pepper*

Brush haddock pieces with butter and sprinkle with bread crumbs. Baste with more melted butter. Bake in a 375°F. oven for 15 to 18 minutes. Cream the unsalted butter and add garlic, chives, parsley, and salt and pepper to taste. Top each portion of fish with a generous serving of the herb butter.
Wine: California Chenin Blanc or French Roussette de Seyssel

PANFRYING—DRY-HEAT PROCEDURE

Reread all instructions given in Chapter VI for breading, panfrying and deep frying.

Fish can be panfried when it is simply floured (the French *meunière*) or when it is breaded. Choose either way. The breading method is easier for beginners, since it "solidifies" the fish considerably. Simple flouring gives a more delicate texture and taste, but it is also more delicate work.

Ideally, frying fat should be only clarified butter, but it may be oil, or half butter and half oil. Make sure that the fat is hot enough to form a crust around the fish immediately. The fillets should, at all times, be able to slide on the bottom of the pan without difficulty. If they stick, neither pan nor butter are hot enough. There should never be less than ⅛ inch of liquid fat in the pan.

A pan with nonstick coating is a great help for beginners attempting the *meunière* way of frying fish.

FILLETS OF SOLE MEUNIÈRE
6 SERVINGS

The simplest and the very best way to cook fillets of sole.

12 single fillets of gray sole	*½ cup clarified butter*
Milk	*¼ cup noisette butter (p. 145)*
½ cup flour	*Lemon juice*
1 teaspoon salt	

Marinate fillets in milk for 30 minutes. Pat dry. Mix flour and salt. Flour the fillets, and pat them to discard any excess flour. Sauté in hot clarified butter until golden on each side. Transfer to a serving platter, baste with *noisette* butter, and sprinkle with lemon juice.
Wine: New York State Vinifera Pinot Chardonnay or French Margaux Blanc

FILLETS OF POMPANO WITH FLORIDA BUTTER
6 SERVINGS

12 single fillets of pompano	*1 teaspoon salt*
Flour	*Dash of pepper*
Clarified butter	*½ cup unsalted butter*
⅓ cup water	*Chopped* cilantro (*Chinese*
1 tablespoon lime juice	*parsley*)
¼ teaspoon fine-grated lime rind	*1 ripe avocado*

Flour pompano fillets and sauté in clarified butter. Mix water, lime juice and rind, salt and pepper. Reduce to 3 tablespoons, then fluff in the unsalted butter, tablespoon by tablespoon. Add as much parsley as you like. Top each sautéed fillet with a paper-thin slice of avocado and spoon the lime-flavored butter over all.

Wine: California Sauvignon Blanc or *French Muscadet*

SALMON SCALLOPS DREI KÖNIGE
6 SERVINGS

From the lovely memory of a delicious lunch at the Drei Könige Hotel in Basel, Switzerland. I take the responsibility for all ingredients and their balance.

6 salmon steaks, ½ inch thick,	*½ cup Rhine wine*
preferably boned	*1 tablespoon Hungarian paprika*
Anglaise (*p. 178*)	*½ teaspoon salt*
1 cup fresh bread crumbs	*⅛ teaspoon pepper*
½ cup clarified butter	*½ cup unsalted butter*
3 cups minced onions	

Brush salmon steaks with *anglaise* and coat with bread crumbs. Sauté in some of the clarified butter until golden on both sides. Meanwhile, sauté onions in clarified butter until brown; do not burn them. Mix wine, paprika, salt and pepper and reduce to 3 tablespoons. Fluff in the unsalted butter, tablespoon by tablespoon. Serve each steak on a bed of onions and spoon paprika butter over all.

Wine: California Grey Riesling or German Rhine or Moselle Auslese

BREADED BRILL FILLETS CALIFORNIA STYLE
6 SERVINGS

½ cup slivered almonds	1 ½ teaspoons lemon juice
Clarified butter (about ⅔ cup)	12 seedless grapes, peeled
2 pounds brill fillets	½ teaspoon salt
Flour	Dash of pepper
Anglaise (p. 178)	½ cup unsalted butter
1 cup bread crumbs	2 tablespoons unsweetened
⅓ cup water	whipped cream

Sauté almonds in butter until brown. Remove almonds to a plate and leave the butter in the pan. Flour the fish, brush with *anglaise,* and coat with bread crumbs. Sauté until golden in the almond-flavored butter. Mix water, lemon juice, grapes, salt and pepper. Reduce to 3 tablespoons and fluff in the unsalted butter, tablespoon by tablespoon. While shaking the pan back and forth, blend in cream and sautéed almonds. Serve the sauce with the sautéed fillets.

Wine: California Blanc de Blancs

DEEP FRYING—DRY-HEAT PROCEDURE

There is no difference between deep frying meat and deep frying fish. Please reread the deep frying section in Chapter VI. Although some cooks dip fish into milk and roll it in bread crumbs before deep frying it, in my opinion the most efficient method for the housewife remains breading with an *anglaise* (p. 178). A fritter batter can also be used.

FRIED SMELTS
6 SERVINGS

36 smelts, cleaned   *Oil for deep frying*
1½ cups milk   *1½ cups flour*
Salt   *Pepper*

Soak the smelts in the milk with ¾ teaspoon salt for 1 hour. Drain on a cake rack. Heat the oil to 375°F. Roll the smelts in flour. Deep fry 6 fish at a time in the oil bath. Serve sprinkled with salt and pepper.

GOUJONNETTE OF SOLE   *fryin clarified butter*

A *goujon* is a small European freshwater fish. The species has probably died out by now from pollution. Other larger fish are sometimes cut into narrow strips, deep fried, and served like the little *goujons*. Cut sole fillets into strips ¾ inch wide. Soak in milk, roll in fresh crumbs, and deep fry in oil heated to 380°F. for a few minutes. Serve with Mustard Hollandaise (p. 129).

FROGS'-LEGS FRITTERS
6 APPETIZER SERVINGS

Although frogs are not fish, we usually think of them with other creatures that live in the water.

12 pairs of frogs' legs   *Oil for deep frying*
Vinaigrette (p. 360)   *Savory fritter batter (p. 189)*

Use tiny frogs' legs if you can get them. Bone the frogs' legs to form nuggets as big as one single muscle. Marinate in the vinaigrette overnight.

Make the fritter batter. Drain the nuggets and pat dry. Heat the oil bath to 375°F. Dip the nuggets into the batter and deep fry until golden. Serve on a folded napkin.

SHELLFISH

Shellfish is delicious only if cooked properly. It can be considered cooked when its proteins are barely coagulated.

Lobster

Ask the fish market for female lobsters if you want the coral, the unlaid lobster eggs, which give flavor and color to the dish. However, the male lobsters are in general somewhat sweeter in flavor.

The most useful size of lobster is "Large," with a weight of 1½ to 2 pounds. Other sizes are "Chicken" lobsters of 1 pound, "Eighths" of 1⅛ pounds, "Quarters" of 1¼ pounds, and "Jumbo," over 2 pounds.

BOILED LOBSTER

There is nothing that can equal the Maine lobster steamed in sea water, but sea water is not within everyone's reach. Instead measure into a large pot enough water to cover the whole lobsters. Add 3 teaspoons salt for each quart of water. Bring to a boil.

Immerse a live 1½-pound lobster in the water and barely simmer for 15 minutes. Drain in a colander.

Tie lobsters to be used for salads to a wooden spatula handle before immersing. It will keep the tail straight.

BAKED LOBSTER

Lobster is not often baked at home because this involves cutting the lobster alive. Scientists say that the nervous system of lobsters is not developed enough for them to feel pain, but since no scientist has ever been a lobster, it is still unnerving for some of us. Hold the lobster by the tail with a thick towel under your hand. Be as quick as you can to cut the head between the eyes, at which point the object of the sacrifice has left you!

Still holding the tail, push the tip of your knife through the cartilage of the main articulation of the claws. Twist to remove the claws and crack them open. Turn the lobster around and cut through the whole body. Remove the gravel bag between the eyes, and the stomach and intestinal tract. Save any tomalley, the green liver, or coral.

Split the lobster into halves, sear in butter for a few minutes, then bake in a 375°F. oven for 15 more minutes. Do not cook a 1½-pound lobster (Large), any longer than this or the texture will be spoiled. Serve it with plenty of butter and lemon juice.

CUTTING A LOBSTER FOR STEW

Put the lobster on a board. Hold down the tail with a thick towel, and cut between the eyes to kill the lobster. Push the tip of your knife through the cartilage of the main articulation of the claws. Twist to remove the claws and crack them open with the back of your knife. Turn the lobster around. Slide the knife blade between each two tail articulations and cut through to remove each "steak" or "medallion." Finish cutting the head. Remove the gravel bag between the eyes, and the stomach and intestinal tract. Save any tomalley or coral.

LOBSTER TAILS

Large Florida or South American lobster tails are tough if they are overcooked. Wrap the open end of each tail in foil. Immerse in boiling water, and barely simmer for 5 minutes. Let cool in the water. They will be tender as butter.

Small South African and Australian tails are better broiled. Broil for 3 or 4 minutes on each side. If you want them boiled, shell them raw and handle them like shrimps (see p. 276).

LOBSTER CIVET
4 SERVINGS

½ cup chopped carrots
½ cup chopped onions
¼ cup chopped celery
10 tablespoons butter
1½ cups excellent red wine
2 tablespoons chopped shallots
2 garlic cloves, chopped
1 teaspoon tomato paste

2 tablespoons meat glaze, or ¼ teaspoon commercial meat extract
Bouquet garni
2 "large" live lobsters, 1½ pounds each
4 tablespoons olive oil
Salt and pepper

6 tablespoons Cognac or brandy   Beurre manié
½ cup red-wine fish fumet   Chopped parsley for garnish
   (p. 83)

Sauté chopped vegetables in 4 tablespoons butter. Add red wine and bring to a boil. Add shallots, garlic, tomato paste, meat glaze or extract, and *bouquet garni.* Reduce to ¾ cup and set aside.

Cut the lobster as for stew (p. 273). Reserve coral and tomalley. Heat the oil and toss lobster pieces in oil until they are bright red. Sprinkle with salt and pepper. Discard the oil. Flambé the lobster with heated Cognac or brandy. Add the wine reduction and the fish *fumet.* Cover and barely simmer for 15 minutes.

Remove lobster pieces to a serving dish. Thicken the sauce with *beurre manié;* use 2 tablespoons butter and 1 tablespoon flour per cup of liquid. Cream the reserved tomalley, if any, with 6 tablespoons butter, and blend into the hot, but not boiling, sauce. Strain on top of the lobster, and serve sprinkled with chopped parsley.

Wine: the red wine used in making the sauce

LOBSTER THERMIDOR

2 SERVINGS

As true as possible to the original recipe, this version received the approval of the great Alexandre Dumaine.

1 "Large" live lobster, 1½
   pounds
4 tablespoons olive oil
Salt and pepper
2 tablespoons chopped shallots
½ cup California Fumé Blanc
   or French Pouilly Fumé
½ cup white-wine fish fumet
   (p. 83)
1 tablespoon meat glaze, or ⅛
   teaspoon commercial meat
   extract

⅓ cup béchamel sauce (p. 110)
   or medium white sauce
½ teaspoon dried chervil
1/16 teaspoon cayenne pepper
¾ cup heavy cream
3 tablespoons butter
1 scant teaspoon dry mustard
¼ cup grated Gruyère cheese
2 tablespoons grated Parmesan
   cheese

Cut the lobster as for baked lobster (p. 272). Keep tomalley and coral, if any. Heat oil in a large frying pan. Add lobster, flesh side down, and cook for 5 minutes. Bake in a 400°F. oven for 10 more minutes. Sprinkle with salt and pepper. Remove the meat of claws and tail and dice. Keep the shells.

In the same oil in which you cooked the lobster, sauté the shallots very quickly. Do not burn them, or the sauce will be bitter. Add the wine, fish *fumet* and meat glaze. Reduce to 3 to 4 tablespoons. Add béchamel, chervil and cayenne. Bring to a boil. Add the cream, little by little, and continue reducing and stirring until the sauce coats the spatula. Turn the heat off. Mix tomalley and coral with the butter and blend into the sauce. Add the mustard last. Mix well, correct seasoning, and strain on top of the lobster meat.

Fill each half shell with the sauced lobster. Sprinkle with both cheeses mixed. Slide under the broiler for a few minutes.

Wine: California Fumé Blanc or *French Pouilly Fumé*

LOBSTER OUZO

2 SERVINGS

This dish was concocted on the day we ran out of Pernod, the French apéritif. The recipe can be made with cooked lobster meat, crabmeat or shrimps.

1 "Large" live lobster, 1½ pounds	1 teaspoon chopped fresh or frozen chives
4 tablespoons olive oil	¼ teaspoon fennel seeds
Greek ouzo (about 3 tablespoons)	6 tablespoons chopped blanched pistachios
Salt and pepper	½ cup unsalted butter
1 teaspoon dried tarragon	¾ cup fresh bread crumbs, made from Italian bread
½ teaspoon dried basil	

Cut lobster as for baked lobster (p. 272). Heat olive oil, and cook the lobster, flesh side down, for 5 minutes. Brush all pieces of lobster with a *little* ouzo and finish baking in a 400°F. oven for 10 to 12 minutes. Sprinkle with salt and pepper. Remove lobster meat and dice it. Reserve tomalley and coral, if any.

Mix tarragon, basil, chives, fennel seeds and chopped pistachios. Add tomalley and coral. Cream the butter with 2 tablespoons ouzo; add the herb mixture, ½ cup of the bread crumbs, and salt and pepper to taste. Blend the diced lobster meat with the butter mixture. Put half of the mixture in each half shell. Sprinkle with the remaining bread crumbs. Slide under the broiler for a few minutes.

Wine: California Sauvignon Blanc or *French Meursault*

Shrimps and Scallops

Shrimps are 10-legged crustaceans that can be found in waters all over the world. The size and color varies, but the familiar pink color appears only when they are cooked. The shrimps we buy in the market are only abdomens and tails with the heads already removed.

A scallop in the United States is only the muscle that opens and closes the shell. The rest is discarded at sea. In Europe the whole mollusk is available, with the coral, which is not unlike cooked lobster coral in color. Sea scallops are large, while bay scallops are small. These more delicate small scallops have a short season, in the early fall.

Neither shrimp nor scallop should ever boil, or the texture will become rubbery. Immerse these shellfish in cold *court-bouillon* and bring very slowly to a boil. Turn off the heat immediately and let them cool completely in the liquid. Should the centers of the shellfish not be completely set, reheating them in butter or sauce will complete the cooking. This cooking method applies to shrimps and scallops of all sizes, fresh or frozen, since the time for the heat to penetrate each shellfish is in proportion to the original temperature of the *court-bouillon* and the size of the shellfish.

Rather than spend hours cleaning shrimps, buy large flash-frozen shrimps. Their quality is remarkable. Immerse solidly frozen shrimps in the *court-bouillon*. They will defrost and cook at the same time.

Handle frozen large deep-sea scallops in the same manner. However, remember that bay scallops taste better when they have *not* been frozen.

CLAM JUICE COURT-BOUILLON FOR
SHRIMPS AND SCALLOPS
TO POACH 2 POUNDS SHELLFISH

6 *cups clam juice*	*Small* bouquet garni
2 *cups white wine*	6 *peppercorns, cracked*
3 *large onions, minced*	Use no *salt*

Simmer all ingredients together for 30 minutes. Let cool completely before using. Strain. This *court-bouillon* can be frozen and re-used several times. Always reboil between uses.

SCALLOPS GRATINÉ
6 SERVINGS

The mussel or clam juice in this dish replaces the natural scallop juices discarded at the fishery. Use scallop shells or individual au gratin dishes for the final step of preparation.

1 ½ *pounds scallops*	*Butter*
1 *onion, chopped*	⅔ *cup heavy cream*
2 *shallots, chopped*	*Salt*
1 ½ *cups mussel or clam juice*	½ *pound minced mushrooms,*
1 ½ *cups dry white wine*	*sautéed*
Dash of pepper	1 *cup fresh bread crumbs*
Small bouquet garni	*Melted butter*
Flour	

Put scallops in a pan; add onion, shallots, mussel or clam juice, wine, pepper and *bouquet garni.* Bring very slowly to a boil. Turn off the heat and let the scallops cool in the cooking juices.

Drain and reserve cooking juices. Cut the scallops into ⅛-inch-thick slices; set aside. Strain the cooking juices through cheesecloth and measure. Make a *roux* with flour and butter, using 2 tablespoons of each per cup of cooking liquor. Add the cooking liquor to make a velouté. As soon as the sauce has thickened, add the cream and reduce over high heat until the sauce coats the spatula. Correct seasoning.

Mix scallops and mushrooms. Spoon 1½ tablespoons sauce into each shell or dish; add scallops and mushrooms. Cover with more of the sauce; sprinkle with bread crumbs and baste with melted butter. Bake in a 425°F. oven for 12 to 15 minutes, until golden brown.

This dish freezes well. Freeze after adding the crumbs and butter and before baking. Place still solidly frozen in a 300°F. oven and bake for 45 minutes.

Wine: California Semillon or French white Graves

SCALLOPS AU PERNOD

Use the recipe for Scallops Gratiné, adding 1½ tablespoons Pernod to the finished sauce.

SCALLOPS OPORTO
6 SERVINGS

Flour	*1 cup white-wine fish* fumet
1½ pounds scallops	*(p. 83) or clam juice*
Clarified butter, or half butter,	*Small* bouquet garni
half oil	*Salt and pepper*
6 ripe tomatoes, peeled and	*6 egg yolks*
seeded, or 2 cups drained	*½ cup heavy cream*
canned tomatoes	*¾ cup fresh bread crumbs*
1 cup white port	*Melted butter*

Flour whole scallops. Sauté them in clarified butter, tossing constantly, for 3 to 4 minutes. Add tomatoes, ⅛ cup of the port, the fish *fumet* or clam juice, and *bouquet garni*. Season with salt and pepper, cover, and barely simmer for another 5 to 6 minutes. Remove the scallops and slice them. Reduce the cooking juices to 1½ cups. Remove the *bouquet garni* and push the sauce through a strainer to purée the tomato pulp.

Return scallops to the pan and add the strained sauce reduction. Add the liaison of egg yolks and cream. Shake the pan back and forth over medium heat until the sauce thickens. Add remaining 2 table-spoons raw port. Put scallops in fireproof dishes, and sprinkle with bread crumbs and melted butter. Slide very quickly under the broiler.

This dish does not freeze, but it can be made ahead and refrigerated. In that case, reheat in a hot-water bath in a 200°F. oven for 40 to 45 minutes; then broil the top.

Note: Use only white port or the dish will be too sweet.

Wine: New York State Vinifera Riesling or *French Sancerre*

SHRIMPS ISTANBUL
6 SERVINGS

To Micky, our dear French baby-sitter, who wolfed the dish with me.

1½ pounds flash-frozen shrimps	*¼ teaspoon dried thyme*
4 cups clam-juice court-bouillon	*1 bay leaf, crushed*
(p. 277)	*¼ teaspoon ground saffron*
2 tablespoons olive oil	*⅛ teaspoon fine-grated orange*
¼ cup white wine	*rind*
½ lemon, cut into very thin	*½ pound mushrooms, minced*
slices	*5 tablespoons butter*
1 teaspoon dried basil	*Salt and pepper*

Poach the shrimps in the *court-bouillon,* and cool. Marinate the shrimps in a mixture of olive oil, wine, lemon slices, basil, thyme, bay leaf, saffron and orange rind for 1 hour.

Sauté the mushrooms in 2 tablespoons butter. Add them to the shrimps and marinade. Transfer to a saucepan and put over high heat. Toss the shrimps in the liquid over heat until the wine has completely evaporated, barely more than 5 minutes. Turn off the heat, remove lemon slices, and correct seasoning. Blend in remaining 3 tablespoons butter. Serve on toast or in croustades.

Wine: Greek white retsina

GRATIN OF SHRIMPS OR SCALLOPS
6 DINNER SERVINGS OR 12 APPETIZER SERVINGS

Inspired by Fernand Point's *gratin de queues d'écrevisses.* Cooked crabmeat can replace the shrimps or scallops.

1 ½ *pounds flash-frozen shrimps*
   or fresh scallops
4 *cups clam-juice* court-bouillon
   (*p. 277*)
9 *tablespoons butter*
2 *cans* (2 *ounces each*) *lobster*
   paste

2 *or 3 drops of red food coloring*
   (*optional*)
Salt and pepper
⅓ *cup Cognac or brandy*
6 *egg yolks*
2 *cups heavy cream*
6 *croustades* (*p. 43*)

Poach the shellfish in the *court-bouillon* and cool. Slice the scallops if you are using them. Cream 6 tablespoons butter with the lobster spread. Color with food coloring, if desired. Keep ready to use. Heat 3 tablespoons butter and in it sauté the shrimps or scallops until hot. Sprinkle with salt and pepper. Heat Cognac and flambé shellfish.

Mix egg yolks and cream and pour on the shrimps or scallops. Thicken over medium heat, shaking the pan back and forth. Turn off the heat and blend in the lobster butter. Correct seasoning. Turn shellfish into a fireproof dish. Slide under the broiler for 2 or 3 minutes, until golden brown. Serve in croustades.

Wine: California Blanc de Blancs or *French Hermitage Blanc*

SHRIMP FRITTERS
4 TO 6 APPETIZER SERVINGS

2 *tablespoons lemon juice*
6 *tablespoons olive oil*
1 *teaspoon dried basil*
1 *teaspoon salt*
1/16 *teaspoon pepper*

12 *jumbo shrimps*
Oil for deep frying
Flour
Savory fritter batter (*p. 189*)

Mix lemon juice, olive oil, basil, salt and pepper. Marinate the shrimps in the mixture overnight.

Drain the shrimps and pat dry. Heat the oil bath to 375°F. Flour the shrimps and dip into the fritter batter. (If you prefer, the shrimps can be brushed with *anglaise* and coated with bread crumbs instead of using fritter batter.) Deep fry until golden. Serve piping hot on a napkin. Serve with Gribiche Sauce (p. 137).

Clams, Mussels, Oysters

Clean clams and mussels by rubbing them with a stiff plastic pot scrubber under running cold water. Pull the beard from mussels. Discard any of the mollusks that are broken or opened.

Steam clams and mussels open with white wine instead of water; the juice obtained will be more nutritious and flavorful. Use ½ to 1 cup liquid according to the number of mussels you are steaming. When the steaming begins, hold the steamer pot by the handles, while holding the cover tightly shut with your thumbs. Toss the shellfish so that the top layers are not undercooked while the bottom layers slowly toughen. Steam mussels for about 5 minutes, or until the shells are open. Discard any shells that have not opened. Clams need a larger time for their shells are much heavier. Usually 15 minutes will open all the clams. Add no salt when steaming mussels or clams, for they are already very salty.

Strain the liquid through a double layer of cheesecloth and use it for sauces.

Although oysters are sometimes available already shucked, positively do not use them unless you buy them in the shell. Have the fish store open them for you in front of you. All of these mollusks are very perishable and must be fresh. Remove the beard of oysters after poaching.

If you are not absolutely sure about the freshness of clams, mussels or oysters, rather than take a chance, boil the shellfish. Discard the meat, which has become tough and inedible, but keep its liquor, which the boiling has sterilized. Boiling also concentrates the flavor.

LES MOULES DE LA MÈRE PIN
6 SERVINGS

Out of my grandmother's kitchen, so nostalgically remembered.

3 quarts black mussels	*1½ cups fresh bread crumbs,*
1 cup dry white wine	*from French bread*
1 onion, chopped fine	*1 cup butter*
2 shallots, chopped fine	*1 small garlic clove, minced*
2 tablespoons chopped parsley	*1 tablespoon fine-chopped*
Dash of pepper	*parsley*
Use no salt.	*Cream, if necessary*

Steam the mussels with wine, onion, shallots, chopped parsley and pepper. Lift mussels from the pan and discard half shells not containing mussels. Strain the cooking juices through several layers of damp cheesecloth. Simmer for 5 minutes.

Sauté the bread crumbs in the butter until golden. Add the mussel juices to make a sauce. Blend in garlic and fine-chopped parsley. Correct seasoning. If the sauce is too thick, thin it with a few tablespoons of cream, light or heavy. Mix mussels in their shells with the sauce. Give each guest a finger bowl of acidulated water and a fresh napkin for the next course.

Wine: California Folle Blanche or French Muscadet

CAPE NEDDICK MUSSEL BOATS
6 SERVINGS

Cape Neddick is 45 minutes away from our house. Whenever we go there, we bring back several quarts of mussels, and the pastry is always ready in the refrigerator.

Basic Pastry Crust (p. 391),	*2 tablespoons chopped shallots*
made with butter	*1 onion, chopped*
1½ quarts mussels	*Several parsley sprigs*
½ cup white wine	*6 peppercorns*

3 tablespoons butter
2 tablespoons flour
1 egg yolk
½ cup heavy cream

1 teaspoon prepared Dijon
    mustard
Salt and pepper

Shape 12 small pastry shells out of the pastry, and bake them. Steam mussels open with wine, shallots, onion, parsley and peppercorns. Strain the mussel juices through several layers of damp cheesecloth, and remove mussels from shells.

Make a *roux* with butter and flour, and add 1½ cups mussel liquid. Enrich with the egg yolk mixed with the heavy cream. Add mustard to the finished sauce and correct seasoning. Mix mussels and sauce and spoon into warm pastry shells. Serve piping hot.

Wine: California Chenin Blanc or *French Sancerre*

OYSTERS WITHOUT A NAME
6 APPETIZER SERVINGS

We make this dish only when we can find Chincoteagues.

18 oysters
¾ pound mushrooms
Butter (about ⅓ cup)
1 tablespoon lemon juice
1 pea-size piece of garlic, mashed
1 tablespoon chopped parsley

Salt and pepper
Heavy cream
Flour (2 to 4 tablespoons)
2 egg yolks
1 cup mixed grated Gruyère and
    Parmesan cheese

Shuck the oysters, and set aside the bottom shells. Drop the oysters into a frying pan with their own juices. Poach them until they curl up and puff up noticeably. Remove their beards. Pour off the juices and keep.

Chop the mushrooms and sauté in 2 tablespoons butter with the lemon juice; add the well-mashed garlic, the parsley and salt and pepper to taste. Divide the mushroom mixture among the oyster shells. Top each with an oyster. Measure the oyster juice, and add the same amount of heavy cream. Make a sauce using 2 tablespoons butter and 2 tablespoons flour per cup of liquid. Enrich with the egg yolks.

Season with salt and pepper. Spoon some of the sauce over each oyster. Sprinkle with cheese, and broil for 2 to 3 minutes.

Wine: the best possible Chablis

Abalone

Abalone is a large mollusk of Pacific waters. The part we eat is the muscle that controls the opening and closing of the shell. In the United States fresh abalone is available only in California, but it is canned or frozen for use elsewhere. Today there is so little left in California that most of it is imported from Australia already sliced and pounded. Pounding breaks the tough fibers of the muscle.

Overcooking abalone will make the bundles of muscle fibers shrink again and toughen beyond repair.

ABALONE BLISS

If you live on the West Coast, you can use fresh abalone and Dungeness crab. Elsewhere use canned or frozen abalone and Maryland blue crab. Do not marinate abalone; the small gain in tenderness is not worth the loss of true abalone flavor.

This is an expensive dish, for sophisticated guests only.

6 tablespoons chopped backfin Dungeness crabmeat	*1 cup bread crumbs*
	Clarified butter exclusively
12 slices of abalone, about 1½ pounds	*Salt and pepper*
	6 tablespoons noisette butter
Flour	*(p. 145)*
Anglaise *(p. 178)*	*Lemon juice*

Place 1 tablespoon crabmeat (not more, or the crabmeat will overpower the abalone) between 2 slices of abalone, making 6 pattylike sandwiches. Flour each patty, brush with *anglaise,* and coat with bread crumbs. Sauté in clarified butter (electric skillet 350°F.) for 2 to 3 minutes on each side, not more. The abalone is cooked when tiny puddles of melted collagen can be seen in the pan. Season with salt

and pepper. The patties will not be brown and should not be. Serve piping hot, basted with *noisette* butter and lemon juice.
Wine: California Fumé Blanc

Snails

Although fresh snails are imported to this country from France, Italy and North Africa, the best and safest snails come out of U.S.-inspected cans! Do not reboil canned snails. The canning has already toughened them.

The snails we eat are not shellfish but land creatures, but we think of them with shellfish because they carry a hard shell like a mollusk.

LO CAGARAULO
4 SERVINGS

This recipe is dedicated to Craig Claiborne. There is no set recipe for this dish, which comes from the Languedoc; there everyone prepares it to his own taste. The hollandaise is my idea to brighten the color of the dish and temper the taste of the greens.

2 dozen canned snails
White wine
Pinch each of dried thyme, basil, chervil, tarragon
3 tablespoons chopped parsley
1 dime-size piece of orange rind
1 very small piece of bay leaf
4 garlic cloves, chopped fine
4 teaspoons chopped shallot
2 tablespoons fine-diced blanched salt pork
2 tablespoons olive oil

1 tablespoon chopped onion
2 tablespoons chopped leek
½ cup each of fine-chopped Boston lettuce, spinach, escarole and chicory
Salt and pepper
9 tablespoons melted unsalted butter
2 anchovies, rinsed and chopped fine
2 tablespoons minced walnuts
2 egg yolks

Drain the snails and measure the liquid. Measure the same amount of the white wine. Make a marinade with the juices, the wine, the dried herbs, 1 tablespoon of the parsley, the orange rind, bay leaf, 2 garlic cloves and 1 teaspoon of the chopped shallots. Simmer for 10 minutes. Turn off the heat and add the snails. Let them marinate for 24 to 36 hours.

Make a green sauce. Render diced salt pork in a heavy pot, preferably enameled cast iron. Add the olive oil, and sauté onion and leek in both fats until golden. Add remaining shallots, 5 teaspoons parsley and all the chopped salad greens. Toss until wilted, then season with salt and pepper. Cover tightly and cook over very low heat for 45 minutes to 1 hour.

Drain the snails from the marinade. Reduce the marinade to ½ cup. Set aside 2 tablespoons of it to make the hollandaise. Mix in a shallow pan 2 tablespoons of the butter, the reduced marinade, the drained snails, the green sauce, one of the remaining garlic cloves, the anchovies and walnuts. Heat gently together until the snails are hot.

To make the hollandaise, mix the egg yolks with the reserved 2 tablespoons marinade, ¼ teaspoon salt, dash of pepper, remaining chopped garlic and remaining 1 teaspoon chopped parsley. Fluff the yolks until foamy, remove from the heat, and dribble in the remaining butter.

Serve snails and green sauce on toasts or in small croustades, and spoon the hollandaise over them.

Wine: California Fumé Blanc or *French Chablis Les Clos*

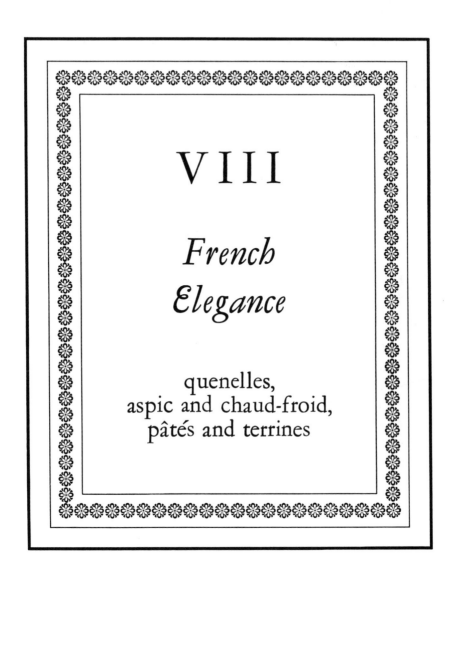

VIII

French Elegance

quenelles,
aspic and chaud-froid,
pâtés and terrines

THE PROCEDURES described in this chapter are generally reserved for professional cooks and chefs and are considered difficult for the lay cook. The truth of the matter is that they are considerably less difficult than is often thought, especially with the equipment and implements of the modern kitchen. Still, it has been my observation that when a student has made *quenelles* or a pâté, she really feels that she is a confirmed cook; so here's your way to confirmation.

QUENELLES

This mysterious word sounds glamorous, but actually a *quenelle* is nothing more than a patty made with uncooked meat or fish, which is then poached. When I am asked what *quenelles* are, I invariably answer, "French gefilte fish."

Quenelles are made with fish, veal and white meat of poultry. Fish *quenelles* are served as a first or a main course; poultry and veal *quenelles* are more usually served as a garnish. Many formulas exist, some made with a bread and milk mixture, some with a base of cream-puff paste. The finest are the *mousseline* type made only with eggs and cream, although the Lyonnaise mixture made with beef kidney suet is nearly as good as the airy *mousselines*. The method of preparation for the following basic recipes is the same.

SOLE OR PIKE QUENELLES
(PERSONAL INTERPRETATION)

1 pound fillet of sole or pike
1 whole egg
1 extra egg white
¼ cup unsalted butter

2¼ cups heavy cream, chilled
1½ teaspoons salt
½ teaspoon ground white
    pepper

SALMON QUENELLES
(PERSONAL INTERPRETATION)

1 pound boneless salmon meat   *1 teaspoon salt*
1 whole egg   *½ teaspoon ground white*
1 extra egg yolk   *pepper*
½ cup unsalted butter   *1 tablespoon lemon juice*
1¾ cups heavy cream, chilled

POULTRY QUENELLES (CLASSIC RECIPE)

1 pound white meat of chicken   *1½ teaspoons salt*
2 egg whites   *½ teaspoon grated nutmeg*
2¼ cups heavy cream, chilled   *Ground white pepper*

VEAL QUENELLES (CLASSIC RECIPE)

½ pound boneless loin of veal   *1½ cups heavy cream, chilled*
½ pound uncooked beef kidney   *1 teaspoon salt*
   suet   *½ teaspoon ground white pepper*
2 medium-size whole eggs   *¼ teaspoon grated nutmeg*
1 extra egg yolk

MAKING QUENELLE PASTE

In all cases the fish or meat should be free of skin and bones. Try to handle the raw meat or fish as little as possible with your hands; use all stainless-steel implements if possible. Cut the meat or fish into ½-inch cubes. Beat whole eggs and egg yolks or whites lightly together. Divide meat or fish and eggs into 3 parts. Put one part of each in the blender container (you may want to invest in a very good blender, which will purée in a minimum amount of time). Blend the meat until puréed. Repeat with the remainder of the eggs and meat or fish. Push the purée through a *tamis* or large conical strainer. Straining is not a must, but if you want a perfectly smooth *quenelle,* you will want to discard all the connective tissues invisible to the naked eye.

Gather the purée in a bowl and deep chill for 2 hours. If the recipe contains butter, cream it; then gradually beat the chilled paste into the butter with a mixer. If you have only 1 pound of meat or fish, gradually beat the chilled cream into it with the electric mixer on medium-low speed, so as not to churn butter. Add all the seasonings. If you have more than 1 pound of meat or fish, place the bowl of paste over ice while you add the cream. Your *quenelle* paste is ready; chill it for at least 2 hours before using it. This chilling allows the flavors to blend and makes the mixture firmer.

POACHING QUENELLES IN STOCK (FISH AND POULTRY)

Butter a large frying pan or *sauteuse.* Roll the *quenelle* paste between 2 spoons until you obtain an egg-shaped nugget. Drop each nugget on the bottom of the buttered pan; or stuff the paste into a pastry bag fitted with a ¾-inch plain nozzle and pipe 3-inch-long strips on the bottom of the pan. Slowly pour boiling stock (fish *fumet* or chicken broth) into the pan until the *quenelles* are well covered. Keep over low heat, *without boiling* or the *quenelles* will split open, for 15 to 20 minutes, depending on the size or until they are firm. The *quenelle*s can wait for service in the warm poaching stock.

POACHING MOLDED QUENELLES (FISH AND POULTRY)

Butter well 3-ounce custard cups or ramekins. Fill with *quenelle* paste. Tap the ramekins on the table top to pack the paste. Set all the ramekins in a deep baking dish, pour boiling water into the baking dish to cover at least two thirds of the ramekins, and cover with a well-buttered paper. Bake in a 325°F. oven for 18 to 20 minutes, or until a knife inserted at the center of a *mousseline* comes out clean.

POACHING QUENELLES IN THE OVEN (VEAL)

Set a piece of baking paper on a cookie sheet; butter the paper well. Pipe 1½-inch-long nuggets of paste on the paper. Bake in a 300°F. oven for about 12 minutes, or until the fat pearls in tiny droplets at the surface of the *quenelles.*

QUENELLES OF SALMON NORDIC
6 SERVINGS

Created for the Wine and Food Society of Philadelphia. A fine dish for a company meal.

Salmon quenelle *paste (p. 290)*
3 tablespoons butter
3 tablespoons flour
2 cups strong white-wine fish
  fumet (p. 83)

5 tablespoons chopped fresh dill
1 cup heavy cream
2 tablespoons butter
Salt and pepper

Make the salmon *quenelle* paste. Butter heavily 6 ramekins or custard cups of 3- to 4-ounce size. Fill the ramekins with the *quenelle* paste and poach as for molded *quenelles* (p. 291).

With butter, flour and fish *fumet* (no clam juice, please, the dish is too delicate) make a fish velouté. Add 3 tablespoons of the dill. Simmer the sauce and skim well. Place the sauce over high heat; add the heavy cream, little by little, stirring all the time, until the sauce coats the spoon. Butter the sauce, strain, and add the rest of the dill. Correct the seasoning. Invert the *mousselines* and serve with sauce. A few puff-paste croutons for garnish are pretty and delicious.

QUENELLES OF SOLE LEXINGTON
6 SERVINGS

To Paul and Julia Child, for whom the dish was created.

Sole quenelle *paste (p. 290)*
10 slices of Nova Scotia salmon
2 ounces Beluga or Sevruga
  caviar, or best available
3 tablespoons butter
3 tablespoons flour

2 cups strong white-wine fish
  fumet (p. 83)
1 cup heavy cream, unwhipped
1/3 cup heavy cream, whipped
Salt and pepper

Make the sole *quenelle* paste. Butter well 6 ramekins of 3- to 4-ounce size. Line each of them with a slice of smoked salmon. Half fill with *quenelle* paste, add ½ teaspoon caviar, then add more *quenelle* paste to fill the ramekins completely. Poach as for molded *quenelles* (p. 291).

With butter, flour and fish *fumet* (no clam juice, please, the dish is too delicate) make a velouté. Simmer and skim well, then reduce over high heat, adding the *unwhipped* heavy cream, little by little, and stirring all the time until the sauce coats the spoon heavily. Strain the finished sauce and whisk the *whipped* cream into it. Add the rest of the smoked salmon cut into fine julienne and the remainder of the caviar. Reheat the sauce well, but do not boil. Correct the seasoning. Invert the *mousselines* on hot plates and spoon the sauce over them. A few puff-paste croutons look lovely.

ASPIC AND CHAUD-FROID

Aspic and chaud-froid are jellied sauces. Aspic is a jellied stock used to coat pieces of meat or poultry that are served cold. It gives a cold dish a royal appearance. A *chaud-froid* is a sauce, white or brown, stabilized with aspic or a small amount of gelatin, that is spread over a cold meat just before the sauce turns solid. To dress a dish with either is time-consuming, and the sauce and the food must be well prepared.

CLASSIC ASPIC

Use the recipe for brown veal stock on page 80. To the amount of meat already mentioned in the recipe, add a large veal knuckle. Let the meat juices caramelize only once at the bottom of the pot, so as to obtain a lighter colored stock. When made according to this recipe, the stock will gel without addition of extra gelatin; the aspic will be soft and refined. Strain, defatten, and clarify the aspic.

MODERN ASPIC

Use the stock of your choice, homemade or canned, but completely defattened and clarified. Stabilize the stock with 1 envelope of gelatin for each 2 cups of stock. Soften the gelatin in ½ cup of the cold stock.

Heat well the remaining 1½ cups of stock and blend in the gelatin, stirring until it has completely dissolved.

FISH ASPIC
Fish *fumet* (p. 83) reduced by half and clarified makes the best fish aspic.

CLARIFYING AND FLAVORING ASPIC
Clarify the stock exactly as described in the recipe for Simple Consommé (p. 89). If the aspic is to be flavored with herbs, add them to the stock before clarifying. If the aspic is to be flavored with wine, use 1½ tablespoons port, Madeira or sherry for each cup of stock and add it to the cooled clarified aspic.

TO APPLY ASPIC TO FOOD
Use a white feather snipped from a feather duster or a turkey feather. If you do not have a feather, even though it is the ideal tool, use a thin flat silk brush that is very supple, like a silk paint brush. Remove any trace of fat from the piece of food to be coated, since aspic will not coat on a fat surface. Chill the food as deeply as possible. Put some aspic in a bowl set on ice. When the aspic feels and looks like oil, remove it from the ice, dip the feather into it, and brush a layer of aspic all over the food. Chill the food again. From then on, you may *spoon* successive layers of aspic over the food; it will coat easily. Chill the food after each layer is applied.

COATING A MOLD WITH ASPIC
This requires time and careful work. Deep-chill the mold for 1 hour. Prepare a large container of crushed ice. Set the mold in the ice. Pour some liquid aspic into the mold and quickly turn the mold to coat evenly. Repeat until the mold is evenly coated with a layer about ⅒ inch thick.

TO DECORATE AN ASPIC
Use your imagination and artistic talents to decorate a mold or an aspic-coated piece of food. Cut out pieces of different shapes. To obtain different colors for your cutouts, use pimiento for red, truffle for

black, egg white for white, and egg yolk for yellow. For green, use blanched leek or watercress leaves rather than green pepper, for green pepper will impart a taste to the aspic.

If you are working on a large piece of food and need many cutouts, prepare the ingredients in sheets; it will be less expensive. For all sheets, oil a 9-inch pizza pan lightly.

EGG-WHITE SHEET

Butter the pan, pour 8 unbeaten egg whites into it, and bake in a 300°F. oven until whites are set. Cool, unmold on a damp cheesecloth, and use. (You may strain the egg whites to remove the ligaments if you wish.)

EGG-YOLK SHEET

Hard-cook 6 egg yolks. Dissolve 3½ tablespoons unflavored gelatin in 1 cup of broth or aspic. Put the mixture and the cooked egg yolks in the blender container and blend until smooth. Pour into the prepared pan and chill.

TRUFFLE SHEET

Mix 6 tablespoons truffle peels with 3 tablespoons unflavored gelatin and 1 cup of broth or aspic. Blend in the blender, pour into the prepared pan, and chill.

ASPIC SHEET

Pour aspic ¼ inch thick in the pan and chill. Cut decorative pieces with cutters or a knife.

Dip all cutouts of egg or vegetable into liquid aspic and apply them to the sides of the mold with a trussing needle, a skewer, or a food pick. Or arrange them on the piece of food after the first layer of aspic has set. Spoon additional aspic layers over the cutouts.

SERVING ASPICS

Unmold the aspic on a chilled serving platter set over ice. Serve on chilled plates.

CHAUD-FROID

A *chaud-froid* sauce is prepared like a warm sauce but is served cold. The classic *chaud-froid* sauces are made with *sauce suprême* for the white sauces and *demi-glace* for the brown sauces. With all the skimming both of these classic sauces require, one can very well imagine how much time goes into their confection; so that there are few cooks around who have not devised their own formulas for pleasant, but less complicated, *chaud-froid* sauces.

WHITE CHAUD-FROID SAUCE

If the butter is not completely removed from a classic *chaud-froid* sauce, it will pit the surface of the finished product badly and make it appear lumpy. The present formula turns around the difficulty of skimming. Adapt the stock in the sauce to the meat presented. If you use homemade aspic stock, you need only 2 teaspoons unflavored gelatin.

2 cups white stock (chicken, veal, or fish fumet), absolutely fat free	2 teaspoons cornstarch
	2 cups heavy cream
	Salt and pepper
4 teaspoons unflavored gelatin	Flavorings

Bring 1¾ cups stock to a boil. Mix the remaining cold stock with the gelatin, and blend into the hot stock. Mix cornstarch with cream. Blend into the simmering stock to thicken. Add seasoning and flavorings to taste. Cool, stirring over ice until the sauce reaches coating consistency. *Chaud-froid* sauce is rather stiff when refrigerated, but will be soft and pleasant when the meat reaches room temperature at serving time.

VARIATIONS OF THE WHITE CHAUD-FROID SAUCE

Wine   Replace ¼ cup of the white stock by Fino or Amontillado sherry, or Sercial Madeira.

Paprika   Flavor with 1 to 2 tablespoons mild Hungarian paprika to taste.

Truffles   Use 3 cups of stock. Simmer as many truffle peels as possible in the stock until it has reduced to 2 cups. Strain. Make the sauce with this truffle-flavored stock.

Tarragon or other herb   Follow recipe and proportions on page 298 for all herbs. For dill, double the amount of the herbs.

Tomato   Add 2 tablespoons tomato paste to the finished sauce. Do not use tomato sauce, for it is too acid and the sauce will turn lumpy.

BROWN CHAUD-FROID SAUCE

Although rarely used in modern cuisine, this sauce will be useful for a beautiful-looking cold roast beef or a cold roast of duck. Adapt the stock to the meat. Use only homemade stock, or the sauce is not worth the time involved in its preparation.

8 cups homemade brown stock (p. 78), made with a large amount of veal bones, or aspic stock prepared with some beef, duck or game-bird bones or meat	*Unflavored gelatin* *2 tablespoons potato starch* *1 cup Madeira, sherry or port*

Reduce the 8 cups of stock to 4¼ cups. To test the gelatin content of the stock, pour ½ inch of it into a small dish and place the dish in the freezer for 5 minutes. Use a timer so that the stock does not freeze. If the sample in the freezer has not jelled, dissolve 1 teaspoon gelatin in the hot stock and make the test again. If necessary, add more gelatin, teaspoon by teaspoon, and test the jelling quality of the stock between additions. (Too much gelatin would make the stock rubbery, therefore testing is important.)

Clarify the stock that remains. You can expect to lose about ¼ cup in the process. Bring 3½ cups of clarified stock to a boil. Dissolve the potato starch in ¼ cup of cold stock and blend into the simmering stock. Turn off the heat and add the wine. Stir the sauce over ice until coating consistency has been reached.

To Coat with Chaud-Froid

This requires care and patience. Have all the pieces to be coated deep chilled and set on a cake rack. Protect the table with parchment paper, or work over a jelly-roll pan. As soon as the *chaud-froid* coats the back of a spoon, remove it from the ice and quickly ladle it over the pieces of meat. If you run short of sauce, pick up what fell on the paper, melt it, and reuse it. If at any time the *chaud-froid* hardens too much, you can do nothing else than be patient and remelt it.

If you cut whole poached birds into serving pieces before coating them with *chaud-froid,* remove their skins. The best home presentation of *chaud-froid* is obtained with chicken cutlets poached and deep chilled, rather than with whole birds. If you are working with a ham, brush it with a layer of clear aspic before covering with *chaud-froid,* to keep the fat in the ham from spoiling the coating.

Repair work is difficult on *chaud-froid.* If you have a lumpy spot, run a hot spatula over it and coat with aspic. Finish the pieces that have been coated with *chaud-froid* by glazing them with a final layer of clear aspic. Without this layer of aspic, the *chaud-froid* would develop a hard surface because of the cornstarch content. Also, the aspic keeps the *chaud-froid* from drying, and gives a professional appearance to the whole dish.

Keep the serving platter containing a *chaud-froid* over ice even on the buffet table, and serve the portions on chilled plates.

TARRAGON CHICKEN CHAUD-FROID

12 SERVINGS

A lovely presentation for a summer dinner party.

6 double chicken breasts	*2 tablespoons fresh tarragon, or*
3 tablespoons melted butter	*1 tablespoon dried*
1 tablespoon lemon juice	*4 teaspoons unflavored gelatin*
Salt and pepper	*2 teaspoons cornstarch*
Poor man's mousse de foie gras	*2 cups heavy cream*
(p. 491)	*2 cups clarified aspic (p. 293)*
3 cups fat-free chicken stock	*12 thin truffle slices or shavings*

Skin and bone the chicken breasts to obtain 12 chicken cutlets. Poach in butter and lemon juice (see p. 218). Drain, cool, and deep chill. Slice each cutlet lengthwise into halves. Spread half of them with a ¼-inch layer of liver mousse, and put both halves together to make a sandwich. Keep deep chilled until ready to coat with *chaud-froid*.

Bring 2¾ cups of the chicken stock to a boil. Add tarragon. Let simmer until reduced to 1¾ cups. Mix the remaining cold stock with the gelatin and blend into the hot stock. Mix the cornstarch with the cream and blend into the simmering stock to thicken. Strain the sauce to discard tarragon, and chill until the sauce reaches coating consistency.

Put chicken cutlets on a cake rack over a large sheet of parchment paper. Spoon *chaud-froid* over cutlets. Deep chill the cutlets again. If you are short of sauce, melt any that has fallen on the parchment paper while coating, and chill again to coating consistency.

Cool 1½ cups aspic over ice. As soon as it has reached the consistency of oil, spoon it over the chicken cutlets. Chill the chicken again. Dip the truffle slices in aspic and use one to decorate the center of each cutlet. Cool the rest of the aspic and spoon a second coat over the truffle slices.

Note: Instead of a pure white sauce decorated with the contrasting black truffles, you can color the sauce pale green with a few drops of green food coloring and decorate the cutlets with blanched fresh tarragon leaves.

FILLET OF BEEF IN ASPIC

12 SERVINGS

1 whole beef fillet (tenderloin), *about 6 pounds*	*4 cups clarified aspic (p. 293)*
Oil	*2 large truffles*
Salt and pepper	*6 hard-cooked eggs*
Double recipe poor man's mousse *de foie gras (p. 491)*	

Trim the beef of all fat and gristle. Brush the meat with oil. Roast in a 400°F. oven to an internal temperature of 135°F. Sprinkle with salt and pepper. Cool completely and chill. Slice the fillet to obtain 24 slices ¼ inch thick. Spread most of the liver mousse ⅛ inch thick on 12 slices, and top with the remaining slices to make 12 sandwiches. Deep chill to set.

Cool 2 cups of the aspic over ice. Arrange meat sandwiches in the center of a large serving platter. Brush aspic over them with a feather. Shave 12 slices from the truffles and chop the rest. Decorate the top of each meat sandwich with 1 small truffle slice dipped in aspic.

Slice eggs lengthwise into halves. Remove the yolks and save them for another recipe (see Hard-Cooked Egg-Yolk Mayonnaise, p. 137, for instance). Fill the whites with more of the liver mousse forced through a pastry bag fitted with a star nozzle. Chill the eggs. Cool another cup of the aspic and dribble aspic over eggs; sprinkle with the chopped truffle. Set 6 half eggs on each side of the beef slices.

Put the platter over a large basin of ice. Let it cool completely. Slowly pour the remaining cup of aspic on the bottom of the platter. Let it gel over ice, then transfer to refrigerator to keep chilled until serving time.

FILLET OF BEEF IN CHAUD-FROID

If you prefer *chaud-froid* to aspic, use Brown Chaud-Froid Sauce (p. 297) to coat the beef slices. However, the stuffed eggs look better coated with clear aspic. When the whole dish is ready, coat everything with a final layer of clear aspic.

HAM IN CHAUD-FROID
8 TO 10 SERVINGS

1 fully cooked whole ham (about 12 pounds), with bones *4 cups clarified aspic*	*Double recipe white chaud-froid sauce (p. 296), flavored with tarragon or paprika* *Truffles, carrot shavings, leaves, etc., for cutouts*

Remove 2 inches of meat all around the shank bone of the ham. Break or saw off the small bone parallel to the shank bone. Remove all the rind but the 3 inches around the shank bone; cut that rind to make it look like a pointed scalloped collar. Trim all the fat, leaving a layer only ¼ inch thick over the whole surface of the ham. Remove a slice of meat about 1½ inches thick from the bottom of the ham so it can sit flat on the serving platter. Chill the ham until it is very cold.

Cool 1 cup of aspic until it reaches the consistency of oil. Put the ham on a rack over a jelly-roll pan. Brush it well with the aspic, using a feather. This first layer of aspic is a must or the *chaud-froid* will not adhere. Refrigerate the ham.

Prepare the *chaud-froid.* Coat the ham as quickly and evenly as possible. Deep chill for 1 hour. Meanwhile, prepare all the cutouts of your design. Dip them into liquid aspic. They should be only very lightly coated so the aspic does not run down the *chaud-froid* and streak it. Arrange the decorations on top of the ham. Chill again. Finally cover with a last layer of clear aspic.

For a very impressive presentation, rest the ham on a wedge of white bread on the platter. Surround the ham with asparagus spears rolled in boiled ham slices, deviled eggs, tomatoes filled with Waldorf salad, all these items first put on a rack and glazed with aspic.

POACHED TROUT IN ASPIC
6 SERVINGS

6 *trout*	36 *small Danish shrimps*
Wine court-bouillon (*p. 257*)	6 *hard-cooked eggs*
Salmon mousse (*p. 493*), *flavored with dill*	3 *cups mayonnaise* (*p. 135*)
	Chopped chives
3 *cups clarified reduced white-wine fish* fumet (*p. 83*)	*Chopped fresh dill*

Remove the fins from the trout but leave heads and tails on. Poach the fish in the *court-bouillon,* and let them cool completely in the *court-bouillon.* Make the salmon mousse.

Remove the top skin of each trout, lift off the top fillets, and remove the backbone. Pipe a layer of salmon mousse ¼ inch thick on the bottom fillets of each fish; then replace the top fillets to reshape the fish. Place the fish on a large serving platter. Cool 2 cups of the clarified *fumet* until it has the consistency of oil. Brush the trout with the jelling *fumet* to make a thin aspic layer. Arrange 6 shrimps on top of each fish. Deep chill trout and shrimps. Brush an aspic layer over the shrimps; deep chill. Spoon a last layer of aspic over the fish; deep chill again.

Cut eggs lengthwise into halves, remove yolks, and mash them. Add yolks to ⅔ cups mayonnaise and whip until smooth. Add chopped chives and dill to taste. Pipe the mixture into the egg-white halves. Arrange the eggs around the fish. Place the platter over a large container filled with ice. Let the platter chill completely, then pour 1 cup aspic into it and refrigerate immediately. Keep deep chilled until serving time. Serve with mayonnaise flavored with chives and dill to taste.

PÂTÉS AND TERRINES

Pâtés are meat pastes in a crust; they are descendants of the fabulous 16th-century meat pies. Terrines are pâtés baked without a crust in a special earthenware casserole called a *terrine* (from the French *terre,* meaning earth or clay). Both pâtés and terrines are filled with the same type of ground meats, called a forcemeat.

The most practical pâté mold for a housewife is a rectangular 6-cup mold with removable hinges. A pâté baked in this mold will serve 12 persons. The shape of a terrine is of no great importance as long as the vessel is fireproof.

PASTRY FOR PÂTÉS

The pastry for pâtés should be made 24 hours ahead of time. Choose a butter crust or a lard crust; a lard crust is better adapted to a meat pâté while a fish pâté tastes better with a butter crust.

Butter Crust	Lard Crust
4 cups sifted flour	*4 cups sifted flour*
¾ cup butter	*⅔ cup lard*
1 egg	*1 egg*
¾ cup water, or less	*½ cup water, or less*

Make the pastry according to the general instructions given on pages 391 to 392.

PÂTÉ IN CRUST (BASIC MIXTURE)

The forcemeat of a hare, duck, turkey or game-bird pâté should be prepared according to these approximate proportions; pack the cup firmly with the various ingredients before measuring.

Fillets of the birds
⅓ cup Cognac or brandy
2 cups 1-inch cubes of poultry meat (all the meat of the bird except the fillets and livers), weight ¾ to 1¼ pounds
½ cup 1-inch cubes of lean veal meat, weight ⅓ pound
¾ cup 1-inch cubes of lean pork meat, weight ⅓ pound
2 cups 1-inch cubes of semifat, semilean pork meat, weight 1 pound

2 cups 1-inch cubes of unsalted pork fatback, weight 1 pound
4 medium-size eggs
⅔ cup port or Madeira
3 teaspoons salt
3 teaspoons spiced salt (p. 27)
Pastry for pâtés (p. 302)
1 pound ⅛-inch-thick sheets of unsalted pork fatback
Livers of the birds
Egg-yolk glaze (p. 421)
2 to 3 cups aspic (p. 293)

It is essential that the pork fatback used for these preparations be *unsalted* fresh pork fat; salt pork is not an adequate replacement; neither is bacon, blanched or not. Ask your butcher to order fatback for you if he does not regularly carry it. He can order it and obtain it easily and at a modest price. If you cannot locate fatback, buy a whole side of *fresh bacon;* farmers' markets always carry it. A whole 3-pound side of fresh bacon will provide you with enough fat and meat to make the forcemeat and the strips to line the terrine or crust.

The forcemeat should be seasoned with the spice mixture that the French call *sel épicé,* or "spiced salt." Use the recipe on page 27, or use a commercial brand, or mix your own blend of nutmeg, Cayenne, cinnamon, cloves, thyme and pepper. Taste the uncooked forcemeat; it must be oversalted if you want the chilled cooked mixture to be salted enough.

Marinate the fillets in the Cognac or brandy. Grind all the rest of the meats and the *cubed* fatback twice with the finest blade of your grinder. Put the forcemeat in a large mixer bowl and add eggs, port or Madeira, *regular* salt and *spiced* salt. Beat well until the mixture is homogenous, then build the pâté or terrine.

Building a Pâté

Butter the pâté mold very well. Roll out two thirds of the dough into a sheet ¼ inch thick. Ease the sheet of dough into the mold without stretching it; do not thin it at the angles of the mold or the meat juices will run out. When the mold is lined, cut the dough all around the edge of the mold, leaving a ¾-inch-wide pastry strip hanging over the edge.

Line the dough with strips cut from the sheets of fatback so that the whole surface is protected from penetration by the meat juices. Build the pâté in layers, starting and ending with a layer of forcemeat. In between, put alternate layers of strips of marinated fillet and pieces of liver wrapped in thin sheets of fatback. Fold in the dough hanging over the edge of the mold to cover the edge of the forcemeat. Brush the dough with egg-yolk glaze.

Roll out the remainder of the dough into a sheet ¼ inch thick and cut a lid to fit over the opening of the pâté; use the bottom of the mold as a pattern. Crimp the lid and decorate to taste. Cut two vents ½ inch wide in the lid to let the steam escape. Brush with egg-yolk glaze. Bake in a 350°F. oven for 20 minutes per pound (1½ to 2 hours for this pâté mixture).

When the pâté is cooked, turn off the oven. Loosen the hinges of the mold but do not remove its sides. Let the pâté cool in the cooling oven for about 30 minutes. Then cool completely at room temperature. Chill only when cold. Pour semiliquid aspic into the vents in the lid only a few hours before serving.

TERRINES

A terrine is built exactly like a pâté, and the vessel itself is lined with fatback strips. Bake, covered with its lid, in a hot-water bath in a 350°F. oven until the fat runs clear. Remove from the oven but leave in the water bath. Remove the lid of the terrine, put a dessert plate over the pâté, and set a heavy weight on the plate. The weight will press the excess fat out of the pâté. Let cool completely with the weight on, then chill.

When the terrine and its contents are chilled, remove the pâté mixture from the terrine. Scrape all the fat from the pâté, which will be firm like a meat loaf. Wash the terrine. Return the pâté to the terrine and pour liquid aspic all around the pâté. Chill. You may, if you want, decorate the top with vegetable cutouts as you would any aspic preparation.

TERRINE OF DUCK

1 duck (5 pounds) and the duck liver
⅓ cup Cognac or brandy
½ cup cubed lean veal (3 loin chops)
¾ cup cubed lean pork
2 cups cubed semilean pork
2 cups cubed fresh pork fatback
4 medium-size eggs
⅔ cup white port or Sercial Madeira
6 teaspoons salt
½ teaspoon grated nutmeg
⅛ teaspoon each of ground allspice, cinnamon and coriander

⅛ teaspoon crumbled dried thyme
Pinch of ground cloves
1 teaspoon ground white pepper
Pinch of Cayenne pepper
1 pound ⅛-inch-thick sheets of unsalted pork fatback, cut into strips
2 large truffles
10 ounces goose liver pâté (optional)
2 cups liquid aspic

Bone the duck; remove fillets and cut them into ⅓-inch-wide strips. Marinate the strips and the duck liver in Cognac overnight. Mix the remainder of the duck meat, the other meats and the cubed fatback to make a forcemeat (see p. 303); add the eggs, port or Madeira, and all the seasonings.

Line the terrine with strips cut from the sheets of fatback. Build the pâté (see p. 304), alternating layers of forcemeat with layers of fillets, duck liver, truffles and goose-liver pâté. Bake in a hot-water bath in a 350°F. oven for 1½ hours. Cool under a weight. Scrape fat from the cold pâté mixture, wash the terrine, and return the pâté to the terrine. Fill the terrine with 2 cups liquid aspic, and chill.

Note: This same mixture can be baked in a crust to make a duck pâté. Use a whole recipe for lard crust (p. 303).

TERRINE OF CHICKEN LIVERS

1 pound chicken livers	*1 small onion, grated fine*
1 duck, goose, or turkey liver, if available	*1 shallot, grated fine*
3 tablespoons Cognac or brandy	*1 teaspoon salt*
7 slices of white bread, crusts removed	*½ teaspoon ground white pepper*
¼ cup heavy cream	*½ teaspoon celery salt*
½ pound fresh pork fatback	*¼ teaspoon grated nutmeg*
2 truffles	*⅛ teaspoon ground cloves*
2 eggs	*Pinch each of ground cinnamon and allspice*
1 tablespoon port or Madeira	*2 Mediterranean bay leaves, or 1 California bay leaf*

Trim all the livers free of connective tissues, fat, or gall. Marinate the livers in 2 tablespoons of the Cognac in the refrigerator for 4 hours.

Moisten bread with the cream. Grind the livers, fatback and truffles twice. Mix the ground ingredients, eggs, remaining Cognac or brandy, the port or Madeira, onion, shallot and seasonings in a large mixer bowl, and whip until smooth. Turn the forcemeat into a buttered 6-cup terrine. Place the bay leaves on top. Bake in a hot-water bath in a 350°F. oven for 1½ hours, or until the fat appears clear. Cool under a weight, and serve chilled.

If you wish, the fat can be scraped off the chilled finished pâté and the space left in the terrine can be filled with aspic. The aspic will not stay clear but will become muddled by the livers, even when you take the greatest precautions.

Note: Calf's liver or pork liver can also be used to make a very good pâté mixture to be baked in a terrine, following this recipe.

COLD SALMON PÂTÉ

To Carolyn Gusman, great friend, great cook and great cooking teacher.

Butter crust for pâtés (p. 303)	*Pinch of Cayenne pepper*
1 pound fish fillets (pike, turbot,	*2 teaspoons dried dillweed*
brill or sole)	*1 pound salmon, cut into*
2 whole eggs	*½-inch-wide strips*
¾ cup milk	*1 egg white, lightly beaten, or*
7 slices of white bread, crusts	*¼ cup flour*
removed	*Egg-yolk glaze (p. 421)*
1 cup unsalted butter	*4 cups fish fumet (p. 83)*
3 teaspoons salt	*2 cups watercress or dill*
1 teaspoon white pepper	*mayonnaise (p. 136)*

Make the pastry and chill it. Roll out two thirds of the pastry into a sheet ¼ inch thick. Fit into the pâté mold. Cut the fish fillets into small pieces, and purée in a blender, using the eggs as liquid. Strain and chill.

Bring the milk to a boil and add the crumbled bread slices. Set over medium heat and dry as you would a cream-puff paste (see p. 522), stirring constantly with a wooden spoon or spatula, until the paste does not stick to the spoon any more. Cool completely.

Cream the butter. Gradually add the cold fish purée, the bread mixture, salt, peppers and dill. Chill the forcemeat. Spread a layer of chilled forcemeat ¼ inch thick around the bottom and sides of the dough lining the mold. Cut the salmon into strips and salt and pepper them. Roll them in lightly beaten egg white or flour. Build the pâté as described on page 304. Roll out the rest of the pastry and cut a lid to fit the mold. Put the lid in place and brush with egg-yolk glaze. Bake in a 350°F. oven for 1½ hours. Let cool completely.

Reduce fish *fumet* to 2 cups, clarify it, and cool. When cold but still liquid, gently pour it into the vents of the cooled pâté. Serve chilled with the mayonnaise.

Note: Instead of mixing dillweed with the forecemeat, the pâté can instead be flavored with 2 large truffles. Cut them into ⅓-inch cubes. Or use 24 peeled whole pistachios. Mix either with the forcemeat.

PÂTÉ PANTIN—MEATS IN A CRUST

A *pantin* is a meat or fish pâté baked in a crust without the help of a mold. The crust is usually an ordinary pastry crust, but you can use any pastry you like. In the *kulebiak*, I use *brioche* dough; for Lutèce's hot salmon pâté, I use puff paste.

The most attractive of all meats in a crust is, of course, a fillet of beef. It was sad, a few years back, to see the famous beef Wellington damaged so much by too many cooks trying to—should I say—democratize it? I include here the original recipe for beef Wellington. Both are expensive and time-consuming to prepare, but beautiful to serve.

KULEBIAK OF TROUT
10 TO 12 SERVINGS

This is a warm pâté of Russian origin. The old-fashioned recipe called for *vesiga,* the dried spinal cord of sturgeon, but even modern Russian cookery seems to have given up using it. The *vesiga* added flavor and had great absorptive powers to dispose of excess moisture developed during the baking. The rice serves the latter purpose today. You may use salmon instead of trout.

Brioche de boulanger (*p. 428*), *or* Wiener Kipfeln (*p. 425*), *made with only 2 tablespoons sugar and without cinnamon and lemon rind*	2 *cups white-wine fish* fumet (*p. 83*)
	6 *large onions, minced*
	1 *pound mushrooms, minced*
	1 *tablespoon lemon juice*
6 *trout*	2 *hard-cooked eggs, chopped*
10 *tablespoons butter*	Egg-yolk glaze (*p. 421*)
1 *cup uncooked long-grain rice*	Clarified butter
	Chopped chives

Prepare the *brioche* dough a day ahead and refrigerate overnight.

Braise the trout, cool them, and fillet them. With 3 tablespoons butter, the rice and fish *fumet,* make a small rice pilaf; cool it. Sauté the minced onions in 4 tablespoons butter; sauté the minced mushrooms in 3 tablespoons butter with the lemon juice; cool.

On a pastry cloth or a large linen towel, roll out well-chilled dough into a rectangle 15 by 12 inches. Build the *kulebiak* in layers down the center of the dough rectangle. Use half of the cooked rice, half of the chopped eggs, half of the sautéed onions, half of the sautéed mushrooms. Then arrange the fillets of trout on top and continue with the remainder of the mushrooms, onions, egg and rice. The whole should be well seasoned. Fold the dough over the filling and seal with egg-yolk glaze. Lift the edge of the pastry cloth near you and roll the *kulebiak* over onto a buttered cookie sheet so the seam is on the bottom. Brush with more glaze and trace crisscross lattice patterns on top with the tines of a fork. Bake in a preheated 350°F. oven for 45 minutes. Serve with clarified butter flavored with chives to taste.
Wine: Bâtard-Montrachet

SALMON PÂTÉ LUTÈCE
6 SERVINGS

This is, with André Soltner's permission, the recipe for Lutèce's beautiful salmon pie.

Puff paste (p. 395)	*Salt and pepper*
Pike quenelle *paste* (p. 289)	*2 egg yolks*
2 cups strong white-wine fish	*⅔ cup heavy cream*
fumet (p. 83)	*1 pound salmon fillets* (*cut*
5 tablespoons butter	*toward the tail*), *sautéed in*
3 tablespoons flour	*butter*
2 cups fresh sorrel, chopped	*Egg-yolk glaze* (p. 421)

Make puff paste a day ahead and chill in the refrigerator. Make a paper pattern in the shape of a fish, about 10 inches long and 5 inches wide at the widest part. Make pike *quenelle* paste.

With fish *fumet,* 3 tablespoons of the butter and the flour, make a fish velouté; skim it well. Sauté sorrel in 2 tablespoons butter until all the moisture has evaporated; season with salt and pepper. Enrich the sauce with a liaison of the egg yolks and heavy cream. Add the sorrel to the sauce and correct seasoning.

Butter a cookie sheet; rinse it under cold water. Roll out half of the puff paste into a sheet ⅒ inch thick. Place the fish pattern on the pastry and cut out one fish exactly along the edges of the pattern. Transfer to the cookie sheet. Put the cooked and cooled salmon fillets on this bottom layer. Pipe the *quenelle* paste on top of it. Brush the edge of the pastry with egg-yolk glaze.

Roll out the remainder of the pastry, and cut another fish ¼ inch larger all around than the paper pattern. Place the second pastry fish on top of the *quenelle* paste. Press the edges of the two layers of pastry well together. Make indentations (*chiqueter*) all around the edges of the fish. Brush the whole surface of the fish with egg-yolk glaze. With the rounded end of a knife blade, mark an outline of scales all over the fish. Also outline an eye and a mouth. Bake in the upper third of a 425°F. oven for 25 to 30 minutes, or until golden. Slice into 6 servings and serve with the sauce.

Wine: Champagne, Crémant Blanc de Blancs Brut

BEEF WELLINGTON
10 SERVINGS

This recipe is as close as possible to the original. If you plan to make this dish, be prepared to spend a great deal of money, for the ingredients are costly.

½ *recipe puff paste (p. 395)*
1 *whole fillet of beef, about 6*
   pounds
1 *pound goose liver pâté* (foie
   gras); *no replacement please*
2 *large truffles*

2 *cups* duxelles *(p. 340)*
Egg-yolk glaze (p. 421)
2 *cups classic Madeira sauce*
   (p. 118), made on a base of
   demi-glace sauce

Make the puff paste a day ahead and chill in the refrigerator.

Trim the fillet completely of connective tissues and fat. Remove tail and head ends to keep only the center part weighing about 5 pounds. Broil under high heat for 5 minutes on each side. Let cool completely.

Whip the *foie gras* until fluffy. Spread it evenly all around the meat. Cut the truffles into sticks, and embed them in the *foie gras.* Then spread the *duxelles* on top of the *foie gras.*

Roll out the pastry on a floured kitchen towel into a sheet ⅛ inch thick. Place the meat at its center. Lift the long side of the pastry opposite you up onto the meat. Brush this pastry edge with egg-yolk glaze. Fold the second long side over the first so they overlap by about 1 inch. Cut away the excess pastry at each end of the roast so that only 5 inches are left. With the rolling pin flatten both thicknesses well until the length is 10 inches on each end. Brush the top of these dough flaps with egg-yolk glaze and fold over the roast. Cut off excess dough so that the flap overlaps only 3 inches on the top at each side.

Place a buttered and rinsed cookie sheet in front of the roast, lift the kitchen towel, and invert the roast on the cookie sheet so the seams are underneath. Cut 2 or 3 vents in the top of the *pantin.* Brush with egg-yolk glaze. Decorate to taste with pastry cutouts. Insert a meat thermometer in one of the vents. Bake in a 425°F. oven until brown; the thermometer should register 130°F. Serve with the Madeira sauce. *Wine: Chambertin-Clos de Bèze; Bonnes Mares*

IX

Colors on Your Plate

vegetable cookery

THE PRETTIEST COLORS on your plate are the vivid green, orange, red or yellow shades or hues of vegetables; but are they always that vivid and pretty? Read the suggestions that follow and bid forever goodbye to soggy, pallid, tasteless vegetables.

This chapter includes among the vegetables such nonvegetables as apples (fruit), chestnuts (nuts), mushrooms (fungi). These are foods we use in the same way as vegetables, and they are cooked by the same methods. At the end of the chapter you will find out how to cook rice and how to make your own noodles.

Vegetable cells are held together by pectic substances, which play a role in plants similar to that of collagen in meats. Each cell has walls made of cellulose, which gives each vegetable its proper texture, and a protoplasma containing the minerals, salts, sugars, acids and starches which make up our nutrients and vitamins. Pigments also present in the cells give the vegetable its color; chlorophyll is green, carotene is orange or yellow, flavones are white, and anthocyanins are reddish purple. A vegetable is still alive after being picked; but as soon as it is submitted to heat, the cells cease all activity; with the help of water or steam, the cellulose softens, the pectic substances dissolve to form pectin, the starches swell and absorb moisture. Like meat and fish, vegetables are cooked by moist- or dry-heat cookery methods.

BOILING OR BLANCHING—MOIST-HEAT PROCEDURE

The term *blanching* is used for two different processes. One is the parboiling of strong vegetables before cooking them to remove some of their pungency. The other is the complete cooking of vegetables in a bath of boiling water.

Boil only young and tender vegetables with little cellulose. Use either of those two methods:

VITAMIN METHOD

Drop the vegetables into a pot containing a small amount of boiling liquid, cover, and cook until tender but still crisp. This way, you will retain a maximum of vitamins; however, if the vegetables are not watched very closely, their texture and color can be damaged beyond repair.

TEXTURE METHOD

Immerse the vegetables in a large amount of rapidly boiling water seasoned with 1½ teaspoons of salt per quart. Bring to a second boil. Keep at a rolling boil, uncovered, until the desired doneness has been reached. Drain and serve. Or, if the vegetable is prepared ahead of time, drain and rinse under cold water to stop the cooking. You will retain less vitamins, but you'll be able to control better the taste, texture and color.

For best results, use the texture method and follow these suggestions.

Never cover green vegetables; they release volatile acids that condense on the pot lid, fall back into the pot, and turn the vegetables from emerald to olive green.

To keep white vegetables from yellowing, add a pinch of cream of tartar to the cooking water.

Cook purplish-red vegetables in water containing an apple or a little vinegar.

Do not add baking soda to the cooking water; it bites through the outer layers of the vegetables, renders them mushy, and completely destroys thiamin, one of the B-complex vitamins.

Never attempt to keep vegetables warm after boiling them; they will become mushy and lose color and texture. Cool them completely under cold water, roll them in a towel to absorb the excess moisture, and reheat them in their seasoning butter or sauce.

To cream 1 pound of boiled vegetables, use cream or a cream sauce made in one of the following ways.

Another way to sauce them is with a compound or flavored butter. Examples of several of these will be found in the chapter on sauces (pp. 145 to 149).

LIQUID	BUTTER	FLOUR
⅔ cup heavy cream, reduced by half	—	—
1 cup chicken broth, milk, or light cream	*2 tablespoons*	*1½ tablespoons*
½ cup cooking water plus ½ cup heavy cream	*2 tablespoons*	*1½ tablespoons*

FROZEN ARTICHOKE HEARTS
6 SERVINGS

Frozen artichoke hearts offer a practical shortcut to small artichokes of even size, without the need for extensive preparations or trimming, In many areas this is the only possible way to enjoy very small artichokes.

Rather than follow the instructions given on the package, bring 3 quarts of water to a boil, add 2 packages (10 ounces each) of frozen hearts, and boil rapidly for 8 minutes. Drain.

Serve with one of these warm dressings:
- ❀ ⅔ to 1 cup Hollandaise or Mousseline Sauce; spoon on top;
- ❀ 1 cup light Béchamel Sauce; mix into the artichokes, then sprinkle with ½ cup grated cheese and broil quickly;
- ❀ Tarragon Butter; toss the artichokes in the butter.

Or use a cold dressing:
- ❀ toss in ¼ cup salad dressing of your choice;
- ❀ toss in ⅓ cup Mayonnaise.

ARTICHOKE BOTTOMS
6 SERVINGS

Remove all the leaves, the choke and the stems of 6 large fresh artichokes. Trim the bottoms with a paring knife and immediately immerse in cold water acidulated with lemon juice.

Mix 2 quarts water with ¼ cup salad oil, ½ cup flour, 2 table-spoons lemon juice and ½ teaspoon salt. This mixture is called a *blanc* (a white solution); in this the combined effects of the flour starches, oil and citric acid, which coat and bleach the artichokes, keep the vegetables from darkening.

Bring the solution to a boil. Add the artichoke bottoms and boil for 8 to 10 minutes. Test the doneness with a large sewing needle. Serve as a vegetable; fill the bottoms with Hollandaise or Mousseline Sauce.

When served as a garnish to a large piece of meat, artichokes can be filled with other small vegetables, boiled and buttered, creamed or braised.

WHOLE FRESH ARTICHOKES
6 SERVINGS

Cut off the stems and leaf tips of 6 large fresh artichokes. Bring 6 quarts of water to a boil. Drop in the vegetables and boil for 35 to 45 minutes, according to size. Drain upside down in a colander. Pry the leaves open and remove the choke with a teaspoon.

Serve with a warm dressing: 1½ cups Virgin Butter or Hollandaise or Mousseline Sauce.

Or use a cold dressing: 1½ cups salad dressing or Mayonnaise.

ASPARAGUS
6 SERVINGS

Use 2 pounds asparagus. Bend each stalk head to stem; it will break at exactly the place where the fibers stop being edible. Peel with a potato peeler from the blossom end down, starting just under the close crop of leaves. Assemble the stalks in bundles of small, medium or large asparagus.

Immerse in 4 quarts boiling water; boil tiny asparagus for 2 to 3 minutes; small asparagus for 5 minutes; medium-size asparagus for 6 to 8 minutes; large asparagus for 8 to 10 minutes; jumbo asparagus for 11 minutes.

Never steam green asparagus, or they will discolor. French and Italian cooks can steam their asparagus because they both use the white variety called Argenteuil or the Italian purple-tipped asparagus.

Serve with a warm dressing: 1½ cups Maltaise, Mikado, Hollandaise or Mousseline Sauce.

Or use a cold dressing: 1½ cups salad dressing or Mayonnaise.

GREEN OR WAX BEANS

The best-tasting green or wax beans are fresh rather than frozen and about ¼ inch wide. At that stage their flavor is at its peak because the starches have not yet started to mature in the tissues. When using larger beans, french them. Frenching means to remove the strings on both sides of the pod with a paring knife.

Use 3 quarts boiling water per pound of vegetable. Boil frenched beans for about 8 minutes, young tender beans ¼ inch wide for about the same length of time, and whole larger beans for up to 15 minutes. Taste often for desired crispness.

Serve with a warm dressing: Ravigote Butter, Snail Butter or Maître d'Hôtel Butter.

Or use a cold dressing: a salad dressing of your choice.

BROCCOLI AND CAULIFLOWER
6 SERVINGS

Separate 1 large head of cauliflower or 1 bunch of broccoli into flowerets. Peel the stems; if you do not, the flowerets will be too soft before the stems are tender. Cut a cross about 1 inch deep in stems that are 1 inch thick or thicker. As soon as peeled, soak in acidulated water to remove insects. Blanch (parboil) only if desired and then only for 1 or 2 minutes.

Boil in 3 quarts of rapidly boiling water. Use unsalted water if you are cooking cauliflower, for salt darkens it considerably. Drain the flowerets upside down in a colander. The cooking time will vary with your personal taste; taste the vegetable often. Broccoli tastes best when the stems are still bright green and appear translucent.

Serve with a warm dressing:

❀ 1½ cups Hollandaise or Caper Hollandaise;
❀ Polish Butter;
❀ ½ cup Noisette Butter in which 2 tablespoons sesame seeds have been slowly fried.

BRUSSELS SPROUTS
6 SERVINGS

Remove the outer leaves of 1½ pounds of sprouts. Cut a tiny cross in the root end of each sprout to keep it from bursting apart while cooking. Blanch (parboil) only large sprouts. Boil in 4 quarts water, 12 minutes for baby sprouts, 15 minutes for larger sprouts.

Serve with a warm dressing:
❀ butter and celery salt;
❀ cream, top with ½ cup grated cheese, then broil quickly;
❀ mix with ½ pound chestnuts, boiled and buttered.

CARROTS
6 SERVINGS

Preferably use fresh carrots; freezing damages the tissue considerably; the large gaps left between the fibers by the thawed ice crystals give the cooked carrot a spongy texture.

Peel 1 pound carrots and cut into pieces 1 inch by ⅓ inch. Immerse in 3 quarts boiling water, and boil for 10 to 12 minutes.

Serve with a warm dressing:
❀ butter and freshly grated nutmeg;
❀ Ravigote Butter or Maître d'Hôtel Butter;
❀ Brandy Glaze: Mix 3 tablespoons butter, 1 teaspoon sugar, ½ cup White Stock (p. 76), 2 teaspoons lemon juice and 2 tablespoons brandy in a small pan. Reduce to 3 tablespoons. Roll the hot carrots in the glaze.

CUCUMBERS
6 SERVINGS

Peel 2 large cucumbers and cut them into halves. Remove the seeds and cut the pulp into small triangles. Boil in 3 quarts of rapidly boiling water for about 5 minutes.

Serve with a warm dressing: an herb-butter of your choice (dill and basil taste best), or cream sauce, plain or with herbs.

PEAS
6 SERVINGS

Boil only medium-size peas; tiny peas taste better pot roasted (see p. 334). Boil 1 pound shelled peas in 3 quarts rapidly boiling water for 5 to 6 minutes. For a special flavor add a sprig of fresh mint or 1 tablespoon dried mint to the boiling water.

Serve with a warm dressing:

❉ butter, a pinch of sugar, salt and pepper;
❉ Mint Butter;
❉ mix with ½ pound Braised White Onions (p. 332);
❉ mix with 2 slices of bacon, cooked until crisp and crumbled.

POTATOES
6 SERVINGS

Potatoes that are being cooked in water should always be started in cold water to allow the starches to swell little by little.

For potatoes boiled in their jackets, use smaller California new potatoes, Red Bliss potatoes, or Maine potatoes. Count 1 potato for each woman or child and 2 potatoes for each man. Scrub them thoroughly, immerse in cold water, and bring to a boil. Add 1 teaspoon salt per quart of water. Simmer for 20 minutes.

Serve with a warm seasoning: plain butter, preferably unsalted.

Or use a cold dressing if the potatoes are used for a salad.

For peeled and cut potatoes, use California new potatoes, Red Bliss or Maine potatoes. Count 1 large potato per person. Trim the vegetables into chunks the size of a very small pullet egg. Take off the sharp angles with a paring knife; if not removed, these angles over-cook, fall off in the water, become mushy, and coat the potatoes with an unpleasant layer of starches. Cover with cold water and bring to a boil. Add 1 teaspoon salt per quart of water and simmer for 18 to 20 minutes.

Serve with a warm dressing: plain butter, or an herb butter.

JARDINIÈRE OF VEGETABLES
6 SERVINGS

This classic vegetable mixture makes a perfect garnish for any red or white meat.

2 large carrots	*1 cup green beans, cut slantwise*
2 large white turnips	*into ½-inch pieces*
1 ½ cups excellent veal or	*1 cup medium-size peas*
chicken stock	*1 head of cauliflower*
Salt and pepper	*⅔ cup heavy cream*
Pinch of sugar	*2 teaspoons chopped chives*
1 ½ tablespoons butter	

Peel and trim carrots and turnips and cut into pieces 1 by ⅓ inch. Round off all the sharp angles with a paring knife so the vegetables can roll in butter without breaking. Cover with cold stock; add ½ teaspoon salt, a dash of pepper, the sugar and butter; cook until the stock has completely evaporated. Boil green beans and peas. Drain them well and add them to the carrots and turnips. Cut the cauli-flower into flowerets, and boil; drain. Reduce the heavy cream by half, and add chopped chives and salt and pepper to taste. Correct the sea-soning of the glazed vegetables. Arrange the glazed vegetables around the meat; at intervals add cauliflowerets topped with reduced and sea-soned cream.

VEGETABLE PURÉES

Only vegetables containing a large amount of starches can be strained through a food mill or fine sieve (*tamis*) to obtain a thick purée, so that the most common purée to be served is mashed white or sweet potatoes. Since green vegetables and some of the yellow vegetables contain mostly cellulose and water, they produce purées that are too liquid; as a result they do not have a pleasant appearance. Your vegetable repertoire will be enlarged considerably if you enrich it with recipes for vegetable purées made by blending green or yellow vegetables with mashed potatoes.

Potatoes should never be puréed in an electric blender. The pulp of potatoes contains gluten-producing proteins, which produce a gummy and stringy purée when subjected to the mechanical action of the blender. Instead, purée potatoes through a food mill or sieve (*tamis*) or large conical strainer. Push the potato pulp downward and toward yourself without the slightest back-and-forth motion that would start gluten development.

Any liquid—stock, milk, cream—that is added to a purée containing a small or large amount of potatoes must be warm, or the finished preparation will acquire a definite taste of stale potato starch.

As with other starches, potato starch has a tendency to hydrolyze if submitted to a burst of violent heat (see Starch-Bound Sauces, p. 104). Therefore it is imperative to reheat a potato purée very gradually; if you proceed too quickly, you will see the purée become rather liquid and soupy. "Dry" any purée by stirring it over medium heat to evaporate excess moisture.

POTATO PURÉE OR MASHED POTATOES

6 SERVINGS

6 medium-size Idaho or Maine potatoes
Salt
⅓ cup heavy cream, scalded
¾ cup butter
Grated nutmeg (optional)

Peel the potatoes, cut into pieces, and cover with cold water. Bring to a boil and add 1 teaspoon salt per quart of water. Simmer for 18 to 20 minutes; drain. Push the potatoes through a *tamis* or conical strainer. Add the scalded heavy cream and the butter. Beat well with a wooden spoon or spatula to homogenize. Correct the seasoning and add nutmeg if desired.

Serve with any meats.

YAM OR SWEET-POTATO PURÉE
6 SERVINGS

6 medium-size yams or sweet potatoes	2 to 3 tablespoons dry sherry
¼ cup heavy cream, scalded	½ cup butter
	Salt and pepper

Peel the yams or potatoes and cut into pieces. Boil until tender. Push through a *tamis* or conical strainer. Add the hot cream, sherry and butter. Beat well with a wooden spoon until homogenous. Correct the seasoning.

PURÉE OF PEAS
6 SERVINGS

2 bags (24 ounces each) frozen large peas	⅓ teaspoon sugar
⅓ cup butter	¼ teaspoon pepper, or more
	Salt

Boil the peas until they are almost overcooked for complete development of the starches; drain. Blend quickly in the blender only long enough to break the pea skins. Then push through a *tamis* or conical strainer. Add butter, sugar, pepper, and salt to taste. Pipe into cooked artichoke bottoms, using a pastry bag, to make a beautiful vegetable garnish.

PURÉE OF LIMA OR NAVY BEANS
6 SERVINGS

2 pounds fresh lima beans,   *¾ cup butter*
cooked, or 1 cup dried navy   *Salt and pepper*
beans, cooked

Push the beans through a *tamis* or conical strainer. Add the butter, season to taste, and beat well with a wooden spoon.

Serve with roast beef or lamb.

CHESTNUT PURÉE
6 SERVINGS

2 pounds chestnuts   *Salt and pepper*
Veal, beef or chicken stock   *⅓ cup heavy cream*
(about 2 cups)   *2 tablespoons dry Madeira*
1 small head of celery, center   *¼ cup butter*
ribs, 2½ inches long

First shell the nuts. Cut a gash ⅛ inch deep on the rounded side of each nut. Immerse them in boiling water. Lift out a few nuts at a time and remove the shells and skins with a paring knife. Keep the rest of the nuts in the water while you are peeling.

Cover the shelled and peeled nuts with cold stock and bring to a boil. Add the celery, ½ teaspoon salt and ⅛ teaspoon pepper. Simmer until the stock has been completely absorbed and the nuts are falling apart. Remove the celery. Push the nuts through a *tamis* or conical strainer. Toss the purée over medium-high heat, stirring well with a wooden spoon or spatula until completely dry. Blend in cream, Madeira and butter. Correct seasoning.

Serve for winter meals with poultry and venison.

ARTICHOKE PURÉE
6 SERVINGS

6 large or 9 small artichoke   ¼ cup butter
    bottoms   Salt and pepper
1½ cups mashed potatoes
    (p. 323)

Cook the artichoke bottoms in a *blanc* (p. 318). Push the cooked artichokes through a *tamis* or conical strainer. Mix with the mashed potatoes. Add butter and salt and pepper to taste. Beat well with a wooden spoon.

Serve with veal and poultry.

PURÉE OF GREEN BEANS
6 SERVINGS

1½ pounds green beans   ⅓ cup butter
1½ cups mashed potatoes   Salt and pepper
    (p. 323)

Boil the green beans (p. 319) and purée them in a blender. Mix with the mashed potatoes. Add butter and salt and pepper to taste. Beat well with a wooden spoon.

Serve with beef and lamb.

LETTUCE PURÉE
6 SERVINGS

6 cups hot chopped braised   ¼ cup butter
    Boston lettuce (p. 331)   3 bacon slices, cooked crisp and
2 cups hot mashed potatoes   crumbled
    (p. 323)

Put the braised lettuce in the container of a blender and purée on medium speed. Mix with the mashed potatoes; add butter and bacon and stir well.

Serve with veal and poultry.

PURÉE OF CARROTS OR YELLOW TURNIPS (RUTABAGAS)

6 SERVINGS

1 pound carrots or yellow turnips	*¼ cup butter*
½ cup heavy cream	*Salt and pepper*
1 cup hot mashed potatoes	
(p. 323)	

Boil the carrots or turnips until tender, and drain. Put the hot vegetables in a frying pan and add the cream. Shake the pan back and forth over low heat until the cream has reduced completely and coats the vegetables. Purée the creamed vegetables in the blender. Mix the purée with the mashed potatoes. Beat in the butter and add salt and pepper to taste.

Serve with poultry, veal, ham.

BRAISING VEGETABLES—MOIST-HEAT PROCEDURE

In braising, which is very close in principle to the braising of red meats (see p. 193), there is constant exchange between the vegetable tissues and the cooking liquid. The vegetables will not retain their color since the volatile acids are given ample time to dissolve in the steam and cooking juices. The vitamins are completely destroyed, and the texture is soft. However, the taste is delicious, since the vegetable essences are mixed with the reduced meat stock.

Braise only vegetables containing a large amount of cellulose and fibers. Line the braising pot or dish with 4 bacon slices or 3 tablespoons butter. Blanch (parboil) the vegetables; start the blanching in cold water if the vegetable is extremely pungent; drain well. Put in the braising pot or baking dish; add enough stock to barely cover, and salt and pepper. Cover with a buttered paper forming an inverted lid, then with the pot lid or a tight-fitting piece of foil. If the juices do not completely reduce by the time the vegetables are cooked—and this does happen—pour juices into a small pot and reduce them to a glaze. Spoon the glaze over the vegetables. The vegetables may be braised in a 325°F. oven or over slow direct heat.

BRAISED BELGIAN ENDIVES
6 SERVINGS

Endives must be perfectly white with barely yellow tips. Should the tips be green, the vegetable will be bitter. To keep endives sweet, keep them tightly wrapped in dark paper in a cool place until you are ready to use them. Remove the root cone with a paring knife if the endive is large.

12 Belgian endives	*1 tablespoon lemon juice*
3 tablespoons butter	*Salt and pepper*
1 cup water	

Do not blanch endives. Wash them quickly under running cold water. Butter the baking dish, arrange the vegetables in it, and add the water and lemon juice. Season with salt and pepper. Cook covered over low direct heat for 35 to 40 minutes.

Excellent with poultry and veal.

BRAISED RED CABBAGE
6 SERVINGS

4 bacon slices	*2 tablespoons flour*
1 head of red cabbage, shredded	*Salt and pepper*
2 apples, grated	*1 cup Zinfandel wine*
¼ teaspoon ground cinnamon	

Do not blanch the cabbage. Line a 3-quart braising pot with the bacon. Add half of the cabbage and 1 grated apple. Sprinkle with half of the cinnamon, half of the flour, and a little salt and pepper. Add the rest of the ingredients in the same order. Add the wine. Bring to a boil over direct heat, then braise in a 325°F. oven for 1¼ hours.

BRAISED WHITE CABBAGE
6 SERVINGS

4 bacon slices
1 head of white cabbage, cut into 6 wedges
2 onions, chopped

1 tablespoon caraway seeds
Salt and pepper
1 cup chicken stock

Line a 3-quart braising pot with the bacon. Add half of the cabbage and sprinkle with 1 chopped onion, ½ tablespoon of the caraway seeds, and a little salt and pepper. Add the rest of the ingredients in the same order. Add the chicken stock. Bring to a boil over direct heat, then braise in a 325°F. oven for 1½ hours.

All cabbage dishes are excellent with roast pork, roast goose, corned beef and all kinds of sausages.

BRAISED CELERIAC AND CELERY
6 SERVINGS

The same method may be applied to celeriac (celery knob or celery root), Golden Heart celery (pale green), or Pascal celery (deep green).

6 small celeriacs, cubed, or 1 whole celery heart, cut into 1-inch chunks

4 bacon slices
Salt and pepper
1 cup veal or chicken stock

Blanch the vegetable, starting in cold water. Line a 3-quart braising pot with the bacon. Add the blanched celery or celeriac, sprinkle with salt and pepper, and add the stock. Bring to a boil over direct heat, then braise, covered, in a 325°F. oven, 35 minutes for celeriac, 1½ hours for celery.

Either vegetable is excellent with all meats.

BRAISED ESCAROLE
6 SERVINGS

2 large heads of escarole	Salt and pepper
3 tablespoons butter, softened	½ cup grated full-cream
⅔ cup boiling veal or chicken stock	mozzarella cheese

Trim the root ends of the escaroles, and wash the heads thoroughly under running cold water. Cut each head into 3 wedges. Blanch in boiling water for 3 minutes; drain well.

Rub the butter on the bottom and sides of a baking dish. With each wedge of escarole, form a tight bundle by wrapping the large outer leaves around the light green center leaves. Put the bundles in the bottom of the baking dish and add the boiling stock and a little salt and pepper. Cover and bake in a 325°F. oven for about 30 minutes. Uncover, sprinkle the greens with the grated cheese, and bake for another 10 minutes.

Excellent with veal, especially *scaloppine* and chops.

BRAISED FENNEL
6 SERVINGS

3 heads of fennel	¼ cup grated Emmenthal or
3 tablespoons butter, softened	Gruyère cheese
¾ cup boiling veal or chicken stock	2 tablespoons grated Parmesan
Salt and pepper	cheese

Trim the core and the tougher outer leaves of the fennel heads. Cut into halves. Blanch in boiling water for 5 minutes. Rub the butter on the bottom and sides of a baking dish. Arrange the fennel in the dish and add the boiling stock and a little salt and pepper. Cover and bake in a 325°F. oven for 1 hour. Remove the cover, sprinkle with the mixed grated cheeses, and bake for 30 minutes more, still at 325°F.

Excellent with roast lamb or lamb chops, chicken cutlets, veal chops and *scaloppine*.

BRAISED LEEKS
6 SERVINGS

12 large leeks, white part only	*Salt and pepper*
4 bacon slices	*⅓ cup heavy cream, whipped*
⅔ cup boiling veal or chicken	*and lightly salted (optional)*
stock	

Wash leeks carefully under running cold water. Blanch in boiling water. Line a baking dish with the bacon, add the blanched leeks, and cover them with the boiling stock. Season. Cover and bake in a 325°F. oven for 35 minutes. Uncover the dish and spoon the whipped cream over the leeks. Slide under the broiler for 1 minute.

Excellent with all types of beef preparations.

BRAISED LETTUCE
6 SERVINGS

3 heads of Boston or Red lettuce	*Salt and pepper*
3 tablespoons butter, softened	*⅓ cup mushroom butter*
½ cup boiling chicken or veal	*(p. 142)*
stock	

Trim the root ends of the lettuces and cut the heads into halves. Wash under running cold water. Wrap the lettuce hearts with the larger outer leaves to make tight bundles. Rub a baking dish with the butter, add the lettuce, and cover with the boiling stock. Season. Cover and bake in a 325°F. oven for 30 to 35 minutes. Drain off the cooking juices and reduce to 1 tablespoon. Blend with the mushroom butter and spoon over the lettuce hearts before serving.

Excellent with chicken, turkey and veal.

BRAISED WHITE ONIONS
6 SERVINGS

1 pound small white onions	*⅓ cup veal or chicken stock*
(silverskins)	*Salt and pepper*
3 tablespoons butter	

Drop the unpeeled onions into boiling water and leave them for 1 minute. Drop into cold water until cool enough to handle, then squeeze them out of their skins. Cut a tiny cross in the root side of each onion so that the moisture can penetrate evenly on both sides of the vegetables; this keeps the onion from breaking open while cooking.

Mix butter and stock in a thick pot and add a little salt and pepper. Add the onions, cover, and cook over medium to low direct heat for about 40 minutes, or until tender.

Excellent with all meats.

BRAISED SPINACH AND OTHER CHOPPED GREENS
6 SERVINGS

2 pounds fresh spinach or other	*3 tablespoons butter*
greens	*½ cup chicken or veal stock*
1 onion, chopped	

Clean the greens thoroughly; remove tough stems and wilted leaves. Chop; there should be about 8 cups. For full taste do not blanch. Sauté onion in butter. Transfer to a baking pot and add the stock and chopped greens. Cover tightly and bake in a 325°F. oven for 20 to 25 minutes. Drain off all the cooking juices and reduce them to 1 to 2 tablespoons.

Toss the greens with any of these dressings:
- ✿ mix reduced cooking juices with 2 tablespoons butter and ¼ teaspoon freshly grated nutmeg;
- ✿ cook 3 bacon slices until crisp, and crumble;
- ✿ chop hard-cooked egg and mix with 3 tablespoons sour cream;
- ✿ reduce ⅔ cup heavy cream to ⅓ cup.

OUR FAMILY SAUERKRAUT
6 SERVINGS

Use a large enameled cast-iron braising pot. The recipe does not contain an apple.

4 pounds sauerkraut, processed without sugar	6 peppercorns
3 large onions, chopped	1 bay leaf
¼ pound lard, or ½ cup rendered goose fat	½ teaspoon caraway seeds
	1 pound slab bacon, blanched
2 cups California Emerald Riesling or French Sylvaner	6 smoked pork chops
	6 frankfurters or knackwurst
2 to 3 cups veal or chicken stock	¾ cup whipped butter
10 juniper berries	Salt if necessary
	6 potatoes (Red Bliss), boiled

Wash sauerkraut under running cold water three times; spread on a thick towel and squeeze dry. Sauté onions in melted lard or goose fat. Add sauerkraut, wine and enough stock to cover the sauerkraut; bring to a boil. Add juniper berries and all the spices. Cover with a buttered paper and the pot lid. Bake in a 325°F. oven for 2 hours.

Add bacon and chops, and bake for another hour. Uncover the pot, add wurst and butter, and bake for another 30 minutes. Pile sauerkraut on a platter; surround with meats and potatoes. Should any cooking juices remain, boil them down quickly to 3 tablespoons and spoon them over the kraut.

Wine: California Emerald Riesling or *French Sylvaner*

POT ROASTING VEGETABLES—
MOIST-HEAT PROCEDURE

This is the French *à l'étuvée* method sometimes called "flavor-sealed" in the United States. The method should only be used for vegetables that are young and contain new cellulose that can be softened in a relatively short time by the vegetables' own moisture.

Zucchini, summer squash, young peas (the typical recipe is that for *petits pois à la française*), frenched young green beans and young carrots can be cooked in this manner. Vegetables containing a little more cellulose can also be cooked in this manner if a very small amount of liquid is added to the pot to produce additional moisture.

Melt a few tablespoons of butter, add the raw vegetables—sliced, shredded or diced—and season with salt and pepper. Cover the pot tightly and cook over very low heat until just tender. Overcooking will result in mushy vegetables. There is no loss of vitamins if the vegetables are kept crisp.

ZUCCHINI BASILICO
6 SERVINGS

Summer squash also can be prepared this way. Change the herb to tarragon, dill or any other you like.

> 6 *small zucchini, unpeeled*   ½ *teaspoon dried basil*
> 2 *tablespoons olive oil*   *Salt and pepper*

Clean zucchini and cut into ¼-inch slices. Heat the oil and add zucchini, basil and a little salt and pepper. Cover and cook for 5 minutes. Toss, cover again, and cook for another 5 minutes. Do not cook for more than 10 to 12 minutes altogether.

Excellent with all meats.

SHREDDED CARROTS
6 SERVINGS

2 small onions, chopped fine	*Salt and pepper*
2 tablespoons butter	*1 tablespoon lemon juice*
1½ pounds carrots, shredded to	*4 tablespoons whipped butter*
fine julienne	*1 to 2 tablespoons fine-chopped*
¼ teaspoon freshly grated	*parsley*
nutmeg (optional)	

Sauté onions in hot butter until soft. Add carrots, nutmeg and a little salt and pepper. Cover tightly, and cook over low heat for 15 to 20 minutes. At regular intervals shake the pot to distribute butter and seasonings; do not use a fork or spoon for either might mash the vegetables. Add lemon juice, whipped butter and chopped parsley, and shake the pot again to blend.

Excellent with all meats.

RAGOUT OF PEAS AND ARTICHOKES
6 SERVINGS

For the proper taste of this French country dish, both of the vegetables must be overcooked.

4 tablespoons butter	*Salt and pepper*
2 packages (10 ounces each)	*1 package (10 ounces) frozen*
frozen artichoke hearts	*early peas (not medium peas)*
1 dime-size piece of lemon rind	*2 tablespoons chopped parsley*
1 teaspoon dried tarragon	
3 tablespoons chicken stock or	
water	

Melt butter; add frozen artichokes, lemon rind, tarragon, stock or water, and a little salt and pepper. Cover the pot tightly and cook over low heat for 10 minutes.

Defrost the peas under running cold water, then add to the artichokes. Toss well, cover the pot again, and continue cooking until the vegetables are tender, 10 to 15 minutes. Remove the lemon rind and correct the seasoning. Add the parsley and serve.

Excellent with chicken cutlets.

MARIE BECKER'S GREEN BEANS
6 SERVINGS

¼ pound slab bacon, unblanched
6 tablespoons butter
1 pound green beans, frenched
Salt and pepper

3 red potatoes, peeled and cut
into rounded chunks (see
p. 322)

Cut bacon into ½-inch pieces. Render slowly until golden. Discard the liquid bacon fat and replace it with butter. Add beans and season with salt and pepper. Cover tightly and cook over very low heat for 15 minutes. Shake the pot, then add 1 or 2 tablespoons of water if necessary. Let cook for another 15 minutes.

Add the potato chunks, hiding them among the beans. Continue cooking for 20 more minutes. The beans will be completely discolored, but the taste will be delicious. Serve without delay.

PANFRYING VEGETABLES—DRY-HEAT PROCEDURE

There is no set rule for panfrying vegetables. Each vegetable is panfried following the procedure best adapted to its texture. The goal in panfrying is to seal the moisture inside the vegetable. If the vegetable is starchy, there will be no problem. If the vegetable is filled with moisture, this moisture will be released by the breaking tissues and constantly interfere with the formation of a crust. Use these guidelines:

Starchy vegetables   Use clarified butter or oil. Keep the initial heat high so as to build a crust and seal the moisture inside the vegetable.

Turn down the heat to give the starches time to absorb the sealed-in moisture and soften. Salt and pepper after frying only. This procedure applies to raw potatoes, raw butternut squash, cooked white and sweet potatoes.

Moist vegetables Use oil. Slice the vegetables into ⅓-inch slices, flour the slices, and sauté, keeping the heat rather high. Salt and pepper after frying only. This applies to tomatoes, zucchini and summer squash, eggplant.

Mushrooms (a special case) Use butter, oil, or a mixture of both. The abundant moisture of mushrooms must be removed before they can be used in a dish or sauce, or the dish will be "flooded" and thinned without remission. Add mushrooms to the hot fat in a frying pan, season with salt and pepper, and sprinkle with lemon juice. Watch the water pour out of the mushrooms; keep cooking over high heat until it has completely evaporated. The mushrooms are ready.

SAUTÉED APPLES
6 SERVINGS

Of course apples are not vegetables, but they are often used in the same way as a vegetable to accompany meats.

6 Red Delicious or Golden Grimes apples	Salt and pepper
¼ cup clarified butter	2 tablespoons applejack or Calvados
¼ teaspoon sugar	

Peel the apples and cut each into 6 slices. Heat the clarified butter until it bubbles well, add apples, and sauté over high heat. Add sugar and a little salt and pepper, and continue sautéing until the apples are browned and all their moisture has evaporated. Add applejack or Calvados and continue to sauté until it has evaporated.

These seasonings may be replaced by 1 tablespoon brown sugar, a pinch of salt and ¼ teaspoon ground cinnamon; in that case use no spirits.

Excellent with roast chicken, sautéed chicken, pork, ham.

SAUTÉED BUTTERNUT SQUASH
6 SERVINGS

2 small butternut squashes	*2 tablespoons chopped pecans*
½ cup clarified butter	*2 tablespoons dry sherry*

Peel squashes and cut them into ⅓-inch slices. Sauté in clarified butter until brown, turn over, and brown on the second side. Remove to a warm serving platter.

Toss pecans in the hot butter left in the pan. Turn off the heat and add the sherry; toss well together and spoon over the slices of squash.

SAUTÉED EGGPLANT
6 SERVINGS

2 small eggplants	*2 tablespoons chopped fresh*
Salt	*parsley or fine-cut basil leaves*
⅓ cup flour	*1 small garlic clove, minced*
⅓ cup olive oil	

Peel the eggplants and cut them into ⅓-inch-thick slices. If you prefer the eggplant not too pungent, sprinkle the slices with salt; let them stand for at least 35 to 40 minutes. Drain off the water that is extracted by the salt, pat slices dry, and flour. Otherwise flour the slices as soon as peeled and cut.

Brown in hot olive oil for 5 to 6 minutes on each side. Remove to a hot serving platter. Add the herbs and garlic to the oil in the pan, toss without letting them brown, and spoon over the eggplant slices.

SAUTÉED MUSHROOMS
6 SERVINGS

1 ½ pounds whole button	*¼ cup butter*
mushrooms, or large	*Salt and pepper*
mushrooms quartered or	*1 tablespoon lemon juice*
minced	

Cut off the mushroom stem ends. Wipe mushrooms clean with a towel. Wash them only if very dirty and then only under running cold water and as fast as possible. Never soak mushrooms or they will become rubbery. Never peel mushrooms or they will lose much of their taste.

Heat the butter until the foam starts receding. Add the mushrooms, a little salt and pepper and the lemon juice. Keep tossing over high heat until mushrooms are brown and dry.

MUSTARD MUSHROOMS
6 SERVINGS

1 ½ pounds mushrooms	*2 tablespoons chopped parsley*
1 tablespoon prepared Dijon-style	*1 very small garlic clove, minced*
mustard	

Sauté the mushrooms as in the preceding recipe until brown and dry. Stir in the mustard, parsley and garlic. Serve immediately.

Excellent with steak, veal chops, sautéed chicken.

CREAMED MUSHROOMS
6 SERVINGS

1 ½ pounds mushrooms	*Salt and pepper*
⅔ cup heavy cream	
2 tablespoons dry Madeira or	
sherry or a little grated nutmeg	

Sauté the mushrooms until brown and dry. Add the cream and wine and a little more salt and pepper. Shake the pan back and forth over medium heat until the cream coats the mushrooms. Do not overcook or the cream will separate into proteins coating the mushrooms and butter coating the bottom of the pan. In case of separation of the cream, add 2 to 3 tablespoons of stock or water to reinstate the cream to its semiliquid coating state.

Excellent with veal chops, chicken, turkey, ham.

MUSHROOM DUXELLES
(A PERSONAL INTERPRETATION)

Duxelles is used as a stuffing, as a filling for tartlet shells, as addition to a white sauce. It was created by François de La Varenne, otherwise known as *Le Cuisinier François*. Since the old form of the adjective *français* was *françois*, it was often believed that this name meant "the French cook," but François here means Francis, the translation of the French first name François.

2 tablespoons fine-chopped onion	*3 tablespoons Madiera or white*
6 tablespoons butter	*wine*
1 pound mushrooms, minced	*3 tablespoons fresh bread crumbs*
2 tablespoons fine-chopped	*(optional)*
shallots	*½ cup heavy cream*
Salt and pepper	*1 truffle, minced (optional)*

Sauté onion in butter until golden. Add mushrooms, shallots, salt and pepper. Sauté over high heat until all the moisture has evaporated. Add the wine and let it evaporate. Add bread crumbs, cream, and truffle if used. Cook over low heat until thick and almost dry.

The method of wringing the chopped mushrooms in the corner of a towel is not recommended, since much of the mushroom flavor goes with the juice and is lost. This method uses all of the juices and concentrates them over high heat. Use at once, or store, or freeze *duxelles*. The best size jar for storing is a 4-ounce baby-food jar.

COOKED POTATOES

For all the variations given here, start with potatoes boiled in their jackets (see p. 321). Wash and scrub medium-size Red Bliss or Maine potatoes. Cover them with cold water. Bring the water slowly to a boil. Add 1 teaspoon salt per quart of water, and simmer for 20 minutes.

HOME FRIES
6 SERVINGS

2 cups of ⅛-inch slices of boiled
  potatoes
¼ cup butter

¼ cup oil of your choice
Salt and pepper
2 tablespoons chopped parsley

Sauté the potatoes in the mixture of butter and oil until golden on both sides. Drain on paper towels. Season with salt and pepper and sprinkle with chopped parsley.

Excellent with eggs or steak.

LYONNAISE POTATOES
6 SERVINGS

2 cups of ⅛-inch slices of boiled
  potatoes
⅓ cup oil
1 cup minced onions

¼ cup butter
1 teaspoon vinegar
Salt and pepper
2 tablespoons chopped parsley

Sauté the potatoes in hot oil until brown on both sides. Meanwhile sauté minced onions in hot butter until golden; add vinegar and a little salt and pepper to the cooked onions. Drain the cooked potatoes on paper towels. Toss onions and potatoes together. Serve immediately, sprinkled with the chopped parsley and with more salt and pepper if needed.

Serve with eggs or red meats.

SWISS RÖSTI
6 SERVINGS

¼ cup lard, butter or oil
1½ cups shredded cooked
  potatoes

Salt and pepper

Heat the chosen fat. Add the shredded potatoes and shape them into a ⅓-inch-thick cake. Brown slowly until a golden crust has formed. Slide onto a plate and reverse in the pan. Fry the other side to the same brown color. Drain on a paper towel. Sprinkle with salt and pepper before serving.

Serve with wurst, eggs and red meats.

UNCOOKED POTATOES

In all cases use enough large Red Bliss or Maine potatoes to obtain 3 cups of cut and trimmed potatoes ready to cook. The potatoes may, if desired, be first blanched (parboiled). Start in cold salted water and blanch for 3 to 4 minutes; drain. Keep the potatoes rolled in towels until they are to be fried.

NOISETTE, CHÂTEAU, PARISIENNE POTATOES
6 SERVINGS

Noisette potatoes are cut into small ¾-inch balls with a "Parisian spoon" or simply with a melon-baller. *Château potatoes* are cut and trimmed into pieces the shape and size of jumbo olives. *Parisienne potatoes* are identical to noisette potatoes, but after they have been sautéed and cooked they are seasoned with 2 tablespoons of melted meat glaze (sorry, no meat extract!) and sprinkled with fine-chopped parsley.

½ cup clarified butter	*2 tablespoons meat glaze, for*
3 cups potatoes	*Parisienne potatoes only*
Salt and pepper	

Heat clarified butter until bubbly and deep yellow. Add the potatoes and sear them well to obtain a crust, then reduce the heat to let the starches cook and dilate slowly. The cooking may be finished in an oven preheated to 350°F. if the potatoes must wait before being served. In any case, sprinkle with salt and pepper, and add the meat glaze where applicable, just before serving.

Use the potato trimmings in a soup or for mashed potatoes or potato pancakes.

Excellent with grilled steaks, Chateaubriand, grilled chicken.

SHREDDED POTATO PANCAKES
6 SERVINGS

Use Maine potatoes. Shred enough potatoes to obtain 2½ cups of
shreds. Shred directly into a bowl of cold water to keep the pulp from
darkening. Drain and pat dry in towels. Shape into 6 pancakes. Panfry
in ½ cup bubbling clarified butter until golden on both sides. Serve
plain with salt and pepper, or with either of the following toppings.

Beginners may find that adding 1 beaten egg to the shredded potato
will help to shape the cakes.

AVOCADO TOPPING

½ cup mashed avocado   *Salt and pepper*
1½ teaspoons lemon juice   *1 tablespoon fine-chopped parsley*
1 pea-size piece of mashed garlic

Mash the avocado until it is very smooth. Immediately add the
lemon juice, garlic, and salt and pepper to taste. Cream with a small
whisk. Spread on the cooked potato pancakes and sprinkle with
chopped parsley.

LEEK TOPPING

1 cup fine-minced leeks, white   *2 tablespoons sour cream*
*   part only, unblanched*   *Salt and pepper*
1 tablespoon butter   *1 tablespoon chopped chives*
2 tablespoons heavy cream

Sauté the minced leeks in butter until soft but not brown. Add both
creams and salt and pepper to taste. Spoon over the pancakes and
sprinkle with chopped chives.

Potato pancakes are excellent with steaks, chops, eggs, grilled chicken.

GLAZED WHOLE ONIONS
6 SERVINGS

1 pound small white onions   *⅓ teaspoon sugar*
   (silverskins)   *Salt and pepper*
⅓ cup clarified butter or oil

Blanch the silverskins in boiling water for 2 minutes; drain well. Sauté in hot fat until brown. Add the sugar; it will caramelize and accentuate the brown color. Season with salt and pepper.

Use as a garnish for browned, stewed and braised meats.

SAUTÉED MINCED ONIONS
6 SERVINGS

4 cups minced yellow onions   *Salt and pepper*
¼ cup clarified butter or oil

Sauté the minced onions in clarified butter or oil until golden. Do not burn, or the bitter taste of the sugar contained in the onions will spoil the flavor and that of any dish to which you add them.

FRIED TOMATOES
6 SERVINGS

3 large tomatoes   *3 tablespoons oil of your choice*
¼ cup flour

Remove the stem end of the tomatoes. Immerse the whole fruits in boiling water for 2 minutes; then peel them. Cut the fruit into ⅓-inch slices, and flour the slices. Fry them in hot oil for 3 to 4 minutes on each side. Sprinkle with any of the following garnishes:

⚘ 1 tablespoon parsley mixed with ½ very small garlic clove, minced;

⚘ fine-grated Parmesan cheese;

⚘ 3 tablespoons butter creamed with 1 tablespoon anchovy paste.

Excellent as a garnish with steaks and chops.

FRIED ZUCCHINI
6 SERVINGS

2 large zucchini	*Salt and pepper*
¼ cup flour	*2 tablespoons fine-chopped*
⅓ cup oil of your choice	*parsley or basil*

Peel the zucchini and cut slantwise into ⅓-inch-thick slices. Flour the slices and fry on both sides until golden. Serve sprinkled with salt and pepper and the herb of your choice.

DEEP FRYING VEGETABLES—DRY-HEAT PROCEDURE

Reread the instructions on deep frying on pages 187 to 189. Immerse starchy vegetables in the oil bath without flouring, but flour vegetables containing some moisture, such as eggplant. Enclose very moist vegetables in a batter (Savory Fritter Batter, p. 189).

Deep-fried vegetables cook as the heat of the oil bath raises the temperature of their water content; the water content eventually vaporizes, thus softening the cellulose and dilating the starches. Notice the large amount of steam escaping when you cut through a deep-fried potato. Drain all deep-fried vegetables on crumpled paper towels. Salt just before serving only, or the moisture produced by the melting salt will render them soggy.

DEEP-FRIED BROCCOLI AND CAULIFLOWER
6 SERVINGS

1 head of cauliflower, or 1 bunch of broccoli	*Oil for deep frying*
½ cup flour	*2 cups tomato sauce (optional)*
1½ cups savory fritter batter (p. 189)	

Blanch (parboil) cleaned and trimmed flowerets. Drain well on paper towels. Coat with flour and dip into the batter. Deep fry in an oil bath heated to 370°F. until golden. Serve with tomato sauce if desired.

Serve separately as an appetizer, or as a vegetable with red meats or grilled chicken.

DEEP-FRIED EGGPLANT
6 SERVINGS

2 small eggplants	*1½ cups savory fritter batter*
Salt	*(p. 189), optional*
½ cup flour	*Oil for deep frying*

Peel the eggplants and cut them into ⅓-inch-thick slices. Sprinkle with salt and let stand for 1 hour. Drain off the water that is extracted by the salt, pat dry, and flour. Dip into batter if desired, or fry in just the flour coating. Deep fry in an oil bath heated to 370°F. until golden. Sprinkle with salt and pepper.

Serve with red meats.

DEEP-FRIED MUSHROOM CAPS
6 SERVINGS

1 pound medium-size mushrooms	*1½ cups savory fritter batter*
2 tablespoons lemon juice	*(p. 189)*
Salt and pepper	*Oil for deep frying*
½ cup flour	

Remove the stems from the mushrooms; the stems can be used to make *duxelles*. Marinate the caps in lemon juice with a little salt and pepper for 15 minutes. Pat dry, flour, and dip into the batter. Deep fry in an oil bath heated to 370°F. until golden. Sprinkle with salt and pepper.

Best used as an unusual appetizer.

DEEP-FRIED TOMATOES OR ZUCCHINI
6 SERVINGS

3 large tomatoes, peeled, or 2	*Oil for deep frying*
large zucchini, peeled	*Salt and pepper*
½ cup flour	*2 cups garlic-flavored tomato*
1½ cups savory fritter batter	*sauce (p. 121), optional*
(p. 189)	

Cut the peeled vegetables into slices ⅓-inch-thick. Coat with flour and dip into batter. Deep fry in an oil bath heated to 370°F. until golden. Sprinkle with salt and pepper. Serve with garlic-flavored to-mato sauce, or plain.

Serve with beef, lamb and veal.

FRENCH FRIES
6 SERVINGS

Use 4 large Maine potatoes. Peel them, do not wash them, and wipe them dry with a tea towel. Cut into sticks ⅓ inch wide and measure 4 cups of the sticks. Wrap tightly in the towel to avoid browning while waiting.

Heat an oil bath to 370°F. Immerse about ⅔ cup of the potato sticks at a time in the hot oil. Cook for 6 to 7 minutes. Remove the fries to crumpled paper towels. This precooking may be done as early as 1 hour before serving.

Just before serving, reheat the oil bath to 380°F. Immerse about 1 cup of potatoes at a time for not more than 1 to 2 minutes, or until golden. Drain on paper towels again and sprinkle with salt just before serving.

Serve with steak, chops, broiled chicken.

Note: With these and other fried potatoes prepared for family use, the second frying is so quick that there is no time for the potatoes to cool off between batches. If you are preparing larger quantities, line a metal colander with paper towels and drop the finished potatoes into it. Set the colander in a 300°F. oven with the door slightly ajar. Do not salt any of the potatoes until all the batches are fried and ready to serve.

STRAW POTATOES
6 SERVINGS

Use 4 large Maine potatoes and prepare them as for French Fries, but cut them into straws only ⅛ to ¹⁄₁₆ inch thick. Measure 4 cups straws. Immerse the potatoes, about 1 cup at a time, in the oil bath heated to 370°F. Raise the heat under the oil bath immediately after immersion. Cook the straws until golden. A second immersion is not necessary.

Serve with steaks, roasts, chops, broiled or roast chicken.

POTATO NESTS
6 SERVINGS

Prepare 4 cups of straw potatoes no thicker than ⅛ inch. Use a metal potato- or noodle-nest frying basket. Line the larger basket with ⅔ cup of potato straws. Put the small basket in place over the potatoes and clamp the handles shut. Heat the oil bath to 370°F. Immerse the basket in the oil and let cook for 7 to 8 minutes. Unclamp the basket handle and deposit the potato nest gently on crumpled paper towels. Repeat with the remainder of the straws, making 6 baskets.

Reheat the oil bath to 380°F. and immerse 2 baskets at a time, without the metal frame, for about 2 minutes, or until golden. Keep pushing the baskets down with a long fork to keep them immersed. Do this just before serving.

Serve with small birds such as quails or squabs, Rock Cornish Game hens, etc.

SOUFFLÉED POTATOES
6 SERVINGS

Souffléed potatoes are elegant, but they should not be attempted for a large dinner party. They are best cooked in two different oil baths. Be scientific about the temperatures, and cook only 5 potatoes at a time. Also, the potato slices must be absolutely even in thickness from one end to the other and no larger than ⅒ inch thick. Cut and trim the sides to obtain a rectangle and then trim off the corners.

Immerse the potatoes in an oil bath heated to 350°F. and let them cook for 3 minutes. For 2 more minutes, let the temperature of the bath fall to 250°F.; for 2 more minutes raise it again to 300°F. Remove the potato slices to crumpled paper towels.

Heat the second bath of oil to 400°F. and immerse the potatoes. They will puff up and bob over by themselves when the under side is cooked. Remove from the bath, sprinkle with salt and pepper, and serve immediately.

Souffléed potatoes puff up because they are very thin and the steam they contain is completely evaporated by the heat of the oil bath. The temperature of the bath is so high that the steam is under high pressure and pushes out the crust of potato starch already built around the potato pulp during the first cooking. Since souffléed potatoes do not contain any more moisture, they harden and become brittle when left to stand. Therefore, they should be eaten as soon as served, or within 8 to 10 minutes.

POTATOES DAUPHINE
6 SERVINGS

2 large Idaho potatoes	Dash of pepper
½ cup chicken stock	Dash of grated nutmeg
¼ cup butter	½ cup flour
½ teaspoon salt	2 eggs

Boil peeled and cut potatoes until tender. Drain and mash. Make a *choux* paste (see p. 521) with the remaining ingredients. Mix with the mashed potatoes. Drop the batter by teaspoons into an oil bath heated to 370°F. and cook until golden. Sprinkle with salt just before serving.

Serve with red meats.

BAKING VEGETABLES

Bake vegetables with a moisture content high enough to soften their cellulose without the help of an external liquid, but containing enough cellulose to retain their shape. Bake vegetables either in their skins or peeled and cut, in a fat. Prick the skins of vegetables cooked in their skins to allow some of the steam to escape and avoid explosions in the oven. Oil the skin of potatoes if you wish, but never wrap them in aluminum foil or they will acquire an unattractive metallic taste. Always use Idaho Russet potatoes for baking.

Cut large round vegetables (tomatoes, eggplant) into halves and sauté the cut sides in fat to insure their complete doneness when they are to be baked stuffed. When you prepare zucchini and green peppers for the same purpose, blanch them first instead.

Vegetables baked in heavy cream in a 300°F. oven are said to be scalloped. Each cup of heavy cream may be replaced by 1 cup of light cream, or 1 cup of milk plus 1 tablespoon of flour. The quality of the prepared dish is better with cream, of course. Potatoes to be scalloped should be precooked in milk. Their starch will dilate and they will be ready to absorb the cream. Scallop vegetables in French pottery, heat-proof glass, or Pyroceram.

For a golden crust at the bottom of the dish, set the baking dish directly on the oven rack; for a soft bottom layer, set the dish in a hot-water bath. A dish of scalloped vegetables with a heavy cream base is ready to serve when the butter starts oozing at its edges.

Bake scalloped potatoes ahead of serving time and keep the dish in a 150°F. oven. If you need the oven for another preparation, set the dish in a hot-water bath over low heat; it will keep warm as long as you desire. *Never* let a dish of scalloped potatoes cool and then reheat it; the starches of the potatoes acquire an unpleasant stale taste that no seasoning or condiment will be able to disguise.

JULIENNE OF BAKED BEETS IN MUSTARD SAUCE
6 SERVINGS

4 pounds red beets, without
   greens
Oil
½ cup heavy cream
1 to 2 tablespoons prepared
   Dijon-style mustard

Salt and pepper
1 tablespoon chopped fresh
   parsley

Scrub the beets but do not peel; rub them with oil. Bake in a 325°F. oven until a skewer penetrates the vegetable easily. The baking time is long and depends on the size of each beet, but it will take at least an hour for a medium-size beet. Peel and cut into ¼-inch julienne strips. Heat the cream, add mustard to your taste, the beets, and salt and pepper to taste. Toss together. Serve sprinkled with chopped parsley. There will be a lot of shrinkage in the beets, but the final taste is worth it.

RATATOUILLE GRATIN
6 SERVINGS

1 large eggplant, sliced
Salt
Flour
⅓ cup olive oil, approximately
2 large sun-ripened tomatoes,
   peeled and sliced, or 2 cups
   peeled whole tomatoes with
   ⅓ cup of the canning juice

¼ cup chopped parsley
1 garlic clove, minced
2 small zucchini, sliced
¼ cup bread crumbs
¼ cup grated Parmesan cheese

Sprinkle the slices of eggplant with salt; let stand for 1 hour; drain off the water that is extracted by the salt. Pat the slices dry and flour them. Fry the slices in olive oil until lightly browned. Rub a baking dish with olive oil. Add half of the eggplant slices, then add the other vegetables in layers in this order: tomatoes, mixed parsley and garlic, zucchini, more eggplant. Salt and pepper each layer lightly. Sprinkle the top with bread crumbs mixed with Parmesan; dribble olive oil over the top. Bake at 325°F. for about 1 hour, or until brown.

For the conventional ratatouille, add 2 chopped onions and 1 chopped green pepper, both sautéed. Cover tightly and cook over low direct heat. Omit the bread crumbs and cheese.

MELANIE'S STUFFED ZUCCHINI
6 SERVINGS

3 cups very thick béchamel sauce (p. 110)	¼ cup diced Gruyère cheese
6 small zucchini	¼ cup pine nuts or chopped almonds
½ cup chopped boiled ham	¾ cup fresh bread crumbs
¼ cup chopped cooked artichoke bottoms	¼ cup grated Parmesan cheese
	6 tablespoons melted butter

Make the béchamel sauce with 4 tablespoons butter and 4 table-spoons flour per cup of milk.

Wash zucchini, cut lengthwise into halves, and blanch (parboil) in boiling water for 3 to 4 minutes. Let cool. Scoop out the halves with a spoon, leaving a shell ¼ inch thick. Chop the pulp and mix with ham, artichokes, Gruyère and nuts. Mix with the béchamel sauce, and correct the seasoning. Fill the zucchini halves with this mixture. Sprinkle with mixed bread crumbs and Parmesan. Baste with melted butter and bake in a 350°F. oven until brown.

BAKED POTATOES GRATINÉ
6 SERVINGS

6 large Idaho potatoes, scrubbed	Grated nutmeg
1 cup (½ pound) butter	1 cup grated Gruyère or Emmenthal cheese
¼ cup heavy cream	
Salt and pepper	

Prick the potato skins, and bake them in a 400°F. oven for 1 hour. Cut the potatoes into halves, and scoop out the pulp, keeping the shells intact. Cream ¾ cup butter in a large mixer bowl, then add the hot potato pulp, little by little. Blend in the heavy cream. Season with salt, pepper and grated nutmeg to taste. Pipe or spoon back into the potato skins. Sprinkle with grated cheese. Cut the rest of the butter into as many parts as there are potato halves, and crown each half with one part. Return the stuffed shells to the oven until golden brown. These freeze well.

Note: The amount of butter is correct, although it is extravagant; of course it may be reduced.

BAKED SHREDDED POTATOES
6 SERVINGS

You may use any of the following flavorings:
- 1 teaspoon dried basil or 1 tablespoon fresh basil;
- 2 tablespoons chopped fresh parsley or *cilantro* (Chinese parsley);
- 1 large truffle, shredded;
- ½ cup *duxelles* or chopped sautéed mushrooms;
- ½ cup diced Gruyère cheese plus 2 tablespoons fine-chopped fresh parsley.

> *3 large Idaho potatoes*   *¾ cup melted butter*
> *Salt and pepper*

Shred the potatoes directly into a bowl of cold water to prevent browning of the pulp. Drain and pat dry between towels. Transfer to a baking dish. Sprinkle the chosen flavoring between each 2 layers of potatoes. Pour the melted butter over the vegetables. Bake in a 325°F. oven for 1½ hours. As the potatoes cook, spoon off the butter; save it to reuse for eggs or other potatoes.

POTATOES ANNA–CORNING
6 SERVINGS

This exquisite French dish is difficult to execute properly without the special copper pan, but an 8-inch round Corning Ware baking dish is the key in your own kitchen. Variations can be made by using the flavorings given in the recipe for Baked Shredded Potatoes.

4 large Idaho baking potatoes	*Salt and pepper*
¾ cup melted butter	*Flavoring*

Slice the potatoes with a slicer to make even slices ¹⁄₁₀ inch thick. Presauté them in melted butter in a frying pan until they start crisping on both sides. Arrange them in the baking dish, building concentric rows of potato slices. Salt and pepper each layer of potatoes, and sprinkle with whatever flavoring you are using. Pour melted butter over each layer; use the same butter that you used for sautéing. Continue until the dish is almost full. Bake in a 400°F. oven until the bottom is golden. Turn upside down on a serving plate. Drain off the butter into a jar and use it again for eggs or other potatoes.

GRATIN OF POTATOES
6 SERVINGS

This is a personal interpretation of the famous *gratin dauphinois*.

3 large Idaho potatoes	*1 garlic clove*
Milk	*2 tablespoons butter*
Salt and pepper	*1 cup heavy cream, scalded*
Freshly grated nutmeg	

Cut the potatoes into ⅛-inch slices. Place the slices in a 2-quart pot and cover them with milk. Bring slowly to a boil. Add a little salt and pepper and a dash of grated nutmeg. Simmer for about 5 minutes.

Slash the garlic clove and rub a baking dish with it. Discard the pieces of garlic; only the garlic juice is needed. Let the garlic juice dry, then rub the dish with the butter; use all of it. Divide the potatoes into 3 equal amounts. With each part build a layer in the baking dish; sprinkle each layer with salt, pepper and nutmeg, and add one third of the heavy cream. Bake in a 300°F. oven until the top is golden brown. Serve in the baking dish.

VARIATIONS OF GRATIN OF POTATOES

For each variation, make 2 layers of potatoes and separate them by a layer of the ingredients used in the particular variation.

MUSHROOM-POTATO GRATIN

Use no garlic on the baking dish. Separate the layers of potatoes by 1½ cups of sautéed mushrooms or *duxelles.*

GRUYÈRE GRATIN

Separate the layers of the potatoes with ¾ cup grated Gruyère cheese mixed with ¼ cup minced flat-leafed Italian parsley. Top the dish with another ¾ cup grated Gruyère.

BLUE-CHEESE GRATIN

Use no garlic on the baking dish. Cream 3 tablespoons butter and mix with ⅓ cup well-crumbled blue cheese (Wisconsin or Danish) or Roquefort. Spread between the layers of potatoes.

ONION GRATIN

Use no garlic on the baking dish. Separate the layers of potatoes with 2 cups minced onions, sautéed in butter.

LEEK GRATIN

Use no garlic on the baking dish. Separate the layers of potatoes with 2 cups unblanched white part of leeks, sautéed in butter.

MUSTARD GRATIN

Make the gratin without garlic and nutmeg. About 15 minutes before taking it out of the oven, top it with a mixture of 1 cup fresh bread crumbs, ¼ cup chicken stock, 3 tablespoons melted butter and 2 tablespoons prepared Dijon-style mustard. Finish baking at 400°F.

MUSHROOMS AND ARTICHOKES GRATIN
6 SERVINGS

This dish is very expensive and time-consuming, but it makes an exquisite vegetable for a special dinner.

1½ pounds mushrooms	Salt and pepper
6 tablespoons butter	¾ cup heavy cream
4 large artichoke bottoms,	2 tablespoons dry Madeira or
uncooked	sherry
1 tablespoon lemon juice	

Sauté the mushrooms (see p. 338) in 4 tablespoons butter, making sure that they do not contain the slightest amount of moisture. Clean the artichoke bottoms and cut into ⅟₁₆-inch slices. Sauté in 2 tablespoons butter for a few minutes, and sprinkle with lemon juice and salt and pepper. Continue tossing for a few minutes longer. Mix mushrooms and artichokes. Divide the vegetables in 3 equal parts. Mix the cream and wine. Arrange the vegetables in a baking dish in 3 layers; cover each layer with one third of the cream mixture. Bake in a 300°F. oven for 1¼ hours, or until the top is golden.

WINTER-SQUASH OR SWEET-POTATO GRATIN
6 SERVINGS

Use butternut or acorn squash, sweet potatoes or yams. Madeira is better for squash, and sherry or tawny port is better for sweet potatoes or yams. The proportions are the same for all these vegetables.

2 acorn squash, or 1 butternut	1 cup heavy cream, scalded
squash, or 3 sweet potatoes or	¼ cup dry Madeira or sherry
yams	or tawny port
4 tablespoons clarified butter	Salt and pepper
(for squash)	½ cup fresh bread crumbs
1 tablespoon butter	½ cup chopped pistachios

Peel the vegetables and cut into enough ¼-inch slices to fill 3 cups. Sauté the squash slices in the clarified butter until delicately browned, or blanch (parboil) the sweet potatoes or yams for about 10 minutes. Butter a baking dish. Make 2 layers of vegetables and cover each layer with half of the mixed cream and wine; sprinkle with salt and pepper. Sprinkle the top layer with mixed bread crumbs and pistachios. Bake in a 325 °F. oven for 1 hour.

MARINATED OR À LA GRECQUE VEGETABLES

This latest addition to vegetable cookery is a complete blanching in a strongly acidulated and flavored mixture of wine and water. According to Prosper Montagné, the method was created in Nice or Monte Carlo during the 1891–92 season. It has remained popular ever since. Vegetables *à la Grecque* can be served as an appetizer, a first course, or a salad.

The same method is used for all vegetables. Mix the same volume of water and wine, add all the seasonings and the raw vegetables, and cook over medium-high heat until the vegetables are tender. The vegetables should then steep overnight in the refrigerator.

It is awkward to serve vegetables in a very large amount of liquid, so I have developed a better way. The vegetables taste and look best when they are removed from the marinade before serving and set on a serving platter. Reduce the marinade to a few tablespoons and spoon the resulting acid glaze over the vegetables.

A very attractive way is to serve vegetables *à la Grecque* deep chilled with a plate of plain unsweetened unfilled cream puffs (p. 522).

ARTICHOKES À LA GRECQUE
6 SERVINGS

¾ cup white wine	*¼ teaspoon dried French thyme*
¾ cup water	*Salt and pepper*
Juice of 2 lemons	*2 packages (10 ounces each)*
4 tablespoons olive oil	*frozen artichoke hearts,*
2 Turkish bay leaves, or 1	*thawed*
California bay leaf	*1½ tablespoons anchovy paste*

Make the marinade with the first 6 ingredients and add salt and pepper to taste. Add the artichokes and cook until tender. Let the vegetables steep overnight, then drain. Reduce the marinade and blend in the anchovy paste. Spoon the glaze over the artichokes.

CAULIFLOWERETS À LA GRECQUE
6 SERVINGS

½ cup each of white wine and
   water
3 tablespoons olive oil
Juice and rind of 1 lemon
1 teaspoon salt

6 peppercorns, 3 black, 3 white
¼ teaspoon dried French thyme
2 Turkish bay leaves, or 1
   California bay leaf
1 pound cauliflowerets, blanched

Make the marinade with the first 7 ingredients, and cook the cauliflowerets. Follow the basic recipe.

CELERIAC À LA GRECQUE
6 SERVINGS

4 celeriac (celery knobs)
1 cup each of white wine and
   water
Juice of 1½ lemons
3 tablespoons olive oil
2 Turkish bay leaves, or 1
   California bay leaf

¼ teaspoon dried French thyme
¼ teaspoon fennel seeds
1 teaspoon salt
6 white peppercorns

Peel the celeriac and cut into ¾-inch cubes. Make a marinade from the remaining ingredients, and cook the celeriac. Follow the basic recipe.

MUSHROOMS À LA GRECQUE
6 SERVINGS

1 pound button mushrooms
½ cup each of water and white
wine
3 tablespoons olive oil
Juice and rind of 1 lemon
1 teaspoon salt

6 peppercorns, 3 black, 3 white
¼ teaspoon dried thyme
2 Turkish bay leaves, or 1
California bay leaf
¼ teaspoon ground coriander

Cook the mushrooms in the marinade made of the other ingredients.

FENNEL À LA GRECQUE
6 SERVINGS

2 large heads of fennel
¾ cup white wine
½ cup water
3 tablespoons olive oil
Juice of 1 lemon
2 tablespoons tomato paste

½ teaspoon coriander seeds
¼ teaspoon dried thyme
1 Turkish bay leaf, or ½
California bay leaf
½ teaspoon salt
6 white peppercorns

Cut the fennel into 1-inch strips and blanch (parboil) before cooking in the marinade.

ZUCCHINI OR SUMMER SQUASH À LA GRECQUE
6 SERVINGS

2 large zucchini or summer
squash
1 cup white wine
½ cup water
Juice of 1 lemon
3 tablespoons olive oil

1 teaspoon salt
¼ teaspoon dried thyme
1 teaspoon dried basil
2 Turkish bay leaves, or 1
California bay leaf
6 peppercorns

Peel the zucchini or squash and cut into slices or chunks. Cook it in the marinade made of the other ingredients.

GREEN SALADS

Whatever the type of green you are using for salad, wash the whole head. Separate the leaves, wash them individually, shake them well, and roll them in a tea towel before refrigerating them to crisp.

Cut the greens into bite-size pieces before putting them in your salad bowl. You may tear the greens with your hands or cut them with a stainless-steel knife, but an ordinary carbon-steel blade leaves rust traces at the edges of the salad leaves.

SALAD DRESSINGS

The basic oil and vinegar dressing is called *vinaigrette.* The oil for the dressing can be olive, corn, peanut or walnut oil. Walnut oil is a rare delicious treat, expensive and not easy to locate. The best olive oil comes from France, but California also produces some very good olive oil, to be located in health-food stores. A dressing made with olive oil tastes better when the acid ingredient is lemon or lime juice.

Good wine vinegar is not always easy to find. You can make your own, using wine leftovers. Let wine stand in the bottle until it turns to vinegar; it will, especially if it is cheap French wine. To speed things a bit, ask among your friends if anyone has a "vinegar mother." A mother is a soft brown lump formed by a colony of *Mycoderma aceti,* the bacteria which transform wine into vinegar. I have been snipping pieces away from my vinegar mother for my friends; the same mother had been a "present" from my own mother. While you are waiting for your vinegar to make itself, tame overacid vinegar by blending it with table wine until it has mellowed to please your taste. Or use cider vinegar.

The oil and vinegar can be combined in proportions to make an acid dressing, using ⅓ vinegar and ⅔ oil, measured by volume; or it can be made mellow by using ¼ vinegar plus ¾ oil, measured by volume. Make the dressing by hand or in the blender, as you prefer. One egg will smooth any rough vinegar and keep the dressing well emulsified.

Combine the seasonings of your dressing to your heart's content; but rather than put garlic in the dressing, rub a garlic clove on the surface of the salad bowl and on tiny croutons.

Enclose chopped shallots in the corner of a towel, squeeze out their juices, and rinse the still enclosed shallots under running water. The taste of the shallots will be much softer, but they will be less difficult to digest.

Steep dried herbs in the vinegar you are using, but add fresh herbs to the already mixed dressing.

Use a glass or china bowl, and chill the bowl. A wooden bowl becomes increasingly rancid with age, even if washed regularly. Toss greens and dressing at the table so that no wilting appears. If you prefer, instead of adding the already mixed dressing, add the dressing ingredients to the salad one after the other, starting with the oil and ending with the vinegar; in this way the greens are first well coated with oil and protected from the acid of the vinegar.

Serve the salad on very cold plates. Serve it at the beginning of the meal if you like. If the meal is rich, serve it after the roast, in the French manner; it lightens the stomach for cheese and dessert.

If thousands of French people every day drink rosé wine with their *salade niçoise,* it can only be because the salad redeems the rosé, for the acid of a dressing is the downfall of any wine. The only beverage that should be served with a green salad or any salad with an acid dressing is a glass of chilled water.

These salad combinations have proved very popular with my students over the years. You may make the the dressing either by hand or in an electric blender. When the blender is recommended, the recipe is labeled "Blender Dressing."

GLORIA'S SALAD
6 SERVINGS

2 Belgian endives
1 head of leaf (curly) lettuce
¾ cup pink grapefruit sections
¾ cup white grapefruit sections

½ cup orange sections
2 tablespoons chopped
   Macadamia nuts

BLENDER DRESSING

2 tablespoons lemon juice
Salt and pepper
4 tablespoons corn oil

3 tablespoons heavy cream
2 tablespoons sweetened coconut
    flakes

SAM'S SALAD

6 SERVINGS

1 head of Boston lettuce
1 head of romaine
2 tablespoons diced Gruyère
    cheese

2 tablespoons fine-chopped
    walnuts

BLENDER DRESSING

2 tablespoons wine vinegar
Salt and pepper
1 teaspoon minced shallot
1/2 teaspoon each of dried
    tarragon and chervil

1 teaspoon each of chopped fresh
    parsley and chives
2 teaspoons chopped walnuts
6 tablespoons corn oil

CURRIED SALAD

6 SERVINGS

1 head of chicory
1 head of Boston lettuce

1 small head of western lettuce

DRESSING

1 teaspoon curry powder
3 tablespoons vinegar
1/2 teaspoon salt
Pepper

2 hard-cooked eggs, separated
6 tablespoons oil
3 tablespoons heavy cream

Mix curry powder, vinegar, salt, and pepper to taste in a small pot. Cook in a hot-water bath for 5 minutes; cool. Strain the hard-cooked egg yolks into the vinegar mixture and fluff in the oil as if making a mayonnaise. Add the cream, and egg whites cut into fine strips.

MARIO'S ESCAROLE
6 SERVINGS

1 head of escarole
1 head of romaine
1 large sweet onion, sliced into thin rings

2 tablespoons grated Parmesan cheese

DRESSING

2 tablespoons lemon juice
2 teaspoons anchovy paste
Pepper

2 tablespoons snipped fresh basil leaves
6 tablespoons olive oil

GOODY'S FAVORITE
6 SERVINGS

½ pound raw mushrooms, sliced
1 pound fresh spinach

⅓ cup tiny goldfish cheese crackers

DRESSING

1½ tablespoons vinegar
1 teaspoon prepared Dijon-style mustard

1 teaspoon anchovy paste
Pepper
4½ tablespoons olive oil

Marinate the mushrooms in the dressing for 5 minutes, then toss mushrooms and dressing with the spinach. Sprinkle with the goldfish crackers.

ALAN'S FOLLY
6 SERVINGS

2 garlic cloves   *1 head of Boston lettuce*
1 slice of white bread, toasted   *1 head of romaine*

BLENDER DRESSING

2 tablespoons wine vinegar   *1 shallot, chopped fine*
½ teaspoon salt   *1 ½ teaspoons prepared Dijon-*
Pepper   *style mustard*
½ teaspoon each of dried   *3 tablespoons heavy cream*
    tarragon and chervil   *3 tablespoons sour cream*
2 teaspoons each of chopped   *3 tablespoons oil*
    fresh parsley and chives

Rub the salad bowl with 1 garlic clove. Rub the toasted bread with the other. Put the garlic toast, which is called a *chapon,* in the salad bowl and toss with the greens just before serving; or cut the toast into small cubes, which you will add to the salad *after* tossing it, so that they do not absorb all the vinegar.

RICE

BOILED RICE
6 SERVINGS

Use 1½ cups converted (parboiled) rice. Immerse in rapidly boiling water and stir well until the water returns to the boil. Barely simmer, covered, for 18 minutes, never more. Drain the rice and rinse under running *warm* not cold water. The warm water washes off the jelled layer of starch surrounding the grains of rice and keeps them from sticking to one another. Continue rinsing under warm water until the water runs clear. Let the rice drain completely.

Transfer the rice to a baking dish. Dot it with butter, and season with salt and pepper. Let it "dry" in a 200°F. oven for 30 minutes, fluffing it occasionally with the tines of a fork. Never use a spoon, for that would cut and break the kernels. Season the dried rice with any compound butter well adapted to the meat you are serving (see pp. 144 to 149).

BRAISED RICE, PILAF METHOD
6 SERVINGS

Sauté 1½ cups converted rice in ½ cup butter until the grains look as white as milk, a sign that the starches of the outside layers of each grain have seared and hardened; this searing keeps the kernels from sticking to one another. Measure the rice by volume always; so add 3 cups stock—beef or chicken or even fish *fumet.* There should always be twice as much stock as there is rice. Bring to a boil, and cover with a buttered paper and the pot lid; or stretch several layers of paper towels over the opening of the pot before closing it with the lid. The paper towels will keep the steam rising from the cooking rice from falling back into the pot. Bake in a 325°F. oven for 18 to 20 minutes. Fluff with a fork. Each grain remains separate. Mold, if desired, in a buttered mold. The mold can be held as long as needed in a hot-water bath in a 175°F. oven.

The richer the stock used, the longer it takes for the rice to absorb it. A pilaf cooked with canned broth cooks faster than one made with rich homemade stock.

BRAISED RICE, RISOTTO METHOD
6 SERVINGS

Use 1½ cups short-grained rice with a round kernel, Italian or California rice. Sauté the rice in a mixture of 3 tablespoons butter and 3 tablespoons olive oil. The total volume of liquid used must be three times that of the rice. Add the stock in 3 successive additions of 1½ cups each. After adding the first part of the stock, let the *risotto* cook over direct heat, not in the oven, until all the liquid has evaporated.

Add then the second part of the liquid; as soon as it has been completely absorbed by the rice, add the last part of the stock. A jelled layer of starches will form around the grains of rice and the dish will appear like a creamy pudding.

Risotto should not be heavy and gummy. If the rice is too dry, do not hesitate to add a little more stock; do the same if the rice is still a bit too hard at the center of the grain after you have added all the stock.

Many variations can be made with both methods. Here are three ideas:

SAFFRON PILAF
6 SERVINGS

¾ cup unsalted butter	*Pinch of freshly grated nutmeg*
1 garlic clove, minced	*Salt and pepper*
2 shallots, minced	*¼ to ½ teaspoon crushed*
2 tablespoons fine-chopped	* saffron*
* parsley*	*Braised rice, pilaf method*
1 teaspoon crushed dried basil	* (p. 365)*

Cream the butter. Add the garlic, shallots, parsley, basil and nutmeg. Mash well with a fork to extract the vegetable juices. Season with salt and pepper and add the saffron to taste. Refrigerate for at least 2 hours. Strain before using.

Make the pilaf, using only 4 tablespoons butter. Blend into the finished pilaf as much of the saffron butter as you wish. Freeze any remaining saffron butter in a small jar.

SHELLFISH PILAF
6 SERVINGS

If no mussels are available, use clams. The fish *fumet* may be replaced by thin chicken broth.

24 mussels, steamed
1 ½ cups white-wine fish fumet
  (p. 83), approximately
1 cup diced cooked shrimps
1 cup diced cooked scallops

1 onion, chopped fine
4 tablespoons butter
1 ½ cups uncooked rice
Additional butter
Pepper

Steam the mussels (see p. 281), shell them, and keep them warm. Strain the juices through a double layer of cheesecloth and measure. Add enough fish *fumet* to make 3 cups liquid. Mix shrimps and scallops with the mussels. Make a pilaf (see p. 365): Sauté the onion in the butter until tender but not browned. Add the rice and sauté until the kernels are white. Add the mixed mussel juice and fish *fumet* and bring to a boil. Cover and cook for 18 to 20 minutes. Blend the warm shellfish with the cooked rice and add as much additional butter as you allow yourself. Season with pepper—no salt.

BRUNO'S RISOTTO
6 SERVINGS

The author of the recipe is Milanese and uses butter rather than olive oil. You may use either of them or a combination of both.

2 large onions, chopped fine
6 tablespoons butter or olive oil
1 ½ cups uncooked short-grain
  round rice
½ cup dry vermouth
2 garlic cloves, completely
  mashed
6 tablespoons tomato paste

3 fresh basil leaves, scissored, or
  ½ teaspoon dried basil
1 ½ teaspoons anchovy paste
4 ½ cups chicken broth
¼ pound mushrooms, shredded
  and sautéed
Grated Parmesan cheese

Sauté the onions in the butter or oil until translucent. Toss the rice in the hot mixture until the grains are milky white. Add the vermouth and toss until evaporated. Add the garlic, tomato paste, basil, anchovy paste and one third of the chicken broth; cook over low heat until all the liquid has been absorbed. Repeat twice with the remainder of the broth. Blend in the mushrooms. Serve with grated Parmesan.

NOODLES

If you try making fresh noodles just once, you will never again want to buy packaged pasta. If you become adept and plan to make noodles often, investing in a noodle-making machine will save you much time and physical effort.

GERMAN-ALSATIAN-AUSTRIAN NOODLE DOUGH

This European recipe is similar to that for the famous Pennsylvania Dutch noodle dough.

5 cups sifted flour	1¾ teaspoons salt
8 medium-size or 7 large eggs	Use no water.
6 extra egg yolks	

Sift the flour into a mound on a mixing board. Make a well in the flour. Add all the other ingredients and gather into a ball of dough. *Fraiser* (see p. 392) twice. Shape into a 4-inch square and refrigerate, preferably overnight.

ITALIAN NOODLE DOUGH

4½ cups flour	1½ teaspoons salt
4 eggs	Use no more than ¼ cup water.
3 to 4 tablespoons oil	

Sift the flour into a mound on a mixing board. Make a well in the flour. Add the eggs, oil, salt and water; gather into a ball. Knead for 7 to 8 minutes. Shape into a 4-inch square and refrigerate, preferably overnight.

To Make Noodles

Cut the dough into 4 identical squares. Roll out one square at a time paper-thin. Flour the top of the sheet of dough and roll it up like a cigar. Cut strips as wide as desired. Unroll the strips; every one of them is a noodle. Let the strips dry on a sheet of wax paper.

Blanch in 5 quarts boiling water with 5 teaspoons of salt. Cook until done *al dente*, i.e., cooked, but still pleasantly firm. Rinse under *warm* water until the water runs clear, to discard the film of liquid starch gel around the noodles.

Store uncooked homemade noodles in a tightly sealed container.

SEASONINGS FOR NOODLES

These seasonings from four different places may be used to flavor ½ pound noodles, homemade or commercially packaged.

ITALIAN-GENOVESE

Cream 6 tablespoons butter, add 1 small garlic clove chopped fine, 2 tablespoons chopped parsley and 6 slices of Italian salami chopped fine. Mix into the cooked noodles.

ITALIAN-PIEMONTESE

Add these ingredients to the hot cooked noodles in the order given: ½ cup heavy cream scalded, 2 tablespoons tomato paste, 2 tablespoons dry Madeira, 2 tablespoons butter and 1 large white truffle shredded (optional).

ALSATIAN-GERMAN

Reduce 1 cup heavy cream to ⅔ cup with 1 teaspoon dried savory; add to the noodles.

Another way is to season the noodles with ½ cup butter, a pinch of sugar and ground cinnamon to your heart's content. This is excellent with pork.

ALSATIAN-FRENCH

Sauté ⅔ cup tiny white-bread croutons in ½ cup clarified butter. Toss with the noodles, adding at the same time another ¼ cup fresh butter.

X

Jewels on Your Plate

poaching fruits,
sugar cookery,
fruit sauces

FRUITS, FRESH OR POACHED, make beautiful desserts. The fruits most often poached are pears, peaches, apricots, cherries. Unfortunately, the long transportation of fruit from one end of the country to the other is not to the advantage of most housewives, who seldom can buy a fresh *ripe* fruit in the market. Sour cherries are still difficult to find, although apricots have become a bit less of a rarity in the last few years. Pears and peaches are plentiful, but present a ripening problem, although not as much as plums, which usually have the single virtue of looking gorgeous.

As you bring fruit home from the market, be gentle with it. Berries will probably be fresh, almost ready to eat, since they have to be sold fast to be profitable. If they are not quite ready for the table, do not hesitate to keep them in the vegetable crisper of your refrigerator for a few days. They will go on ripening; watch them carefully, though.

The greatest trouble comes from pears and apples that are stored green. After a fruit has been severed from the tree, it relies entirely on its own supply of water, and several very complicated reactions take place inside of the pulp. It has been assumed for a long time that starches are changed into sugars as fruit ripens; but although glucose, sucrose and fructose are present in a ripe fruit, no one has really established what their true source is. Apples and pears need some help on your part to ripen properly. When you bring them from the store, they are often very cold. If they are, do not expose them immediately to the relatively high temperature of your kitchen. Keep them in the vegetable crisper of the refrigerator for a few days, then let them acclimate to a warmer place every day. It may take a week or more for a pear to ripen and be ready for cooking or eating. Even if you are careful, the pear may, instead of ripening, turn brown and spoil. This "sleepiness" very often happens during the winter months.

Serving fresh fruits needs no description, but we are less familiar with cooked fruits other than stewed prunes. Poaching is a good method to use, for this gentle cooking will help to keep the shape of the fruits and will add lusciousness.

Poach fruits in syrups of different density depending on their nature:

APPLES
Use a light syrup—½ to ⅓ cup of sugar per cup of water.

APRICOTS, PEACHES, CHERRIES, PEARS
Use a medium syrup—½ to ¾ cup sugar per cup of water.

BANANAS
Use a medium or heavy syrup—1 cup of sugar per cup of water.

Instead of water, the poaching liquid may be wine or a fruit juice, or a combination of both. If the wine is sweet, reduce the amount of sugar. Too much sugar in a syrup will shrivel the fruit and draw the juices out of it, but not enough sugar will cause the fruit to break down completely and mush up; the best example is apples, which fall apart when cooked without sugar and become applesauce.

COOKING A SUGAR SYRUP
The first step to successful sugar cookery is a perfectly clean pot. Any trace, even the smallest, of dried food or fat may provoke the crystallization of the sugar. Even if your pot seems clean, wash it again, rinse it several times, and dry it *with paper towels exclusively.* The cleanest cloth kitchen towel always contains undetectable, but chemically active, fat residues.

Mix the sugar with some water, usually ¾ cup water with 1 cup sugar, and add a pinch of cream of tartar or a few drops of lemon juice. Left to stand, this cold mixture will form a saturated solution; while some sugar granules will melt in the water, others will sink to the bottom of the pot and melt only if the syrup is submitted to heat. When heated, the syrup will become a true solution, entirely liquid and transparent. Sugar bought in stores is called *sucrose.* An acid (cream of tartar or lemon juice) added to sucrose transforms it while the syrup cooks into two different sugars called *glucose* and *fructose.* This chemical reaction called *inversion* prevents recrystallization of the sugar.

To cook sugar accurately, use a candy thermometer; put it in the syrup before the cooking starts. As soon as the syrup has reached the desired temperature, immerse the thermometer in hot water to keep the sugar from hardening on it.

Soon after the syrup has come to a boil, bubbles will appear, very close to one another and very small, a sign that the water has evaporated and that the sugar has started to cook. Sugar refined in the United States is usually so clean that barely any scum forms. Should some materialize at the edges of the syrup, remove it with a clean silver spoon. Do not let flames rise around the pot, for this extreme heat will start the sugar caramelizing at its edges. Should this happen, wrap a linen cloth dipped into ice water around the prongs of a fork and rub all around the pan to remove all traces of burned sugar; then do not touch the syrup any more.

As sugar cooks, it reaches higher and higher temperatures and passes through successive "stages." In old-fashioned recipes, you will sometimes see the expression, "cook the syrup to the thread stage," or "to the ball stage." The old-fashioned way of testing the temperature of a syrup was with the tips of the fingers. The fingers were dipped into ice water before being dipped quickly into the syrup. As the sugar reached various temperatures, it would form a thread or ball when pulled or rubbed between thumb and index finger.

215°F.—a thin thread
219°F.—a thick thread
230° to 240°F.—a soft ball
242° to 252°F.—a hard ball
260°F.—light-crack
310°F.—hard-crack
350° to 355°F.—caramel

From 260° to 310°F., the sugar passes successively from the light- to the medium- to the hard-crack stages. From 260°F. on, the stages of cooking are separated only by intervals of seconds. From the hard-crack on, the syrup forms a brittle sheet that cracks or breaks when cooled. It starts coloring and reaches the *caramel* stage at 350° to 355°F. Caramel is recognizable by its candylike smell. If the cooking is continued too long, caramel becomes acrid and burns.

To poach fruits, the sugar syrup needs to be heated only long enough to make a true solution. The other stages are used for other dessert preparations.

Test the doneness of poached fruit with a large sewing needle, the trace of which will not be visible in the fruit pulp after cooking.

Leftover syrups of poached fruit are very popular on old-fashioned flapjacks; cool the syrup at room temperature. It will stay refrigerated without granulating for about a week.

PEELING FRUITS

When you peel a fruit such as an apple or a pear, the knife leaves a bruise at its surface and a browning immediately occurs. This is caused by the presence of an enzyme which, combined with the air, provokes an oxidation of the phenol-type material present in the fruit pulp. An antioxidant will stop or slow enzymatic reactions. Rub the fruit immediately with lemon juice; its citric acid will go to work at once. Then, as soon as you immerse a fruit in a sugar syrup, the enzyme is destroyed by the heat and the browning stops.

Peel pears and apples very gently with a vegetable peeler to remove a very thin layer of skin and cause a minimum of bruising. Remove apple cores with a corer, and pear cores with the small scoop of a melon baller dipped into lemon juice.

Peaches also turn brown when peeled, but not as fast. You may rub them with lemon juice if you plan to poach them; or, if you plan to macerate them in wine, immediately sprinkle them with sugar. The sugar will draw out some of the fruit juice, but it will also build a protective layer of concentrated sugar syrup all around the fruit. Remove the skins of peaches, apricots, nectarines (and tomatoes) by immersing them in boiling water for 30 to 45 seconds. A layer of steam builds between skin and pulp, and the peel can be lifted without damaging the appearance of the fruit pulp.

Citrus fruits do not darken when peeled and exposed to the air because they do not contain these enzymes. The rinds of these fruits are often candied to use as a garnish for the fruit slices themselves. Lift the rind with a potato peeler, applying just enough pressure to obtain only the outer layers of the rind and none of the white cottonlike cellulose.

Thousands of small sacs containing an oil (oil of lemon or orange) are visible at the surface of the rind. After cutting the rind into fine strips, blanch it to remove some of that oil and prevent the bitterness that too much of it would give to the candied peel.

To remove the white skin of a citrus fruit, cut a small portion at each end of the fruit so it can stand without rolling. With large strokes of a very sharp and thin knife blade, remove the white skin from top to bottom. The fruit looks elegant only if your hand is steady and if all traces of white cellulose are removed. Make an effort to be light handed and not to damage the fruit.

APRICOTS JOLIE MADAME
6 SERVINGS

1 *cup sugar*	¼ *teaspoon bitter-almond extract*
1½ *cups water*	*Liquid honey* (2 *to* 4
1-*inch piece of vanilla bean*	*tablespoons*).
12 *large apricots, ripe but still*	1 *cup heavy cream, whipped*
firm	*Sugar* (*about* 2 *tablespoons*)
½ *cup fine-ground blanched*	2 *tablespoons Kirsch or Apry*
almonds	(*apricot liqueur*)
½ *cup chopped blanched*	
pistachios	

Prepare sugar syrup (p. 374), using sugar and water. Cut the vanilla bean open and drop the seeds into the syrup. Cut the apricots into halves and remove the pits, but do not peel. The skins keep the fruit from falling apart during poaching. Immerse apricot halves in the syrup and simmer very gently for 3 to 4 minutes. Do not overcook the fruit. Remove to a plate and chill. Reserve the cooking syrup.

Mix together almonds, pistachios and almond extract; bind with just enough honey for the mixture to hold together. Fill the cooled apricot halves with a nugget of the mixture. Whip the cream, sweeten to taste, and flavor with the liqueur of your choice. Serve apricots in small dessert dishes; baste each serving with 2 tablespoons of the cooking syrup and top with the whipped cream.

DUBONNET PEARS
6 SERVINGS

A variation on the classic *poires au vin;* the flavor is somewhat different.

2 cups red Dubonnet
½ cup orange juice
1 teaspoon grated orange rind
1¼ cups granulated sugar
6 ripe pears
1 lemon, halved

1 cup heavy cream
2 tablespoons Curaçao
1 tablespoon minced candied
   orange peel
Sugar (about 1 tablespoon)

Mix Dubonnet, orange juice, grated rind, and 1¼ cups sugar. Bring to a boil. Simmer for 5 minutes. Peel and core the pears carefully; work with only 2 pears at a time. Rub with the lemon and immediately immerse in the boiling syrup. Simmer for 8 to 10 minutes, or until tender. Chill pears as soon as all have been poached. Reduce the cooking syrup to 1 cup and cool.

Whip the cream to the Chantilly stage (p. 20). Add Curaçao, candied peel, and sugar to taste. Continue whipping until stiff. Pipe 1 teaspoon of cream into the center of each pear half and reshape whole pears by putting 2 halves together. Pipe a large rosette of cream in each of 6 dessert dishes. Set 1 pear in each dish. Serve deep chilled. Pass the cooled syrup in a sauceboat.

POIRES BELLE DIJONNAISE
6 SERVINGS

Each French cook has his own interpretation of this dish, but it always requires a small amount of black-currant preserves or liqueur.

2 cups water
1⅓ cups sugar
1-inch piece of vanilla bean
6 ripe pears
2 boxes (10 ounces each) frozen
   raspberries

Black-currant jam
3 to 4 tablespoons Cassis
   (black-currant liqueur)
1 cup heavy cream
1 pint fresh raspberries

Make a syrup with the water, sugar and vanilla bean. Peel and core the pears and poach them. Put the frozen raspberries in a strainer and drain completely. Purée them. Add black-currant jam to your taste to sweeten the purée and 1 tablespoon of the Cassis. Strain to discard seeds and currant skins. Whip the cream to the Chantilly stage (p. 20); gradually add remaining Cassis. Clean the fresh berries.

Arrange the pear halves in a ring or crown on a serving plate. Put the Chantilly cream in the center and top with the fresh berries. Serve the raspberry-currant sauce in a sauceboat. To savor, cut through pear, cream, berries and sauce all at once.

PEACHES KOTJA
6 SERVINGS

To my dear friend Dr. Konstantin Frank, who produces the best Riesling in America. Use fragrant fresh white peaches if you can locate them, but the euphoric effect is identical with yellow peaches.

> 6 *firm ripe peaches*   *1 bottle Spätlese Riesling*
> 6 *teaspoons* powdered *sugar*

Bring water to a boil and immerse peaches for a few seconds to peel them easily. Halve and pit the peaches. Immediately sprinkle each peach half, inside and outside, with about ½ teaspoon of the sugar. Place the peaches, pit side down, in a shallow dish and pour the wine on top. Refrigerate for at least 5 hours. Shake the dish gently at regular intervals to mix fruit juice and wine.

CHERRY SLICES
6 SERVINGS

This is often served in the Black Forest of Germany with leftover slices of *Schwarzwälder Kirschtorte* (Black Forest cherry cake).

> 6 *slices of chocolate cake*   *1 ½ pounds fresh sour cherries,*
> *Butter* (*2 to 3 tablespoons*)   *pitted*
> *Superfine sugar* (*about 6*   ½ *teaspoon arrowroot*
>   *teaspoons*)   ½ *cup heavy cream*

1½ cups ruby port or sweet   *2 tablespoons Kirsch or*
     white wine   *Maraschino*
    1 cup granulated sugar   *¼ cup macaroon crumbs*

Lightly butter the cake slices, sprinkle them with the superfine sugar, and broil until the sugar starts caramelizing. Mix port and granulated sugar, bring to a boil, and simmer for 5 minutes. Immerse the cherries in the boiling syrup and *boil,* do not simmer, for 4 minutes. Drain the cherries and reduce the syrup to ¾ cup. Spoon half of it over the slices of cake. Deep chill.

Thicken remaining syrup with the arrowroot. Add the cooked cherries and mix well. Cool. Whip the cream to the Chantilly stage (p. 20), gradually adding Kirsch or Maraschino. Fold in the macaroon crumbs. Top each slice of cake with some of the cherries in syrup and a serving of macaroon cream. Serve chilled.

GRAPEFRUIT MARTINIQUE
6 SERVINGS

An imitation of Lasserre's *oranges orientales* made with our lovely white and pink grapefruit. The mixture of lime and lemon rind in the syrup gives it a haunting flavor.

3 red or pink seedless grapefruit   *2 cups sugar*
3 white seedless grapefruit   *1 cup water*
Rinds of 2 limes   *1 teaspoon lemon juice*
Rind of 1 lemon   *3 tablespoons rum*

Remove the rinds of 2 pink grapefruit and 2 white grapefruit, the limes and lemon. Cut the rinds into very fine julienne, and blanch the tiny slivers in boiling water for 2 minutes. Drain and blot dry. Mix together sugar, water and lemon juice; heat slowly. Add the blanched rinds, bring to a boil, and simmer until the rinds are candied and transparent (syrup temperature about 240°F.). Drain the rinds and cool the syrup.

Peel and section all the grapefruit; discard all membranes (they are too difficult to cut on a plate). Arrange in a shallow crystal dish, alternating pink and white sections. Cover with rum and refrigerate. Just before serving, arrange the candied rinds carefully on top of the sections. Serve the syrup in a bowl.

PRUNEAUX PINOT
6 TO 8 SERVINGS

A perfect dessert for a country dinner. The preparation is as old as dried prunes, and as old as Burgundy wine which Gaul's Vercingetorix was already drinking. The suggested wines are listed in order of price. You may use a claret if you prefer; in that case, choose a Pauillac.

*1½ pounds unpitted jumbo
   prunes
1 bottle Nuits-Saint-Georges, or
   Hermitage, or Juliénas, or
   California Pinot Noir
1-inch piece of vanilla bean
½ teaspoon ground ginger
¼ teaspoon each of ground
   allspice and cinnamon*

*⅛ teaspoon ground cloves
1 teaspoon fine-grated lemon
   rind
½ cup sugar
1 cup heavy cream, whipped and
   slightly sweetened*

Cover the prunes with water and let them soak overnight. Drain. Bring the wine to a boil and add the seeds from the vanilla bean, all the spices, the grated lemon rind and the sugar. Stir until the sugar is dissolved. Cover the prunes with the hot wine and let them stand in a warm place for 24 to 48 hours. Chill then, until ready to serve. Serve with the whipped cream.

WEST COAST FRUIT SALAD
6 SERVINGS

*6 large ripe Bartlett or Comice
   pears
Juice of 2 lemons*

*2 cups grapes, preferably Muscat
2 cups raspberry sauce (p. 384)*

Peel the pears, cut into ⅟₁₆-inch slices, and immediately sprinkle with some of the lemon juice. If you cannot cut slices this thin, make them as thin as possible so that they absorb the lemon juice. Peel the grapes if you wish, then cut each grape into halves and sprinkle them too with lemon juice. Put the fruits in a large crystal dish, alternating layers of pears and grapes and sprinkling with more lemon juice. Cover the dish with plastic wrap and refrigerate for at least 4 hours. Sweeten the raspberry sauce to your taste and pour over the fruits at serving time.

FLAMBÉED PEACHES AUGUSTE ESCOFFIER
6 SERVINGS

This recipe is not to be found in Escoffier's *Le Guide Culinaire,* but the method is.

6 ripe peaches, preferably white	*8 tablespoons (4 ounces)*
1 ½ cups sugar	*Framboise or Kirsch*
1 cup water	*3 egg yolks*
2 cups raspberry sauce (p. 384)	*⅓ cup white wine*

Peel the peaches and halve and pit them. Poach in a syrup made with 1 cup of the sugar and 1 cup water. Flavor the raspberry sauce with 3 tablespoons of the liqueur, but sweeten it very slightly. Put the peach halves in a flambéing pan. Pour the sauce over the peaches. Reheat until the mixture steams well.

Meanwhile, make a *sabayon* (p. 66) with the yolks, remaining ½ cup sugar and the wine; flavor with 2 tablespoons Kirsch or Framboise. Heat the remaining liqueur in a small pot and flambé the peaches with it. Serve the *sabayon* separately. The sweetness of the *sabayon* is tempered by the tartness of the raspberry sauce.

STRAWBERRIES MADELEINE
6 SERVINGS

Use Louisiana berries if you can find them, or take the time to ripen berries very well in your vegetable crisper. The same recipe can be made with fresh raspberries.

1 quart strawberries or
* raspberries*
4 tablespoons (2 ounces)
* Framboise or Kirsch*
2 cups raspberry sauce (p. 384)
2 egg yolks
2 tablespoons sugar

½ cup milk, scalded
1 teaspoon unflavored gelatin
½ cup heavy cream, whipped to
* the Chantilly stage (p. 20)*
¼ cup chopped blanched
* pistachios*

Macerate the cleaned fruit in 3 tablespoons Kirsch or Framboise for 2 hours. Prepare raspberry sauce.

With egg yolks, sugar and scalded milk, make a stirred English custard (p. 62). Melt the gelatin and add it to the custard. Flavor with the remaining Kirsch or Framboise, or with more liqueur to taste. Stir over ice until the mixture starts thickening. Gently fold in the whipped cream. Pour the custard cream into a crystal dish. Refrigerate to gel, but the mixture will stay very soft. Arrange the berries on top of the custard cream. Pour the raspberry sauce on top and sprinkle with chopped pistachios.

FRUIT SAUCES

Fruit sauces do not present the slightest technical difficulty. They are fruit purées, often flavored with a liqueur or brandy. Fruit sauces can be thickened, if their consistency makes it necessary, with a slurry of 1 teaspoon cornstarch per cup of sauce.

Some of these recipes are year-round formulas made with dried or frozen fruits. Use fresh fruits when available; they should be absolutely ripe and naturally sweet. Use fruit sauces on rice pudding, upside-down vanilla custard, molded English custard, ice cream, and other desserts.

APRICOT SAUCE

½ pound dried apricots *2 tablespoons Kirsch, rum or*
Sugar *brandy*

Soak the apricots in water to cover overnight. Discard the soaking water and replace with enough water to cover the fruit. Simmer until apricots are tender. Drain, reserving the juices. Purée the apricots in a blender and strain to discard the skins. Add enough cooking water to obtain the desired consistency. Sweeten to taste and flavor with desired liqueur.

RASPBERRY SAUCE

2 packages (10 ounces each) *Sugar*
frozen raspberries in syrup
2 tablespoons Kirsch or
Framboise

Thaw the berries. Drain off the juices and reserve. Purée the berries in a blender and strain to discard all seeds. Add enough of the reserved juices to obtain the desired consistency. Add sugar if needed. Flavor with Kirsch or Framboise.

STRAWBERRY SAUCE

3 cups individually frozen *2 tablespoons Kirsch, Framboise,*
unsweetened strawberries *Triple Sec or Curaçao*
Sugar

Thaw the berries and purée them in a blender. Strain to discard as many seeds as possible. Sweeten to taste and flavor with desired liqueur.

CHERRY SAUCE

1 pound fresh Bing cherries
¾ cup sugar
½ cup orange juice
1 dime-size piece of lemon rind

Pinch of ground ginger
2 tablespoons Kirsch or cherry
brandy

Pit the cherries. Mix them with sugar and orange juice, and bring to a boil. Add lemon rind and ginger; simmer for 6 to 8 minutes. Purée in a blender and strain. Add more sugar if desired and flavor with liqueur.

ORANGE SAUCE

⅔ cup orange juice
1 jar (12 ounces) Scottish
orange marmalade

2 tablespoons Cognac

Mix juice and marmalade and simmer together for 10 to 15 minutes. Strain to discard orange peels. Flavor with Cognac.

XI

Wrapped in Dough

pastry doughs;
pies, tarts, and turnovers

To MASTER pastry making, it is important to read the introductory notes before starting to prepare a specific recipe.

ELEMENTS OF A PASTRY DOUGH

FLOUR

Mix ¼ cup flour with enough water to make a dough. Work and work and work that nugget until it becomes as hard as rubber. Now wash it under cold water. The water will run white at first as the flour starches leach out, but the water will clear up little by little until you are left with a grayish piece of tough material containing roughly two thirds water and one third *gluten.*

Gluten is the gummy elastic material obtained when the proteins contained in flour are submitted to the mechanical action of hands or mixer in the presence of water. Gluten plays a most important role in pastry making. If you overwork a dough, gluten will overdevelop and the pastry will be tough and elastic. If, on the contrary, the dough is not given a slight amount of work, it will crumble, tear, and be difficult to roll out. The perfect technique depends on developing just enough gluten to obtain a manageable dough that will remain flaky after baking. *Always sift the flour before making a pastry dough.*

FAT

Fat enters the composition of a pastry dough to act as a softener on the gluten strands. When these strands are coated with fat, they do not cling to each other any more to form a solid structure but, rather, slide against each other, forming short separated strands. Fat gives the crust its flakiness. The colder and the harder the fat used, the flakier the crust will be. Soft unsaturated fats like margarine and oil, and melted butter as well, produce a sandy and mealy crust.

Use the fat you like best, but consider how each kind works in making the pastry.

Lard   has the best shortening power on the gluten strands; it is too bad that its "meaty" flavor makes it more appropriate for savory pies than for dessert tarts and pies.

Vegetable shortening,   which is 100 per cent fat, gives the next flakiest pastry, but it also results in a colorless crust, in which taste is entirely sacrificed to texture.

Butter,   which is only 80 per cent fat, gives a definitely firmer texture, but is positively unbeatable for taste and color. Do not add additional salt to your pastry if you use salted butter.

A mixture of *two thirds butter* with *one third vegetable shortening* helps the beginner cope with gluten problems, but it never tastes as good as butter alone.

Margarine,   because it has very little taste or flavor, should not be used for pastry making unless the most stringent dietary rules require it. If you must use margarine, place it in the freezer 15 minutes before making the pastry.

The ratio of flour to shortening should be 2 to 1 by weight and 3 to 1 by volume.

WATER AND OTHER LIQUID INGREDIENTS

Eggs used in a pastry crust are considered liquid ingredients. The coagulation of their proteins makes the pastry firmer and more resistant to the penetration of moisture seeping from fillings.

Water acts as a melting agent for salt and sugar if used. It allows the starch cells of the flour to dilate and the gluten to develop. Exactly how much water is needed to make a pastry dough cannot be predetermined. It depends on many factors, among which the absorbing power of the flour starches and the dexterity of the operator are most important. Chilled water slows down the formation of the gluten strands.

You may have seen pastry recipes calling for lemon juice or vinegar. These ingredients, as well as sour cream or soured milk, are often used because their acid content works as an additional softener on the gluten strands.

EQUIPMENT

Throw away pastry cloth, cutter and stockinet. All you need are your bare hands, the counter top and, of course, a rolling pin. The best is one made with ball bearings, which help weak feminine forearms. A marble slab is indeed a help but not a necessity. I have up to now worked without it.

BASIC PASTRY CRUST OR SHORT PASTE

This pastry is all-purpose. It can be used for savories as well as for dessert pies, quiches, flans and tarts. The recipe makes 2 one-crust 9-inch pies, or 1 two-crust pie, or 24 paper-thin tartlet shells.

Notice the ratio of water to fat. In a basic short paste this ratio is always 2 to 1, so that in this recipe calling for 9 tablespoons butter the maximum amount of water used should be 4½ tablespoons. If you have a recipe based on 1 cup butter, remember that the total amount of water should never exceed ½ cup. It is possible to complete a short paste with slightly less water than this exact ratio, but never use more.

1½ cups sifted flour　　　　*1 teaspoon salt*
3 to 4½ tablespoons chilled　*9 tablespoons butter, chilled*
　water

Put the flour on the counter top; make a well in the center and put in it ½ tablespoon water, the salt and the butter cut into ½-inch cubes. Working with the tips of the fingers, rub flour and butter together until the mixture forms particles the size of a pea. In culinary jargon, this is called *sabler,* which means "reduce to sand," but very rough sand. Now add the remainder of the water, ½ tablespoon at a time. Mix it into the mixture with the tips of the fingers of both your hands extended down toward the counter in such a way as to form a natural pastry cutter; the palms face each other. Push the dough from left and right, throwing it up from the bottom and fluffing it about 2 inches above the counter top. The more water you add, the more difficult it becomes to break the lumps until large lumps form that cannot be broken anymore.

Take the dough in one hand; using the dough ball as a mop, gather all the loose particles remaining on the counter. Put your right hand and wrist flat on the counter in front of the ball of dough. Leave your wrist on the counter, but extend your hand upward at a 45-degree angle with the counter. *Do not knead,* but with heel of the hand slide the dough 6 to 8 inches forward only—not sideways—flattening nut-size pieces of it on the counter. When all the dough has been used, re-form all the pieces to a ball and repeat the same operation. This procedure is called *fraiser*. This action flattens the fat in extremely thin leaves between layers of flour, gives the pastry homogeneity and, most important, develops just enough gluten to give the dough a certain plasticity for easy handling. This procedure is not kneading, which is reserved for yeast doughs; you will read about them in the next chapter. Shape the pastry into a circular 3-inch cake about 1 inch thick. Test it by poking your finger into it. If the hole remains, you may use the pastry within 15 minutes. The more that hole closes, the more gluten you have developed and the more the dough needs rest in the refrigerator.

When you roll out the pastry, you further flatten the fat in very thin sheets between thin layers of flour. In the heat of the oven, the fat melts and is absorbed by the starches, while the steam resulting from the boiling of the water contained in the dough applies pressure on the leaves of the baking dough and separates them from one another. The result is a flaky pastry.

STORING AND FREEZING PASTRY DOUGHS

Preferably make your pastry doughs at least 24 hours ahead of time. They will oxidate and bake with a better color. Wrap the doughs in wax paper and keep refrigerated. All pastry doughs freeze well wrapped in sealed foil. The thawing time for the Basic Pastry Crust, above, is 2 hours; thawing may be done at room temperature.

MRS. REEVES' ENGLISH LARD PASTRY

From the kitchen of a friend from Frinton, Essex; the best lard pastry I have ever tasted.

1½ cups sifted flour	1 teaspoon sugar
6 tablespoons lard	½ teaspoon salt
3 tablespoons butter	2 to 3 tablespoons water

Proceed as for basic pastry crust, but do not *fraiser*.

SOUR-CREAM PASTRY

Replace the water in the basic recipe by 2 to 3 tablespoons sour cream. The pastry is very flaky and very fragile.

CREAM-CHEESE PASTRY

Add 3 ounces cream cheese to the basic recipe when rubbing the flour and fat together (*sabler*). Use only 1½ to 2 tablespoons water.

SANDY PASTRY

Use the basic recipe, but melt the butter.

SWEET PASTRY

For fruit tarts if you like it, although the sour-cream pastry and the basic pastry are better and lighter.

1½ cups sifted flour	*1 teaspoon salt*
½ cup butter	*Vanilla extract, or grated citrus*
¼ cup sugar	*rinds*
1 egg	

Rub flour and butter together; add sugar, lightly beaten egg, salt and flavoring to taste. Mix together, fluffing with the fingers as indicated on page 391, and *fraiser* twice. Refrigerate for at least 2 hours before using.

PIE PLATES

Use a 9-inch aluminum pie plate 1¼ inches deep; or a French fluted china pie plate; or a flan ring set on a buttered cookie sheet; or an 8-inch round deep baking dish for upside-down pies.

Do not use an American cake pan with a detachable bottom or a French fluted pie plate with a detachable bottom. The double thickness of the metal results in uneven heat conduction, and the bottom of the pie remains soggy.

Butter the pie plate well.

ROLLING THE DOUGH

Let the dough warm up a little. If it is still too hard, give a gentle tapping with the rolling pin, but do not beat or pound heavily. Your friend the gluten is always ready to start working again.

Without stretching or pushing, roll the dough from the center out, forming a circle barely ⅛ inch thick and 1½ inches larger than the pie plate or flan ring. Dust the surface of the dough with a veil of flour. Fold the dough in quarters. Place the wedge of dough in the pie plate with the point of the wedge at the center. Open the dough, and pat it gently but firmly against the sides and the bottom of the plate to fit it neatly in the plate.

If you work with a pie plate, cut the dough all around the edges of the plate with scissors. Twist the edge of the dough between thumb and index finger to obtain a fluted rim. If you work with a flan ring, roll the pin once over the edge of the ring, to cut off the excess dough. With the left hand, push the dough over the edge of the ring while you pinch it with a pie crimper, or flatten it with the dull side of a knife blade or the tines of a fork.

ONE-OPERATION PIES AND TARTS

Cook crust and filling of "one-operation pies" at the same time. The temperature of the oven must be high at the beginning to bake the crust very quickly and seal it against penetration of moisture from the filling. Bake on the lowest rack of a preheated 400°F. oven for about 10 to 15 minutes. Then move the pie to the upper middle part of the oven and finish baking at 350°F. for an additional 20 to 30 minutes.

BLIND-BAKED PIES AND TARTS

A pie is baked "blind" when the empty crust is baked first and it is filled afterwards with a precooked filling.

If your crust is very soft and does not contain much gluten, roll it out ⅟₁₆ inch thick. Set it in the pie plate or ring, prick it very heavily with a fork, and refrigerate it for 1 hour. Then bake it in a preheated 425°F. oven for 7 to 8 minutes. If the bottom of the crust lifts, prick it again with a fork to let the air escape. This will be the very finest crust for fruit tarts—paper-thin and especially delicious if you sprinkle it with a little sugar, which will caramelize while baking.

If you are not sure of the quality of your pastry, use the classic method of fitting a foil snugly inside the unbaked shell and filling it with 4 to 5 cups of dried beans. Bake in a preheated 425°F. oven for 7 to 8 minutes. Remove the beans and foil and continue baking for another 4 to 5 minutes.

TARTLET SHELLS

The recipe for basic pastry crust (p. 391) will yield 24 tartlet shells. Buy 24 small tart pans. Butter 12 pans well. Cut 12 circles or ovals from half of the dough as close as possible to the pan size. Fit each piece of dough in a pan. Butter the second set of pans *on the bottom*, then force each one into one of the others on top of the dough, so that the dough is squeezed between the 2 pans. Scrape the excess pastry off the edges of each set of pans with the dull side of a knife blade. Fill the upper pan with dried beans. Bake in a preheated 425°F. oven for 5 minutes. Remove beans and upper pan and continue baking for another 3 to 4 minutes. The shells are paper-thin. Repeat the process for the other 12 shells.

PUFF PASTE

Read the recipe completely before you start to work. In spite of all the ado, puff paste will give you more fun than trepidation. There exist as many ways of making puff paste as there are pastry cooks. I have seen over twenty experts make it, and each one had a different technique.

The idea of the pastry is ancient, but apparently the definitive method was established at the end of the 16th century by a French cook named Saupiquet. This original method in connection with intelligent use of refrigeration gives the very best results.

Work on a large amount of paste; it is easier. These ingredients will make a large 2-pound square of dough.

2 tablespoons cornstarch *1¼ to 1⅓ cups water*
3⅞ cups sifted flour *2 cups (1 pound) unsalted*
1½ teaspoon salt *butter*

FLOUR AND WATER PASTE, OR DÉTREMPE

Put the cornstarch in a 4-cup measuring cup, and sift enough flour on top to make a total volume of 4 cups. Pour the mixture onto the counter top and mix. Make a large well in the center and put salt and ¼ cup water in it. Dissolve the salt in the water. Slowly bring some of the flour into the water with the tip of the finger. When the liquid looks like a crêpe batter, start fluffing up the flour as for an ordinary piecrust (see p. 391). Continue fluffing, adding the water tablespoon by tablespoon, until the lumps of dough will not be broken any more by the fingertips. Stay as close as you can to the butter-water ratio of 2 to 1.25 by volume, which is the most common, but the ratio for each pastry dough depends, of course, on the absorbing power of your flour and on the humidity of the day.

Gather all the lumps in one ball. Wipe all particles off the counter, using the dough ball as a mop. Holding the dough in both hands, break it open twice as you would a piece of bread. *Do not knead or handle it any more,* whether it is smooth or not. What is essential at this point is that the *détrempe* contain as little gluten as possible. You may have heard of kneading a *détrempe* for 20 minutes before enclosing the butter in it. This method is perfectly correct, for the more you knead a dough beyond 10 minutes, the more the gluten strands lose their rigidity. At 20 minutes, they have completely slackened and the *détrempe* will assimilate the butter easily. Choose: either no kneading at all or 20 *full minutes* of kneading, but *never* in between. Cut a cross ½ inch deep in the top of the dough, and refrigerate it *uncovered* for 30 minutes.

PATON

After 30 minutes, remove the butter from the refrigerator. Let it stand at room temperature for 5 minutes; during those 5 minutes soak your hands in water as cold as you can stand it. Remove the wrappers from the butter and knead the butter with your bare hands until the water drips out of it and it has become soft enough for a finger to sink into it without resistance. Do not let the butter get oily. Notice the water dripping on the counter; should you leave that water in the butter instead of removing it by kneading, that water would start acting on the flour proteins to form gluten in your paste the minute you started handling the mixture. For puff paste you do not need this gluten.

Take the *détrempe* out of the refrigerator. Poke it with a finger. If the hole stays, without shrinking, the flour and water paste is ready to use. If the paste puckers slightly, let it rest for another 30 minutes. If the hole closes completely, make another *détrempe;* the gluten has been worked too much.

With the heel of the hand, gently pat the dough into a 9-inch square. Flatten the butter into a 7-inch square. Put the butter on the *détrempe* with each corner of the butter square in the center of one of the long sides of the *détrempe* square. Fold the four corners of the *détrempe* over the butter, edge to edge and without overlapping; the points of the four corners of the *détrempe* square meet exactly in the middle, looking something like the back of an envelope. The dough and butter package is now a *paton.* Let it stand for 5 minutes, the rolling pin resting on it.

TURNS I AND II

Roll the *paton* 9 inches away from you and 9 inches toward you, keeping it 7 inches wide and never less than ½ inch thick. Do not bear down on the dough; roll the dough parallel, not perpendicular, to the counter top. You want to flatten the butter between the two layers of dough and keep it as much as possible in one unbroken sheet. Do not roll the dough in small hesitant strokes but in one or two decisive ones.

If the *paton* becomes wider than 7 inches, block it on each side by placing the rolling pin parallel to the edge of the dough and tapping it gently. The edge will straighten up. Fold the dough in three. Now turn it by 90 degrees so that it looks like a book ready to be opened. With a bit of pressure applied with the rolling pin at the top and bottom seams, pinch the layers of dough together slightly to prevent the butter escaping. Roll out the dough again and fold it a second time exactly as described above. You will have given 2 *turns.* If the dough is less than 7 inches wide, tap it gently to flatten it a little. To keep track of the turns, punch 2 small depressions at the surface of the dough with a fingertip.

Put the dough on a lightly floured plate, cover loosely with a sheet of foil, and put it to cool *in the vegetable crisper* of the refrigerator. Should you put it on a rack in the cold part of the refrigerator, the butter—which is still in a thick layer—would harden and break through the layers of flour and water dough as soon as you started working again. Let the dough rest for 1 complete hour, or longer if you wish.

TURNS III TO VI; THE HALF TURN

Finish the dough by giving 2 more series of 2 turns each, exactly as described above. The rest period, always in the vegetable crisper of the refrigerator, should never be less than 30 minutes so that the gluten produced by the mechanical action of your rolling pin has time to loosen up again. You may leave it for a longer time without adverse effects, but never for less. After turns III and IV, punch 4 small depressions at the surface of the dough. After turns V and VI, trace an X. That will remind you that the paste is finished and may be used.

While you give the turns, it may happen, and probably will, that the butter will "break out" of the dough layers. It happens even to experts, so do not panic. If the tear is small, sprinkle it with a little flour. If it is an inch long or so, cut off a little piece of paste at one of the edges. Flatten the little piece and use it to patch the hole. Continue working as if nothing had happened.

If, after giving 4 turns, there are still pieces of butter visible between layers of paste—there should not be any more at this point— give 1 *half turn*. Roll out the dough only 6 inches long in each direction and fold the paste in two instead of three. Let it rest in the crisper for a good 20 minutes before giving the last 2 turns. The dough will be perfect; it never fails.

Now, behold the finished paste! You have, while giving 6 turns, produced 730 layers of flour and water paste enclosing 729 layers of butter,* so that you can realize how very small the sheets of butter and paste are. At the same time, you have enclosed air between the layers. When you cut the paste, you will feel its resistance under your knife blade. When you bake the paste in a very hot oven, the thin layers of butter will melt and be absorbed by the starches. The pressure of the

* Madame Lucie Belime-Laugier, *Les Clés de la Cuisine Française*, page 139.

steam produced by the evaporation of the water contained in the dough will push those layers apart at the same time as the imprisoned air will dilate, and the result will be gorgeous puff pastries.

If you give more than 6½ turns, the layers of butter will integrate completely in the flour and water paste and the dough will remain an overrich short paste, which will not puff very much. The quality of a puff paste can be judged by the length of its flakes. Long uninterrupted flakes give a tender but solid crust. When the butter is introduced in the paste in small pieces, the flakes are small and interrupted and the baked product is more fragile.

ROLLING OUT, CUTTING AND FREEZING PUFF PASTE

Roll out the dough when it is deep chilled and very stiff. Cut the dough neatly, perpendicular to the counter top, so as not to produce stragglers that would prevent the paste rising. After cutting patty shells or squares of dough, put them *upside down* on the cookie sheet. This keeps the baked product from being narrower at the top than at the bottom, since a slight shrinking always occurs at the surface of the dough when it is first cut. Set the cutouts on a buttered cookie sheet rinsed under cold water; the water will vaporize while in the oven and keep the bottom of the pastries from scorching.

If you do not own pastry cutters, make rounds with a coffeepot lid. With the tip of a paring knife, cut small indentations ⅛ inch deep into the paste at the edges to replace the scalloped edge; this process is called *chiqueter.* Use the same procedure when you cut the dough following a paper pattern. For a lovely color, brush the top of all pastries with an egg-yolk glaze made of egg yolk mixed with 3 tablespoons milk. To decorate the tops of pastries, trace superficial parallel lines with the dull side of a knife blade after you have applied the egg-yolk glaze; this is called *rayer.*

Finished puff paste freezes beautifully; you may freeze it in a lump, or you may cut it into shapes such as patty shells or *vol-au-vent* and freeze it that way. Wrap a lump in wax paper and a double layer of foil. As soon as it is taken out of the freezer for defrosting, remove all wrappers and bundle the dough in a thick towel, which will absorb the thawing condensation. Defrosting should be done entirely in the refrigerator; it will take from 6 to 8 hours. Transfer cutouts directly from the freezer to a 425° oven; turn the oven down to 400° as soon as the dough has been put to bake.

SEMI-PUFF PASTE

> 3 cups sifted flour   1 teaspoon salt
> 1½ cups butter   ⅓ cup water

Make an ordinary short paste with all the ingredients. Chill for 30 minutes and give 2 turns. Chill for another 30 minutes and give another 2 turns. The dough is ready to use. Excellent for meats in a crust.

SWEETBREAD TOURTE
6 SERVINGS

Serve a salad with this country pie and a light fruit dessert for a delightful meal.

> 2 large sweetbreads
> Butter (4 to 6 tablespoons)
> 1 cup artichoke hearts
> 2 cups mushrooms, quartered
> 1 shallot, chopped fine
> 1 cup asparagus tips, blanched
> 2 tablespoons Madeira
> 2 tablespoons meat glaze, or ¼
>   teaspoon commercial meat
>   extract
>
> Salt and pepper
> ½ recipe basic pastry crust
>   (p. 391)
> ⅔ cup heavy cream
> 1 egg
> 2 teaspoons chopped chives
> ½ cup grated Gruyère or
>   Emmenthal cheese

Blanch the sweetbreads, slice them, and sauté in butter until brown on both sides. Dice sweetbreads and keep ready to use. Boil artichoke hearts until tender; cut into quarters. Sauté quartered mushrooms in butter until brown and dry. Add shallot and asparagus tips to the frying pan containing the mushrooms and sauté together for 2 minutes. Mix sweetbreads and vegetables in the same frying pan. Add Madeira and meat glaze. Mix well. Correct seasoning.

Roll out pastry and fit into a 9-inch pie plate. Fill with the sweetbread and vegetable mixture. Mix cream, egg, chives, and salt and pepper to taste; pour on the filling. Bake on the lowest oven rack of a preheated 400°F. oven for 20 minutes. Top with grated cheese and continue baking at 375°F. for an additional 15 minutes, until golden brown. Serve piping hot.

Wine: California Johannisberg Riesling or French Hermitage Blanc

POTATO PIES
12 TINY PIES

No diet has ever held its own against these little beauties.

Basic pastry crust (p. 391)	*1 cup heavy cream*
2 large Idaho potatoes	*Salt and pepper*
3 large truffles, grated, or 1 cup	
duxelles (p. 340), or chopped	
chives	

Roll out the pastry and fit it into 12 muffin tins. Parboil peeled whole potatoes for 8 minutes. Grate the potatoes; they will be lightly gummy. Fill each pastry-lined tin half full with potatoes. Add grated truffles or *duxelles* and top with more grated potato. Fill each mold with seasoned heavy cream. If you use chives, mix them with the cream. Bake on the lowest rack of a preheated 400°F. oven for 5 minutes. Raise to upper middle rack and continue baking at 325°F. until the top of the pie is golden.

DEEP-DISH ENDIVE PIE
6 SERVINGS

To *Maman* and Goody, not knowing which loves endives more.

12 small Belgian endives	*Salt and pepper*
1 tablespoon lemon juice	*⅔ cup heavy cream, scalded*
Butter (about 4 tablespoons)	*½ recipe basic pastry crust*
12 slices of hickory-smoked	*(p. 391)*
bacon	*Chopped parsley*

Braise the endives with butter and lemon juice (see page 328).
Render bacon until the slices are crisp but not brittle. Butter a 9-inch
pie plate. Arrange endives on the bottom of the plate and season with
salt and pepper. Top with bacon slices and add scalded heavy cream.
Roll out the pastry into a thin sheet and cut a circle to fit the top of the
pie. Cover the filling with the lid and cut vents in the lid with the tip
of scissors. Bake in a preheated 400°F. oven for 20 minutes, then at
325°F. for another 20 to 25 minutes. Invert on a serving platter and
sprinkle with chopped parsley; or serve in the baking dish.
Wine: Mountain White Chablis

NOVA SCOTIA QUICHE
6 SERVINGS

You may prebake the pastry for 7 to 8 minutes if you wish; then fill
the pie and bake at 375°F. for only 25 minutes. In Lorraine, however,
no one goes to all this trouble! Use fresh herbs if you can locate them;
the pie will be much better.

1 cup light cream
½ teaspoon each of dried
tarragon, chervil and chives
½ recipe basic pastry crust
(p. 391)
6 small slices of smoked Nova
Scotia salmon (no lox; it will
be too salty.)

2 eggs
1 tablespoon chopped fresh
parsley
Salt and pepper

Scald the cream and add the dried herbs; let them infuse for 1 hour.
Roll out the dough and line a 9-inch pie plate. Arrange the salmon
slices on the pastry. Mix cream, eggs, parsley, very little salt and
pepper to taste. You may wish to strain the cream if you are using
dried herbs, but it is not necessary. Definitely do not strain it if using
fresh herbs. Pour over the salmon. Bake on the lowest rack of a preheated 400°F. oven for 10 minutes. Reduce temperature to 300°F.
and bake on the middle rack of the oven for another 20 to 25 minutes.
Serve piping hot.
Wine: California Fumé Blanc

MUSHROOM TART

6 SERVINGS

To Elaine Tait, Food Editor of the *Philadelphia I*,
the dish was created.

*1 pie shell, 8 or 9 inches, baked
   blind
1 pound mushrooms, minced
Butter (about 4 tablespoons)
1 teaspoon lemon juice
1 tablespoon minced shallots
Salt and pepper*

*2 tablespoons Madeira, or grated
   nutmeg
¾ cup heavy cream
1 tablespoon chopped parsley
⅔ cup grated Gruyère or
   Emmenthal cheese*

Make the pie shell and keep ready to use. Sauté mushrooms in hot
butter; add lemon juice, shallots, and salt and pepper to taste. Toss
over high heat until all the moisture has evaporated. Add Madeira and
let evaporate; or season the mushrooms with nutmeg to taste. Add
cream and cook gently until it coats the mushrooms. Correct seasoning. Add parsley. Pour filling into prepared shell. Sprinkle with cheese
and baste with 1½ tablespoons melted butter. Protect the edge of the
pastry with foil. Broil for 2 minutes, or until golden. Serve warm.
Wine: California Semillon Blanc or French Seyssel or Quincy

VOL-AU-VENT OR PATTY SHELLS

A *vol-au-vent* is a large patty shell made of puff paste. A filled *vol-
au-vent* can serve 6 persons.

Roll out puff paste ½ inch thick. Cut 2 round pieces, using an 8-
inch saucepan lid as a pattern. Wrap the first circle of pastry over the
rolling pin and transfer it, upside down, to a buttered and rinsed
cookie sheet. Brush with egg-yolk glaze.

With a 4-inch coffeepot lid, cut a smaller circle in the center of the
second circle of pastry; remove the small circle. Lightly flour the top
of the ring that is left, fold it in quarters, and place it on top of the first
circle. Open the ring and press ring and circle edges together. Crimp

...nt the edges (see *chiqueter,* p. 399). Brush the top with egg-..k glaze. Decorate the top of the pastry as you wish (see *rayer,* p. 399). Bake on the upper rack of a preheated 425°F. oven for 30 minutes.

During baking a thin layer of the pastry will rise from the center of the bottom circle. This thin layer will serve as a lid for the pastry case. It is very thin and requires no drying. Remove the lid and the uncooked dough from the center underneath it. Turn off the oven and return the *vol-au-vent* to the oven to dry until ready to fill.

Patty shells are made in the same way. For lunch or dinner shells, use a 3½- to 4-inch cutter or coffeepot lid, and cut shells from the pastry rolled ⅓ inch thick. For cocktail shells, use a 2½-inch cutter or pot lid and cut shells from the pastry rolled ¼ inch thick. Bake on the upper rack of a preheated 425°F. oven for 20 to 25 minutes. Remove lids and uncooked inside dough, and let dry in the turned-off oven for 4 to 5 minutes.

SWEETBREAD FILLING FOR VOL-AU-VENT OR PATTIES
ENOUGH FOR 1 LARGE VOL-AU-VENT
OR 6 PATTY SHELLS

4 sweetbreads	⅓ cup plus 2 tablespoons
1 carrot, minced	Madeira or dry sherry
1 onion, minced	1 pound mushrooms, quartered
4 tablepoons butter	8 egg yolks
½ cup veal stock, or best	2 cups heavy cream
available stock	Salt and pepper

Blanch the sweetbreads. Flatten between 2 plates overnight (see p. 238). Sauté the minced carrot and onion in 2 tablespoons butter until soft but not brown. Add the sweetbreads, stock and ⅓ cup Madeira, and braise the sweetbreads in a 325°F. oven for 25 to 30 minutes. Sauté the mushrooms in 2 tablespoons butter. Dice the sweetbreads and mix with the mushrooms. Reduce the cooking juices of the sweetbreads to ¼ cup; mix with sweetbreads and mushrooms in a large *sauteuse* or frying pan. Make a liaison with egg yolks and cream, pour into the pan, and shake back and forth until the sauce coats the meat

(see p. 144). Correct seasoning, add 1 or 2 more tablespoons Madeira, and spoon into the *vol-au-vent* or patty shells.
Wine: California Fumé Blanc or *French Hermitage Blanc*

BLUE CHEESE OR ROQUEFORT TURNOVERS
ABOUT 18 TURNOVERS

Very successful as hot appetizers.

3 tablespoons unsalted butter	*½ recipe puff paste (p. 395)*
1 cup crumbled blue or	*Egg-yolk glaze (p. 421)*
Roquefort cheese	

Cream the butter, and add the crumbled cheese to obtain a paste. Roll out the puff paste ⅛ inch thick. Cut with a 5-inch cutter or the lid of a large coffeepot. Put ½ tablespoon filling in the center of each circle of dough. Brush the edges of each circle with egg-yolk glaze, and fold over to make a turnover. Press the edges to seal, and crimp them (*chiqueter*). Brush with egg-yolk glaze. Freeze.

When ready to use, preheat oven to 425°F. Put the turnovers on a baking sheet in the oven and immediately turn down the heat to 400°F. Bake for 35 to 40 minutes, or until golden. Serve when slightly cooled.

MY APPLE TART
6 SERVINGS

I have been known to eat the whole pie by myself.

3 large Stayman, Winesap or	*½ recipe for pastry of your*
Golden Grimes apples	*choice*
1 tablespoon lemon juice	*⅓ cup heavy cream*
3 tablespoons Calvados or	*2 to 3 tablespoons sugar*
applejack	

Peel and core the apples and cut into quarters. Macerate them in a mixture of lemon juice and Calvados or applejack for 2 hours, turning often. Roll out pastry and fit into an 8- or 9-inch pie plate. Arrange the drained apples in the pastry-lined plate. Beat together the Calvados from the marinade, the heavy cream and the sugar. Pour on the apples. Bake in a preheated 400°F. oven for 30 to 35 minutes. Serve lukewarm.

ZWETSCHKEWEIHE
6 SERVINGS

From Alsace, where Italian prunes are called *Zwetschke*.

½ recipe for pastry of your choice	*½ cup heavy cream*
	Pinch of salt
1½ pounds Italian prunes (small blue plums)	*¼ cup sugar*
	Grated rind of 1 lemon
1 egg	

Roll out the pastry and fit into an 8- or 9-inch pie plate. Halve the prunes and discard pits. Arrange prune halves in concentric circles on the pastry. Bake on the bottom rack of a preheated 400°F. oven for 20 minutes. Beat together egg, cream, salt, sugar and lemon rind. Pour over the prunes and continue baking in a 350°F. oven for another 20 minutes. Let cool. Serve in the pie plate.

BLACK-CURRANT PEAR TART
6 SERVINGS

To Selma Kasser, who tested the recipe.

1 pie shell, 8 or 9 inches, baked blind	*1 cup sugar*
	1 tablespoon vanilla extract
3 very ripe Bartlett, Comice, Anjou or Bosc pears	*2 boxes (10 ounces each) frozen raspberries, thawed*
1 cup water	*2 tablespoons black-currant jam*

2 to 3 tablespoons Cassis liqueur   1 cup heavy cream, whipped
    or Kirsch   2 tablespoons chopped pistachios

Bake and cool the pie shell. Peel the pears carefully, cut into halves, and core. Make a syrup with water, sugar and vanilla. Poach the pears in the syrup until they can be pierced easily with a pin. Cool the pears and drain well. (Use the drained syrup on pancakes.)

Drain the syrup from the thawed raspberries. (Use raspberry syrup for making colorful drinks.) Purée the berries in an electric blender. Sweeten the purée with black-currant jam and flavor it with the Cassis or Kirsch. Strain to remove seeds. Whip the cream to the Chantilly stage. Add the raspberry purée and continue beating until stiff. With a pastry bag, pipe some of the cream into the pastry shell. Put the pear halves on the bed of cream. Pipe the remainder of the cream between the pear halves and in the center of the pie in attractive rosettes. Sprinkle with the chopped pistachios.

CHESTNUT TARTS
12 TINY TARTS

The work is in the shells. The filling is done in a few minutes. Make very small shells, for this dessert is very rich.

Pastry of your choice   1 can (8¾ ounces) French
2 egg yolks   candied chestnut spread
⅓ cup sifted confectioners' sugar   ½ cup chopped blanched
½ cup unsalted butter   pistachios
2 tablespoons rum or Kirsch

Make pastry, shape small shells, and bake; cool. Ribbon egg yolks and sugar; cream in the butter. Add rum or Kirsch and finally blend in the chestnut spread. Pipe the filling into the shells through a pastry bag fitted with a star nozzle. Sprinkle with chopped pistachios.

CANTALOUPE TART
6 SERVINGS

Great and juicy for a summer dinner.

1 pie shell, 8 or 9 inches, baked blind
2 ripe cantaloupes

¼ cup tawny port
⅓ cup sugar
½ cup heavy cream

Bake and cool the pie shell. Cut 2 cups melon balls and steep in port for 2 hours. Purée the cantaloupe scraps to obtain 1 cup of purée. Add the sugar and cook until ⅓ cup of very thick purée is left. Flavor with half of the port in which the melon balls steeped.

Whip cream, flavor with the remainder of the port, and sweeten with 1 or 2 tablespoons of the melon purée. Spread the cream on the bottom of the baked shell. Set the cantaloupe balls on top. Reheat the sweet purée and glaze the melon balls with it. Serve as soon as possible after glazing.

RASPBERRY TART
6 SERVINGS

This exquisite tart must be made exclusively with fresh berries. Strawberries, strawberry jam or jelly, and strawberry liqueur can be used instead.

2 pints fresh ripe raspberries
2 tablespoons Framboise
1 pie shell, 8 or 9 inches, baked blind
1 egg
¼ cup sugar

¼ cup unsalted butter
¾ cup chopped blanched pistachios
3 tablespoons Kirsch
½ cup strained raspberry jam or jelly

Steep the raspberries in the Framboise for 2 hours. Bake and cool the pie shell.

Ribbon egg and sugar, and cream in butter. Pulverize ½ cup of the pistachios in the blender. Add to the egg mixture with the Kirsch. Continue beating until smooth. Spread in the prepared pastry shell. Drain the berries, reserving the liqueur, and arrange the berries on top of the pistachio mixture in the pie shell. Melt strained jam or jelly, and flavor with the Framboise drained from the berries. Brush this glaze on top of the berries; sprinkle with remaining chopped pistachios.

AVOCADO-LIME CREAM TART
4 TO 6 SERVINGS

1 pie shell, 8 inches, baked blind	*Pinch of salt*
1 avocado	*2 drops of green food coloring*
2 tablespoons dark rum	*1 teaspoon fine-grated lime rind*
2 teaspoons confectioners' sugar	*1 teaspoon unflavored gelatin,*
1 teaspoon and 2½ tablespoons	*melted*
lime juice (about 2 limes)	*¾ cup heavy cream, whipped*
3 egg yolks	*¼ cup chopped unsalted Brazil*
⅓ cup granulated sugar	*nuts*

Bake and cool the pie shell. Mash avocado with rum, confectioners' sugar and 1 teaspoon lime juice. Spread on the bottom of the pastry shell. Ribbon egg yolks, granulated sugar, salt, food coloring and lime rind over heat (see p. 484) until warm to the finger. Still beating, add remaining lime juice, then the melted gelatin. Remove from heat and beat until cold and foamy. Fold in the whipped cream. Pour over the avocado purée. Sprinkle with chopped nuts and deep chill.

BLUEBERRY NAPOLEONS
6 SERVINGS

Blueberry Bavarian cream	*1 pint fresh blueberries*
(p. 503)	*Confectioners' sugar*
½ recipe puff paste (p. 395)	
1 cup heavy cream, whipped and	
lightly sweetened	

410 ❊ WRAPPED IN DOUGH

Make Bavarian cream, and turn the mixture into an oiled 9-inch-square baking pan. When ready to use, unmold and cut into 6 rectangles 4½ by 1½ inches.

Roll out puff paste in 2 sheets 17 by 14 inches and ⅒ inch thick. Squeeze each sheet of pastry between 2 unbendable aluminum cookie sheets of the same size, buttered and rinsed under cold water. Clip the sides of the sheets with strong art clips. Put on the middle rack of a preheated 425°F. oven. Set a large roasting pan filled with boiling water on the cookie sheets. The weight keeps the pastry from rising. Bake for 12 to 15 minutes. Remove the pan of water, clips and upper cookie sheet. Raise to the top oven rack, and let the pastry brown for 5 to 6 minutes more.

Gently slide the baked sheets on a rack to cool. With a saw-edged knife, cut the cooled pastry into rectangles 4½ by 1½ inches. The pastry is fragile. Build Napoleons as follows: 1 slice of pastry, 1 slice of Bavarian cream, 1 slice of pastry spread with whipped cream, 1 layer of blueberries, 1 slice of pastry spread with whipped cream and inverted on berries. Sprinkle the finished pastries with confectioners' sugar.

PUFF-PASTE PASTIES
32 PASTIES

The nut filling can be made with blanched almonds (like French *Pithiviers*) or with walnuts, pecans, hazelnuts, pistachios. Follow the same procedure with all nuts. Or instead of the nut filling use 1 cup of your own or canned mincemeat, doctored up with a little rum.

1½ cups chopped nuts	*3 tablespoons dark rum or Kirsch*
⅓ cup sugar	*Puff paste (p. 395)*
5 tablespoons butter	*Egg-yolk glaze (p. 421)*
2 egg yolks	*Superfine powdered sugar*
½ teaspoon vanilla extract	

Put nuts and sugar in the blender container, and blend until completely pulverized. The mixture will be reduced to 1 generous cup of a thick and sticky paste. Add butter, egg yolks, vanilla and rum, and blend until the mixture is a smooth paste.

Roll out puff paste ⅛ inch thick. With a 2½-inch flower-shaped or scalloped cutter, cut as many rounds as possible. Put 1½ teaspoons filling on half of the rounds; brush the edges with egg-yolk glaze, and top with another round to form a pasty. Press edges together, and brush tops with egg-yolk glaze. Bake in a preheated 425°F. oven for 10 minutes. Sprinkle with superfine powdered sugar and bake for another 5 minutes.

XII

Staple of Life

yeast bakery

I N G R E E K, *sakcharon* means sugar and *mykes* mushroom; *cerevisiae* is the genitive of the Latin word for beer, and *Saccharomyces cerevisiae* is what you reach for on the supermarket shelf when you buy yeast. *Saccharomyces* is a plant made of only one cell; it has no chlorophyll; it lives and reproduces best between the temperatures of 80° and 110°F. Its characteristic of feeding on sugars is used in the manufacture of beers and breads. Our grandmothers baked with beer yeast or a batterlike starter kept from one baking session to the other. We use a special strain of yeast packaged in neat little cakes or envelopes and put on the market by reputable houses like Fleischmann or Red Star.

ACTIVATION OF A BATTER

When you mix yeast with flour and a liquid, you obtain a batter which is said to be activated. The term "inoculation" is also used. The activation can be initiated by several methods.

STARTER METHOD

Mix half to one third of the total volume of the flour and half of the total volume of liquid ingredients with the yeast. Gather into a ball, cut a cross in the top, and immerse the dough ball in a large bowl of water heated to 105° to 110°F. The cross allows faster penetration of the water's warmth into the "starter." Watch the ball of dough; within 10 to 15 minutes it will come floating to the surface of the water; it is then ready for blending with the rest of the ingredients.

DIRECT METHOD

Dissolve the yeast in the total amount of liquid ingredients heated to barely lukewarm; beat in half of the flour, then hand-knead remaining flour into the dough. Starter and direct methods are interchangeable in any recipe.

RAPID-MIX METHOD

This is the most modern method of activation. It allows the cook to gain a noticeable amount of time. Mix one third of the flour with the yeast. Dilute with all of the liquid ingredients heated to 110°F. Blend well, and mix with an electric mixer for 3 minutes, until a pancakelike batter is obtained. Add all the remaining ingredients on low speed.

Remember that: FLOUR + LIQUID + YEAST = ACTIVATED BATTER.

EFFECTS OF MECHANICAL ACTION ON AN ACTIVATED BATTER

To transform an activated batter into a dough, mechanical action must be used. It may come from the beaters of a mixer or from hand-kneading. The two methods are interchangeable. When you handle batter, you develop the *gluten* in the flour (see p. 389). Gluten is a protein which develops only when you handle a mixture of flour and liquid. The more handling the mixture receives, the tougher and harder it becomes.

To knead, put the batter on the counter top and push it forward with the heel of your right hand. *Use only one hand.* Raise your wrist up and down and push very rhythmically; three strokes of the hand will push the whole ball of dough forward. Turn it over and at a right angle; start kneading again. Do not knead down, but slide the dough parallel to the counter or table top. As the kneading progresses, more and more gluten forms and long strands and streaks become visible through the dough, which becomes increasingly elastic and sticks less and less to hands and counter top. After 10 minutes, it does not stick anymore, the gluten has been developed to its maximum, and you have now a *dough ready to be fermented.* Continuing the kneading beyond 10 minutes slackens the gluten again and makes the dough gummy. Underkneading, on the contrary, results in a wet, coarse, doughy bread.

A dough is *lean* when it contains only flour, water, yeast and a very small amount of fat; a dough is *rich* when in addition to flour, water and yeast, it also contains eggs, sugar and a larger amount of fat.

The richer in fat a dough is, the less you should knead it. In an overkneaded rich dough the starch is tightly enclosed in the strands of gluten and unable to absorb the fat that oozes out of the dough during baking. Rather than knead very rich doughs (*brioche,* Danish pastry, *croissants*), crash them rhythmically on the counter top until they become silky and smooth. If the recipe is that of a batter bread, pull the batter rhythmically by hand or with a spatula until the strands of gluten develop. Recipes are usually explicit about this step.

Wheat flour is the only cereal capable of developing gluten. Other flours such as rye must be blended with some wheat flour to obtain a solidly structured dough that will shape beautifully.

Remember that: ACTIVATED BATTER + MECHANICAL ACTION = DOUGH.

FERMENTATION OF THE DOUGH

Grease the finished dough very lightly to prevent the formation of a hard crust; let it ferment in a lightly greased large mixing bowl; heatproof glass, pottery, or stainless steel will do, but I prefer glass because it conducts heat well; do not use wood because it absorbs flavors. Place the bowl in an unlit oven (preheat an electric oven to 100°F., then turn off 10 minutes before putting in the dough).

The dough starts rising slowly at first. As times goes on, the yeast cells wake up and start their activity. They breathe and feed on the sugars (sucrose from the flour starch and from the sugar used to sweeten the dough). The result of their life functions is the formation of waste products: carbon dioxide and alcohol. The carbon dioxide finds itself trapped in the strong net of gluten built when kneading; the gas applies pressure on the gluten walls and forms bubbles, which leaven the dough and lighten it. More carbon dioxide is formed as the yeast cells multiply and the newborn cells start activity themselves; in 4 hours, one cell may give rise to three new generations. Alcohol is easily detectable in the pleasant smell of the unbaked dough.

The chemical and physical changes in the dough are multiple. The sugar feeds the yeast and speeds the development of carbon dioxide, but it is interesting to note that very sweet doughs rise more slowly than lean ones; it is possible that, in this case, the yeast is somewhat stupefied by a larger production of alcohol and its activity is slowed down. A similar reaction takes place in fortified wines, where brandy stops the fermentation of the wines by numbing their yeasts. Milk contains enzymes endowed with the power of slackening the gluten frame of the dough so that you must always scald and cool milk before using it so as to suppress enzymatic activity. Salt hardens the gluten, while fats have a slowing effect on the fermentation, so that very fat doughs will rise more slowly than lean ones. Whole eggs and egg whites give color and body to the dough, and you will often find a dough containing a gluten-softening acid ingredient like buttermilk or yogurt reinforced by one or several egg whites.

Let the fermentation proceed until the dough has doubled in bulk for lean doughs, or is 1½ times its original bulk for rich doughs, which undergo only what is called a "young fermentation."

The dough has fermented enough when it retains the impression of a finger. Overfermented doughs turn acid and become unpleasantly sour when baked. Their gluten structure overstretches and collapses. Sourdough breads are made with overfermented starters, which communicate their sour taste to the bulk of the dough.

Punch down the fermented dough and listen to all that hissing and puffing as the carbon dioxide is released into the atmosphere; smell, also; it is a pleasure! The handling of the dough as you punch it down will again reinforce the strength of the gluten frame. Let the dough rest for about 10 minutes before shaping the bread.

PROOFING OR PROVING THE DOUGH

Proofing or proving (both expressions are used) means letting the dough double in bulk again after it has been shaped and before baking it. Punching down the dough removes most of the carbon dioxide. By letting the shaped dough stand, you give the yeast time to produce more gas, which again distends the gluten walls and brings the bread or roll very close to its final shape and size.

COOL RISE

In the last few years, the yeast laboratories have developed the procedure of fermentation known as "cool rise." Cool rise is often used in conjunction with the "rapid-mix" activation. The fermentation starts as the dough is allowed to stay at room temperature for 20 minutes. The bread or rolls are shaped and refrigerated. They may be baked at any time after 2 hours of refrigeration, but an overnight stay in the refrigerator gives the best results. There is no proofing stage; the bread or rolls are allowed to reach room temperature and baked.

Remember that: FERMENTED SHAPED DOUGH + PROOFING = BREAD READY TO BAKE.

BAKING

Bake lean doughs at 425°F. and rich doughs at 375°F. Observe the bread after 5 minutes of baking. The heat of the oven makes the carbon dioxide dilate, and the bread swells by one third of its unbaked volume. This last rising, called "ovenspring," is a joy to behold. The lovely smell immediately following the ovenspring is that of evaporating alcohol.

While the dough gathers internal heat, the following changes occur. At 120°F. the yeast stops its activity and 10 degrees later succumbs to the heat of the oven. At 150°F. the starch of the flour mixed with the water contained in the dough thickens and gelatinizes. The browning occurs after the water contained in the dough has reached the boiling point of 212°F.; browning is due partly to the caramelization of sugars and partly to the dextrinization of the flour. The bread or roll is baked when it sounds hollow when tapped with the finger; when it is brown; when no smell of alcohol can be detected anymore on opening of the oven door.

Remove bread or rolls from their baking pans immediately, and cool them on racks to allow the steam to evaporate.

Homemade breads stale proportionally faster in the refrigerator than outside. The very best way to have fresh bread always available is to freeze it.

FREEZING UNBAKED DOUGH OR BREAD

The fermentation of a yeast-leavened dough can be postponed by freezing. Freezing can be done at any stage. Freezing the dough before the fermentation sets in requires a minimum amount of space in the freezer. Label packages of dough as in the following example:

Type of Dough: Sourdough bread
Date: 12/12/70
Next Step: Fermentation

Baked breads may be frozen; defrost them by reheating them at the temperature at which they were baked.

In the recipes that follow the best stage for freezing is listed at the end of each recipe.

TYPES OF BREAD

BATTER BREADS

These are made of a batter too liquid to be kneaded and are, instead, beaten with a wooden spoon or a mixer or by hand. To this type belong *Kugelhopf* and *brioche*.

KNEADED BREADS

The dough of these breads contains enough flour to allow kneading. Kneaded breads may be made of lean dough (French, Italian, sourdough) or rich dough (cinnamon buns).

CRASHED AND ROLLED BREADS

These breads (Danish pastry, *croissants*) are made with dough undergoing a double leavening process; they contain yeast, and the butter is incorporated in the dough by giving it "turns" (see puff paste, p. 395). The kneading is replaced by crashing so as to develop just enough gluten for the bread to hold its shape, but still allow the starch to absorb the butter.

The fermentation period is divided into two stages. The first stage takes place in the refrigerator and lasts about 1 hour. It should not last longer or the yeast develops too much carbon dioxide, which renders the turns difficult if not impossible.

The second stage coincides with the proofing. Different countries use different proofing methods; see the difference between Danish and French *croissants*.

BASIC PROPORTIONS

The exact amount of water or milk used in a recipe cannot ever be given in advance. The amount depends on the absorbancy of the flour and the humidity of the day, and it will vary from day to day and from flour to flour in any recipe.

Generally 1 cake or 1 envelope of yeast will leaven 3 cups of flour in lean doughs, but only 2 to 2½ cups in rich doughs.

Bread of 100 per cent whole wheat can be made, but rye flour, which develops no gluten, must be blended with all-purpose flour. Use half and half, or two thirds rye and one third all-purpose flour.

GLAZES

Breads acquire browner tops and crusts when they are glazed because the proteins of the glazing material coagulate and darken on contact with the heat of the oven. These glazes are used for pastry as well as for bread.

EGG-WHITE GLAZE

For lean breads. Mix 1 egg white with 3 tablespoons water. Brush on bread once before baking and twice while baking.

EGG-YOLK GLAZE

For rich breads. Mix together 1 egg yolk plus 3 tablespoons milk. Brush on rolls before baking.

BATTER BREAD (BASIC RECIPE)

¾ cup scalded lukewarm milk	*2 eggs, lightly beaten*
4 teaspoons sugar	*½ cup soft butter*
1 envelope yeast	*3 cups unsifted flour*
1¼ teaspoons salt	*Egg-yolk glaze*

Place the milk in a large mixer bowl. Add the sugar and sprinkle yeast over its surface. Let stand for 10 minutes. Add salt, lightly beaten eggs and soft butter. Little by little add half of the flour and mix in on slow speed. Add chosen flavoring, if any. Add remainder of the flour and continue beating until the batter shreds from the mixer beaters. Place the batter in a greased bowl and let rise until double in bulk.

Punch down the dough. Beat with a spatula for a few minutes and turn into a buttered 1½-quart casserole. Let it rise again until almost double in bulk. Brush with egg-yolk glaze. Bake in a preheated 375°F. oven for 35 minutes.

VARIATIONS

Viennese Bread Flavor with ⅛ teaspoon ground cardamom or ¼ teaspoon ground cinnamon and ½ teaspoon fine-grated lemon rind.

German Bread Flavor with 1 tablespoon caraway seeds; replace salt with celery salt.

Cheese Bread Add ½ cup fine-diced cheese; use Cheddar, Jack, smoked Cheddar or Swiss.

Danish Bread Add ½ teaspoon cracked white pepper and 3 tablespoons minced fresh dill.

Raisin or Currant Bread Increase the amount of sugar to 2 tablespoons; add ½ cup dried currants or raisins.

Best Freezing Stage for Batter Breads and Variations: BEFORE FERMENTATION.

FRENCH BREADS

True French bread contains *no sugar* and *no milk*. Breads containing milk that are sold in French bakeries bear the name of *baguettes viennoises*. The method is the same for both.

ORDINARY FRENCH BREAD
  Starter
    1½ cups unsifted flour
    2 envelopes yeast

    1 scant cup water

  Dough
    4½ cups unsifted flour
    2½ to 3 teaspoons salt
    3 tablespoons oil (corn or olive)
    1½ to 2 cups water

    White cornmeal
    Egg-white glaze (p. 421)

BAGUETTE VIENNOISE
  Starter
    1½ cups unsifted flour
    2 envelopes yeast
    1 tablespoon sugar
    1 scant cup water

  Dough
    4½ cups unsifted flour
    2½ teaspoons salt
    3 tablespoons butter, softened
    1½ cups scalded and cooled milk
    2 egg whites
    White cornmeal
    Egg-white glaze (p. 421)

For both breads: Make a starter with 1½ cups unsifted flour, the yeast, sugar if applicable, and scant cup of water.

It is impossible to be more exact about the amounts of water used in the starter, because it depends on the absorbing power of the flour starches. Immerse the starter ball in a bowl of water heated to 110°F., and let it bob to the surface of the water. Put 4½ cups unsifted flour on the counter top. Make a well in the flour, and add salt, oil or soft butter, water or milk, and egg whites if applicable. Gather all ingredients into a ball. Blend starter and the bulk of the dough together. Knead for 10 minutes, or until the dough is smooth and does not stick any more to either counter top or hands. Place in a greased bowl; let rise until 2½ times its original volume.

Punch down the dough. Before you shape the bread, grease or butter 1 or 2 large baking sheets 17 by 14 inches; sprinkle them with white cornmeal.

Bâtards   A *bâtard* is a large French bread 2½ to 3 inches in diameter when baked. Cut the dough into 2 portions. Roll each portion into a rectangle 14 by 17 inches. Roll up each rectangle tightly to make a bread. Taper both ends by rolling them back and forth with the flat of the hand. With a razor blade or steak knife, cut diagonal slashes ½ inch deep through the top of each loaf. The recipe will make 2 large *bâtards*, 17 inches long.

Baguettes   A *baguette* is that well-known long loaf of bread about 2 inches in diameter when baked. In French bakery shops they are about 32 inches long. You will not be able to make yours longer than 17 inches. Cut the dough into 4 portions. Roll each portion into a rectangle 7 by 17 inches. Roll up each rectangle tightly to make a bread. Taper both ends by rolling them back and forth with the flat of the hand. With a razor blade or steak knife cut diagonal slashes ⅓ inch deep through the top of each loaf. The recipe will make 4 *baguettes* 17 inches long.

Ficelles   These loaves are not as well known as *baguettes* although they are much more delicious. Since they are not as thick, they are crisper when baked. The *ficelles* you make will look quite authentic since those sold in French bakeries are only half as long as *baguettes*. Cut the dough into 8 portions. Roll each portion into a rectangle 4 by 17 inches. Roll up each rectangle tightly to make a bread. Taper both ends by rolling them back and forth with the flat of the hand. With a

razor blade or steak knife cut diagonal slashes ¼ inch deep through
the top of each loaf. The recipe will make 8 *ficelles* about 1 inch in
diameter and 17 inches long.

Place whichever breads you have shaped on the prepared baking
sheets; you will need 1 sheet for the *bâtards,* 2 sheets for the *baguettes*
or *ficelles.* Let the loaves prove until double in bulk.

Bake in a preheated 425°F. oven for 15 to 25 minutes, according
to size. Brush with egg-white glaze three times during baking.

Best Freezing Stage: BEFORE FERMENTATION.

THE KIDS' BREAD

The family booster for iron deficiencies. Inspired by the Alsatian
Birewecke.

2 cups whole-wheat flour	*¼ cup each of whole pecans,*
1 cup unsifted all-purpose flour	*hazelnuts and walnuts*
⅓ cup milk, scalded and cooled	*¼ cup dark raisins*
3 tablespoons blackstrap molasses	*2 tablespoons water*
1 envelope yeast	*3 tablespoons dark brown sugar*
½ teaspoon salt	*Ground cinnamon, allspice and*
3 eggs, slightly beaten	*cloves*
½ cup soft butter	*Egg-yolk glaze (p. 421)*
1 pound mixed dried fruit	

Mix both flours; put on the counter top and make a well. Put milk,
molasses and yeast in the well. Let stand for 15 minutes. Add the salt,
slightly beaten eggs and the butter cut into tablespoon-size pieces.
Gather into a dough; knead for 10 minutes. Put in a greased bowl and
let rise until double in bulk.

Meanwhile, chop the dried fruit; chop the nuts if you like, or leave
whole. Mix with raisins, water, brown sugar, and spices to taste. Let
stand until ready to use.

Roll the dough into a rectangle 10 by 8 inches and ¼ inch thick.
Sprinkle the fruit mixture on the dough; roll tightly to form a loaf.

Let prove for 45 minutes to 1 hour. Brush with egg-yolk glaze. Bake in a preheated 375°F. oven for 40 to 45 minutes.

Best Freezing Stage: BAKED.

WIENER KIPFELN OR WIENER SPITZWECKEN

This dough is the ancestor of both the French *croissants* and the Danish pastry on pages 427 and 426. It came to France with Marie Antoinette and traveled to Denmark, where it is still called *Wienerbrød.*

5 cups unsifted flour	*1½ to 2 teaspoons salt*
¼ cup granulated sugar	*2 medium-size whole eggs*
1⅓ cups lukewarm milk	*2 extra egg yolks*
1 envelope yeast	*1 cup plus 6 tablespoons butter*
¼ teaspoon ground cinnamon	*Egg-yolk glaze (p. 421)*
¾ teaspoon fine-grated lemon rind	

Put the flour on the counter top and make a well in the center. Put sugar and milk in the well and sprinkle yeast on the surface of the milk. Let stand until the yeast starts to bubble. Add cinnamon, lemon rind, salt, slightly beaten whole eggs and yolks. Slowly incorporate the flour in the liquid ingredients. Add the 6 tablespoons soft butter without kneading. Crash the dough on the counter top until it no longer sticks either to counter or hands. Refrigerate, wrapped in floured aluminum foil, for 1 hour.

Knead the cup of butter with bare hands until it has the same consistency as the dough. Pat the dough into a 9-inch square 2 inches thick, and flatten the butter into a 7-inch square ¼ inch thick. Put the butter on the dough. Fold in the four corners of the dough as you would those of an envelope. Give the dough 6 "turns" (see Puff Paste, p. 395), refrigerating between each 2 turns for 30 minutes.

Cut the dough into 3 pieces and roll each into a circle 9½ inches in diameter. Cut each circle into 8 or 12 wedges; roll each wedge from base to point and bend to form a crescent. Brush with egg-yolk glaze.

Prove until double in bulk. Bake in a preheated 375°F. oven for 15 minutes.

Best Freezing Stage: AFTER ALL TURNS HAVE BEEN COMPLETED.

DANISH PASTRY

A personal interpretation. To Marjorie Fine, the best 12-year-old baker in Lexington, Massachusetts. Buttermilk or sour cream may be used instead of milk and lemon juice. The acid mellows the gluten strands.

STARTER

2 cups sifted flour	*2 envelopes yeast*
¼ cup sugar	*½ cup water*

DOUGH

3 cups sifted all-purpose flour	*2 whole eggs*
¼ cup cornstarch	*2 extra egg yolks*
2 teaspoons salt	*2¼ cups butter*
½ cup milk	*Egg-yolk glaze (p. 421)*
1 tablespoon lemon juice	

Make the starter and immerse the dough ball in water heated to 110°F. until it bobs to the surface of the water.

Make the bulk of the dough. Mix the flour and cornstarch on the counter top and make a well in the center. Put salt, milk, lemon juice, slightly beaten whole eggs and egg yolks in the well. Mix together and gather into a ball. Mix the starter with the bulk dough.

Crash the dough on the counter top ten times. Add ¼ cup of the butter, softened, tablespoon by tablespoon, while continuing to crash the dough. *Positively do not knead.* Crash steadily for 10 to 12 minutes, until the dough is smooth and leaves hands and counter freely. Shape into a rectangle 8 by 6 inches. Wrap in foil and refrigerate for 1 hour.

Give the turns. Flatten the dough to a 10-inch square. Knead the rest of the butter with bare hands, and flatten it to an 8-inch square. Put the butter square on the dough square and fold corners over the butter. Give 6 turns (see Puff Paste, p. 395), two at a time, at a 30-

to 45-minute interval each time. Put the dough-butter package in the vegetable crisper of the refrigerator between turns.

Shape finished dough in desired shapes. To shape crescents, follow the procedure for *croissants* (p. 427). To shape *schnecken,* roll out the dough into 2 large rectangles 17 by 14 inches and ½ inch thick. Sprinkle or spread the surface of each rectangle with the chosen filling —jelly, cheese, almond paste, etc.—and roll up the dough again to form a long loaf. Cut the loaf into ⅓-inch-thick slices. Put slices on a buttered cookie sheet and refrigerate for 2 hours. Let stand at room temperature for 15 minutes before baking. Glaze with egg-yolk glaze. Bake in a 375°F. oven for 20 to 25 minutes.

Best Freezing Stage: AFTER THE SIX TURNS.

CROISSANTS

There is a wide variation in the quality of *croissants.* The two formulas given here are executed according to the same method. No overnight stay in the refrigerator is absolutely necessary, but the baked product tastes better if the dough is kept refrigerated one or two days before baking.

CROISSANTS DE BOULANGER	CROISSANTS DE PÂTISSIER
Starter	Starter
½ cup unsifted flour	*¾ cup sifted flour*
1 envelope yeast	*1 envelope yeast*
3 to 4 tablespoons water	*3 to 4 tablespoons water*
1 tablespoon sugar	*2 tablespoons sugar*
Dough	Dough
1¾ cups unsifted flour	*1¾ cups sifted flour*
½ to ⅔ cup water	*½ to ⅔ cup milk*
1 teaspoon salt	*¾ teaspoon salt*
¾ to 1 cup butter	*1 cup butter*
Egg-white glaze (p. 421)	*Egg-yolk glaze (p. 421)*

Make the starter, immerse in water, and let rise to the surface. Meanwhile, make the bulk of the dough by mixing flour, water or milk, and salt. Blend starter and dough and crash on the counter until the dough does not stick to either hands or counter top. Flatten to an 8-inch square ⅓ inch thick.

Knead the butter with bare hands; spread in the center of the dough. Enclose the butter in the dough and give 6 turns (see Puff Paste, p. 395), refrigerating in the vegetable crisper for at least 30 minutes between turns. Let finished dough rest in the refrigerator for about 30 minutes before cutting.

Cut dough into three parts; roll each one to a circle 10 inches in diameter. Cut each circle into 6 wedges. Roll each wedge from base to point and bend both ends to form a crescent. Set on a buttered cookie sheet. Let rise until double in bulk. Brush with appropriate glaze. Bake in a preheated 375°F. oven for 15 to 18 minutes.

Best Freezing Stage: AFTER THE SIX TURNS.

PETITS PAINS AU CHOCOLAT
24 PIECES

The afternoon snack of millions of French children.

1 ½ pounds semisweet chocolate	Croissants de boulanger
(24 one-ounce pieces)	*Egg-yolk glaze (p. 421)*

Cut each ounce of chocolate lengthwise into halves. Roll the dough to a rectangle 18 by 16 inches and ⅛ inch thick. Cut the sheet into 24 smaller rectangles 3 by 4 inches. Place 2 pieces of chocolate end to end on each rectangle, and roll up the dough around the chocolate. Place the rolls on a buttered cookie sheet; let prove until double in bulk. Brush with egg-yolk glaze. Bake in a preheated 375°F. oven for 20 to 25 minutes.

BRIOCHES DE BOULANGER

Use the electric mixer and the rapid-mix and cool-rise methods.

3 cups unsifted flour	*¼ cup water*
1 envelope yeast	*2 large or 3 small eggs*
2 tablespoons sugar	*¾ cup butter*
¾ teaspoon salt	*Egg-yolk glaze (p. 421)*

Mix ½ cup of the flour, the yeast, sugar and salt. Add water and mix on medium speed. Add 1 egg and 1 additional cup of flour, and blend well. Add another egg, then the butter, tablespoon by table-spoon, and another 1 cup of flour. Beat on medium speed for 1 min-ute, or until the dough shreds from the beaters. Place ½ cup flour on the counter and incorporate it in the dough, kneading lightly. Roll the dough into a ball and place it in a greased mixing bowl. Let stand at room temperature, covered with clear plastic wrap and a kitchen towel, for 20 minutes.

Butter 12 *brioche* molds or muffin tins. Shape 12 balls large enough to fill two thirds of each mold, and 12 smaller pear-shaped pieces. Cut a cross at the center of each large ball and fit one of the small pieces in each opening. Place the molds on a jelly-roll pan and cover loosely with clear plastic wrap. Refrigerate overnight.

Let the *brioches* stand at room temperature for 15 minutes. Bake in a preheated 350°F. oven for 10 minutes. Brush with egg-yolk glaze and continue baking for another 10 to 12 minutes.

Best Freezing Stage: BAKED.

BRIOCHE MOUSSELINE

This is the aristocrat of all *brioches*. Compare with the rapid-mix and cool-rise *brioche*. Use the starter method and work entirely by hand, because the electric mixer would develop too much gluten for the very large amount of butter in the recipe.

STARTER

⅔ cup sifted flour	2 tablespoons sugar
1 envelope yeast	¼ cup water

DOUGH

1⅓ cups sifted flour	1 cup unsalted butter, very soft
½ to ¾ teaspoon salt	but not melted
1 tablespoon milk	Egg-yolk glaze (p. 421)
3 eggs, slightly beaten	

Make the starter, immerse in water, and let rise to the surface. Put the remainder of the flour on the counter top and make a well in the center. Put salt in the well and dissolve it in the milk. Add the eggs and ¼ cup of the butter. With fingertips mix butter and eggs and slowly gather the flour to obtain a smooth but thin batter. Remove the starter from the water, and mix it with the dough. Pull the dough toward you until a little elasticity develops.

Take 2 tablespoons of the remaining butter at a time and work it into the dough with the fingertips. Repeat until all the butter has been used. *Do not knead or crash any more;* the dough will be elastic enough. Put it in a large bowl and let rise until 1½ times larger in bulk.

Punch down the dough and let it rise again until 1½ times larger in bulk. The total time for rising is 3 to 4 hours. Turn the dough into 2 heavily buttered Charlotte molds, and let it rise again until it reaches the rim of each mold. Brush the tops with egg-yolk glaze. Bake in a preheated 425°F. oven for 20 to 25 minutes.

It is possible to make the dough at 7:30 P.M., let it rise until 9:30 P.M., then refrigerate it overnight. Mold it and let it prove the next morning for breakfast.

SEMISWEET ROLL DOUGH

For dinner rolls.

1⅓ cups lukewarm scalded milk	*1 cup butter, softened*
2 tablespoons sugar	*2 teaspoons salt*
2 envelopes yeast	*6 cups unsifted flour*
4 eggs, beaten	

Place lukewarm milk and sugar in a larger mixer bowl. Sprinkle yeast over milk. Let stand for 10 minutes. Add beaten eggs, soft butter and salt. Mix well. Add 3 cups flour. Place the remainder of the flour on the counter top; gradually work it into the dough by hand. Knead for 10 to 15 minutes, or until smooth. Place the dough in a lightly greased bowl, and let rise until double in bulk.

Punch down, shape, let prove until double in bulk again, and bake. This recipe will make:

- ✿ 18 to 24 crescents. Bake in a preheated 425°F. oven for 12 to 15 minutes.
- ✿ 36 muffins. Bake in a preheated 425°F. oven for 12 to 15 minutes.
- ✿ 2 large braids. Bake in a preheated 425°F. oven for 20 to 25 minutes.

SWEET YEAST DOUGH

Follow proportions for semisweet roll dough, but increase the amount of sugar to ⅓ cup. Make the recipe according to the directions for semisweet roll dough.

Best Freezing Stage for Semisweet and Sweet Roll Doughs: BE-FORE FERMENTATION.

STICKY BUNS

To Charlotte Sheedy, to bring back Philadelphia memories.

Sweet yeast dough	*1 teaspoon ground cinnamon*
¾ cup unsalted butter	*½ cup dried currants or raisins*
1 ¼ cups dark brown sugar	*½ cup chopped pecans or*
2 tablespoons dark corn syrup	*walnuts*

Make the recipe for sweet yeast dough, let it rise, and punch down.

Cream ½ cup butter with ¾ cup brown sugar and the corn syrup. Spread over the bottom of a 10-inch cast-iron skillet with heatproof handle.

Roll the dough to a rectangle 15 by 12 inches. Brush the whole surface of the dough with the remaining ¼ cup butter, melted. Sprinkle with remaining ½ cup brown sugar, the cinnamon, currants and pecans. Add more cinnamon if you like. Roll the dough in a long roll. Cut across in slices 1 to 1½ inches thick. Set the slices close to one another on the bottom of the pan. Let rise until the dough reaches the rim of the skillet. Bake in a preheated 375°F. oven for 25 to 30 minutes, or until brown on the top.

Best Freezing Stage: BAKED.

ABGESCHLAGENER KUGELHUPF

This recipe comes from the hand-written cookbook of one of my grandmothers. It can be traced back about 150 years in the family. For best results, use a *Bundtkuchen* pan lined with nonstick coating.

½ cup raisins	*1 cup unsalted butter*
¼ cup rum	*1½ teaspoons salt*
⅔ cup milk	*6 eggs*
2 tablespoons sugar	*2⅔ cups sifted flour*
1½ envelopes yeast	*½ cup whole blanched almonds*

Soak the raisins in rum overnight; the rum will be all absorbed. Scald the milk; cool to lukewarm. Add 1 tablespoon sugar. Sprinkle yeast over the mixture and let stand for 10 minutes. Meanwhile, cream the butter and the second tablespoon of sugar until white. Add salt, then the eggs, one at a time, beating well between additions. Blend yeast mixture into egg and butter mixture. Gradually add flour on slow speed. Beat on medium speed for 2 minutes. Add the soaked raisins. Butter the cake pan heavily. Sprinkle almonds on the bottom, and fill with the batter. Let the batter rise till it reaches the rim of the pan. Bake in a preheated 375°F. oven for 25 to 30 minutes.

Best Freezing Stage: BAKED.

OLD-FASHIONED SAVARIN

Also from my grandmother's cookbook. Notice the heavy cream; it makes all the difference in the world.

STARTER

1 cup sifted flour	*2 tablespoons sugar*
1½ envelopes yeast	*3 to 4 tablespoons water*

DOUGH

2¼ cups sifted flour   Fine-grated rind of 1 lemon
6 eggs   1 cup melted unsalted butter,
¾ teaspoon salt   cooled
½ cup heavy cream

SYRUP AND CREAM

1 cup sugar   ⅓ cup Curaçao or Triple Sec
2 cups water   1 cup sweetened whipped cream
¼ cup Kirsch
⅓ cup Noyau de Poissy or
   Crème de Noyau (almond
   liqueur)

Make the starter, immerse in water, and let rise to the surface. Meanwhile, mix together on slow speed of the electric mixer, so as to obtain a loose batter, the 2¼ cups flour, the eggs, salt, heavy cream and lemon rind. Add raised starter and blend well. Gradually add the melted butter on slow speed. Mix on medium speed for 2 minutes. Let rise in the mixing bowl for 1 hour.

Punch down with a spatula. Turn into a well-buttered *Bundt-kuchen* pan lined with nonstick coating. Let rise until the batter reaches the rim of the pan. Bake in a preheated 375°F. oven for 35 minutes. *Do not unmold.*

Make the syrup with sugar and water. Add liqueurs. Slice off the hard top crust of the cake. Gradually spoon the syrup on the cake and around the inside of the cake pan. Let the *savarin* cool to lukewarm. Unmold on a serving platter and serve with sweetened whipped cream.

Best Freezing Stage: BAKED.

BABAS

Use the recipe for *savarin,* but replace the liqueurs in the syrup with pure rum. Bake the dough in muffin tins. Immerse the baked *babas* in the syrup. Push on each with a soup ladle to squeeze the air out. Release the pressure gradually until each cake is soaked with syrup. Drain the *babas* on a cake rack. Serve with sweetened whipped cream.

XIII

Light and Airy Relatives

cakes

CAKES ARE breadlike products resulting from the mixture of protein foams with flour, shortening, flavorings and leavening agents. Each of the elements entering the composition of a cake batter plays a special role in its making and baking.

FLOUR

Flour starches and gluten mix with egg protein to form the structure of a cake. Use the flour called for in the recipe, and always sift it. Too much flour will result in a heavy, compact cake; not enough flour will result in a cake that collapses in the oven before its baking time is completed. Blend flour into batters using the slow speed of a mixer, or gently by hand, to prevent too much gluten development. *All these recipes are based on all-purpose flour.*

EGGS

Eggs are considered part of the liquid ingredients of a cake batter. They give the batter taste, color and richness. Last but not least they give volume when they are beaten; they are the main leavening agent for old-fashioned spongecake and poundcake.

SUGAR

Sugar sweetens the batter and gives it color as it bakes and browns in the oven. The more sugar a cake contains, the more the gluten development of the flour will be slowed down, and the longer the egg and flour proteins will need to coagulate in the oven. A cake containing 1 cup or more of sugar per cup of flour is called a high-ratio cake. High-ratio cakes have a fine texture because the cell walls of their batters take a very long time to stretch.

FAT

As in a pastry dough, the fat coats the gluten strands of the flour, allowing them to slide against one another. Fat tenderizes the cake batter. The tenderest cakes are made with vegetable shortening, but the most flavorful ones are made with butter. The creaming of either shortening or butter introduces air into the batter; that air is an important leavening agent.

LEAVENING

Double-acting baking powder, as everyone knows, is the leavener of modern cakes. It contains acids, which are released when they come in contact with the liquid ingredients in the batter and thus produce carbon dioxide. The carbon dioxide develops in the oven and dilates under the influence of the heat, thus making the cake rise. Baking soda to become active must be put in contact with an acid—lemon juice, vinegar, sour cream or buttermilk. The procedure of dissolving baking soda in the liquid acid should be disregarded in modern bakery. Baking soda is ground fine enough to be added as a powder to the batter, so that the carbon dioxide which was formerly lost in the surrounding atmosphere is now retained in the batter. In foam cakes or poundcakes, the leaveners are the air beaten into the eggs and creamed into the butter, and the steam resulting from the vaporization, during baking, of the water contained in the butter and eggs.

In modern bakery, three main types of cakes exist: shortened cakes, poundcakes and foam cakes (including angel, sponge, chiffon, torten). All types are mixed following the very definite patterns and ratios listed here:

BUTTER OR SHORTENED CAKES

The recipe will start: "Cream the butter . . .", except when the one-bowl method is used.

ONE-BOWL METHOD

Always use vegetable shortening. Beat liquid ingredients into dry ingredients.

Leavening agent: baking powder, 100%.

Ratios per cup of sifted flour:

¾ *cup sugar*   *1 teaspoon baking powder*
¼ *cup shortening*   *1 to 1½ eggs*
½ *cup milk*

Baking temperature: 350°F.

CREAMING METHOD

Use vegetable shortening or butter, or a combination of both. Cream the butter, add sugar, and beat until fluffy. Add alternately dry and liquid ingredients.

Leavening agents: air introduced by creaming, 15%; baking powder, 85%.

Ratios per cup of sifted flour are the same as above.

POUNDCAKES

Only true poundcakes made without baking powder are considered here. Poundcakes owe their name to their composition, which is always 1 pound each of flour, sugar, eggs and butter. In French, they are called *quatre-quarts,* or "four-quarters," for ¼ pound of each main ingredient. The only liquid ingredients are the eggs.

Cream the butter and add sugar. Add egg yolks, one at a time, beating after each addition. Blend in dry ingredients. Fold in beaten egg whites.

Leavening agents: air introduced by creaming, 25%; egg-white foam, 75%.

Ratios per cup of sifted flour:

½ *cup plus 2 tablespoons butter*   ½ *cup sugar*
2 *eggs*

Baking temperature: 325°F.
The top of the cake will crack due to internal steam pressure.

FOAMCAKES

The recipe will start: "Beat egg yolks and sugar until thick and lemon-colored . . ." or "Ribbon egg yolks and sugar. . . ."

BAKING-POWDER SPONGECAKE

Ribbon egg yolks and sugar. Slowly beat in dry ingredients and water (hot or cold). Fold in beaten egg whites.

Leavening agents: egg-yolk and egg-white foams, 40%; baking powder, 60%.

Ratios per cup of sifted flour:

> *3 eggs, separated*   *1 teaspoon baking powder*
> *1 cup sugar*   *⅓ cup water*

Baking temperature: 325° to 350°F.

OLD-FASHIONED SPONGECAKE

Ribbon egg yolks and sugar. Fold in beaten egg whites and dry ingredients at the same time (see p. 61).

Leavening agents: egg-yolk and egg-white foam only.

Ratios per cup of sifted flour:

> *4 eggs, separated*   *¼ to ½ cup butter (optional;*
> *½ cup sugar*   *a true sponge is butterless)*

Baking temperature: 325°F.

WHOLE-EGG SPONGECAKE

Whole-egg sponge is an old European cake known in France under the name of *génoise*, in England under the name of *gâteau*, and in German countries under the name of *warme Teigmasse* or *Genueser*.

Ribbon whole eggs and sugar (see p. 443). Fold in flour. Fold in melted butter.

Ratios per cup of sifted flour:

> *4 to 6 eggs*   *½ cup butter or less, or even no*
> *½ to 1 cup sugar*   *butter at all*

Baking temperature: 325° or 350°F.

CHIFFON CAKES

Made with oil exclusively.

Blend flour, sugar, baking powder and salt; mix with oil, egg yolks and liquid ingredients. Fold in beaten egg whites. Bake in a tube or loaf pan only.

Leavening agents: egg foam, 50%; baking powder, 50%.

Ratios per cup of sifted flour:

> *¾ cup sugar*   *3 egg yolks*
> *1½ teaspoons baking powder*   *6 tablespoons water*
> *¼ cup oil*   *4 egg whites*

Baking temperature: 325° to 350°F.

ANGEL CAKE

Made with egg whites only.

Beat egg whites and granulated sugar. Fold in flour and confectioners' sugar.

Leavening agent: egg-white foam, 100%.

Ratios per cup of sifted flour:

> *1 cup granulated sugar*   *12 egg whites*
> *1½ cups confectioners' sugar,*
>   *sifted*

Baking temperature: 375°F.

TORTEN (FLOURLESS CAKES)

WHOLE-EGG TORTEN

Ribbon egg yolks and sugar. Fold into them the beaten egg whites together with nuts.

Ratios per cup of ground nuts:

3 eggs, separated   *⅓ cup sugar*
⅓ cup bread crumbs or cake crumbs

Baking temperature: 350°F.

EGG-WHITE TORTEN

Beat egg whites. Fold in sugar and nuts.

Ratios per cup of ground nuts:

3 egg whites   *⅓ cup plus 1 tablespoon sugar*

Baking temperature: 325°F.

GENERAL BAKING PROCEDURES

Before you start mixing the cake batter, apply soft butter generously and evenly to the bottom and sides of baking pans; use your fingertips or a pastry brush, never a wax paper or the pan will be unevenly buttered.

Whatever the type of cake baked, the same physical transformations take place in a batter when it bakes. The heat provokes the dilatation of the air and/or carbon dioxide in the cell walls of the batter at the same time that it causes the vaporization of the water. The combined effect of gas dilatation and steam pressure provokes the stretching of the starch and egg-protein walls. When most of the steam has evaporated, the cake is baked. Test its doneness by inserting a metal skewer at the center of the cake. If it comes out dry, shiny and too hot to be bearable for more than a few seconds when applied to the back of your hand, the cake is done. Most cakes are cooled in the baking pan, but not a *génoise* (see p. 444). Let a poundcake cool in its pan for 10 minutes. Invert chiffon and angel cakes by putting the cone in the center of the tube pan over an upside-down funnel.

Cutting a Cake into Layers

Slice a cake into layers only when it is completely cold. Cut 2 pieces of wax paper or foil. Put the cake on one of them. Exactly in front of you, cut a small vertical groove ¹⁄₁₆ inch deep in the side of the cake; it will help you to match the layers after filling and icing the cake. Holding a very sharp knife in your right hand, press the tip of the blade against the side of the cake while your right hand remains motionless on the counter top. Rest your left hand on top of the cake and with it turn the cake around in a circle. The tip of the knife will trace a line all around the cake. Fit a strong but thin thread in this line, cross both ends of the thread, and pull to separate the layers. Slide the second piece of wax paper or foil between the layers and lift off the top layer. If the cake contains nuts use a knife.

Icing a Cake

To ice a cake, set it on a cake rack. Melt 2 to 3 tablespoons jelly (currant for berry cakes, apricot for chocolate cakes), and brush it on the surface and around the sides of the cake to trap the crumbs and keep them from breaking through the icing. Pour a thin icing at the exact center of the cake top and let it drip around the sides. To ice with a thick icing, spread the icing on the sides first and on the top of the cake last.

To transfer a cake to a serving platter, cross two long spatulas under it, take hold of their handles in each hand with confidence, and deposit the cake at the center of the platter without problem or complications.

SPECIAL TECHNIQUES FOR OLD-FASHIONED CAKES

To Fold Dry Ingredients into an Old-Fashioned Sponge

Start beating the egg yolks and let them foam well. Separate the whole amount of sugar into 4 equal parts. Start adding the first part in one long stream; continue beating for 1 minute before you add the second part, and so on until you have used all the sugar. Whip the egg whites. Mix one quarter of their volume into the egg-yolk foam. Slide the remainder of the whites on top of the yolk foam; sift or sprinkle the dry ingredients on top of the whites. With a spatula cut down at the center and fold the three elements into one another until the batter is homogenous.

The Difficult Technique of Génoise

PLAIN 4-EGG GÉNOISE

4 eggs	1 tablespoon vanilla extract or
1 cup sifted flour	liqueur
½ cup sugar	½ cup melted butter
¼ teaspoon salt	

Bake in 2 buttered 8-inch pans.

FINE 6-EGG GÉNOISE

6 eggs	½ teaspoon salt
1 cup plus 2 tablespoons sifted flour	1½ tablespoons vanilla extract or liqueur
1 cup sugar	6 tablespoons clarified butter

Bake in 2 buttered 9-inch pans.

COCOA GÉNOISE

6 eggs	¼ teaspoon salt
¼ cup sifted flour	1½ tablespoons vanilla extract or liqueur
½ cup sifted cocoa	½ cup clarified butter
2 tablespoons sifted cornstarch	
¾ cup sugar	

Bake in 2 buttered 8-inch pans.
On your first try, make an ordinary 4-egg génoise.

Butter the baking pan or pans and lightly dust with flour the bottom of the pan only. Warm unbroken eggs in warm water. Sift the flour. Preheat a 3- to 4-quart mixing bowl with boiling water; dry it. Break the eggs into the bowl and place it on a protective pad over a stove burner on medium low heat; use a metal protector for an electric stove, asbestos or metal for a gas stove. Start beating the eggs immediately with the electric mixer. Add the sugar little by little in a regular stream. Add the salt. Within seconds the batter will swell considerably. Continue beating until a light ribbon forms and the mixture feels frankly *warm* to the finger; the eggs start poaching and the sugar forms a syrup, trapping the already dilating air in the foam. Remove the bowl from the heat, add the flavoring, and continue beating until cold; a twisting ribbon will fall from the beaters. Do not let the batter reach the soft-peak stage or the cake will look and taste cotton-like.

Return the already sifted flour to the sifter. Sift one third of its total volume on top of the egg foam. Fold the flour into it, using a large rubber spatula or your right hand with the fingers extended. Repeat the same operation with the other two thirds of the flour. Do not add the flour in more than three additions or the cake will be overfolded.

Gently pour half of the butter on top of the batter. Try to catch it with your spatula before it has time to fall to the bottom of the bowl. Fold only until the butter is incorporated; repeat with the remainder of the butter.

Holding the bowl very low over the prepared cake pan, pour the batter into it very slowly. Bake the cake on the lowest rack of a preheated 325°F. oven for the 4-egg recipe, and in a 350°F. oven for the 6-egg and cocoa recipes. The air dilatation and steam pressure will continue regularly and evenly. Test doneness as you would any other cake. Do not let the cake shrink too much from the pan sides. Invert on a cake rack as soon as removed from the oven. Baking time: 40 minutes.

EUROPEAN FILLINGS AND ICINGS
FOR EUROPEAN CAKES

Europeans fill their cakes with pure buttercreams. Since there must be over the whole continent about 20 different formulas for buttercream, I have decided to include here the easiest and the finest. Everything else is "in-between" in difficulty and quality.

CONFECTIONERS' SUGAR BUTTERCREAM

5 egg yolks   *½ pound* unsalted *butter*
1 cup sifted confectioners' sugar   *Flavoring*
Pinch of salt

Ribbon together yolks, sugar and salt until very light. The sugar should not be detected when you taste the mixture. Cream half of the butter into the base. Add the flavoring and the remainder of the butter, tablespoon by tablespoon. Use immediately, or store in the refrigerator. If stored, rebeat before using.

Should the emulsion of this buttercream break, add 1 or 2 more tablespoons of butter.

FLAVORINGS
Vanilla   Seeds of 1 vanilla bean or 3 teaspoons vanilla extract.
Citrus fruit   Extracts to taste, or a few tablespoons of fruit juice to taste.
Coffee   Use a good brand of instant coffee powder; dissolve amount to taste in a very small amount of water.
Chocolate   Add up to 4 ounces melted unsweetened or Swiss bittersweet chocolate to taste.
Liqueurs   Add liqueur of your choice to taste.

MOUSSELINE BUTTERCREAM
(SUGAR-SYRUP CREAM)

This cream will require only 5 more minutes of your time, and the difference is worth the small extra work involved. It is pure velvet.

½ cup sugar   *½ pound* unsalted *butter*
¼ cup water   *5 egg yolks*
3 drops of lemon juice   *Flavoring*

Cook sugar, water and lemon juice to the thread stage minimum and the soft-ball stage maximum (230° to 234°F.). While the sugar cooks, cream the butter in the large mixer bowl and keep it ready to use. Clean the mixer beaters and start whipping the egg yolks in a smaller bowl until they are foamy and already very pale yellow. Keep the electric mixer on high speed and pour the hot syrup in a thin stream over the egg yolks. Continue beating until the mixture forms soft peaks. Set aside the small bowl with the yolk mixture.

Place the large bowl containing butter under the beaters. Reduce speed to "creaming" (7 on Mixmaster). Pour half of the yolk mixture into the creamed butter. Beat well. Add the flavoring and the remainder of the yolk mixture. Scrape the sides of the bowl often and continue beating until the cream is smooth.

If the emulsion breaks, add 1 or 2 more tablespoons of butter.

FLAVORINGS

Vanilla   Add vanilla seeds to the syrup while it cooks.

Coffee   Add instant coffee powder to syrup before it starts cooking.

Chocolate   Add 2 to 4 ounces melted unsweetened chocolate to half-finished cream.

Praline, Ground Nuts, Liqueurs   Add to taste to half-finished cream.

Citrus fruit   Infuse rinds of orange or grapefruit in juice of the fruit. Make the syrup with the strained juice. Infuse lemon rind in the water used for the syrup before cooking. In all cases, strain rinds out of juice or water before making syrup.

If you prefer to use citrus extract, add it to taste to the half-finished cream.

PASTRY CREAM

Pastry cream, the flour-based cream most used in pastry cooking, offers another illustration of the principle that egg yolks mixed with flour can and must boil. Pastry cream is made according to the principle of stirred pudding (*bouillie*).

This recipe is for an all-purpose pastry cream, made by combining several classic methods. It gives a light and pleasant cream, the taste of which can be varied. The teaspoon of gelatin will cause the cream to appear rather stiff when refrigerated, but at room temperature it will be mellow and remain very light. The cream is used to fill pastries (éclairs, cream puffs, tarts).

3 eggs, separated	*1 cup scalded milk, cooled*
⅓ cup sugar	*2 teaspoons vanilla extract*
¼ teaspoon salt	*1 teaspoon gelatin, melted*
¼ cup sifted flour	*½ cup heavy cream, whipped*

Ribbon egg yolks, sugar and salt well. Whisk in the flour, tablespoon by tablespoon. Whisk in the cooled milk in two additions, scraping well the whole surface of the pot bottom. Bring slowly to a boil, stirring constantly and very fast. The increase of heat must be regular and not too fast, to allow the flour cells to dilate gradually. As the mixture starts to thicken, whip faster and faster to break any lumps that may form. As soon as the cream boils, remove it from the heat or the taste of uncooked flour (it was not cooked in a *roux*) will be accentuated. Add vanilla and melted gelatin. Strain into a mixing bowl and let cool slightly. Whip egg whites and fold into the warm, not hot, cream. Let cool completely. Fold in the cream whipped to a stage between Chantilly and stiff.

FLAVORINGS

Almond   Make pastry cream with almond milk and flavor with Crème de Noyau or Noyau de Poissy to taste; or simply flavor the plain cream with 1 teaspoon almond extract and almond liqueur to taste.

Coffee   Add as much instant coffee powder as desired to the hot milk before making the custard.

Chocolate   Add 3 ounces melted Swiss bittersweet chocolate to the pastry cream before adding the egg whites.

Citrus fruit   Infuse 2 tablespoons grated rind in the milk before making the custard.

Butterscotch Replace granulated sugar with dark brown sugar and add 2 tablespoons butter before adding the egg whites.

Liqueurs Add any liqueur to taste before adding egg whites.

UNCOOKED ICING

For large cakes or éclairs and cream puffs. Sift 1¼ cups of confectioners' sugar. Mix with 1 to 2 tablespoons water or liqueur. Pour onto large cakes, or brush on small pastries.

CHOCOLATE ICING

Melt 6 ounces Swiss bittersweet chocolate; add 3 tablespoons liqueur and whisk in 3 tablespoons soft butter.

EGG-WHITE ICING

Mix 2 cups sifted confectioners' sugar with 1 to 1½ egg whites and 3 drops of lemon juice. Work with a whisk until smooth and liquid enough to pour onto a cake.

FONDANT

A marble slab is useful but not necessary.

Wash a large broiler pan with soap and water. Dry it with paper towels only, and freeze it for 2 hours. Or if your freezer is not large enough for this, chill the pan until it is as cold as you can make it by filling it with a plastic bag of ice cubes.

Cook 1 pound sugar and 1 cup water acidulated with 3 drops of lemon juice to 238°F. Pour immediately onto the prepared broiler pan. Let cool until warm only to the back of the hand (110° to 115°F.). Work with a spatula, bringing the mixture constantly from the outside to the center of the pan until milky white. Let the mixture rest for 2 minutes, then knead with the heel of the hand until a ball forms.

FLAVORINGS

Flavor preferably only with coffee, chocolate and liqueurs. Add instant coffee powder to taste to the syrup before cooking; add melted chocolate to the finished icing; add liqueurs to the finished icing.

PAIN D'ÉPICES, AMERICAN STYLE

The "butter-cake" method applied to an old French favorite. The spices could be right out of Taillevent's *Viandier*.

½ cup butter	1 teaspoon baking soda
⅔ cup liquid honey	1 teaspoon aniseeds
⅓ cup molasses	¼ teaspoon each of ground
½ cup milk	allspice, cardamom and
1 tablespoon lemon juice	coriander
2 cups unsifted flour	¼ teaspoon grated nutmeg
½ teaspoon salt	⅛ teaspoon ground cloves

Cream the butter, gradually add the liquid honey and molasses, and beat until smooth. Add milk and lemon juice. Mix well all the dry ingredients including the spices, and blend with the liquids. Turn into a heavily buttered and lightly floured 1-pound loaf pan (9 by 5 by 3 inches). Bake in a preheated 375°F. oven for 45 to 50 minutes. The top will crack. Cool completely.

Wrap the cake in foil and let it mellow in the refrigerator for 2 days before eating. Slice while cold and smother with fresh unsalted butter.

RAISIN POUNDCAKE (CREAMING METHOD)

My mother's recipe; she used to mix it by hand.

¼ cup light raisins   *½ teaspoon salt*
¼ cup dark raisins   *Fine-grated rind of 1 lemon*
¼ cup dark rum   *4 eggs, separated*
1¼ cups butter   *2 cups sifted flour*
1 cup sugar

Soak raisins in rum overnight. Cream the butter until very white. Add sugar and salt and beat again. Add lemon rind, then the egg yolks, one at a time, beating well after each addition. Blend in flour and raisins. Beat egg whites; mix one quarter of their volume into the batter and fold in the remainder. Turn into a well-buttered loaf pan (9 by 5 by 3 inches). Bake in a preheated 325°F. oven for 1¾ hours.

GÂTEAU BRETON

It took me years to find a formula that would resemble the true home-made Brittany cake. Do not exceed the amount of baking powder; there is just enough water in the butter to make it react just enough! Buy orange-flower water in a specialty shop. Orange rind is good, too, but not quite the same.

1 cup salted *butter*   *1½ cups sifted flour*
1 whole egg   *2 tablespoons sifted cornstarch*
1 extra egg yolk   *⅓ teaspoon baking powder*
½ cup sugar   *⅓ cup pulverized almonds*
2 teaspoons orange-flower water   *Egg-yolk glaze (p. 421)*
¼ teaspoon almond extract

Cream the butter until white. Add the whole egg, egg yolk and sugar, and beat for 10 minutes (speed 9 on Mixmaster). Add flavorings and blend well.

Mix all dry ingredients and almonds and blend slowly into the batter. Turn into a buttered and lightly floured 9-inch round pan. Brush generously with egg-yolk glaze. Trace a decorative crisscross pattern on top of the cake with the tines of a fork. Bake in a preheated 350°F. oven for 30 to 35 minutes. Let cool in the pan.

Unmold the cake and wrap it in foil. Let mellow in the refrigerator overnight.

MISTAKE CAKE (CREAMING METHOD)

Otherwise known as "what it tastes like when you mix the bottle of vanilla extract with the bottle of lemon extract."

1 ¼ cups butter	2 cups sifted flour
1 cup sugar	¼ cup sifted powdered cocoa
¼ teaspoon salt	2 teaspoons baking powder
1 ½ teaspoons lemon extract	Cream filling (below)
1 teaspoon vanilla extract	2 ounces semisweet chocolate,
¼ cup weak prepared coffee	cut into fine shavings
4 eggs, separated	

Cream the butter until white, add sugar and salt, and beat for 5 minutes. Add lemon and vanilla extracts and coffee. Add egg yolks, one at a time, beating for 1 minute after each addition. Mix flour, powdered cocoa and baking powder, and sift together twice. Beat egg whites; alternately add egg whites and dry ingredients on lowest mixer speed. Turn into 2 heavily buttered 8-inch round layer-cake pans. Bake in a preheated 325°F. oven for 30 to 35 minutes.

Cool cakes on a cake rack. Fill and ice cake with cream filling and cover with chocolate shavings.

CREAM FILLING

1 cup heavy cream	1 teaspoon lemon extract
2 tablespoons confectioners' sugar	
2 tablespoons sifted powdered cocoa	

Whip cream until stiff. Little by little add sugar, powdered cocoa and lemon extract.

PRALINE CHOCOLATE CAKE
(OLD-FASHIONED SPONGE)

You may use rum instead of Kirsch, but the taste is not as delicate.

3½ ounces unsweetened
   chocolate
¼ cup butter
5 egg yolks
⅔ cup plus 1 tablespoon sugar
½ teaspoon salt
1 tablespoon vanilla extract
7 egg whites
½ cup sifted flour

¼ cup sifted cornstarch
1½ cups sliced toasted almonds
1 cup heavy cream
Confectioners' sugar
½ teaspoon unflavored gelatin
  (optional)
3 tablespoons water
3 tablespoons Kirsch
½ cup strained apricot jam

Melt chocolate and butter together; let cool and keep ready to use. Ribbon together yolks, ⅔ cup sugar, salt and vanilla. Add the cooled chocolate mixture. Whip egg whites. Mix one quarter of their volume into the chocolate-yolk mixture. Slide the remainder of the whites onto the chocolate-yolk mixture, and sift flour and cornstarch on top. Fold until homogenous. Turn into a heavily buttered 10-inch round or square baking pan. Bake in a preheated 350°F. oven for 35 minutes. Cool completely.

Make almond cream filling. Grind ½ cup of the almonds very fine. Whip the cream, sweeten to taste with confectioners' sugar, and stabilize with gelatin if desired (see p. 20). Fold ground almonds into cream.

Make Kirsch syrup. Melt remaining 1 tablespoon sugar in the water and add Kirsch.

Split cake into two layers. Set the bottom layer on a serving platter, and moisten with 3 tablespoons of the prepared Kirsch syrup. Spread almond cream filling evenly on the bottom layer of cake; top with second layer. Moisten top layer with the remainder of the syrup. Refrigerate while preparing the icing jam.

Melt apricot jam. Brush on the whole surface of the cake. Immediately sprinkle the rest of the sliced almonds on top. Sprinkle with confectioners' sugar. Let mellow for half a day before serving.

LADYFINGERS
24 LADYFINGERS

3 eggs, separated	*1 teaspoon vanilla extract*
⅓ cup sugar	*1 teaspoon hot water*
Pinch of salt	*⅔ cup sifted flour*

Prepare 4 bands of baking paper 4 inches wide and as long as your cookie sheet, 2 buttered cookie sheets, 1 pastry bag fitted with a ½-inch nozzle, 1 large sheet of wax paper covered with a ⅛-inch layer of confectioners' sugar. Preheat oven to 375°F.

Ribbon egg yolks, sugar, salt, vanilla and the teaspoon of hot water very heavily. Beat egg whites. Mix one quarter of the total volume of the whites into the egg-yolk base. Slide the remainder of the whites onto the surface of the yolks. Sift the flour on top of the whites, and fold in whites and flour together until the mixture is homogenous.

Stuff the mixture into the prepared pastry bag. Pipe 6 ladyfingers 3 inches long on each paper band. Holding the ends of the paper, invert the band on the sheet of wax paper covered with confectioners' sugar. Don't worry, the strips of dough will adhere to the paper. When you lift up the paper band, the tops of the ladyfingers will be coated with sugar; they are coated on one side only. Transfer the paper bands of ladyfingers to the buttered cookie sheets; the buttering will keep the paper band in place. Place on the middle rack of the oven and bake at 375°F. for 7 minutes, then at 325°F. for 5 more minutes.

As soon as baked, remove the paper bands from the cookie sheets. Roll the paper bands over the angle of a counter or table and the cakes will loosen from the paper by themselves. Cool on a cake rack.

CHESTNUT GÉNOISE

My students called this cake exquisite; it is perfect for Christmas dinner. Make a plain 4-egg *génoise* (p. 444), flavored with Kirsch instead of vanilla. Slice into layers when completely cold.

CHESTNUT FILLING

2 egg yolks	*2 tablespoons Kirsch*
⅓ cup sifted confectioners' sugar	*1 can (8¾ ounces) candied*
½ cup unsalted butter, softened	*chestnut spread*

Ribbon egg yolks and sugar. Add soft butter, tablespoon by tablespoon. Add Kirsch and chestnut purée. Mix until smooth. Spread chestnut filling on the bottom layer of the *génoise*.

CREAMY CHOCOLATE ICING

1 cup sifted confectioners' sugar	*2 ounces unsweetened chocolate,*
3 tablespoons unsalted butter,	*melted*
softened	*2 egg yolks*
2 tablespoons heavy cream	*1 to 2 tablespoons Kirsch*

Put sugar, soft butter, cream, melted chocolate and egg yolks into a mixing bowl. Mix to spreading consistency. Thin with 1 to 2 tablespoons Kirsch, depending on the consistency of the mixture. Ice the cake, and let it mellow in a cool place for at least half a day before serving.

LIME RUM SHRUB CAKE

Made with all the ingredients of the rich Southern Lime Rum Shrub, an old colonial drink. This is a perfect example of using American ingredients and assembling them with French cooking techniques.

Fine 6-egg génoise (p. 444),	*2 tablespoons warm strained*
flavored with grated rind of	*lime or lemon marmalade*
1 lime	*1¼ cups sifted confectioners'*
Confectioners' sugar buttercream	*sugar*
(p. 446)	*2 drops of green food coloring*
9 tablespoons dark rum	*½ cup chopped pistachios*
2 tablespoons lime juice,	*Crystallized violets*
approximately	

Make the *génoise* batter and bake in one piece in a 10-inch spring-form pan; cool. Cut into 3 layers. Make the buttercream and flavor it with 4 tablespoons rum and the lime juice to taste. Sprinkle each cake layer with 1 tablespoon rum. Spread the layers with the buttercream, and reshape the cake.

Brush the top of the cake with strained melted lime or lemon marmalade. Mix confectioners' sugar, remaining 2 tablespoons rum and the green coloring; whisk until smooth. Pour onto the cake. Apply the chopped nuts all around the cake. Decorate the top of the cake with crystallized violets just before serving.

LOUISIANA STRAWBERRY PATCH

Use Louisiana strawberries for this cake; they are the best in the Union, and more flavorful than the overrated French *fraises des bois*.

> *Fine 6-egg* génoise (*p. 444)* *Pinch of salt*
> *5 cups strawberries* *¾ to 1 pound butter*
> *½ cup Kirsch* *Green food coloring*
> *8 egg yolks*
> *1½ cups sifted confectioners'*
> *sugar*

Make the 6-egg *génoise* batter and bake in a rectangular pan (13 by 9 inches). Cool, and cut into 2 layers. Macerate 4 cups of the berries in ¼ cup Kirsch for 2 hours.

Mash remaining 1 cup strawberries. Cook until only 3 tablespoons of very thick purée are left; strain. Make buttercream with egg yolks, confectioners' sugar, salt and butter. Flavor with remaining ¼ cup Kirsch and the strained strawberry purée.

Sprinkle the bottom layer of the cake with half of the Kirsch in which the berries were macerated. Spread with one quarter of the buttercream. Cover with part of the strawberries cut into halves. Spread the top layer with another quarter of the buttercream, and invert that layer on the berries to reshape the cake. Sprinkle the top layer with the remainder of the Kirsch. Spread a layer of buttercream ⅛ inch thick on the top and sides of the cake. Decorate with whole berries casually spread over the top of the cake. Color the remainder of the buttercream green, spoon into a pastry bag, and pipe stems and leaves among the berries. This cake will make 24 servings.

CANADIAN TORTE

This uses the spongecake method, but the torte is made without flour or starch. Use maple sugar if available.

6 eggs, separated	*⅔ cup plus 3 tablespoons*
⅔ cup sugar	*vanilla-wafer crumbs*
¼ teaspoon salt	*1 cup heavy cream*
1 teaspoon instant coffee powder	*2 tablespoons maple syrup*
½ teaspoon maple flavoring	*¾ cup chopped walnuts*
2 cups fine-ground walnuts	

Ribbon egg yolks, sugar, salt, coffee powder and ¼ teaspoon of the maple flavoring heavily. Beat egg whites. Immediately mix one quarter of the total volume of the egg whites into the yolk base. Slide the remainder of the whites on top of the yolk mixture, and sprinkle with the ground walnuts and ⅔ cup of the vanilla-wafer crumbs. Fold together until homogenous. Sprinkle 2 buttered 8-inch layer-cake pans with remaining vanilla-wafer crumbs. Turn the batter into the pans and bake in a preheated 350°F. oven for 25 to 30 minutes. Cool. Slice each cake layer into halves.

Whip the cream, add remaining ¼ teaspoon maple flavoring, and sweeten with maple syrup. Fill the cake layers with two thirds of the cream. Spread the remainder of the cream around and on top of the cake. Sprinkle top and sides of the cake with chopped walnuts. Keep the torte chilled, but remove from refrigerator 10 minutes before serving for full flavor.

CREOLE PECAN TORTE

This torte is modeled on the French *Succès,* and a success it is with those Southern pecans. The cake must mellow for 24 hours.

6 eggs, separated	1 teaspoon lemon juice
¾ cup plus ½ cup granulated sugar	⅔ cup chopped pecans
1 tablespoon vanilla extract	3 tablespoons dark brown sugar
2 cups fine-ground pecans	1 to 1¼ cups unsalted butter
¼ cup water	⅓ cup rum
	Confectioners' sugar

Butter and flour 3 cookie sheets. Trace a circle on each with a 9-inch pot lid. Whip egg whites, adding 3 tablespoons granulated sugar and the vanilla toward the end of the beating. Fold in a mixture of 9 tablespoons sugar and the ground pecans. Spread on prepared cookie sheets, and bake in a preheated 325°F. oven for 20 to 25 minutes. If only one oven and one cookie sheet are available, make one sheet at a time; keep the batter refrigerated while waiting.

Make a praline powder (see p. 23) with ½ cup granulated sugar, the water, lemon juice and chopped pecans. Pulverize in the blender. Ribbon egg yolks, brown sugar and praline powder. Cream in 1 cup of the butter, tablespoon by tablespoon. Add the rum. If the filling separates, add 1 to 2 more tablespoons of butter.

Trim edges of meringue layers neatly, and fill with praline buttercream. Refrigerate the cake and let it mellow for 24 hours. Sprinkle the top with confectioners' sugar before serving.

PISTACHIO RASPBERRY ROLL

A bit of work but worth it. The baking powder captures water from the eggs and dries the batter, which would otherwise be too moist.

6 eggs, separated	2 drops of green food coloring
⅔ cup granulated sugar	2 cups ground blanched pistachios
2½ tablespoons Kirsch or Framboise	¾ teaspoon baking powder

4 boxes (10 ounces each) frozen   *Confectioners' sugar*
    raspberries, thawed   *1 pint fresh raspberries*
1 ½ cups heavy cream

Fit baking paper into a slightly greased jelly-roll pan (15 by 12
inches). Butter the paper.

Ribbon egg yolks and granulated sugar; add 1 tablespoon Kirsch
and the food coloring. Whip egg whites; mix one quarter of their
volume into the yolks. Slide the remainder of the whites over the yolk
mixture. Sprinkle with ground pistachios and the baking powder, and
fold until homogenous. Pour the batter into the prepared pan. Bake in
a preheated 325°F. oven for 12 to 15 minutes. Remove from oven.
Cover the cake with 2 layers of wet paper towels. Let stand until cool.

Drain thawed berries from their syrup. (Use the drained syrup for
some other purpose.) Purée in a blender, strain, and cook down to ¼
cup thick purée. Whip the cream, and flavor with cold raspberry
purée and 1 ½ tablespoons Kirsch or Framboise or more to taste.
Sweeten with 2 to 3 tablespoons confectioners' sugar to taste. Spread
cream over the cake, top with fresh raspberries, and roll. Sprinkle with
a thin layer of confectioners' sugar and serve.

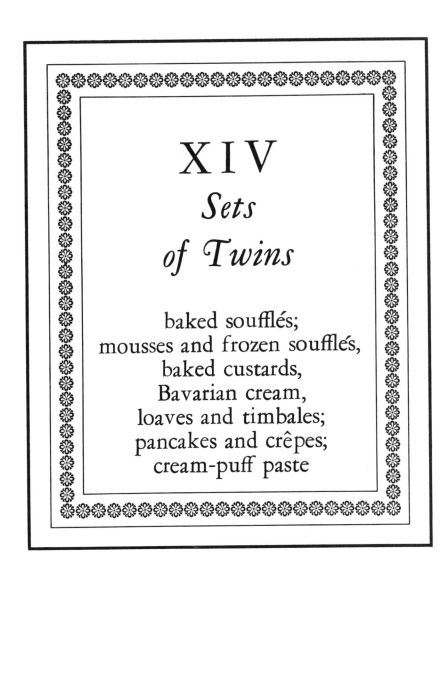

XIV

Sets
of Twins

baked soufflés;
mousses and frozen soufflés,
baked custards,
Bavarian cream,
loaves and timbales;
pancakes and crêpes;
cream-puff paste

THE DISHES featured in the different sections of this chapter have been grouped together because, whether prepared as a main course or as a dessert, they are made according to the same techniques. You have already become acquainted with one "Twin" in Chapter XI, for pies and tarts for main course or dessert are prepared following the same methods.

SOUFFLÉS

Soufflé is the past participle of the French verb *souffler,* which means "blow up"; it has become a noun designating a culinary preparation, other than a cake, containing a large amount of beaten egg whites and baked in the oven. The cold soufflé, *soufflé glacé,* is not a baked dish and consequently not a true soufflé, but a kind of mousse. You will find more about this in the next section.

A soufflé is made of two parts—the base (sauce, purée or beaten egg yolks), which contains all the elements that give the soufflé its taste and flavor, and the whipped egg whites. A soufflé puffs up when baked because the air beaten into the egg whites and trapped in the foam walls dilates when submitted to the heat of the oven. This dilatation is further helped by the pressure applied on the foam walls by the steam produced when the water present in the batter boils.

After you have chosen a soufflé recipe, prepare all your ingredients. Make sure that you are familiar with the basic techniques involved:

- making a basic white flour-bound sauce (pp. 108 to 110) or a *bouillie* (p. 474);
- ribboning egg yolks and sugar (p. 57);
- folding (p. 61);
- whipping egg whites (pp. 58–59).

Remember that, savory or sweet, a soufflé always contains at least *one more egg white* than egg yolks.

SOUFFLÉ DISH

If at all possible, use a classic round soufflé dish with striated sides. The striations together with the perfectly straight sides of the dish insure even penetration of the oven heat through the whole batter. However, many other dishes such as heatproof glass casseroles and Charlotte molds may be used. The most practical dish to acquire is a 1¾-quart round Corning Ware casserole; although its sides are not quite straight enough, this dish gives excellent results.

COLLAR MATHEMATICS

As the soufflé bakes it rises. If your dish is just the right size for your batter, the soufflé will rise in the dish, making a beautiful crown. If your dish is not large enough, the batter will rise out of the dish and spill over before it is firm enough to hold its shape. In such a case you need a collar. It all depends on the bulk of the recipe and the capacity of the dish you own. Measure the capacity of your dish with water. Then calculate the volume of your batter, adding:

the volume of the base;

the volume of each egg yolk (2½ tablespoons per yolk);

the volume of each egg white properly beaten (1 cup per white).

Remember, however, that the folding loss of volume for each egg white is about ⅓ cup if you are experienced, a bit more if you are not.

For example, the hickory-smoked cheese soufflé on page 470 can be calculated as follows:

base	1½ cups
volume of cheese and bacon	¼ cup
5 egg yolks	¾ cup
6 beaten egg whites, less folding loss	4 cups
total volume of soufflé batter:	6½ cups

Probably the actual volume will be a little less if you are inexperienced; since the dish should be from two thirds to five sixths full, you need an 8-cup dish.

If you need it, make a collar. Measure a piece of parchment paper 1⅓ times as long as the diameter of the dish and twice as high. Butter it well. Wrap the paper around the dish, its lower edges resting on the counter top and the buttered side facing the center of the dish. Secure the paper at the top with a paper clip and tie a kitchen string around the dish.

Soufflé Sequence

Preheat the oven to the desired temperature. Butter the dish, and collar it if necessary. Sprinkle the dish lightly with grated cheese, bread crumbs or sugar, whichever is applicable. Cook the base; add the egg yolks one by one and whisk well. After adding the egg yolks, reboil the batter if you like a very firm soufflé, but do not reboil if you prefer a lighter consistency. Correct seasoning now. Mix one fourth to one third of the whites in the *warm,* not hot, base; fold in the remainder. Fill the dish and bake.

Filling a Soufflé Dish

Do not pour a soufflé batter into its baking dish; *spoon* it in, using a very large serving spoon. You will lose less air and be able to control the thickness of the layer of batter, which must be even throughout the dish. If the soufflé contains a heavy garnish (diced meat, cake, candied fruit), do not mix it in the batter. Spoon half of the batter into the dish, add the garnish, then cover it with the second half of the batter.

To obtain a round-hat soufflé (medium-heat cookery only—see section on oven temperature), shape the top of the batter so it mounds slightly toward the center. One inch away from the sides of the dish and at 1-inch intervals, cut ½-inch-deep openings in the batter with scissors. The cuts will form the round hat.

To obtain a top-hat soufflé (high-heat cookery only—see section on oven temperature), fill the mold up to the brim, allowing the batter to mound a little. Push the excess batter out of the mold with one stroke of a long spatula to obtain a perfectly smooth surface. Slide your right thumb between dish and batter; turning the dish from left to right with your left hand, trace a rim all around the top of the batter. The soufflé will rise straight out of the mold and look like a top hat.

OVEN TEMPERATURE

If you desire a soufflé evenly cooked to the center, bake it in a medium oven (325°F.). All savory soufflés must be cooked at this temperature. Heavy batters need slow ovens.

If you desire a French-style soufflé with about 1½ inches of cooked batter enclosing a soft creamy center, bake at a high temperature (400°F.). Light dessert batters can be baked according to either method.

The goal to achieve is to coagulate the proteins as soon as the batter is pushed out of the dish by the oven heat. In a *too low oven,* the soufflé will flatten at its top and spill over the edges of the dish. In a *too high oven,* the soufflé will build a hard crust on the outside and stay liquid in the center. To obtain a "mushroom" top, put the soufflé in a 400°F. oven and turn the heat down immediately to 375°F.; the soufflé top will show the difference of temperatures.

Always bake a soufflé on the lowest rack of the oven or as close as possible to the source of heat. For a crisp outside, bake directly on the rack. For a firm but unbrowned outside, bake in a hot-water bath.

FREEZING SOUFFLÉS

All uncooked soufflés, unless otherwise mentioned in the recipe, may be frozen. Turn the refrigerator to its coldest setting. Cover soufflé top with clear plastic wrap. Set the dish flush on the bottom of the freezing unit so that the batter stays level during freezing. Let the batter freeze solid.

When ready to use, if the soufflé is in a Corning Ware dish, put it immediately in the oven. The dish is worth its price just for that. If it is in a regular china dish, let the soufflé stand at room temperature for 30 minutes before baking. In both cases, bake twice as long as the same batter uncooked. At freezing time label the dish with the contents and the regular cooking time multiplied by two. This is a well-tried method.

SERVING A SOUFFLÉ

To serve, break a soufflé top open with two large serving spoons with their convex sides facing each other. Slide one spoon between batter and dish and with the help of the other, lift portions out of the dish.

Although you can make large soufflés in rectangular roasting pans with collars, it is better, if you are not an expert, not to serve soufflés to large groups. Keep them for small intimate dinners where people can appreciate their grace and elegance.

Generally, a savory soufflé baked in a 6-cup mold will make 6 servings as a first course, 4 servings as a main course. A savory soufflé baked in an 8-cup mold will make 8 servings as a first course, 6 servings as a main course.

As for dessert soufflés, if baked in a 4-cup mold you can expect 4 servings, and 6 servings from a 6-cup mold, 8 servings from an 8-cup mold.

These indications cannot be considered precise, however, since the amount of soufflé served depends to some degree on the composition of the rest of the meal.

Savory Soufflés

The base of a savory soufflé can be a purée of meat, fish or vegetable, a thick white, béchamel or velouté sauce, or a combination of vegetable purée or cheese with any of these sauces. Savory soufflés follow the rules outlined in the preceding paragraphs. You can make up your own soufflés using ¼ cup of base per egg. Do not forget the traditional additional egg white for lightness. Serve soufflés made of a meat or fish base accompanied by a sauce derivative of the velouté, but serve cheese or vegetable soufflés without a sauce.

Roulades are soufflés baked in jelly-roll pans lined with baking paper. You may add chopped vegetables such as *duxelles* (p. 340) or braised spinach to the batter, making sure that the vegetables are completely free of moisture. *Roulades* are filled with diced ham, chicken, shrimp or mushrooms, bound with a béchamel sauce or velouté. You may vary them according to your own taste.

POULTRY SOUFFLÉ
4 SERVINGS

Use white meat of chicken, turkey, rabbit. Adapt your sauce to the meat. With this method, there is no stale reheated poultry taste.

12 ounces white meat of poultry,   *Pepper*
   without skin, gristle or bone   *½ teaspoon grated nutmeg*
1 whole egg   *⅛ teaspoon four spices (p. 27),*
2 tablespoons soft butter   *optional*
1 cup heavy cream, chilled   *1 tablespoon lemon juice*
1 teaspoon salt   *4 egg whites*

Cut the meat into small pieces. Beat the whole egg until liquid. Blend half of the meat in the blender (see Quenelles, p. 290), using half of the egg as liquid. Repeat with the rest of the meat and egg. Strain, if desired, and chill for 1 hour.

Cream the butter, add the chilled meat gradually, and then beat in chilled cream with the electric mixer on slow speed. Add salt, pepper to taste, spices and lemon juice. Whip egg whites and fold into the mixture. Spoon into a buttered 6-cup soufflé mold and set in a hot-water bath. Bake in a 325°F. oven for 40 minutes.

ONION SAUCE

1½ cups chopped onions   *1 cup medium-thick chicken*
2 tablespoons butter   *velouté (p. 108)*
1½ tablespoons Hungarian   *½ cup heavy cream*
   sweet paprika   *Salt and pepper*

Sauté onions in butter until very soft; add paprika. Add velouté and simmer together for 10 minutes. Add heavy cream and correct seasoning. Serve sauce over soufflé portions.
Wine: California Johannisberg Riesling

FISH SOUFFLÉ
4 SERVINGS

½ *pound raw fish* (*sole,*
    haddock, cod, etc.), *without*
    bone or skin
1 whole egg
1 extra egg yolk
⅔ *cup heavy cream*

¾ *teaspoon salt*
Pepper
⅛ *teaspoon four spices*
    (*p. 27*), *optional*
4 egg whites

Cut fish into small pieces. Using whole egg and extra egg yolk as liquid, purée the fish in the blender. Strain if desired. Put in a large mixing bowl and refrigerate for 1 hour.

With electric mixer on slow speed, add the heavy cream to the purée. Add salt, pepper to taste and spices if used. Whip egg whites and fold into the fish purée. Spoon into a buttered 6-cup soufflé dish and set in a hot-water bath. Bake in a 325°F. oven for 40 minutes.

HERB SAUCE

2 tablespoons butter
2 tablespoons flour
1¼ cups white-wine fish fumet
    (*p. 83*)
2 teaspoons chopped shallots
¼ *cup wine vinegar*

2 tablespoons each of chopped
    and quickly blanched spinach
    and watercress
1 tablespoon chopped chives
4 tablespoons butter
Salt and pepper

Make a velouté with butter, flour and fish *fumet.* Cook shallots and vinegar until the vinegar has evaporated. Add the sauce and simmer together for 5 minutes. Strain. Add blanched herbs and chives. Whisk in the butter and correct seasoning. Serve over soufflé portions.
Wine: California Pinot Blanc or *French Pouilly Fuissé*

HICKORY-SMOKED CHEESE SOUFFLÉ
6 SERVINGS

A true American flavor and a new twist to an old favorite.

5 tablespoons butter	*6 ounces hickory-smoked cheese*
4½ tablespoons flour	*8 slices of bacon, cooked crisp*
1½ cups scalded milk	* and crumbled*
¼ teaspoon grated nutmeg	*Salt and pepper*
5 egg yolks	*6 egg whites*

With butter, flour and scalded milk, make a white sauce. Season with nutmeg. Add egg yolks, one by one, whisking well. Grate two thirds of the cheese; reserve 1 tablespoon to sprinkle around the dish. Dice the remaining third of the cheese into ¼-inch cubes. Add both grated and diced cheese to the sauce; add fine-crumbled bacon. Correct seasoning. Whip egg whites; mix one quarter of the whites into the batter; fold in the rest. Turn into a buttered 8-cup soufflé mold sprinkled with the reserved grated cheese. Bake in a 325°F. oven for 45 minutes.

Wine: California Zinfandel or French Hermitage

BLUE-CHEESE SOUFFLÉ
6 SERVINGS

Use Wisconsin Blue, Danish Blue or Roquefort.

1 onion, chopped fine	*5 egg yolks*
5 tablespoons butter	*1 cup crumbled blue cheese*
1 tablespoon caraway seeds	*Salt and pepper*
4½ tablespoons flour	*6 egg whites*
1½ cups scalded milk	

Sauté onion in butter until golden. Add caraway seeds and flour. Add scalded milk and thicken to make a sauce; add egg yolks, one by one, whisking well. Add crumbled cheese; mix well. Correct seasoning. Whip egg whites; mix one quarter of their volume into the bat-

ter; fold in the rest. Turn into an 8-cup soufflé mold, and bake in a
325°F. oven for 45 minutes.
Wine: California Pinot Noir or *French Châteauneuf-du-Pape*

ALASKAN KING-CRAB SOUFFLÉ
4 TO 6 SERVINGS

You may also use shrimp or lobster, Maryland crab, or Dungeness
crab. This makes a good first course.

1 cup Alaskan crab meat	*½ cup heavy cream*
6 tablespoons butter	*3 egg yolks*
1 ounce Cognac or brandy	*2 tablespoons Fino sherry*
4 tablespoons flour	*Salt and pepper*
½ cup white-wine fish fumet	*4 egg whites*
(p. 83)	

Cut crabmeat into ⅓-inch cubes. Sauté in 2 tablespoons of the
butter, and flambé with Cognac or brandy. Make a velouté with 4
tablespoons butter, the flour, fish *fumet* and heavy cream. Add egg
yolks, one by one, whisking well. Add sherry, and correct seasoning.
Whip egg whites; mix one quarter of their volume into the base; fold
in the remainder. Turn half of the batter into a buttered 6-cup soufflé
mold. Add the crabmeat, then top with the remainder of the batter.
Bake in a 325°F. oven for 40 minutes.
Wine: New York State Vinifera Pinot Chardonnay or *French Meursault Perrières*

MOUSSAKA SOUFFLÉ
6 SERVINGS

All the elements of the Greek *moussaka* in a soufflé dish.

1 large onion, chopped	*2 tablespoons tomato paste*
Olive oil (about ½ cup)	*Pinch of dried thyme*
1½ cups freshly ground lamb	*1 garlic clove, mashed*
¼ cup red retsina wine or dry	*½ teaspoon ground coriander*
red wine	*Salt and pepper*

2 small eggplants
3 tablespoons flour
1 cup milk
5 egg yolks

3 tablespoons each of grated
   Parmesan and Romano cheese
6 egg whites

Sauté onion in 2 tablespoons olive oil. Add lamb and brown well; discard fat. Add wine, tomato paste, thyme, mashed garlic, coriander, and salt and pepper to taste. Cover and simmer for 20 minutes, or until all the liquids have evaporated.

Peel the eggplants and cut into large dice. Sprinkle with salt and let stand for 1 hour. Drain off the water extracted by the salt. Sauté the eggplant dice in olive oil over very low heat, letting the vegetable soften slowly and fall apart. Add flour and cook for a few minutes. Add milk and thicken. Add egg yolks, one by one, whisking well. Add all but 1 tablespoon of the mixed cheeses. Whip egg whites; mix one quarter of their volume into the *moussaka;* fold in the remainder. Butter an 8-cup soufflé mold and sprinkle with remaining tablespoon of cheese. Spoon half of the soufflé batter into the dish. Top with the lamb and onion mixture, and add the remainder of the batter. Bake in a 325 °F. oven for 45 minutes.

Wine: red retsina wine from Greece

HAM AND MUSHROOM ROULADE
6 SERVINGS

A pleasant luncheon or brunch dish.

1½ pounds mushrooms,
   quartered
Butter
Salt and pepper
3 cups medium-thick chicken
   velouté (p. 108)
4 egg yolks

½ cup heavy cream
1½ tablespoons lemon juice
Grated nutmeg
1½ cups diced cooked ham, with
   no fat
Chopped parsley

Make the filling first: Sauté mushrooms in hot butter seasoned with salt and pepper, and cook until all the juices have evaporated. Enrich the velouté with the egg yolks mixed with the heavy cream.

Add lemon juice and nutmeg, salt and pepper to taste. Add sautéed mushrooms and diced ham to 2 cups of the sauce. Set aside the filling mixture, the extra cup of sauce, and the parsley.

4 egg yolks	*2 tablespoons flour*
½ teaspoon salt	*Pepper*
1 tablespoon Madeira or sherry	*5 egg whites*
½ teaspoon four spices (p. 27)	

Now make the *roulade*. Whip egg yolks with salt, Madeira and spices until as white as possible. Blend in flour. Add pepper to taste. Whip egg whites and fold into the yolk base. Line a lightly greased jelly-roll pan (14 by 11 inches) with baking paper. Spread the mixture in the pan, and bake in a 375°F. oven for 10 to 12 minutes. Remove from oven and turn upside down on a sheet of wax paper. Remove baking paper.

Fill the *roulade* with the mushroom and ham mixture, and roll. Pour the last cup of velouté over the *roulade* and sprinkle with parsley.

Wine: Mountain White Chablis

Dessert Soufflés

Sweet soufflés are made according to not less than five different methods!

METHOD A—PASTRY CREAM BASE

In a restaurant, you can almost be sure that the pastry chef has used a small amount of pastry cream to make your soufflé, after blending it with a few more egg yolks and flavorings. Use the pastry cream on page 448, omitting the egg whites and the cream. For a 6-cup dish, use the following proportions:

¼ cup pastry cream	*3 tablespoons sugar*
3 egg yolks	*5 egg whites*

Bake at 325°F. for a firm center and at 400°F. for a creamy center. See Macaroon Soufflé (p. 475) for an example.

METHOD B—BOUILLIE OR STIRRED PUDDING BASE

The base of a homemade soufflé is more often than not a *bouillie,* or stirred flour pudding, in which the raw flour is mixed with sugar and cold milk and brought to a boil. The *bouillie* can be used for a soufflé base because the flour has time to finish cooking while the soufflé bakes.

You can make your own combinations by using the following proportions per egg yolk:

> *1 tablespoon sugar*   *2 tablespoons milk*
> *1 ½ teaspoons flour*

See your collar mathematics, and remember that you need 1 more egg white than the total number of egg yolks. Bake at 400°F. for a soft creamy center, or at 325°F. for a firm center. See Rum Raisin Soufflé (p. 476) for an example.

METHOD C—EGG-YOLK BASE

These soufflés are the easiest and the fastest. Use the same amount of yolks and whites. Make the base by ribboning the yolks heavily with the sugar and the flavoring, and finish the batter by folding the whites into the yolks. Perfect for a soufflé "to order"; the French call it a "minute soufflé." Bake only at 400°F. for 12 to 14 minutes; the center will be creamy. See Cappuccino Soufflé (p. 480) for an example.

METHOD D—SUGAR SYRUP AND FRUIT PURÉE BASE

Use per egg white:

> *¼ cup sugar*   *½ cup fruit purée*

and always use 1 additional egg white.

Cook the total amount of sugar with some water to 264°F. (small-crack stage). Blend syrup and fruit purée and recook together for a few minutes. Mix one quarter of the whites into the purée and fold in the remainder. Bake only at 400°F. A 6-cup mold bakes in

13 to 14 minutes and will be firm to the center. See Apricot Soufflé (p. 478) for an example.

METHOD E—SOUFFLÉED PUDDINGS

These soufflés *cannot* collapse and *can* be unmolded; their flavoring can be varied to your choice. Use the same amount of yolks as whites. Use per egg:

> 1½ tablespoons butter 1 tablespoon sugar (*a little*
> 2½ tablespoons sifted flour *more if desired*)
> 3 tablespoons milk, scalded

Cream the butter and add the flour; stir in the scalded milk with the electric mixer. Cook over medium heat until the dough leaves the sides of the pan and forms a ball. Beat in the sugar and the egg yolks one by one. Whip egg whites and fold into the base. Turn into a heavily buttered dish. Bake in a hot-water bath in a 325°F. oven.

Let the pudding cool in the cooking vessel. Push the top lightly down. Invert on a platter, and serve covered with a stirred custard. You may replace flour with cornstarch; in this case, use cold milk. See Dried Fruit Souffléed Pudding (p. 481) for an example.

MACAROON SOUFFLÉ
6 SERVINGS

A typical restaurant-type soufflé.

> 2 large almond macaroons ¼ cup pastry cream (*pp. 448*
> Rum, Kirsch or Curaçao *and 473*)
> 3 egg yolks 5 egg whites
> 2 tablespoons sugar 1 tablespoon butter

Crumble the macaroons and soak in rum or liqueur to taste. Ribbon heavily egg yolks and sugar, and blend in warm pastry cream. Add macaroon-liqueur mixture, which should be almost a paste. Beat egg whites and fold into the base. Turn into a buttered and lightly sugared 6-cup soufflé dish. Bake in a 400°F. oven for 15 to 20 minutes.

SPICED TEA SOUFFLÉ
6 SERVINGS

A variation on the *soufflé au thé,* a rage in the French bourgeois circles of my young days.

½ cup boiling water	Pinch of salt
1 heaping teaspoon (1 teabag) Earl Grey tea	4 egg yolks
	5 egg whites
¼ teaspoon fine-grated orange rind	1 tablespoon butter
	1½ tablespoons fine-ground Macadamia nuts
Dash of ground cloves	
¼ to ⅓ cup sugar	¼ cup chopped crystallized gingerroot
2 tablespoons flour	

Bring water to a boil. Pour on tea, add orange rind and cloves, and let steep until dark and cold. Strain. Mix sugar, flour, salt and cold tea, and thicken over medium heat. Add egg yolks, one by one, whisking well after each addition. Whip egg whites and fold into the batter. Turn half of the batter into a buttered 6-cup soufflé dish sprinkled with chopped Macadamia nuts. Sprinkle with crystallized gingerroot. Top with the remainder of the batter. Bake in a 400°F. oven for 15 minutes.

RUM RAISIN SOUFFLÉ
6 SERVINGS

A great success with my students of The Alliance Française de Philadelphia.

3 tablespoons each of dark and light raisins	Pinch of salt
	4 egg yolks
6 tablespoons white rum	5 egg whites
½ cup light cream	1 tablespoon butter
1½ tablespoons flour	English or stirred custard
¼ cup sugar	(p. 62), flavored with rum

Soak raisins in ¼ cup rum overnight, turning them several times. Mix cream, flour, sugar and salt; thicken over medium heat. Add egg yolks, one by one, whisking well after each addition. Flavor the batter with 2 more tablespoons of rum and any rum left in the raisin dish. Whip egg whites and fold into the base. Turn half of the batter into a buttered and lightly sugared 6-cup soufflé mold. Sprinkle raisins on top, and add the rest of the batter. Bake in a 325°F. oven for 10 to 25 minutes. Serve with rum-flavored English custard as sauce.

AVOCADO SOUFFLÉ
6 TO 8 SERVINGS

To Gloria, so doubtful about freezing soufflés.

2 tablespoons lime juice	*3 egg yolks*
3 tablespoons rum	*⅓ cup chopped Macadamia nuts*
1 large avocado	*6 egg whites*
1 tablespoon flour	*1 tablespoon butter*
⅓ cup sugar	*English or stirred custard*
Pinch of salt	*(p. 62), flavored with lime*
½ cup milk	

Put lime juice and rum in a blender container. Add peeled pitted avocado and purée well.

Mix flour, sugar, salt and milk. Thicken over medium heat; add egg yolks, one by one, whisking well after each addition. Add avocado purée and nuts. Whip egg whites and fold into the batter. Turn into a buttered 8-cup soufflé dish. Bake in a 400°F. oven for 14 minutes. Serve with lime-flavored stirred custard as a sauce.

SNOW-WHITE ALMOND SOUFFLÉ
6 SERVINGS

Different in taste and texture.

ALMOND MILK

> 1 ⅓ cups whole blanched   1 ⅓ cups boiling water
>   almonds   1 ¼ teaspoons bitter-almond
> ⅓ cup superfine powdered sugar   extract

With almonds, sugar, boiling water and almond extract, make almond milk as directed on page 22. Strain and squeeze through damp cheesecloth to obtain 1 ⅓ cups milk.

SOUFFLÉ AND SAUCE

> 2 tablespoons sugar   4 tablespoons almond liqueur
> 2 tablespoons flour   (Noyau de Poissy)
> Pinch of salt   5 egg whites
> 1 ⅓ cups almond milk   ⅓ cup heavy cream
> 1 ¼ teaspoons almond extract   1 teaspoon cornstarch

Mix sugar, flour, salt and ⅔ cup of the almond milk. Thicken over medium heat; add 1 teaspoon almond extract and 2 tablespoons of the almond liqueur. Whip egg whites and fold into the base. Turn into a buttered and lightly sugared 6-cup soufflé dish. Bake in a 400°F. oven for 15 minutes.

While the soufflé bakes, mix the remaining ⅔ cup almond milk with heavy cream and cornstarch. Thicken; add remaining almond extract and almond liqueur. Serve over soufflé.

APRICOT SOUFFLÉ
6 SERVINGS

Year-round formula. Use fresh apricots when in season.

> ½ pound dried apricots   5 egg whites
> 1 ⅓ cups sugar   3 egg yolks
> ¼ cup water   ½ cup white wine
> 2 ounces Cognac, rum or Kirsch

Soak dried apricots in cold water overnight. Drain off water, cover with fresh water, and cook until soft. Purée and strain. Make a syrup with 1 cup of the sugar and ¼ cup water. Cook to 264°F. Blend with the apricot purée and cook together a few minutes. Flavor with 1 ounce of the liqueur. Beat egg whites and fold into the purée. Turn into a heavily buttered and lightly sugared 6-cup soufflé dish. Bake in a 400°F. oven for 20 to 25 minutes.

Meanwhile, make a Zabaglione (see p. 66) with the egg yolks, remaining ⅓ cup sugar, the white wine and remaining liqueur. Serve over the soufflé as a sauce.

RASPBERRY SOUFFLÉ
6 SERVINGS

My interpretation of a specialty of La Grenouille in New York.

2 cups fresh raspberries or strawberries	*3 boxes (10 ounces each) frozen raspberries*
2 tablespoons Kirsch or Framboise	*4 egg whites*
	2 tablespoons sugar

Steep the fresh berries in the liqueur for 2 hours.

Thaw the frozen raspberries. Do not drain. Purée in the blender and strain to discard the seeds. Cook down the purée to ½ cup. Beat egg whites, adding sugar toward the end of the beating. Fold whites into the purée, and turn into a buttered and lightly sugared 6-cup soufflé dish. Bake in a 400°F. oven for 12 to 14 minutes.

Serve the fresh berries over the soufflé. Do not sugar the berries, for the soufflé is sweet enough.

CHOCOLATE SOUFFLÉ
4 TO 6 SERVINGS

There is enough starch as a basic component of chocolate to obtain a good and solid soufflé base without additional corn or potato starch. This soufflé is very rich.

4 egg yolks
⅓ cup sugar
Pinch of salt
4 ounces Swiss bittersweet
    chocolate
1 ounce unsweetened chocolate
2 tablespoons heavy cream

1 teaspoon instant coffee powder
2 tablespoons Cognac or rum
5 egg whites
English or stirred custard
    (p. 62), flavored with rum
    or Cognac

Ribbon egg yolks, sugar and salt heavily. Meanwhile, melt bittersweet and unsweetened chocolate together; cool. Add heavy cream, instant coffee powder and liqueur, and blend into the ribboning yolks. Whip the egg whites and fold into the base. Turn into a buttered and very lightly sugared 6-cup soufflé dish. Bake in a 400°F. oven for 12 to 14 minutes. Serve with warm English custard as a sauce.

CAPPUCCINO SOUFFLÉ
6 SERVINGS

Inspired by the luscious Italian coffee.

4 egg yolks
1 tablespoon instant coffee
    powder
½ teaspoon fine-grated lemon
    rind
⅓ cup granulated sugar

Pinch of salt
5 egg whites
½ cup whipped cream
1 teaspoon powdered cocoa
1 tablespoon confectioners' sugar

Ribbon egg yolks with coffee powder, lemon rind, sugar and salt. Whip egg whites and fold into the base. Turn into a buttered and lightly sugared 6-cup soufflé mold. Bake in a 400°F. oven for 12 to 14 minutes. Serve with the whipped cream flavored with cocoa and only lightly sweetened so as not to overpower the purposely bitter flavor of the soufflé.

DRIED-FRUIT SOUFFLÉED PUDDING
8 SERVINGS

This may be made with any kind of dried fruit—apricots, pears, prunes, etc.

12 ounces dried fruit
⅔ cup heavy cream
5 tablespoons cornstarch
½ cup brown sugar
4 eggs, separated
1 teaspoon flavoring: almond
* extract for apricots; vanilla*
* extract for pears; lemon extract*
* for prunes*

English or stirred custard
* (p. 62)*
2 tablespoons liqueur: Kirsch for
* apricots; pear brandy, Kirsch*
* or Grand Marnier for pears;*
* rum or Slivovitz for prunes*

Soak the fruit overnight. Purée in a blender and strain if desired. Mix fruit purée, cream, cornstarch and brown sugar. Thicken over medium heat. Add the egg yolks, one by one, whisking well after each addition. Add the flavoring. Whip egg whites and fold into the base. Turn into a buttered 8-cup soufflé mold set in a pan of hot water. Bake in a 325°F. oven for 40 to 45 minutes.

Unmold on a serving platter. Flavor the custard with liqueur and pour on the inverted pudding. Serve lukewarm or chilled.

MOUSSES AND FROZEN SOUFFLÉS

Mousses and frozen soufflés are preparations made with proteins whipped to build foam walls: eggs, heavy cream or combinations of several of these. A frozen soufflé is made, in French culinary language, from *appareil de mousse à la crème,* so you can see that these two preparations are closely related.

Dessert Mousses

A mousse may be served chilled or frozen. The flavor of a mousse is contained in a base into which egg whites and/or whipped cream are folded. The base may consist of:

a purée of uncooked fruit (banana), or a sweetened purée of cooked fruit (berries, chestnuts). The fruit purée may be used raw, but cooking it with sugar removes the edge of the natural acids and keeps the mousse from acquiring a faint cheeselike flavor (raspberries, strawberries);

a ribboned mixture of egg yolks and sugar flavored with a liqueur, a citrus-fruit rind, cocoa or coffee, and eventually stabilized with a small amount of gelatin;

melted chocolate, sometimes mixed with melted butter;

a custard made with egg yolks; this method is old-fashioned and on its way to disappearance.

The base must be completely cold before you add egg whites and whipped cream or you will obtain nothing more than a sweet sauce. Before setting out to make a mousse, you must be familiar with the techniques of ribboning (p. 57), folding (p. 61), and whipping cream (pp. 19–20).

You may make up your own mousse with the flavor of your choice. Fill a 3-cup dish or 6 large sherbet glasses with this mixture:

for fruit-flavored purées, 1 cup fruit purée per cup of heavy whipped cream;

for liqueur- or nut-flavored mousses, 3 egg yolks ribboned with 1/3 cup sugar and 3 beaten egg whites per cup of heavy cream.

You may use gelatin as a stabilizer at the ratio of 1/2 to 3/4 teaspoon per each 2 cups of mousse mixture made on a base of egg yolks. Melt the gelatin as indicated on page 21. Add it to the yolk and sugar mixture while they are ribboning. Use gelatin sparingly; its presence is always detectable and does not enhance the texture and flavor of the finished product. Fats and fruit acids act as stabilizers for chocolate and fruit mousses.

Frozen Soufflés

Frozen soufflés are very rich mousses frozen in small soufflé dishes fitted with a collar. When the collar is removed, the dessert stands frozen above the rim of the dish, giving the illusion of a soufflé.

To fit the collar and calculate the capacity of your mold, study the "Collar Mathematics" on page 464. Lightly oil the side of the paper which will be in contact with the batter. You can expect all your ingredients to double in volume; also expect one third loss of volume when folding. Before freezing the dessert, turn the refrigerator to its coldest setting to obtain small crystals.

To remove the collar, let the soufflé stand at room temperature for 5 minutes, then gently pull off the paper. If for any reason the sides of the soufflé have been damaged in the freezer and do not look perfectly smooth, cover them with crushed praline powder (p. 23) or crumbled macaroons.

LIQUEUR-FLAVORED SOUFFLÉS

Frozen soufflés are the dessert *par excellence* for large dinner parties. Make up your own formulas. For a liqueur-flavored soufflé for a 3-cup soufflé mold fitted with collar, use for each 2 cups of heavy cream:

½ to ¾ cup sugar	*2 extra egg yolks*
3 whole eggs	*6 tablespoons liqueur*

Ribbon eggs and yolks over heat until warm, remove from heat, and continue beating until cold. Fold in whipped cream.

FRUIT-FLAVORED SOUFFLÉS

The old-fashioned formula made on a base of English or stirred custard is not in use anymore. Although frozen soufflés with a fruit base are more often made according to the following formula, it is not rare to find them also prepared with a whole-egg base (see Blueberry Soufflé, p. 489).

2 cups fruit purée	*¼ cup water*
6 tablespoons liqueur	*5 egg whites*
1 cup sugar	*1 cup heavy cream, whipped*

Prepare fruit purée and flavor with liqueur. Make sugar syrup by cooking the sugar and water to 238°F. Whip egg whites; pour syrup onto whites and beat until cold. Add fruit purée; fold in whipped cream. See Raspberry Frozen Soufflé (p. 491) for an example.

POACHING EGG-YOLK BASES AND WHOLE-EGG BASES

Mousses and frozen soufflés made on a base of egg yolks are the most difficult. The egg yolks must be poached so that the finished product will not separate. Yolks and sugar must be at room temperature for several hours before starting the ribboning. Ribbon eggs and sugar in a large mixing bowl placed on a protective pad (metal or asbestos) over medium to low heat. Beat the mixture until it feels warm to the finger. Remove the bowl from the heat and continue beating until cold. Only then fold beaten egg whites and/or cream into the base.

WHIPPING CREAM FOR MOUSSES AND FROZEN SOUFFLÉS

Beat the cream so it stays soft and remains at the Chantilly stage. It is essential to keep the cream soft since folding it into the base stiffens it further. Cold desserts made with overbeaten cream are heavy and butterlike in taste. When the cream is overbeaten, it starts separating during the folding, and the texture of the dessert presents very visible globules of fat separated by ice crystals if it is frozen, and the very same globules with the seepage of liquid at the bottom of the dish if the dessert is only deep chilled. The general folding method described on page 61 must be applied.

Entrée Mousses

Cold meat and fish mousses are the staples of a cold buffet. They follow the same rules as the dessert mousses. The base is made with béchamel or velouté; no gelatin is needed when aspic enters the composition (see Fish Mousse, p. 493). Mousses can be molded in decorated molds or used as a stuffing for larger pieces of food coated with *chaud-froid*. In this case, the mousse must be used for stuffing before it gels completely.

APRICOT MOUSSE
6 TO 8 SERVINGS

This recipe resulted from my grandfather's apricot crop, and it has been adapted to dried apricots to make it enjoyable year round.

12 ounces large dried apricots	*1 cup heavy cream*
6 tablespoons sugar	*2 tablespoons chopped blanched*
½ cup water	*pistachios*
2 tablespoons Kirsch	

Cover apricots with cold water and soak overnight. Discard the water, add the sugar, and cook apricots with ½ cup water over medium heat until they are mushy. Strain to remove all skins. Chill.

Add the Kirsch to the purée. Whip the cream and fold into the purée. Serve deep chilled, sprinkled with the pistachios.

BANANA MOUSSE
6 TO 8 SERVINGS

A childhood memory. Use only very ripe bananas, full of sugar spots, those tiny brown flecks.

4 tablespoons butter	*2 tablespoons lemon juice*
6 tablespoons sugar	*1 ounce unsweetened chocolate*
3 tablespoons rum	*1 cup heavy cream*
5 large bananas	

Cream the butter with 5 tablespoons of the sugar, add 2 tablespoons rum, and continue beating until fluffy. Mash 3 large bananas with 1 tablespoon of the lemon juice. Grate the chocolate into the banana purée. Blend creamed butter and banana purée. Whip the heavy cream, and fold into the banana purée. Deep chill.

Slice the remaining 2 bananas, and sprinkle with 1 tablespoon sugar and 1 tablespoon lemon juice mixed with 1 tablespoon rum. Arrange slices of bananas on top of the chilled mousse before serving.

COFFEE MOUSSE
6 TO 8 SERVINGS

To make a very quick coffee mousse, simply flavor heavy cream with instant coffee powder and whip. This slightly more complicated formula is best when made with New Orleans type coffee.

¼ cup boiling water
¼ cup fine-ground coffee
1 teaspoon instant coffee powder
1 teaspoon unflavored gelatin
3 eggs, separated

⅓ cup sugar
2 tablespoons Tia Maria, rum or
Cognac
1 cup heavy cream

Drip the boiling water through the ground coffee. Drip the coffee again through the same grounds. Squeeze the filter to extract as much liquid as possible. Dissolve the instant coffee powder in the prepared extract. Place the extract in a small pot over hot water, add the gelatin, and let it dissolve. Keep warm until ready to use.

Ribbon egg yolks with sugar over heat. Add the coffee-gelatin mixture and beat until warm to the finger. Remove from the heat, add liqueur, and continue beating until cold. Whip egg whites; mix one third of their volume into the base and fold in the remainder. Whip the cream and fold into the mousse. Serve chilled or frozen, sprinkled with a little instant coffee powder.

CREAM-CHEESE MOUSSE
8 OR MORE SERVINGS

Inspired by Crémêt d'Anjou and Fontainebleau, two lovely, airy, fresh French cheeses made with cream and egg white. This mousse is very rich.

Use only whipped cottage cheese without the tiniest trace of a curd. If unable to buy it, blend cottage cheese and sour cream together in the blender until the mixture is like a purée. *Use no salt, no sugar;* if you like either, sprinkle it on the mousse before eating. Serve with fresh berries and douse liberally with unsweetened, unwhipped heavy cream, or with raspberry sauce (p. 384).

> *4 ounces whipped cottage cheese*   *4 ounces cream cheese*
> *2 tablespoons sour cream*   *2 cups heavy cream*

Line a 4-cup *coeur à la crème* basket, or any other small bread basket, with a triple layer of cheesecloth rinsed in cold water and squeezed dry. Purée cottage cheese and sour cream in the blender, if necessary. Put in a large mixer bowl. Add the cream cheese and whip until fluffy. Whip the heavy cream to the semi-stiff stage, mix one third of its volume into the cheese mixture, and fold in the remainder. Spoon the mousse into the prepared basket. Place over a plate to catch the drippings; 3 to 4 tablespoons of whey will escape. Refrigerate overnight. Invert on a serving platter and gently remove the cheesecloth. Serve with red berries, if desired.

Note: If the cream is too soft, the whey will be retained and the mousse will not unmold.

LEMON-LIME MOUSSE
6 TO 8 SERVINGS

Use only lemon to make a lemon mousse, or only lime to make a lime mousse, if you prefer. Serve the dessert either chilled or frozen. It looks better after having been frozen. You can make an orange or tangerine mousse with the same proportions.

> *2 tablespoons milk*   *1½ tablespoons each of lime*
> *1 tablespoon each of fine-grated*   *and lemon juice*
> *lime and lemon rinds*   *2 tablespoons light rum*
> *⅔ cup sugar*   *1 cup heavy cream*
> *3 eggs, separated*   *Candied violets*

Scald milk, add grated rinds, and let steep, covered, for 2 hours; strain. Mix the sugar and egg yolks, and ribbon together over heat. Remove from heat when the mixture feels warm to the finger. Add the flavored milk, the juices and rum, and continue beating until cold. Whip the egg whites, mix half of their volume into the base, and fold in the remainder. Whip the cream and fold into the mousse. Serve frozen or deep chilled. Decorate with candied violets.

MAPLE MOUSSE
6 TO 8 SERVINGS

This mousse is very sweet, but the relatively large amount of walnuts provides a contrast between two totally opposite tastes and textures.

6 egg yolks	1½ teaspoons unflavored gelatin
⅔ cup maple syrup	3 tablespoons water
Pinch of salt	1 cup heavy cream
¼ teaspoon maple flavoring	½ cup chopped walnuts

Ribbon egg yolks and maple syrup over heat. Add salt and maple flavoring. Melt gelatin in the 3 tablespoons water in a double boiler; add to the ribboning mixture. Continue beating until the mixture feels warm to the finger. Remove from the heat and continue beating until cold. Whip the cream and fold into the mousse. Freeze or deep chill. Cover with a thick layer of chopped walnuts.

PRALINE CHOCOLATE MOUSSE
6 TO 8 SERVINGS

This mousse tastes like the chocolate French Christmas confections called *boules pralinées.*

5 ounces Swiss bittersweet chocolate	4 eggs, separated
¼ cup water	2 teaspoons instant coffee powder
¾ cup sugar	2 tablespoons Cognac or rum
¼ cup chopped blanched almonds or hazelnuts	1 cup heavy cream
	Candied violets

Melt the chocolate and let it cool. With water, sugar and almonds or hazelnuts, make a praline powder (see p. 23). Ribbon egg yolks with the praline powder. Add coffee powder and liqueur, and blend in the cooled chocolate. Whip the egg whites, mix one third of their volume into the base, and fold in the remainder. Whip heavy cream to the Chantilly stage. Fold two thirds of it into the mousse. Whip the remainder of the cream until stiff and use it to pipe decorative rosettes on the top of the mousse. Top each rosette with a candied violet.

STRAWBERRY MOUSSE
6 TO 8 SERVINGS

If you use frozen berries, they must be the kind that are frozen individually without syrup or added sugar; defrost before using. Fresh berries must be very ripe.

1 quart strawberries	*2 to 3 tablespoons Kirsch or*
6 tablespoons confectioners'	*Framboise*
sugar	*1¼ cups heavy cream*
1 tablespoon lemon juice	

Purée strawberries. Add sugar and lemon juice. Cook until reduced to 1 cup; chill. Add liqueur to the purée. Whip cream and fold into the fruit purée. Chill.

BLUEBERRY FROZEN SOUFFLÉ
6 TO 8 SERVINGS

This soufflé tastes better with wild berries. Do not strain the berry purée; the skins will melt while cooking.

3 cups blueberries	*2 extra egg yolks*
¾ cup sugar	*Pinch of salt*
1½ tablespoons lemon juice	*½ teaspoon grated lemon rind*
1½ cups heavy cream	*2 tablespoons bourbon*
3 whole eggs	*Confectioners' sugar*

Purée the berries in the blender. Mix with sugar and lemon juice, and cook down to 1½ cups. Whip cream to the Chantilly stage and keep chilled.

Ribbon whole eggs, egg yolks, salt and lemon rind, gradually beating in the hot berry purée, which will poach the eggs. Continue beating until cold. Add whiskey during the last 2 minutes of beating. Fold the whipped cream into the mousse and turn into a collared 3-cup soufflé mold. Freeze immediately. Serve sprinkled with confectioners' sugar.

PECAN-PRALINE FROZEN SOUFFLÉ
6 TO 8 SERVINGS

3 whole eggs
2 extra egg yolks
¼ cup dark brown sugar
Pinch of salt

1½ cups pecan praline powder
(p. 23)
6 tablespoons dark rum
2 cups heavy cream

Ribbon whole eggs, egg yolks, brown sugar, salt and ½ cup praline powder over heat until the mixture feels warm to the finger. Remove from the heat and gradually add rum; continue beating until cold. Whip heavy cream to the Chantilly stage and fold into the base. Turn into a collared 3-cup soufflé mold this way: add a layer of soufflé mixture and sprinkle with one third of the remaining praline powder; repeat twice with the remaining soufflé batter and praline powder. Freeze immediately.

RASPBERRY FROZEN SOUFFLÉ
6 SERVINGS

A favorite of my students. Keep the cream very soft, and do not over-fold.

4 boxes (10 ounces each) frozen　¼ cup water
raspberries, thawed　¼ teaspoon lemon juice
7 tablespoons Kirsch or　5 egg whites
Framboise　6 ladyfingers
1 cup heavy cream　2 tablespoons chopped pistachios
1 cup sugar

Drain thawed berries completely. (Use the syrup for another purpose.) Purée in the blender and strain to remove seeds. Flavor the purée with ¼ cup Kirsch or Framboise. Whip the cream and keep it chilled. Mix sugar, water and lemon juice, and cook to 238°F. While the sugar cooks, whip the egg whites; when they reach the soft-peak stage, pour the sugar syrup on them while you continue whisking. As soon as the syrup has been absorbed, gradually whip the purée of raspberries into the whites; the meringue will be cold by then; immediately fold in the softly whipped cream. Turn half of the soufflé into a collared 3-cup mold. Add the ladyfingers, diced and soaked in 3 tablespoons Kirsch or Framboise. Top with the remainder of the soufflé. Freeze immediately. Serve sprinkled with chopped pistachios.

POOR MAN'S MOUSSE DE FOIE GRAS
2 TO 2½ CUPS

This mousse can be molded and unmolded, and it spreads at room temperature. Use 1 duck or goose liver, if available, with enough chicken livers to make up 1 pound. The color and consistency are that of *foie gras,* but the taste, although delicious, will fool no one.

1 pound chicken livers　½ cup unsalted soft butter
2 tablespoons butter　¼ teaspoon four spices
1 onion, chopped fine　(p. 27)
2 shallots, chopped fine　⅛ teaspoon grated nutmeg
1 teaspoon unflavored gelatin　Salt and pepper
¼ cup tawny port　½ cup heavy cream
½ cup medium-thick white or　1½ cups liquid aspic (for
béchamel sauce (p. 110)　molding)
1 large truffle (optional)

Clean the livers and trim free of all gristle and ligaments. Heat 2 tablespoons butter and in it sauté the onion until soft. Add shallots and sauté for 2 minutes. Add livers and sauté over high heat until just stiff.

Soften gelatin in port, blend into the hot béchamel sauce, and stir until gelatin has dissolved. Put béchamel mixture in a blender, and add livers and peeled diced truffle if used. Blend until smooth, strain, and let cool.

Cream the unsalted butter in a small mixer bowl. Add spices and nutmeg and little by little the liver purée. Add salt and pepper to taste. Continue beating until light and fluffy. Whip the cream and fold into the liver mixture. Deep chill.

To mold: Line a 2-cup mold with a ⅛-inch layer of aspic. Decorate with truffle shavings if desired. Pipe the mousse into the mold with a pastry bag. Deep chill. Invert on a deep-chilled serving platter, and unmold.

POULTRY OR HAM MOUSSE
6 SERVINGS

This mousse can be made with cooked white meat of chicken, capon or turkey, or with duck or ham. With duck, use only the filets and make a stock with the duck carcass.

1 ⅓ cups chicken stock or broth (p. 76)	*1 envelope unflavored gelatin*
½ teaspoon four spices (p. 27)	*2 cups fine-chopped cooked meat*
1 teaspoon salt, or more	*1 large truffle, peeled and chopped fine*
½ teaspoon fine-ground white pepper	*½ teaspoon grated nutmeg*
4 egg yolks	*1 cup heavy cream, whipped*

Scald ⅔ cup of the stock and add spices, salt and pepper. Mix with egg yolks and thicken over medium heat. Dissolve the gelatin in remaining cold stock and blend into the thickened sauce; let cool. Put the sauce in a blender container with the meat, truffle and nutmeg, and blend until smooth. Stir over ice until the mixture is starting to set, then fold in whipped cream. Mold, if desired, in 6 individual 4-ounce custard cups.

FISH OR SHELLFISH MOUSSE
6 SERVINGS

1 pound fish or shellfish, with no skin, bone or shells	*Salt and pepper*
	1 cup heavy cream
1 cup cold medium-thick white or béchamel sauce (p. 110)	*Green herbs (dill, chives, fennel greens), chopped fine*
1½ cups white-wine fish fumet *(p. 83)*	

Poach the fish or shellfish, and cool completely. Shred into fine flakes and mix with béchamel. Reduce fish *fumet* to ¾ cup, and let cool completely. Put fish *fumet* in the blender container with the fish mixture, and blend until smooth; strain. Season if necessary. Whip cream until barely mounding and fold into the base. Mold and chill.

At serving time unmold and decorate with the chopped fresh herbs.

VARIATION

Spoon half of the mousse into the mold, add a layer of well-drained blanched asparagus tips, and top with remainder of the mousse.

BAKED CUSTARDS, BAVARIAN CREAM, LOAVES AND TIMBALES

Custards, timbales and loaves are the solid products you can obtain when you mix eggs with milk, cream and purées of vegetables or meat and bake the mixture in the oven with the help of a hot-water bath.

Custards

CUSTARDS WITH AN EGG-YOLK BASE

These custards are often called creams; they are thicker versions of the basic English or stirred custard on page 62, and are used mainly for desserts. Make up your own recipes with different flavors by mixing 2 cups cream with 6 to 8 egg yolks and ½ cup sugar. If the recipe contains 2 to 3 ounces of chocolate, omit enough egg yolks to achieve a ratio of 1 egg yolk per each ½ cup of liquid. Serve the custards in the dishes in which they have been baked.

CUSTARDS WITH A WHOLE-EGG BASE

To have a baked custard that will unmold, you must use at least 6 whole eggs per each quart of milk. If you serve the custard in the dish in which it has been baked, use only 1 egg per cup of milk. Additional egg yolks reinforce the solidity and richness of the custard. Use from ½ to ⅔ cup of sugar. If the custards are made with chicken broth or tomato sauce, you can obtain a garnish for consommés (Royale) or small savory custards called *timbales*.

Loaves

You may prepare vegetables or meats as "loaves" by adding to them eggs and a certain amount of bread crumbs or béchamel sauce. The basic proportions are:

> FOR MEATS
>> 1 pound raw meat, chopped very fine or blended
>> 1 whole egg
>> 3 extra egg yolks
>> 1 cup very thick cold béchamel sauce (p. 110)
>
> FOR VEGETABLES
>> 4 cups shredded or fine-chopped cooked vegetables
>> 4 slices of white bread plus ⅔ cup milk or cream, or 1 cup very cold béchamel sauce (p. 110)
>> 4 eggs

The meat may be blended, but the vegetables have a better and more pleasant texture if they are only chopped; when they are blended they give a preparation too reminiscent of baby food. Additional egg yolks bring richness to the dish. However, fish and meat require considerably fewer eggs because they contain a large amount of protein.

Preparing and Baking a Custard

All custards and loaves are prepared according to this procedure. Always scald the milk and add it to the eggs while still warm so as to prepare the eggs for the heat of the oven. Do not beat the egg and milk mixture too much to avoid the formation of foam and obtain a smooth top surface. Generously butter the baking dish, or dishes, and put them in a cake pan. Strain the custard mixture into the dishes and fill them completely. Bring a kettle full of water to a rolling boil and pour the water into the cake pan around the dishes so that they will be two thirds immersed in water.

Cover the cake pan with a large lid so that the heat of the oven cannot solidify the top of the custard too fast and thus build a hard crust. Do not use the small lids of small custard *pots de crème* during cooking, but place them on the *pots* only after the custard is cold and ready to chill. Bake in a 300°F. oven for pure egg custards and 325°F. for loaves.

If overheated or cooked too long, a custard separates, i.e., the proteins form large blocks that release water, and the baked product is both grainy and watery. This physical phenomenon, called *syneresis*, does not occur in loaves where the starch absorbs the released water. Custards can be considered done when a skewer inserted 1½ inches deep halfway between the edge and the center of the dish comes out clean. Even if the center of the custard does not look quite firm, remove the water bath from the oven. The heat accumulated in the custard will penetrate to its center and finish coagulating it.

Let the custard cool in its water bath until lukewarm. Keep it at room temperature until completely cold; only then, refrigerate it. Unmold upside-down custards only after chilling them for several hours.

COATING A MOLD WITH CARAMEL

Cook the caramel in a small pot. Pour it into the ungreased custard mold. Tilt the mold back and forth to coat all sides evenly. When the caramel starts to harden, turn the mold upside-down over a plate to allow it to dribble evenly all over the sides of the mold. Butter whatever part of the mold that is not covered with caramel.

Bavarian Creams

Another preparation, usually with a custard base, which is finished in a mold and turned out of the mold to serve is the Bavarian cream. Instead of being made firm by baking, this preparation is made firm by chilling, like a mousse. A Bavarian cream, however, is always stabilized with gelatin.

A true Bavarian cream contains no egg whites, only a large amount of whipped cream folded into a base that can be an English or stirred custard, a fruit purée, or an English or stirred custard sweetened and flavored with a fruit jam or jelly (see Blueberry Bavarian Cream, p. 503).

When you use a fresh fruit purée, heat it first to 190°F. to destroy possibly existing enzymes that keep gelatin from setting. Also the gelatin can be dissolved in the heated purée.

Preparing a Bavarian Cream

Brush a mold with sweet almond oil or an oil without taste; turn it upside down on a paper towel. Whip cream as you would for a mousse or a frozen soufflé (see p. 484), and keep it refrigerated. Make custard, or heat fresh fruit purée, and dissolve gelatin in it. Cool the base (over ice if desired) until the gelatin starts setting. Fold the properly whipped cream into it.

Overwhipped cream or overfolding of the cream into the base will result in a "mortar-like" Bavarian; instead it should be positively ethereal. An already too solid base will have the same adverse effect. If the base solidifies too fast, remelt it over low heat and start the cooling process again.

Turn the cream immediately into the prepared mold, and deep chill for several hours.

Unmolding a Bavarian Cream

Run the tip of a knife around the edges of the cream, center the mold upside down over a platter, and invert. If the mold has been oiled properly, the cream will unmold without problem. If you have difficulties, cover the mold with a hot damp towel, but *do not dip into hot water* or half of the cream will melt.

TO MAKE A CHARLOTTE WITH BAVARIAN CREAM

Turn a Charlotte mold upside down. With your left hand hold a piece of parchment paper over the bottom of the mold and with your right press the dull side of a large kitchen knife blade against the edges to cut a circle of paper the exact size of the bottom. Fit this circle of paper on the inside bottom of the mold. Butter the sides of the mold well and line it with homemade ladyfingers (p. 454); arrange the flat side of the cakes facing the center of the mold. Fill the mold with Bavarian cream. Cover with a sheet of wax paper and a plate; put a weight on the plate and refrigerate overnight. Unmold on a serving platter, remove the paper, and decorate with rosettes of whipped cream.

BASIC PROPORTIONS FOR BAVARIAN CREAMS

To fill a 3-cup mold or 6 large sherbet glasses

Cream Base

4 egg yolks
⅓ to ½ cup sugar
1 cup scalded milk
2½ teaspoons unflavored gelatin
1 cup heavy cream, whipped

Fruit Base

1¼ cups thick purée of fresh fruit
⅓ to ¾ cup sugar, depending on fruit acidity
1 tablespoon unflavored gelatin
1 cup heavy cream, whipped

CREOLE CREAM

8 SERVINGS

A variation on the *crème au chocolat.*

1¾ cups medium or light cream
¼ cup light molasses
Pinch of salt
3 ounces milk chocolate, melted
1 ounce unsweetened chocolate, melted

4 egg yolks
2 tablespoons dark rum
Chopped pecans

Mix cream and molasses; scald but do not boil; add salt. Melt chocolate. Whisk egg yolks until just broken. Slowly add the cream-molasses mixture. Blend custard and melted chocolate; blend in rum. Strain into 3-ounce custard cups or ramekins. Bake in a hot-water bath in a 300°F. oven for 20 minutes. Cool and chill. Serve topped with chopped pecans.

BUTTERSCOTCH CREAM
6 SERVINGS

Perfect dessert for a dinner party.

½ cup dark brown sugar	8 egg yolks
2 tablespoons unsalted butter	2 teaspoons vanilla extract
2 cups medium or light cream	Chopped toasted almonds
Pinch of salt	

Mix brown sugar and butter and melt over medium heat to make butterscotch. Scald cream, and gradually blend with butterscotch. Add salt. Blend with egg yolks; add vanilla. Strain into 3-ounce custard cups or ramekins. Bake in a 300°F. oven for 20 to 25 minutes. Serve sprinkled with toasted almonds.

VIENNESE CUSTARD
6 SERVINGS

1 cup granulated sugar	4 extra egg yolks
5 tablespoons water	2 drops of lemon juice
2 cups milk	½ cup heavy cream
1 tablespoon vanilla extract	Confectioners' sugar
¼ teaspoon salt	2 tablespoons Tia Maria
2 whole eggs	

Measure ½ cup of the sugar and add 3 tablespoons water. Cook until the syrup reaches a dark caramel color; let cool. Add milk and heat slowly, stirring to dissolve the caramel. Add ¼ cup more of the sugar and let it dissolve. Add vanilla and salt. Beat whole eggs and egg yolks lightly and mix with the milk and caramel.

Make a second caramel with remaining ¼ cup sugar, remaining 2 tablespoons water and the lemon juice. Use it to coat a 1-quart Charlotte mold. Strain the custard mixture into the prepared mold. Bake in a hot-water bath in a 300°F. oven for 35 to 40 minutes. Cool and refrigerate. Invert on a serving platter.

Whip the cream, sweeten with confectioners' sugar to taste, and flavor with Tia Maria. Use to decorate the custards. Don't forget the whipped cream, for it adds the true Viennese touch.

LIME UPSIDE-DOWN CUSTARD
6 SERVINGS

Ideal after a rich meal.

2 cups milk	¼ cup white rum
Fine-grated rind of 2 limes	3 drops of green food coloring
⅓ cup sugar	3 whole eggs
¼ teaspoon salt	2 extra egg yolks

Scald the milk, and add lime rind; let steep for 2 hours. Mix lime-flavored milk with sugar and salt, and reheat until sugar has melted. Add rum and coloring. Beat whole eggs and egg yolks; slowly add the warm milk and sugar. Strain the mixture into a buttered 1-quart Charlotte mold. Bake in a hot-water bath in a 300°F. oven for 35 to 40 minutes. Cool and refrigerate. Unmold the custard, pour sabayon on top, and serve deep chilled.

SABAYON

2 egg yolks	Juice of 1 lime
¼ cup sugar	1 tablespoon rum
Pinch of salt	

Ribbon egg yolks, sugar and salt, add lime juice, and thicken over low heat. Add rum, whisk until cool, and refrigerate.

ALMOND OR PISTACHIO UPSIDE-DOWN CUSTARD
6 SERVINGS

ALMOND

2 ¼ cups milk	3 whole eggs
¾ cup blanched almonds	2 extra egg yolks
⅓ cup sugar	½ cup heavy cream, whipped
Pinch of salt	Kirsch or almond liqueur for
1 ½ teaspoons bitter-almond extract	flavoring cream

PISTACHIO

2 cups milk	3 whole eggs
¾ cup blanched pistachios	2 extra egg yolks
⅓ cup sugar	½ cup heavy cream, whipped
Pinch of salt	Kirsch for flavoring cream
¼ cup Kirsch	

Scald milk. Put nuts in the blender container and pour the hot milk over them. Blend on high speed until the nuts are ground. Let steep for 2 hours. Add sugar and salt; reheat until sugar has melted. Add almond extract or Kirsch. Beat whole eggs and egg yolks lightly and blend with milk. Strain the custard into a buttered 1-quart Charlotte mold. Bake in a 300°F. oven for 35 to 40 minutes. Unmold on a serving platter. Serve with whipped cream flavored with liqueur.

CANTALOUPE BAVARIAN CREAM
6 SERVINGS

The melon must be very ripe and fragrant or the cream will be flat.

1 cup cantaloupe purée	*1 envelope unflavored gelatin*
2 to 3 tablespoons sugar	*1 cup heavy cream*
5 tablespoons ruby or tawny	
port	

Purée enough ripe cantaloupe in the blender to obtain 1 cup. Sweeten with sugar to taste. Soften gelatin in port; add to cantaloupe purée heated to 190°F., and stir until melted. Place the mixture over ice and stir until thickening begins. Whip cream and fold into the base. Turn into an oiled 3-cup mold and chill for 4 hours.

MADEIRA BAVARIAN CREAM
6 SERVINGS

Fine-grated rind of 2 lemons	*4 egg yolks*
¾ cup undiluted frozen orange	*½ cup sugar*
juice, thawed	*2½ teaspoons unflavored gelatin*
⅔ cup dry (Sercial) Madeira	*1 cup heavy cream*

Grate lemon rind into orange juice. Cook together until reduced to ⅓ cup. Mix juice and Madeira. Ribbon very lightly egg yolks and sugar. Dilute with the strained Madeira mixture and thicken over medium heat as you would a stirred English custard. Melt gelatin in a double boiler, add to the custard, and stir until dissolved. Stir custard over ice until it starts setting. Fold in the softly whipped cream. Turn into an oiled 3-cup mold. Chill for 4 to 6 hours. Unmold, and decorate with whipped-cream rosettes if desired.

PEAR BAVARIAN CREAM
6 SERVINGS

If pear brandy is not available, use Grand Marnier or Noyau de Poissy. The cream is snow white.

1 envelope unflavored gelatin	*¼ cup pear brandy or almond*
3 jars (4½ ounces each)	*liqueur*
strained baby-food pears	*1 cup heavy cream*

Melt gelatin in a double boiler. Heat puréed pears without boiling, add gelatin, and mix well; add pear brandy. Cool over ice until the mixture starts setting. Whip the cream very soft and fold into the fruit base. Turn into an oiled 3-cup mold, and chill for 4 to 6 hours. Unmold, and decorate with whipped-cream rosettes topped with candied violets if desired.

ITALIAN RICE PUDDING
8 SERVINGS

From the Italian side of Mont Blanc, but the principle is that of the French *riz à l'Impératrice*.

½ cup uncooked long-grain rice	*2 teaspoons unflavored gelatin,*
2 cups scalded milk	*melted*
3 almond macaroons, crushed	*1 cup heavy cream*
6 tablespoons Maraschino	*2 cups (16-ounce can) canned*
4 egg yolks	*sweet cherries with their juices*
⅓ cup sugar	*1 teaspoon cornstarch*

Bring a large pot of water to a boil. Immerse the rice and simmer for 18 minutes; drain. Mix 1⅓ cups of the scalded milk and the rice; simmer until all the milk has been absorbed. Add the crumbled macaroons and 4 tablespoons of the Maraschino.

Ribbon egg yolks and sugar. Dilute with remaining ⅔ cup scalded milk and thicken over medium heat. Blend in melted gelatin. Mix rice and custard, and let the mixture cool.

Whip the cream to the Chantilly stage and fold into the rice. Turn into an oiled 6-cup Charlotte mold, and chill.

Make the cherry sauce. Mix canning juices with cornstarch and thicken over medium heat. Add sugar, if desired, and flavor with remaining 2 tablespoons Maraschino. Add the cherries to the sauce.

Unmold the pudding and serve with the sauce.

BLACK-CURRANT OR BLUEBERRY BAVARIAN CREAM
6 SERVINGS

Use imported English black-currant or blueberry jam.
Correct the color artificially or the finished product will have a green
hue.

1 envelope unflavored gelatin
1 cup milk
½ teaspoon fine-grated lime rind
4 egg yolks
½ cup strained black-currant or
blueberry jam

3 drops of blue food coloring
¼ teaspoon red food coloring
2 tablespoons Cassis liqueur (for
black currant), or 1 tablespoon
bourbon (for blueberry)
1 cup heavy cream

Melt the gelatin in a double boiler. Scald the milk, add lime rind,
and let steep for 2 hours. Mix egg yolks and milk and thicken over
medium heat. Be careful: the mixture will heat fast since it does not
contain any sugar. Add melted gelatin and strained jam. Add both
food colorings and the appropriate liqueur. Stir over ice until the
mixture starts setting. Whip the cream and fold it into the base. Turn
the cream into an oiled 3-cup mold. Serve topped with whipped
cream.

QUICK SPINACH LOAF
6 SERVINGS

This quick method can be used with any green leafy vegetable or with
Brussels sprouts.

4 packages (10 ounces each)
frozen chopped spinach (4
cups)
4 tablespoons butter
4 tablespoons flour

1 cup milk, scalded
½ teaspoon grated nutmeg
Salt and pepper
4 whole eggs

Boil the spinach, drain in a colander, and squeeze well in your hands to extract as much moisture as possible. In a pot, place the butter, spinach and flour. Add scalded milk, nutmeg, and salt and pepper to taste. Stir until thickened. Beat eggs and mix into the spinach mixture. Turn into a buttered 1-quart Charlotte mold. Bake in hot-water bath in a 325°F. oven for 35 to 40 minutes.

FISH LOAF
6 SERVINGS

Use any fish—flounder, whitefish, pike, haddock.

1 whole egg	*1 cup very thick cold béchamel*
3 extra egg yolks	*sauce (p. 110)*
1 pound fish, without bones or	*½ cup heavy cream*
skin	*Salt and pepper*

Beat whole egg and egg yolks. Purée the fish in the blender, using the eggs as liquid. Strain if desired. Mix with cold béchamel; add cream, and salt and pepper to taste. Turn into a buttered 1-quart Charlotte mold. Bake in a hot-water bath in a 325°F. oven for 30 to 35 minutes. Unmold on a serving platter and serve with the fish velouté.

FISH VELOUTÉ

3 tablespoons each of butter and	*⅛ teaspoon fine-grated orange*
flour	*rind*
1½ cups white-wine fish fumet	*½ teaspoon dried basil*
(p. 83)	*Salt and pepper*
½ teaspoon anchovy paste	*6 tablespoons butter*

Make a velouté with butter, flour and fish *fumet*. Bring to a boil and add anchovy paste, orange rind and basil. Simmer for 5 minutes and skim if necessary. Add salt and pepper to taste and whisk in the butter.

SHRIMP TOMATO TIMBALES
6 SERVINGS

A pleasant first course.

1⅓ cups essence of tomatoes II   *4 whole eggs*
    (p. 121), or ⅔ cup water plus   *2 extra egg yolks*
    ⅔ cup tomato paste   *3 tablespoons heavy cream*
½ teaspoon dried basil   *Salt and pepper*
¼ teaspoon each of tarragon and   *1 cup cooked tiny shrimps*
    chervil   *Tomato sauce (p. 121) or*
1 teaspoon chopped chives   *mousseline sauce (p. 129)*

Bring tomato essence (or water and tomato paste) to a boil; add all herbs. Beat whole eggs and egg yolks together. Mix with tomato essence; add heavy cream, salt and pepper to taste, and the shrimps. Turn into 6 buttered 3-ounce custard cups. Bake in a hot-water bath in a 300°F. oven for 20 to 25 minutes. Serve with desired sauce.

CRÊPES, PANCAKES, PANNEQUETS, BLINI

Pannequet is the phonetic translation in French of the English word "pancake," and this is the name mostly given to savory crêpes. Pancakes are the oldest form of unleavened bread. They appear in the cooking of all nations under different names. *Blintzes, blini, blinchiki, plättar, Pfannkuchen, Palacsinta* or *Palatschinken* and *tortillas* are variations on the theme. In the German part of Switzerland, they are even called *Omeletten,* which always gives rise to confusion with real omelets. The cereal grain used in the batter and the consistency of the batter vary; the other elements are invariably milk or cream and eggs, sometimes butter and sometimes baking powder, which appears in the Anglo-Saxon countries, while in Eastern Europe fresh yeast is used liberally. While pancakes are mainly breakfast fare in England and America, all over Europe they are either hors-d'oeuvre or dessert. They are perfect for making leftovers into an enjoyable dish that may be served to company.

BATTER FOR BASIC SAVORY CRÊPES
18 TO 24 CRÊPES

¾ cup sifted flour	*4 tablespoons melted butter*
3 eggs	*½ teaspoon salt*
1 cup milk	

Put the flour into a mixing bowl. Make a well in it and put the eggs in the well. With a wooden spatula, a wire whisk, or an electric mixer on slow speed, mix eggs and flour until the mixture is shiny and shreds. The gluten (p. 389) of the flour should be developed just enough to give the finished crêpes a certain plasticity so they flip easily. *Do not whip too much;* if you do, long strands of gluten will form, and the batter will be too cohesive to absorb the milk. Add the milk gradually. In our era of pasteurized milk, no scalding is required before making the batter. Add last the melted butter, salt and any other flavorings used.

The finished batter is lighter than heavy cream and must be strained to remove very small flour lumps. Let the batter stand from 10 to 20 minutes to allow the starch to absorb some of the milk and to swell, or the first crêpes will be thinner than the later ones. Before cooking a crêpe, stir the batter to avoid the slightest separation. Any leftover batter can be stored in the refrigerator and used up to 24 hours after its confection. The separation can easily be observed then.

BATTER FOR CORNMEAL CRÊPES
18 TO 24 CRÊPES

Delicious as part of a sauced dish or by themselves with sugar or jam.

½ cup white bolted cornmeal	*1 cup milk*
¼ cup sifted flour	*4 tablespoons melted butter*
3 eggs	*½ teaspoon salt*

Proceed exactly as with batter for savory crêpes, but *do not strain* the batter.

BATTER FOR DESSERT CRÊPES
18 TO 24 CRÊPES

There are as many batters for dessert crêpes as there are cooks. The following is a good all-purpose batter. Change the liqueur to adapt it to the general taste of the dish you are preparing.

¾ cup sifted flour	*2 extra egg yolks*
¼ teaspoon salt	*1 cup milk, less 2 tablespoons*
1 tablespoon confectioners'	*4 tablespoons melted butter*
sugar	*2 tablespoons liqueur*
2 whole eggs	

Put the flour, salt and sugar in a mixing bowl, make a well in the center, and add whole eggs and egg yolks. Mix as for savory crêpes. Add milk slowly, then butter and liqueur. Let the batter stand before baking the crêpes.

PAN FOR CRÊPES

With skill, crêpes can be made in any type of skillet or frying pan 4 to 6 inches in diameter. You will obtain the best heat conduction with a French crêpe pan conditioned like an omelet pan (p. 44). Sizes numbered 18 to 22 are the most convenient. Preheat the pan on a protective pad (metal or asbestos) placed over low heat for some time. Put a little oil in the pan when you heat it. When it is hot enough, wipe the pan dry with a paper towel and butter it for cooking. Use either method of buttering; both are used extensively and both are good.

POURING METHOD

Melt 3 tablespoons butter in a small pot. Pour about 1 teaspoon butter into the crêpe pan, swish it around the pan, and pour it back into the butter pot. The butter will clarify by itself, and only a thin film of it will be left in the pan. You will need 3 tablespoons butter to cook 24 crêpes.

BRUSHING METHOD

Put 3 tablespoons clarified butter in a small pot. Dip the tip of a small pastry brush in it. Brush the butter on the bottom and sides of the crêpe pan.

COOKING CRÊPES

To pour the batter, tilt the pan forward. Using a large serving spoon, pour the batter into the front of the pan and slowly tip the pan backward. The batter will run and deposit evenly on the bottom of the pan. A characteristic pitting will develop as tiny air bubbles are caught between the pan and batter. *Do not tilt the pan wildly* back and forth in all directions, or you will have a starfish-shaped crêpe, which will have to be patched and will look sick.

If the pan is not hot enough, there will be no pitting. If the pan is too hot, the batter will immediately fold upon itself as you start tilting the pan. The crêpe will be thick, since the batter cooks too fast, and you will need twice as much batter to obtain an inferior grade of crêpes. The crêpe is cooked on the first side when tiny droplets of butter appear at its surface. To turn it over, flip or turn with a spatula. *Safety first!* Do not, in any case, use a fingernail or the tip of your fingers to turn the crêpe; remember, the pan is hot.

Slide the spatula between crêpe and pan and turn the cake over. Flipping is no great achievement, just fun. Hold the pan below waist level. Shake the crêpe gently from left to right until one third of it hangs over the lip of the pan. Give one twist of the wrist, and the crêpe will flip and fall right back into the pan. Do not aim for the ceiling; 4 to 5 inches above the pan is impressive enough!

CLAFOUTIS

Sweet crêpes batters are also used for the country desserts called *clafoutis*, which are nothing more than fruit cobblers without baking powder. The batter is never made according to fixed rules and is always left to the cook's fancy and mood. A *clafouti* contains as much fruit as you can afford to include in it. It is a great dessert for the summer months and a good way to use bruised and partly overripe fruit.

To be able to cut a *clafouti* into wedges like a true flan, pour one third of the batter into a buttered pie plate and cook it like a huge crêpe without turning it over. Failure to do so will see all the fruit fall to the bottom of the plate and stick there. *Clafoutis* are usually juicy enough to be able to wait without drying out, but they taste best luke-warm, generously sprinkled with confectioners' sugar.

Dessert Crêpes and Flambéed Crêpes

For dessert crêpes, much of the preparation can be done ahead of time. The crêpes can come from the freezer. If you plan to flambé and sauce them, make them and fill them with the buttercream. They will wait for hours without hardening. Reheat them slowly in a low oven. Also prepare the flambéing sauce up to the point when you are supposed to add the crêpes.

Make sure that crêpes to be flambéed are completely heated through before pouring the flambéing liqueur over them, or the flames will die right then and there.

COTTON CAKES

12 FOUR-INCH CAKES

Although every woman in America has her favorite pancake batter, this is a particularly delicious one.

4 eggs	*1 tablespoon lemon juice*
2 tablespoons sugar	*1 cup sifted all-purpose flour*
½ teaspoon salt	*1 teaspoon baking soda*
1 cup light cream	

Ribbon 1 whole egg and 3 egg yolks heavily with sugar and salt. Keep electric mixer on high speed and add cream mixed with lemon juice. Blend in flour mixed with baking soda. Whip the egg whites and fold into the batter. Cook promptly.

BASIC BLINI BATTER
36 THREE-INCH BLINI

1¾ cups lukewarm milk	2 eggs, separated
1 envelope yeast	½ teaspoon salt
1 teaspoon sugar	4 tablespoons heavy cream
2 cups sifted all-purpose flour	

Handle this batter very gently to avoid any gluten development. Make the starter: Mix 1 cup of the lukewarm milk, the yeast, sugar and 1 cup sifted flour and let rise for about 1 hour. The yeast starts developing, and the mixture becomes frothy and bubbly (see p. 417). Gradually add 1 more cup of sifted flour and the egg yolks, and dilute again with remaining ¾ cup lukewarm milk. Add salt. Separately whip egg whites and cream, then fold into each other. Slowly pour the batter into the cream and egg-white mixture, whisking constantly and gently. Let the batter stand for another hour before using.

COOKING PANCAKES AND BLINI

PANCAKES
Use a well-preheated griddle or electric frying pan set at 425°F. Brush the griddle or pan with clarified butter. Drop the batter by large spoonfuls to make 4-inch cakes. Cook them until their tops are full of bubbles ready to break. Do not let the bubbles break, or the cakes will be dry. Turn over, cook for 2 more minutes, and serve piping hot.

BLINI
Blini are usually cooked in tiny crêpe pans not easy to locate in the United States. Use a cast-aluminum pan or a cast-iron griddle. An electric frying pan does not get hot enough for *blini* even at 425°F.

Cooking *blini* is a compromise between cooking a crêpe and a pancake. Grease the pan exactly as for crêpes. Pour 1 large serving spoon of batter into the pan and cook until the bubbles start breaking on the uncooked side but the batter is still wet. Then turn over and finish cooking. The total cooking time is 1½ to 2 minutes on the first side, but only 1 minute for the second side.

Storing and Freezing Crêpes, Pancakes and Blini

Keep crêpes, pancakes, or *blini* warm, loosely covered with a foil, in a medium oven; but use them as fast as possible.

To freeze crêpes, wrap them in foil two by two; do not use wax paper, which steam would make soggy. Wrap while they are still warm and put them in the freezer immediately. When ready to use, put the small packages in a 400°F. oven for 6 to 7 minutes. Unwrap, fill, and sauce. The sauce will mask the imperfection of the already frozen crêpes. Whenever possible, freeze a whole dish of sauced crêpes rather than the crêpes alone.

Pancakes and *blini* can be frozen, but they lose most of their flavor in the process.

BREAKFAST FOLLY

Our favorite breakfast fare with hickory-smoked bacon. Make the recipe for cotton cakes (p. 509), replacing sugar with maple syrup and adding ¼ teaspoon maple flavoring.

Whip ½ cup unsalted butter until foamy white and slowly beat in as much maple syrup as it will absorb without separating (about 1 cup). Serve the maple butter on hot cakes.

THE SHAH'S PANNEQUETS
6 SERVINGS

This dish is too expensive to be a full course. Use only 1 crêpe per person as a first course. Use fish *fumet;* the ingredients are much too fine for clam juice. Also do not use Lox instead of Nova Scotia salmon; the extra salt will spoil the crabmeat.

6 *crêpes*	1 ½ *cups white-wine fish* fumet
8 *small slices of smoked Nova*	(*p. 83*)
Scotia salmon	2 *tablespoons caviar* (*the best*
3 *cups basic béchamel sauce*	*you can afford*)
(*p. 110*)	*Salt and pepper*

1 pound picked-over backfin crabmeat or sliced Alaskan King crab	*6 tablespoons butter* *2 egg yolks* *⅔ cup heavy cream*

Down the center of each crêpe arrange 1 slice of salmon. Mix béchamel sauce with fish *fumet* and reduce to 3½ cups. Whisk in 4 tablespoons of the butter and the caviar. Correct seasoning. Heat crabmeat gently in 2 tablespoons butter, and mix with 1 cup of the sauce. Fill crêpes with an equal amount of filling.

Butter 6 individual fireproof dishes. Put some sauce in each, then a rolled crêpe, then a little more sauce. Chop the remaining 2 slices of salmon. Put in the blender container with egg yolks and cream. Blend on medium speed until smooth; do not overbeat. Correct seasoning. Spoon 1½ tablespoons of the mixture on top of each dish and glaze quickly under the broiler.

This dish can be frozen, but it loses flavor.

Wine: California Fumé Blanc or French Bâtard-Montrachet

HERR KRAEMER'S PALATSCHINKEN
6 SERVINGS

"Das, Fräulein Madeleine, ist ein Palatschinken!" said Herr Kraemer from Austrian Zillertal while he was making crêpes. The dear man cooked with his Tyrolean hat on.

12 crêpes	*½ cup flour*
4 large onions, minced	*2 cups hot chicken broth*
2 tablespoons plus ½ cup butter	*2 cups hot milk*
1 teaspoon caraway seeds	*Salt and pepper*
1 cup julienne of boiled ham	*1 cup heavy cream, scalded*
1 cup julienne of Austrian or *Wisconsin Swiss-type cheese*	*1 cup grated Austrian or* *Wisconsin Swiss-type cheese*

Make crêpes. Make the filling: Sauté 2 onions in 2 tablespoons butter until soft; add half of the caraway seeds and let cook, covered, over very low heat for 8 to 10 minutes. Cool. Mix with ham and julienne cheese.

Make the sauce: Heat ½ cup butter and sauté remaining 2 onions until soft. Add flour and cook for 2 minutes. Add broth and milk, and stir until thickened. Add remaining caraway seeds and salt and pepper to taste. Simmer for 15 to 20 minutes; strain. Correct seasoning.

Add 1½ cups sauce to the filling; mix well. Fill each crêpe with 1 large tablespoon of the mixture, and roll up. Butter a large baking dish, and spread 1 cup of the sauce on the bottom. Arrange the crêpes on the sauce, cover with the rest of the sauce and the hot cream, and sprinkle with grated cheese. Reheat in a 350°F. oven until golden.

This dish freezes very well.

Wine: Veltliner Gumpoldskirchner

CHICKEN-LIVER CRÊPES
6 SERVINGS

A favorite first course with gentlemen. Do not burn the onions or overcook the livers.

6 crêpes	*12 chicken livers*
1 cup heavy cream	*⅓ cup white or tawny port*
2 tablespoons butter	*Salt and pepper*
1 onion, chopped fine	*1 tablespoon chopped fresh*
1 shallot, chopped fine	*tarragon*

Make the crêpes. Reduce heavy cream by half. Heat the butter, add onion, and sauté until soft. Add shallot and toss for a few seconds. Raise the heat and add the livers; toss over high heat for 3 minutes. Add port, and salt and pepper to taste. Simmer gently for another 3 minutes. Add reduced heavy cream and heat thoroughly together. Correct seasoning, and add tarragon. Fill each crêpe with 2 livers basted with 2 tablespoons of the sauce. Fold the crêpes and baste each one with an additional tablespoon of sauce. Serve piping hot.

This recipe does not freeze.

Wine: French Barsac. Serve a glass of club soda to clean the palate for the next course.

MORVANDELLES
6 SERVINGS

My name for small crêpes flavored with an herb and filled with creamed ham, the specialty of Burgundy, here in its old-fashioned 100 per-cent pure cream sauce.

6 *crêpes*	*⅓ cup Madeira*
4 teaspoons chopped chives	*1 cup heavy cream*
2 tablespoons butter	*Pepper*
6 slices (⅛ inch thick) cooked	
ham, with no fat	

Make crêpes with Batter for Basic Savory Crêpes (p. 506), and flavor with 3 teaspoons of the chives. Keep ready to use. Heat the butter and quickly sauté ham in it on both sides. Add Madeira and simmer together for 3 to 4 minutes. Add cream, and let simmer until only ⅔ cup sauce is left. Add remaining chives and pepper to taste. Add salt if needed. Roll each slice of ham in a crêpe and spoon sauce over.

This recipe does not freeze.

Wine: California Blanc de Blancs or French Petit Chablis

SOUFFLÉED CRÊPES

Make crêpes, and make your favorite soufflé batter. Fill each crêpe with ⅓ cup of the batter. Cover crêpes with a few tablespoons of velouté or béchamel sauce or with grated cheese; or simply baste them with butter and cover them with a buttered paper. Bake in a 375°F. oven for 10 to 12 minutes. Serve immediately.

CRÊPES AMERICANA
6 SERVINGS

The most American of foods, assembled according to the best rules of classic French cuisine.

12 cornmeal crêpes (p. 506)
1 Rock Cornish Game hen
5 cups chicken stock or broth
    (p. 76)
1½ cups shoepeg corn (one
    12-ounce can, drained)
2 tablespoons plus ½ cup butter
6 tablespoons pine nuts
½ pound medium-size shrimps,
    cooked and diced
½ cup flour

1 strip of lime rind
1 garlic clove, crushed
1 cup heavy cream
2 tablespoons chopped Italian
    parsley
1 teaspoon lime juice
Salt and pepper
1 avocado, diced
½ cup fresh bread crumbs
3 tablespoons melted butter

Make cornmeal crêpes. Poach the hen in the chicken broth for 35 minutes; discard the skin and dice the meat; reserve the stock. Make the filling: Drain the corn. Heat 2 tablespoons butter and toss the pine nuts in it. Add shrimps, drained corn and diced Rock Cornish Game hen meat. Heat thoroughly.

Make a velouté sauce with ½ cup butter, the flour and 4 cups of the cooking stock from the bird. Add lime rind and garlic. Simmer for 15 minutes. Add cream, and let the sauce reduce to coating consistency; strain. Add parsley and lime juice; correct seasoning.

Mix the filling with 1½ cups sauce. Fill crêpes with equal amounts of filling. Pour half of the remaining sauce into a baking dish. Arrange the crêpes in the dish and cover with the rest of the sauce. Sprinkle with diced avocado and bread crumbs, then with melted butter. Bake in a 350°F. oven for 15 to 20 minutes.

This recipe freezes well.

Wine: California Grey Riesling or New York State unblended Niagara

BLINI AND CAVIAR

Make *blini* with Basic *Blini* Batter (p. 510). Use as much caviar as you can afford.

The best caviar comes from Russia and Iran, where the Caspian Sea is rich in sturgeons. Their roe is salted, strained, and packed in 4-pound tins called "originals." The names *Beluga, Sevruga, Osetrova* and *Sterlet* are the names of the sturgeons producing the caviar. The tin bears only the name of the district where the fish was caught. *Malosol* means that the caviar is only slightly salted (Russian *malo*, "little," and *soleny*, "salted").

A 4-pound tin of Beluga costs a small fortune; Sevruga is barely more reasonable, but red caviar (red *Keta*) from the Pacific salmon is a more accessible replacement.

When serving caviar, keep it in its original container placed in a bed of ice. If the caviar is oversalted, serve it with chopped hard-cooked egg; if it is fishy, with chopped onion. Or if it is slightly sour, with lemon juice as a redeemer.

CARROT BLINI
6 SERVINGS

An inexpensive variation on the classic *blini*. As silly as it may sound, they sell like "hot cakes" at a party.

1 cup fine-shredded carrots	*2 cups sour cream*
Basic blini *batter (p. 510)*	*3 tablespoons fine-chopped*
1 small garlic clove	*parsley*
Salt and pepper	

Shred the carrots, and add them to the finished *blini* batter just before cooking the cakes. Cook in the usual manner. Mash garlic with salt and pepper in a small bowl. Blend with sour cream and chopped parsley. Serve with hot *blini*.

CHIVE BLINI
6 SERVINGS

Very successful as an hors-d'oeuvre with the cheese dip. Try these also as a change of pace, well basted with melted butter, as an accompaniment for a main dish.

Basic blini *batter (p. 510)*
2 tablespoons chopped chives
8 ounces cream cheese
1 cup sour cream
2 tablespoons chopped parsley

2 tablespoons fine-chopped
  scallions
¼ teaspoon four spices (p. 27)
Salt and pepper

Make the *blini*, flavoring the batter with 1 tablespoon of the chives.
Cream the cheese, and blend in the sour cream. Add remaining chives,
the parsley, scallions, spices, and salt and pepper to taste. Refrigerate
for at least 2 hours before serving. Serve as a dip with *blini*.

MAPLE WALNUT CRÊPES
6 SERVINGS

Inspired by a visit to Canada, where the hot cakes are cousins to pancakes rather than sisters to crêpes.

Batter for dessert crêpes
  (p. 507)
3 tablespoons plus ⅓ cup maple
  syrup
½ teaspoon maple flavoring
3 egg yolks
Pinch of salt

¼ cup sifted all-purpose flour
⅔ cup milk
1 tablespoon butter
⅓ cup chopped walnuts
1 cup heavy cream, whipped

Make the crêpe batter, using 2 tablespoons of the maple syrup as
sweetener and ¼ teaspoon of the maple flavoring. Make 12 crêpes.
  Make a pastry cream (see p. 447) with egg yolks, ⅓ cup maple
syrup, the salt, flour and milk. Cut the butter into tiny pieces at the
surface of the cream to prevent formation of a skin; cool. Add walnuts
to the pastry cream, and fold in ½ cup of the heavy cream, whipped
to the Chantilly stage.
  Fill the crêpes with the cream, and fold in half. Put the crêpes on a
serving platter, and cover them with the rest of the heavy cream, also
whipped to the Chantilly stage, sweetened with remaining tablespoon

of maple syrup and flavored with the rest of the maple flavoring, or to taste. Serve lukewarm.

CHERRY BRANDY FLAMBÉED CRÊPES
6 SERVINGS

Batter for dessert crêpes   7 tablespoons cherry brandy
   (p. 507)   (not Kirsch)
6 tablespoons Cognac   1 tablespoon granulated sugar
¾ cup unsalted butter   1 tablespoon lemon juice
1 tablespoon confectioners' sugar   ⅓ cup brandied cherries

Prepare the batter and flavor it with 2 tablespoons of the Cognac. Make 12 crêpes. Cream ½ cup of the butter; add the confectioners' sugar and 3 tablespoons of the cherry brandy. Beat until white and frothy; spread equal amounts of filling in the crêpes and fold them in quarters. Melt remaining 4 tablespoons butter and mix with the granulated sugar, lemon juice and remaining Cognac in a flambéing or frying pan; reduce to ⅓ cup. Add crêpes and reheat thoroughly. Flambé with remaining cherry brandy and add brandied cherries. Serve immediately.

CRÊPES FLAMBÉED SOUTH PACIFIC
6 SERVINGS

1 cup milk   2 tablespoons confectioners'
1 cup sweetened coconut flakes   sugar
¾ cup flour   2 tablespoons chopped
2 whole eggs   Macadamia nuts
2 extra egg yolks   ¼ cup granulated sugar
3 tablespoons plus ⅓ cup white   ½ cup unsweetened pineapple
   rum   juice
¾ cup unsalted butter

Make a crêpe batter: Scald the milk, and add the coconut flakes. Let stand for 2 hours. Put in the blender container and purée on medium speed. Strain to discard all traces of coconut meat, but do not remove the coconut oil, which takes the place of butter. Make the batter with the flour, whole eggs and egg yolks, and the coconut milk. Flavor with 2 tablespoons of the rum. Make the crêpes.

Make the filling: Cream ½ cup of the butter with the confectioners' sugar and 1 tablespoon of the rum. Add the nuts and beat until frothy. Fill the crêpes and fold them in four.

Heat remaining ¼ cup butter, the granulated sugar and pineapple juice; reduce this sauce by half. Put filled crêpes in the sauce and reheat well. Flambé with the rest of the rum and serve immediately.

TIPSY DIXIE
6 SERVINGS

To Linda Fisher, who tested the recipe. A happy marriage of luscious Southern ingredients with French techniques.

Batter for dessert crêpes (p. 507)	*¾ cup unsalted butter*
5 tablespoons brown sugar	*2 tablespoons plus ⅓ cup cream*
3 tablespoons dark rum	*sherry*
5 tablespoons bourbon	*½ cup chopped pecans*

Make the crêpe batter, using 1 tablespoon of the brown sugar as sweetener and 1 tablespoon each of rum and bourbon as flavoring. Make 12 crêpes.

Make the filling: Cream ½ cup of the butter, add 2 tablespoons of the brown sugar and 2 tablespoons of the sherry; beat until frothy. Spread the filling on the crêpes and fold in four.

In a flambéing pan or frying pan, mix remaining 4 tablespoons butter, the pecans, and remaining brown sugar, sherry and rum; reduce to ⅓ cup. Add folded crêpes and heat well. Flambé with the rest of the bourbon. I hope you can get up from the table.

RASPBERRY SOUFFLÉED CRÊPES
6 SERVINGS

A favorite of my classes; you may replace the raspberry sauce by a stirred custard, flavored with the liqueur of your choice.

Batter for dessert crêpes (p. 507)   *¼ cup fine-ground blanched*
Kirsch or Framboise   * almonds*
4 eggs   *Clarified butter*
¼ cup sugar   *Raspberry sauce (p. 384)*
¼ teaspoon almond extract
Pinch of salt

Prepare the crêpe batter and flavor it with Kirsch or Framboise. Make 12 crêpes.

Separate eggs. Ribbon yolks, sugar, almond extract and salt very heavily. Whip egg whites. Put the bulk of the whites on the ribboned yolks. Sprinkle the ground almonds on top and fold together until homogenous.

Fill each crêpe with 2 tablespoons of the soufflé batter. Taper the end of each crêpe to keep the soufflé mixture from running out. Brush a heatproof serving platter well with clarified butter. Arrange the crêpes on it. Brush the top of each crêpe generously with butter. Cover with parchment paper and bake in a 400°F. oven for 5 to 6 minutes. Serve immediately with warm raspberry sauce.

ITALIAN PLUM CLAFOUTI
6 SERVINGS

Use exclusively blue Italian prune-plums; any other type will juice hopelessly. If you wish to use some spirit, replace 3 tablespoons of the milk with an equal amount of Slivovitz or French Quetsch (not always easy to find outside of New York). Grated lemon rind is another excellent flavoring if the spirit is not available.

1 pound Italian prune plums   *2 tablespoons sour cream*
½ cup flour   *⅔ cup milk*
3 tablespoons sugar   *Fine-grated rind of 1 lemon*
¼ teaspoon salt   *Confectioners' sugar*
2 eggs

Cut open the plums and remove pits, but do not peel to preserve the fresh sweet-sour taste. In a mixer bowl put the flour, 2 tablespoons of the sugar, the salt, eggs and sour cream; mix until smooth. Dilute with milk, add lemon rind, and give one last good beating on high speed.

Butter a 9-inch pie plate. Pour one third of the batter on it and cook like a large crêpe. Arrange the fruit on top in concentric circles. Sprinkle with remaining 1 tablespoon sugar, cover with the remainder of the batter, and bake in a preheated 375°F. for 35 to 40 minutes. Serve sprinkled with confectioners' sugar.

CREAM-PUFF PASTE (PÂTE À CHOUX)

Ask any French cook or chef what he first made in the kitchen where he apprenticed, and the answer is sure to be ". . . *de la pâte à choux* . . ." or cream-puff paste. It is common in a French restaurant kitchen to see a young fellow standing on a box in front of a blazing stove and laboriously stirring cream-puff paste. Let the poor child ask the chef whether the paste is dry enough and the *gros bonnet** will answer crossly: "Are you kidding? Do you call this a dry paste? Go on, fellow, at least five more minutes!" The poor *marmiton*† is disgusted, but the *gros bonnet* knows what he is talking about.

PÂTE À CHOUX FOR GNOCCHI AND FRITTERS

1 cup water, chicken stock or milk	*1 teaspoon sugar*
	1 cup sifted flour
¼ to ⅓ cup butter, diced	*3 to 4 eggs*
¾ teaspoon salt	*Flavorings*
Pepper	

Use only ¼ cup butter for fritters, and only 3 eggs for *gnocchi*.

* *Gros bonnet* = "big hat"; the chef wears the biggest in the kitchen!
† *Marmiton* = apprentice cook.

PÂTE À CHOUX FOR PASTRIES AND SHELLS

1 cup water	*1 cup sifted flour*
½ cup butter, diced	*5 eggs*
½ teaspoon salt	*2 teaspoons vanilla extract*
1 tablespoon sugar	

Mix liquid, diced butter, salt, pepper (for *gnocchi* and fritters), and sugar. Bring slowly to a boil to give the butter time to melt. As soon as the boiling point is reached, the mixture will foam up like milk due to the presence of casein in the butter. Remove the pot from the heat and add all at once the whole amount of sifted flour. Stir and mix until a ball forms.

Replace the pot over medium heat and dry the paste, i.e., keep it constantly in movement on the bottom of the pan so that as much as possible of its volume is exposed to the heat. Hold the pan handle with the left hand, a wooden spatula in the right hand. In three strokes, flatten the paste on the bottom of the pan, bringing it against the side of the pan closest to you. With one flip of the spatula, throw the bulk of the paste back to the opposite side of the pan. Repeat this operation as many times as possible until the butter starts oozing in tiny bubbles out of the paste. Reaching this stage may take 5 to 6 minutes, depending on the dexterity of the operator. On the bottom of the pan, a film of paste will coagulate and appear slightly sandy. Do not let it burn. While you work and acquire a tired arm, you extract excess water from the paste. The large amount of water used to make the paste was there only to make mixing easy and give the flour-starch cells a chance to start swelling. The more water you extract from the paste, the more eggs it will be able to absorb and the lighter and hollower the baked product will be. Old-fashioned Austrian cooks gave that paste the picturesque name of *Windnudeln* (wind noodle); in modern German, cream puffs have remained *Windbeuteln* (wind bags). The "wind" can exist only if the paste can absorb enough eggs. When the paste is really dry, remove the pot from the heat.

Beat the eggs slightly to avoid coagulation of the whites on contact with the hot pot. Add the value of 1 egg at a time, stirring as fast as possible until it has been absorbed in the paste. Repeat until the total volume of eggs has been added; you may use the electric mixer. Add vanilla (for cream puffs) or other flavoring.

For cream puffs, the paste should fall from the spatula in a heavy, smooth, shiny ribbon; for *gnocchi* and fritters, it should be considerably stiffer and duller in appearance.

The paste is best when used as soon as finished, but it can wait for a good hour in a warm place. Rub the surface of the paste with a piece of butter to prevent formation of a skin.

BAKING CREAM PUFFS

Butter a cookie sheet generously and rinse it under cold water. The layer of water will vaporize while the puffs bake and prevent scorching of the bottoms of the puffs.

Fit a round plain nozzle into a pastry bag; twist the part of the bag just above the nozzle and stuff it in its cone. The thickness of the material will keep the paste from flowing onto the table. Open your left hand wide, and wrap the top of the bag back over your extended fingers. With a large spoon or spatula, fill the bag with the paste. Close the bag and apply pressure. The paste will fall into the nozzle as the bag untwists. Squeeze the bag with your right hand while you guide it with your left hand, or vice-versa.

Pipe small balls ½ inch in diameter for cocktail puffs and 1 inch in diameter for cream puffs and shells. Leave 3 inches between puffs, for they will triple in size while baking. The top of each puff must be smooth; any *toupe* of paste left twisting on the top of a puff will dry out and burn before it has time to rise. You may also shape the puffs with a spoon.

Before baking the puffs, brush them with an egg-yolk glaze made of 1 egg yolk and 3 tablespoons milk; use a pastry brush. Make sure that no egg yolk rolls down onto the base of a puff or the pastry will not rise.

Bake puffs on the third or fourth rack of a preheated warm oven. Keep the heat at a steady 400°F. for 20 to 30 minutes, according to the size of the puffs.

The puffs must be dry and brown before being removed from the oven, or they will flatten without hope at room temperature. Cool the puffs on a cake rack, not on a plate or table, where they would become soggy from absorbing each other's steam.

The large amount of water contained in the egg whites makes the shells puff. In the warm oven when flour and eggs form a solid structure of coagulated proteins, the steam produced by the evaporation of the water contained in the egg whites applies pressure on the protein walls and distends them. When the steam has almost completely evaporated, a large hole is left at the center of the puff, and the puff is cooked. If the paste has not been dried enough, the puffs must be "emptied." By the time you have emptied 1 dozen puffs, you will quickly realize that you could have obtained 3 or 4 more puffs out of the wasted paste if you had not underdried it.

COOKING GNOCCHI

Gnocchi are little dumplings that must be poached in a large amount of boiling water. Bring at least 5 quarts of water to a boil. Stuff the *gnocchi* paste into a pastry bag fitted with a ½-inch nozzle. With your left hand, apply pressure on the contents of the bag so as to push out a small ½-inch-long piece of dough. Cut off the dough with the dull side of a knife blade and let it fall into the boiling water. As soon as the whole amount of paste has been used and the water comes back to a boil, lower the heat to a bare simmer. Cover the pan and poach the *gnocchi* for about 8 minutes. They are cooked when they come floating to the surface. Drain them on paper towels and season to taste.

It may interest you to know that *gnocchi* made of *choux* paste are not the only kind. In Italy *gnocchi* are made of potatoes or semolina. Potato *gnocchi* are poached like those made of *choux* paste. Semolina or farina *gnocchi* start with a porridge made of the grain and enriched with egg yolks. The porridge is spread in a pan until cooled, then cut into small squares or circles which are drenched with butter and cheese and baked in the oven until golden. Nearly every Italian cookbook has recipes for these gems.

PASTRY RAMEKINS

Make one recipe for cream puffs (p. 522). Press out the paste for cocktail-size puffs. Fill with any of the following combinations:

SWISS FILLING

1 cup grated Swiss Gruyère cheese   *2 tablespoons minced parsley*
2 tablespoons chopped walnuts

Mix cheese, parsley and walnuts. slice the bottom of each puff, and fill with 1 teaspoon of the mixture. Let some cheese pass between the top and the bottom shell. Reheat the puffs in a 350°F. oven for 6 to 7 minutes. Melted cheese will seal the puffs closed.

AMERICAN FILLING

8 ounces cream cheese   *2 tablespoons minced chives*
1 cup heavy cream   *Pinch of Cayenne*

Cream the cheese. Whip the cream to the Chantilly stage. Beat one third of the whipped cream into the cheese, fold in the remainder, and add chives and Cayenne. Stuff in a pastry bag. Punch a hole in the bottom of each puff to fill it with some of the mixture.

FRENCH FILLING

2 chicken cutlets, poached   *Salt and pepper*
1 cup heavy cream   *1 small truffle, chopped fine*

Blend chicken and half of the cream in the blender. Whip the remainder of the cream and fold into the mixture. Add salt and pepper to taste and the truffle. Remove a tiny lid from the top of each puff. Fill with mixture and replace lid.

RUSSIAN FILLING

¼ pound Nova Scotia salmon   *Salt and pepper if needed*
1 cup heavy cream   *1 tablespoon caviar*

Blend salmon and half of the cream in the blender. Whip the rest of the cream and fold into the mixture. Add salt and pepper to taste and the caviar. Fill the puffs with the mixture.

BURGUNDY GOUGÈRE

A personal interpretation. Serve with Kir for cocktails.

1 cup chicken stock or broth	*¾ cup sifted flour*
7 tablespoons butter, diced	*4 whole eggs*
¼ teaspoon grated nutmeg	*⅔ cup grated Gruyère cheese*
Pinch of Cayenne	*1 extra egg yolk*
½ teaspoon salt	*3 tablespoons milk*
Freshly ground pepper	*½ cup diced Gruyère cheese*

Prepare dough like a cream-puff paste. Mix chicken stock, butter and seasonings. Bring slowly to a boil, remove from heat, and add flour. Stir until a ball forms, then dry the paste. Add whole eggs, one by one. Add grated cheese to the finished batter.

Butter an unbendable pizza pan and rinse it under cold water. With a large serving spoon, drop large spoonfuls of batter on the pan, forming a crown. Brush with egg yolk mixed with milk; sprinkle the diced cheese on the pastry. Bake in a 400° F. oven for 35 to 40 minutes.

Serve lukewarm; the bread will rise considerably and deflate rather fast, since it is weighted by the cheese.

KIR

⅓ cup Cassis (black currant)	*3⅔ cups dry white wine*
Liqueur	*(Pouilly Fuissé)*

HICKORY-SMOKED GOUGÈRE

Use the recipe for Burgundy Gougère (above), but use hickory-smoked cheese, and add 3 slices of bacon, cooked and crumbled, to the batter.

GNOCCHI

Use the *Pâte à Choux* for *Gnocchi* and mix the batter according to the basic directions. Season with any of the following mixtures:

Reduce ½ cup heavy cream to about 5 tablespoons. Add 1 tablespoon chopped chives and salt and pepper. Roll the cooked *gnocchi* in the mixture.

Whip fresh butter with 2 tablespoons chopped fresh tarragon. Roll the *gnocchi* in the melted butter.

Serve the *gnocchi* au gratin. Roll the *gnocchi* in reduced and seasoned heavy cream. Put the *gnocchi* in a baking dish, sprinkle with ½ cup grated cheese, and pass under the broiler until golden.

Reduce ½ cup heavy cream to 5 tablespoons. Add 2 tablespoons sautéed chopped onions and 1 tablespoon imported paprika. Roll the *gnocchi* in the mixture.

DUTCH CHEESE PUFFS

Use the *Pâte à Choux* for *Gnocchi,* but use only 3 eggs. Mix the batter according to the basic directions. Dice enough cheese—Edam, Cheddar, Gruyère, Monterey Jack, etc.—to make 1 cup. Add the diced cheese to the finished paste.

Drop the batter by nuggets approximately the size of a walnut into an oil bath heated to 360°F. on a frying thermometer. Slowly increase the temperature of the oil bath to 380°F. The puffs will bob over by themselves. Serve piping hot on a folded napkin. Salt lightly.

BERRY CREAM PUFFS
12 CREAM PUFFS

Pâte à choux *for pastries*
(*p. 522*)
Egg-yolk glaze (*p. 421*)
*1 pint raspberries, strawberries
or blueberries*

Liqueur (*according to the fruit*)
*2 cups heavy cream
Confectioners' sugar*

Make the batter, shape puffs, and brush with egg-yolk glaze. Bake and cool. Slice the puffs open at the top to make a lid. Steep berries in an appropriate liqueur for 2 hours. Whip the cream, sweeten to taste, and flavor with the same liqueur. Fill the bottom of each puff one-third full with cream, top with berries, squeeze more cream on top, and put the lid on. Sprinkle lightly with confectioners' sugar.

BUTTERSCOTCH CREAM PUFFS
12 CREAM PUFFS

Pâte à choux *for pastries*   *Pastry cream (p. 448), flavored*
   (p. 522)   *with butterscotch*
Egg-yolk glaze (p. 421)   *Confectioners' sugar*
½ *cup sliced almonds*

Make cream puffs. Brush with egg-yolk glaze and sprinkle with sliced almonds. Bake as usual. Cut open to form a lid and squeeze pastry cream into the puffs. Top with lids and sprinkle lightly with confectioners' sugar.

LIME ÉCLAIRS
12 ÉCLAIRS

A favorite at ladies' luncheons.

Pâte à choux *for pastries*   *Uncooked icing (p. 449), made*
   (p. 522)   *with lime juice*
Egg-yolk glaze (p. 421)   *2 drops of green food coloring*
Pastry cream (p. 448), flavored   *1 drop of yellow food coloring*
   with lime rind and rum

Pipe 12 strips (½ inch by 4 inches) of cream-puff paste on a buttered and rinsed cookie sheet. Brush with egg-yolk glaze. Bake in a preheated 400°F. oven for 20 to 25 minutes to obtain 12 éclairs.
Make pastry cream; stuff it in a pastry bag. Fill each cooled éclair

by punching a hole at each end with the nozzle of the pastry bag and squeezing the cream inside each cake. Brush the top of each éclair with uncooked icing colored with mixed green and yellow food coloring.

GRAPEFRUIT RING

The idea is that of the French *Paris-Brest;* I did not have the heart to call the present confection New York-Miami.

Pâte à choux *for pastries* (*p. 522*)	Pastry cream (*p. 448*)
	1½ teaspoons unflavored gelatin
Egg-yolk glaze (p. 421)	*Rum*
2 seedless pink or ruby-red grapefruit	*1 cup heavy cream, whipped*
	Confectioners' sugar

Make the batter. Trace a 6- to 7-inch ring with a pot lid on a buttered and rinsed cookie sheet. With a ½-inch nozzle, pipe 2 circles of batter, one on the outside of the traced ring, the second on the inside. Pipe a third circle of batter exactly over the space separating the two first circles. Brush with egg-yolk glaze. Bake in a preheated 375° F. oven for 35 to 40 minutes.

Infuse the fine-grated rind of 1 grapefruit in the 1 cup of milk used to make the pastry cream. Make the cream with 1½ teaspoons gelatin. Flavor it with rum to taste, and fold into it 1 cup heavy cream, whipped, instead of ½ cup.

Cut a lid from the top of the cooled cake. Pipe half of the pastry cream into the bottom of the cake. Lay the skinless sections of both grapefruits on the cream so that they have no contact with the pastry at all. Pipe the remainder of the cream on top of the fruit. Close the lid and dust with confectioners' sugar.

PROFITEROLES PONTRESINA
6 SERVINGS

From a Swiss ski vacation memory.

Pâte à choux *for pastries*
   (*p. 522*)
1 cup heavy cream
½ cup praline powder (*p. 23*)

6 ounces milk chocolate
¾ cup water
1 teaspoon instant coffee powder

Make the batter and shape and bake 3 dozen cocktail-size puffs. Whip cream; fold in the praline powder. Stuff in a pastry bag and squeeze into puffs. Pile the puffs in a deep crystal dish.

Melt chocolate with water and coffee powder in the top of a double boiler; stir until smooth and warm. Let cool slightly and pour over the puffs. Serve immediately, 6 profiteroles for each serving.

Index

Abalone Bliss, 284

Abbacchio e Finocchi, 206

Abgeschlagener Kugelhupf, 432

Acid
  in pastry doughs, 390
  for stabilizing egg-white foam, 40, 59
  in sugar cooking, 374

Aïoli, 134

Aïoli the American Way, 136

Alan's Folly (salad), 364

Alan's Oxtail (soup), 99

Alan's Poached Eggs, 52

Alaskan King-Crab Soufflé, 471

Alliance Française de Philadelphia, 476

Almond(s)
  cream filling, *see* Praline Chocolate
    Cake, 453
  Custard, Upside-Down, 500
  flavoring, 23
  Milk, 22, 478
  Pastry Cream, 448
  Snow-White Soufflé, 477
  Stirred Custard, 63
  to blanch, 22
  to chop, 22
  to grind, 22
  to toast, 22
  Zabaglione, 67

Alsatian-French seasoning for noodles, 370

Alsatian-German seasoning for noodles, 369

American Filling (for pastry ramekins), 525

Anchovy Hollandaise, 128

Anchovy and Olive Sauce, 118

Angel Cake, 441

Anglaise and Breading, 178

Apple(s)
  Chicken and Apples, 210
  Mayonnaise, Swedish, 138
  My Apple Tart, 405
  peeling, 376
  poaching, 374
  Sautéed, 337

Apricot(s)
  Jolie Madame, 377
  Mousse, 485
  poaching, 374
  Sauce, 384
  Soufflé, 478
  to remove skins, 376

Arrowroot for binding sauces, 105

Artichoke(s)
  Bottoms, boiling or blanching, 317
  Fricassee of Chicken and Artichokes, 205
  à la Grecque, 357
  Hearts, Frozen, boiling or blanching, 317
  and Mushrooms Gratin, 356

Artichoke(s) (*continued*)
  and Peas, Ragout of, 335
  Purée, 326
  Sweetbreads Cara Mia, 239
  Whole Fresh, boiling or blanching,
    318
Asparagus, boiling or blanching, 318
Asparagus Tips, as Variation for Fish or
  Shellfish Mousse, 493
Aspic, Aspic Dishes
  Aspic, 293
  Aspic Sheet, 295
  clarifying and flavoring aspic, 294
  Classic Aspic, 293
  coating a mold with aspic, 294
  Egg-White Sheet, 295
  Egg-Yolk Sheet, 295
  Fillet of Beef in Aspic, 299
  Fish Aspic, 294
  Modern Aspic, 293
  Poached Trout in Aspic, 301
  serving aspics, 295
  to apply aspic to food, 294
  to decorate an aspic, 294
  Truffle Sheet, 295
  See also *Chaud-Froid*
Aurore sauce, 110
Avocado
  -Lime Cream Tart, 409
  Mayonnaise, 138
  Soufflé (dessert), 477
  Topping (for potato pancakes), 343
  Velouté (soup), 98

Babas, 433
Baguette, 423
Baguette Viennoise, 422
Baking
  fish, 265–266; fillets, 265; to test for
    doneness, 266; whole fish, 265
  vegetables, 350
Baking-Powder Spongecake, 440
Baking utensils, necessary supplies, 7
Ballottine of Braised Duck Old English
  Style, 199

Banana Mousse, 485
Bananas, poaching, 374
Bar Harbor Chowder, 93
Barnagaud, M., 92
Basil Butter, 147
Basil-Tomato Butter, 148
Bass, Poached, 258
Bass, Sea Bass, Broiled, 265
Bâtard, 423
Bauer, Joan, 219
Bavarian Cream, 496–497
  Black-Currant or Blueberry, 503
  Cantaloupe, 500
  cream base, 497
  fruit base, 497
  gelatin for stabilizing, 496
  heating fresh fruit purée, 496
  Madeira, 501
  Pear, 501
  preparing, 496
  to make a Charlotte with, 497
  unmolding, 496
Bay leaf, 25
Beans
  Green, boiling or blanching, 319;
    Marie Becker's, 336; Purée of,
    326
  Lima, Purée of, 325
  Navy, Purée of, 325
  Wax, boiling or blanching, 319
Béarnaise Sauce, 132
  Brazier, 133
  Choron Sauce, 133
  Valois Sauce, 133
Béchamel, Louis de, 109
Béchamel Sauce, 109, 110
Beef
  Bitoques, 185
  Boeuf à la Ficelle, 218
  Braised, Horseradish, 196
  Brown Sauce, Classic and Short-Cut,
    114
  Chateaubriand, 175
  Côte de Boeuf Paris-Londres, 168;
  Fillet of, in Aspic, 299
  Fillet of, in *Chaud-Froid*, 300
  heart, *see* Heart

Beef (*continued*)
    kidney, *see* Kidney(s)
    liver, *see* Liver(s)
    Onion Steaks, 179
    Ribs of, Standing, with Gravy, 168
    roasting, 161–162; thermometer
        readings, 162
    spit-roasting, 162
    Steak, Beefsteak *à Cheval*, 50; Break-
        fast Steaks, 190; Steak Diane, The
        Ancestor of, 180; Peppered Steak,
        Modern, 180
    Stew, Guinness, 203
    tongue, *see* Tongue(s)
    tripe, *see* Tripe
    Wellington, 311
Beets, Baked Julienne of, in Mustard
    Sauce, 351
Bercy sauce, 110
Berry Cream Puffs, 527
Beurre blanc, 139
Beurre blanc angevin (Classic French
    White Butter), 140
Beurre manié, 119–120
Beurres composées (flavored or com-
    pound butters), 144–145; *for
    recipes, see* Butters
Bitoques, 185
Black-Currant Bavarian Cream, 503
Black-Currant Pear Tart, 406
Blanc (a white solution), 318
Blanquettes, 202
Blender, 8; for puréeing vegetables for
    soup, 87
Blueberry(ies)
    Bavarian Cream, 503
    Berry Cream Puffs, 527
    Frozen Soufflé, 489
    Napoleons, 409
Blue cheese, *see* Cheese
Bocuse, Paul, 262
Boeuf à la Ficelle, 218
Boiling or Blanching—Moist-Heat Pro-
    cedure, Vegetables, 315–316
Bordelaise Sauce, 118
Bouquet garni, 25
Bouillie (stirred pudding), 447, 463;

for soufflé base, 474
Brains, 224
    Court-Bouillon for, 225
    in Green Butter, 225
    preparation for cooking, 224
    to poach, 225
Braisière (braising pot), 191
Braising—Moist-Heat Procedure, 190–
    192
    defattening and thickening juices of
        a braise, 194
    fish, 260
    meats, 190–196
    pot for, 191
    red meats, 193–194
    reheating and freezing braises, 196
    searing, 193
    stock for, 194
    vegetables, 327–328
    white meats, 195
Brandy, 32–33
    fruit-flavored, 33
    Glaze, 320
Brazier Béarnaise Sauce, 133
Bread
    Baguette, 423
    Baguette Viennoise, 422
    Bâtard, 423
    Batter, 420; Basic Recipe, 421; varia-
        tions, 422
    Brioche Mousseline, 429
    Brioches de Boulanger, 428
    Buns, Sticky, 431
    Cheese, 422
    crashed and rolled, 420
    Croissants de Boulanger, 427
    Croissants de Pâtissier, 427
    Currant, 422
    Danish, 422
    Ficelles, 423
    freezing, baked, 420; unbaked, 419
    French, 422
    German, 422
    Glazes, 421
    Kids' Bread, 424
    kneaded, 420
    Petits Pains au Chocolat, 428

Bread (*continued*)
Raisin, 422
Viennese, 422
Wiener Kipfeln or *Spitzwecken,* 425
Breakfast Folly, 511
Breakfast Steaks, 190
Brill Fillets, Breaded, California Style,
270
Brill, Western, Poached, 259
Brioche(s), see Bread
Broccoli, boiling or blanching, 319
Broccoli, Deep-Fried, 346
Broiling—Dry-Heat Procedure
fish, 263
meats, 173–174
to check doneness of meats, 174
Brown Sauce, 112
Classic, chef's method, 115; home
method, 114
enrichment, 117
Lazy Cook's, 113
Short-Cut, 113
thickening, table of measures, 115
variations, 114
Brown Stews, 202
Brown Stock, 78
Brown Veal Stock, 80
Brunoise, 12
Bruno's Risotto, 367
Brussels Sprouts
boiling or blanching, 320
Loaf, *see* Spinach Loaf, Quick
Pork and Sprouts, 215
Buns, Sticky, 431
Burgundy Gougère, 526
Butter, 17
beurre manié, 119–120
clarified, 17–18; freezing, 13, 18; for
panbroiling and panfrying, 177;
for panfrying breaded meats, 179;
for panfrying chicken cutlets,
178; for panfrying starchy vegetables, 336; in *roux,* 106, 107
creaming, 18
Crust, 303
for omelets, 45
in pastry doughs, 390

in soups, 88
in white sauces, 111
Buttercream, *see* Fillings and Icings
Butter Sauces, 139–140
Caper Butter, 143
emulsified on an acid base, 139
emulsified on a glaze base, 139
Geneva Butter, 141
Green Butter, 143
keeping and freezing, 143
Mushroom Butter, 142
Mustard Butter, 141
Provençal Butter, 142
Virgin Butter, 140
White Butter (*beurre blanc*), 139
White Butter, Classic French (*beurre
blanc angevin*), 140
Butters—Flavored or Compound
(*beurres composées*), 144–145
Basil, 147
Caraway, 149
Colbert, 146
Maître d'Hôtel, 146
Mint, 148
Mustard, 147
Noisette, 145
Polish (polonaise sauce), 149
Ravigote, 145
Saffron, *see* Saffron Pilaf
Snail, 146
Tabasco, 148
Tarragon, 147
Tomato-Basil, 148
Butterscotch
Cream, 498
Cream Puffs, 528
Pastry Cream, 449
Stirred Custard, 63

Cabbage
Our Family Sauerkraut, 333
Red, Braised, 328
White, Braised, 329
Cagaraulo, Lo, 285

Cake(s), 437–445
    Angel, 441; cooling, 443
    baking procedures, 442–443
    butter or shortened, 438–439;
        creaming method, 439; one-bowl
        method, 438
    Canadian Torte, 457
    Chiffon, 441; cooling, 443
    Creole Pecan Torte, 458
    cutting into layers, 443
    eggs in cakes, 437
    fat in cakes, 437
    fillings, *see* Fillings and Icings
    flour in cakes, 437
    foam cakes, 440–442
    Gâteau Breton, 451
    Génoise, Chestnut, 454; Cocoa, 444;
        cooling a baked *génoise,* 445;
        Fine 6-Egg, 444; Plain 4-Egg,
        444; special techniques, 444–445
    gluten development, 437
    icings, *see* Fillings and Icings
    Ladyfingers, 454
    leavening in cakes, 438
    Lime Rum Shrub Cake, 455
    Louisiana Strawberry Patch, 456
    Mistake Cake, 452
    Pain d'Épices, American Style, 450
    Pistachio Raspberry Roll, 458
    Poundcake, 439; cooling, 443; Rai-
        sin, 450
    Praline Chocolate Cake, 453
    serving, 443
    Spongecake, Baking-Powder, 440;
        Old-Fashioned, 440; to fold in dry
        ingredients, 443–444; Whole-
        Egg, 440
    sugar in cakes, 437
    to ice, 443
    Torten (flourless cakes), 442; Egg-
        White, 442; Whole-Egg, 442
Calf's Liver, *see* Liver(s)
California Muscat Chicken, 212
California Rabbit Fricassee, 204
Canadian Torte, 457
Cantaloupe Bavarian Cream, 500
Cantaloupe Tart, 408

Cape Neddick Mussel Boats, 282
Caper Butter, 143
Caper Hollandaise, 128
Cappuccino Soufflé, 480
Caraway Butter, 149
Carrot(s)
    Blini, 516
    boiling or blanching, 320
    Purée of, 327
    Purée of (soup), 96
    Shredded, 335
Casserole roasting, French, 207–208
Catfish Stew, 255
Cauliflower
    boiling or blanching, 319
    Cauliflowerets *à la Grecque,* 358
    Deep-Fried, 346
    Purée of (soup), 94
Caviar, 515–516
    Blini and Caviar, 515
    and Lobster Mayonnaise, 138
    Mousseline, 130
Cayenne pepper, 26
Celeriac, Braised, 329
Celeriac *à la Grecque,* 358
Celery, Braised, 329
Chapon (garlic toast) for salad, 364
Charlotte, 497
Chateaubriand, 175
Château Potatoes, 342
Chaud-Froid, 296
    Fillet of Beef in, 300
    Ham in, 298, 300
    Sauce, Brown, 298
    Sauce, White, 296; variations, 296–
        297
    Tarragon Chicken (with truffles),
        298; with tarragon leaves, *see
        Note,* 299
    to coat with, 298
Cheese
    American Filling, 525
    Blue-Cheese Gratin, 355
    Blue-Cheese Soufflé, 470
    Blue Cheese Turnovers, 405
    Bread, 422
    Burgundy Gougère, 526

Cheese (*continued*)
  Cream-Cheese Mousse, 486
  Cream-Cheese Pastry, 393
  filling for omelets, 47
  garnish for scrambled eggs, 42
  Gruyère Gratin, 355
  Hickory-Smoked Gougère, 526
  Hickory-Smoked Soufflé, 470
  Jack Chicken, 212
  Liederkranz Chicken Cutlets, 187
  Mornay sauce, 110
  Puffs, Dutch, 527
  Roquefort Mousseline, 129
  Roquefort Turnovers, 405
  Swiss Filling, 525
  to mince, 12
Cherry (ies)
  poaching, 374
  Sauce, 385
  Slices, 379
Cherry Brandy Flambéed Crêpes, 518
Chestnut
  Filling, 455
  Génoise, 454
  Purée, 325
  Purée of, Soup, 97
  Tarts, 407
Chicken
  and Apples, 210
  aux Aromates, Broiled, 176
  and Artichokes, Fricassee of, 205
  breasts, to bone, 157
  broiled, to check doneness, 174
  California Muscat, 212
  Cutlets, 157; with *chaud-froid,* 298;
    deep-fried, 190; with Green
    Onions, 184; in Hazelnut Cream,
    183; Hickory, 186; Judy, 223;
    Liederkranz, 187; panfrying, 178;
    poaching in butter, 218; Quat-
    trocento, 222; to cut pockets in,
    157
  freezing, 12–13
  French Filling, 525
  Jack Chicken, 212
  liver, *see* Liver(s)
  Pojarski, 185

  pot-roasting, 208–209
  Poularde Demi-Deuil, 219
  Poularde Piemontaise, 220
  Poultry *Quenelles,* 290
  roasting, 165–167; timetable, 167
  Roast, Tarragon, 170
  stock, *see* White Stock
  Succotash, 211
  Tarragon, *Chaud-Froid* (with truf-
    fles), 298; with tarragon leaves,
    see Note, 299
  to cut for sautéing, 158
  to truss, 166
  whole, to bone, 157
Chiffon Cakes, 441; cooling, 443
Chiffonnade, 12
Child, Paul and Julia, 292
Chiqueter (to make indentations at
  the edges of pastry), 310, 399
Chive *Blini,* 516
Chocolate, 21–22
  Buttercream, 446
  Cocoa *Génoise,* 444
  Icing (uncooked), 449
  Icing, Creamy (uncooked), 455
  Mousseline Buttercream, 447
  Pastry Cream, 448
  Petits Pains au Chocolat, 428
  Praline Cake, 453
  Praline Mousse, 488
  Soufflé, 479
  Stirred Custard, 63
  to add melted chocolate to ribboned
    egg yolks, 22
  to melt, 21
  to mince, 12
  Zabaglione, 67
Chopping boards, 8
Choron Sauce, 133
Chowder, *see* Soup
Cilantro (fresh coriander), 25
Ciseler (to cut slashes), 266
Citrus Fruits, 376–377
  Buttercream, 446
  flavorings, 23
  Mousseline Buttercream, 447
  Pastry Cream, 448

Citrus Fruits (*continued*)
  Stirred Custard, 63
  to blanch rinds, 377
  to peel rinds, 376–377
  to remove white skin, 377
  Zabaglione, 67
Clafouti, 508
Clafouti, Italian Plum, 520
Claiborne, Craig, 285
Clam(s)
  cleaning, 281
  importance of freshness, 281
  Juice *Court-Bouillon* for Shrimps and Scallops, 277
  juice to replace fish *fumet,* 82
  steaming to open, 281
Clarifying butter, 17–18
Clarifying consommé, 89
Cocoa *Génoise,* 444
Cod, Braised, Riviera, 261
Cod, Poached, 259
Coffee
  Buttercream, 446
  Cappuccino Soufflé, 480
  flavoring, 23
  Mousse, 486
  Mousseline Buttercream, 447
  Pastry Cream, 448
  Stirred Custard, 63
  Zabaglione, 67
Colbert Butter, 146
Collagen in meats, 76, 153, 159
Confectioners' Sugar Buttercream, 446
Confit d'oie (preserved goose), 29
Confit de Pigeons (squabs), 201
Consommé, *see* Soup
Cool rise (in yeast doughs), 418–419
Cornmeal Crêpes, Batter, 506
Cornstarch, to bind sauces, 104, 105, 383; to stabilize whipped cream, 20
Côte de Boeuf Paris-Londres, 168
Cotton Cakes, 509
Coulis (broth plus purée of meat or vegetable), 84
Court-Bouillon
  for Brains, 225

Clam Juice, for Shrimps and Scallops, 277
  for fish poaching, 256
  Milk, 257
  re-using, 258
  Vinegar, 258
  Wine, 257
Crab, Crabmeat
  Abalone Bliss, 284
  Alaskan King-Crab Soufflé, 471
  Gratin of, *see* Gratin, Shrimps or Scallops
  Ouzo, *see* Lobster Ouzo
  Shah's Pannequets, The, 511
Cream, 19
  Filling, 452
  sauce for vegetables, table of measures, 317
  in soups, 88
  Whipped, 19–20; for mousses and frozen soufflés, 484; to flavor, 20; to stabilize, 20
  in white sauces, 111
Cream cheese, *see* Cheese
Cream Port Sabayon, 68
Cream Puffs, 524
  baking, 523
  Berry, 527
  Butterscotch, 528
  Paste (*Pâte à Choux*), 521
  Pastry Ramekins, 524
  Profiteroles Pontresina, 530
Crème anglaise (English or stirred custard), 62–64
Crème anglaise collée (stabilized stirred custard), 64
Crème Chantilly, 19, 20
Creole Cream, 497
Creole Pecan Torte, 458
Crêpes, *see* Pancakes and Crêpes
Croissants de Boulanger, 427
Croissants de Pâtissier, 427
Croustade, American-Style, 43–44
Croustade, French Method, 43
Cucumbers, boiling or blanching, 321
Currant, Black-Currant Bavarian Cream 503

Currant, Black-Currant Pear Tart, 406
Currant Bread, 422
Curried Salad, 362
Curry Mousseline, 130
Custard Sauces, 144
Custards—Baked, 493–495
  baking, 495
  egg-yolk base, 493
  preparing, 495
  separation, 495
  syneresis, 495
  to coat a mold with caramel, 495
  to test doneness, 495
  whole-egg base, 494
Custards—Dessert
  Almond Upside-Down Custard, 500
  Black-Currant or Blueberry Bavarian
    Cream, 503
  Butterscotch Cream, 498
  Cream Port Sabayon, 68
  Creole Cream, 497
  Eggs Praline, 65
  Eggs Tia Maria, 64
  English or Stirred Custard (*Crème
    anglaise*), 62; flavoring varia-
    tions, 63; to stabilize, 64
  Frau Pelizaeus Weinsauce, 67
  Italian Rice Pudding, 502
  Lime Upside-Down Custard, 499
  Madeira Bavarian Cream, 501
  Molded Scarlet Custard, 65
  Muscatel Sabayon, 68
  Pistachio Upside-Down Custard, 500
  Viennese Custard, 498
  Zabaglione, Classic, 66; to stabilize
    for chilling, 66; variations, 67
Custards—Savory
  Fish Loaf, 504
  Spinach Loaf, Quick, 503

Danish Bread, 422
Danish Pastry, 426
Daube (meat stew), 202, 241
Deep Frying—Dry-Heat Procedure,
  187–189

fish, 270
oil for, 19
Savory Fritter Batter, 189
vegetables, 345
Deglazing, 139, 161
Demi-Glace Sauce, 115, 117
Dessert flavorings, 23
Dessert sauces, see Sauces—Dessert
Détrempe (flour and water paste), 396
Diablotins (mustard croutons), 54
Dill Mayonnaise, 136
Dover sole, 246
Dubonnet Pears, 378
Duck(s)
  Ballottine of, Braised, Old English
    Style, 199
  Brown Sauce, Classic, 115; Short-
    Cut, 114
  Pâté, *see Note,* 306
  Roast, Citrus, 172
  roasting, 167
  Terrine of, 305
  to truss, 166
  whole, to bone, 157
Dumaine, Alexandre, 274
Dutch Cheese Puffs, 527
Duxelles, 340

Éclairs, Lime, 528
Egg(s)
  in cakes, 437
  chemical and physical properties,
    39–40
  in cocottes, 41
  Coddled (soft-cooked), 40
  cooking on gas or electric heat, 13,
    46
  foaming capacity of egg protein, 39–
    40
  foams, 57–62
  folding, 61
  Fried, 41
  Fried, Saint Vincent, 53
  grading, 37
  Hard-Cooked, 43; to peel, 43

Egg(s) (*continued*)

for hollandaise and other emulsified sauces, 123

how to measure, 38–39

ligaments or chalazas, 57

Oeufs Mollets, 43; to peel, 43

Omelet(s), *Omelette(s),* 44–48; Basic, 48; beaten, 46; butter for, 45; *Cagouillarde,* 55; *Chamonix,* 54; Creamed Salmon, 56; Devil's, 54; fillings, 47; *Lyonnaise,* 55; Millionaire's, 56; pan, 44; Potato, 53; preparations, 45–46; scrambled, 47; shaken, 47; to condition an omelet pan, 44–45; to invert, 47

in pastry doughs, 390

Poached, 42–43; Alan's, 52; Beefsteak *à Cheval,* 50; Budapest, 51

Praline, 65

in ramekins, 41

ribbon, 57–58

room temperature for best use, 38, 57, 58

Scrambled, 41–42; Avocado, 49; Brown Butter, 48; Buttered Almond and Pistachio, 49; *Duxelles,* 48; Super, 50

separating, 57

Shirred, 40–41

storing, 38

Succotash Ramekins, 52

temperatures for coagulation of egg protein, 39

Tia Maria, 64

vitamin content, 37

white(s), 37; acid for stabilizing, 40, 59; beating, 58–59; copper bowl and wire whisk, 9, 59; Glaze, 421; electric mixer for beating, 59, 60; Icing, Uncooked, 449; Sheet, 295; sugar added to beaten whites, 59, 61; to incorporate dry ingredients, 61–62

whole, base for custard, 494

yolk(s), 37; base for custards, 493; base for soufflés, 474; Glaze, 399, 421, 523; Hard-Cooked, Mayonnaise, 137; mixed with starch, 88, 111; Sheet, 295

Eggplant

Deep-Fried, 346

Fried Eggs Saint Vincent, 53

Moussaka Soufflé, 471

Sautéed, 338

Einbender, Gloria, 95

Elastin in meats, 76

Emulsions, 121–122

Endive, Belgian, Braised, 328

Endive Pie, Deep-Dish, 401

English Poached Leg of Lamb, 219

English or Stirred Custard (*crème anglaise*), 62–64

Escarole, Braised, 330

Escarole, Mario's (salad), 363

d'Escars, Duc, 109

Escoffier, Auguste, 27, 74, 112, 208, 382

Espagnole Sauce, 115, 116

Fat

butter, 17, 390

in cakes, 437

effect on fermentation of yeast doughs, 418

lard, 390

margarine, 390

for panbroiling, 176–177

for panfrying, 176–177; fish, 268

for pastry doughs, 389–390

vegetable shortening, 390

See also Butter

Fegato, 235

Fennel

Abbacchio e Finocchi, 206

Braised, 330

à la Grecque, 359

Ficelles, 423

Filberts, *see* Hazelnuts

Fillings and Icings (for cakes and pastries), 445

Almond Cream filling, *see* Praline

Fillings and Icings (*continued*)
  Chocolate Cake
  Buttercream, Chocolate, 446; Citrus Fruit, 446; Coffee, 446; Confectioners' Sugar, 446; Liqueur, 446; praline, *see* Creole Pecan Torte; Vanilla, 446
  Buttercream, Mousseline (Sugar-Syrup Cream), 446; Chocolate, 447; Citrus Fruit, 447; Coffee, 447; Ground Nuts, 447; Liqueur, 447; Praline, 447; Vanilla, 447
  Chestnut Filling, 455
  Chocolate Icing (uncooked), 449
  Chocolate Icing, Creamy (uncooked), 455
  Cream Filling, 452
  Fondant, 449; flavorings, 450
  Pastry Cream, 447; Almond, 448; Butterscotch, 449; Chocolate, 448; Citrus Fruit, 448; Coffee, 448; Liqueur, 449
  Uncooked Icing, 449; Chocolate, 449; Chocolate, Creamy, 455; Egg-White, 449
Fillings for savory dishes
  American (for pastry ramekins), 525
  Duxelles, 340
  French (for pastry ramekins), 525
  Russian (for pastry ramekins), 525
  Sweetbread, for *Vol-au-Vent* or Patties, 404
  Swiss (for pastry ramekins), 525
Fine, Marjorie, 426
Fish
  Aspic, 294
  baking, 265–266; fillets, 265; to test for doneness, 266; whole fish, 265
  braising, 260
  broiling, 263; preparing, 263; steaks, 263; whole fish, 263
  buying, 245
  deep frying, 270
  Fillets of, Martini, 251
  fresh, 245

  frozen, to defrost, 245
  Fumet, 81, 83, 247
  Glaze, 83
  Green Fish Pot (soup), 92
  Loaf, 504
  Mousse, 493
  panfrying, 268; *à la meunière,* 268
  poaching, 248–249; cooking temperatures, 249; fillets and small steaks, 248; sauce, 249; small pieces, in small amount of liquid, 248–249; whole fish or large pieces in *court-bouillon,* 256–257
  Quenelles, Poaching, 291
  Red-Wine Fish *Fumet,* 83
  sauces for, 247
  serving, 247–248
  some varieties in United States, 246
  Soufflé, 469
  soups, 85
  Steaks, Lemon-Lime, 252
  Steaks *au Persil,* 250
  to bone a long fish, 247
  to fillet a flat fish, 246
  Velouté (sauce), 504
  White-Wine Fish *Fumet,* 83
Fisher, Linda, 519
Flambéed Dishes
  Cherry Brandy Crêpes, 518
  Crêpes South Pacific, 518
  dessert crêpes, 509
  Lamb Chops Marinated, 181
  meats, 158
  Peaches Auguste Escoffier, 382
  Peppered Steak, Modern, 180
  poultry livers, 235
  Steak Diane, 180
  Typsy Dixie (crêpes), 519
Flour, 20
  in cakes, 437
  gluten formation, 105, 389, 396, 397, 398, 416, 417, 418; in cakes, 437; in crêpe batter, 506
  for sauce thickening, 104, 105
  to measure, 20
  to soften all-purpose flour for pastry, 20

Foam cakes, 440–442
Foie gras, 29
Fondant, 449
Fonds de braise, 191, 193
    for fish, 260
    for white meats, 195
Forcer (to homogenize egg foam), 59
Forelle Blaue (blue trout), 259
Four Spices (*quatre épices*), 27
Fraiser (to flatten pastry dough), 392
Frank, Dr. Konstantin, 30, 379
Frau Pelizaeus Weinsauce, 67
Freezer, 12–13
Freezing utensils, 9
Frei, Mrs. Walter, 183
French Bread, 422, 423
French Filling (for pastry ramekins), 525
French Fries, 347
French White Butter, Classic (*beurre blanc angevin*), 140
Fricassee, 202; for recipes, *see* Stews
Fritter(s)
    Batter, Savory, 189
    Chicken-Liver, 190
    Frogs'-Leg, 271
    Pâte à Choux for, 251
    Shrimp, 280
Frogs'-Leg Fritters, 271
Fruits, 373
    Clafouti, 508
    Dried, Souffléed Pudding, 481
    fresh, purée for Bavarian cream, 496
    peeling, 376
    poaching, 373–374; to test doneness, 376
    purée and sugar-syrup base for soufflés, 474
    Salad, West Coast, 381
    sauces, 383
    storing unripe fruits, 373
    syrup for poaching, 374
    to prevent browning, 376
    wine for poaching, 374
    See also Citrus Fruits, *and names of individual fruits*
Frying utensils, 8

Fumet, 81, 83, 247

❀

Game Birds Brown Sauce, Short-Cut, 114; Classic, 115
Garlic
    aïoli, 134
    Aïoli the American Way, 136
    Hollandaise, 128
    and Parsley Sauce, 119
Garnish
    artichoke bottoms filled with purée of peas, *see* Peas, Purée of
    aspic sheets, 295
    brunoise, 12
    citrus-fruit rinds, 376–377
    Croustade, 43–44
    custard (*royale*) for consommé, 494
    mirepoix, 12
    Onions, Glazed Whole, 344
    Potato Nests, 348
    Tomatoes, Fried, 344
Gâteau Breton, 451
Gelatin, 21
    to stabilize Bavarian cream, 496
    to stabilize mousses, 482
    to stabilize whipped cream, 20
Geneva Butter, 141
Génoise, 443–445; for details, *see* Cake(s)
George, Jimmy, 255
German-Alsatian-Austrian Noodle Dough, 368
German Bread, 422
Glace de viande (meat glaze), 79
Glazes for breads and pastries, 399, 421, 523
Gloria's Salad, 361
Gluten development, 105, 389, 396, 397, 398, 416, 417, 418
    in cakes, 437
    in crêpe batter, 506
    in puréed potatoes, 323
Gnocchi, 523
    cooking, 524
    Pâte à Choux for, 521

Gnocchi (*continued*)
   serving variations, 527
Goody's Favorite (salad), 363
Goose
   fat, 167
   foie gras, 29
   roasting, 167
   Tante Else's Gans, 171
   to truss, 166
Gordon, Mel, 171
Goujonnette of Sole, 271
Grapefruit
   Martinique, 380
   Ring, 529
   Zabaglione, 67
Grapes, West Coast Fruit Salad, 381
Grater and shredder, 8
Gratin
   Gruyère, 355
   Leeks, 355
   Mushrooms and Artichokes, 356
   Potatoes, 354; variations, 355
   Shrimps or Scallops, 280
   Sweet-Potato, 356
   Winter-Squash, 356
Green Butter, 143
Greens, Chopped, Braised, 332
Gribiche Sauce, 137
Gruyère Gratin, 355
Guinness Beef Stew, 203
Gusman, Carolyn, 307

Haddock
   Baked, Emergency, 267
   Braised, Riviera, 261
   Fish Steaks *au Persil,* 250
   Poached, 259
Halibut, Fish Steaks *au Persil,* 250
Ham
   in *Chaud-Froid,* 298, 300
   Morvandelles (crêpes), 514
   Mousse, 492
   and Mushroom Roulade, 472
Hazelnuts or Filberts, to skin, 22
Heart, 226–227

preparation for cooking, 226
Scaloppine, Sautéed, 227
Herbs, 24–25
   dried, for emulsified sauces, 123;
     for salad dressings, 361
   dried, to revive, 24
   Sauce, 469
Herr Kraemer's Palatschinken, 512
Hickory Chicken Cutlets, 186
Hickory-Smoked Cheese Soufflé, 470
Hickory-Smoked Gougère, 526
Hollandaise Sauce, 121–129
   Anchovy, 128
   Blender, 123, 126
   Caper, 128
   Cold Butter, 123, 126
   curdling, 125
   Double-Boiler, 124
   Garlic, 128
   Horseradish, 127
   ingredients, 123
   Mousseline Sauce, 129
   Mustard, 129
   Professional, 124, 127
   separation, 124
   saucepan, 123
   stabilizing, 125
Hors-d'Oeuvre
   Alaskan King-Crab Soufflé, 471
   Blini and Caviar, 515
   Blue Cheese or Roquefort Turnovers,
     405
   Broccoli, Deep-Fried, 346
   Burgundy Gougère, 526
   Cape Neddick Mussel Boats, 282
   Carrot *Blini,* 516
   Cauliflower, Deep-Fried, 346
   Chicken-Liver Crêpes, 513
   Chive *Blini,* 516
   Dutch Cheese Puffs, 527
   Hickory-Smoked Gougère, 526
   Moules (*Les*) *de la Mère Pin,* 282
   Mushroom Caps, Deep-Fried, 346
   Oysters Without a Name, 282
   patty shells, cocktail size, 404
   Poor Man's *Mousse de Foie Gras,*
     491

Hors-d'Oeuvre (*continued*)
  Potato Pies, 401
  Shah's Pannequets, The, 511
  Shrimp Tomato Timbales, 505
  Vegetables *à la Grecque*, 357
Horseradish Braised Beef, 196
Horseradish Hollandaise, 127

Icings, *see* Fillings and Icings
Indian Purée (soup), 95
Infusion, 122
Inversion in sugar cooking, 374
Irish Sauce, 130
Italian-Genovese seasoning for noodles, 369
Italian Noodle Dough, 368
Italian-Piemontese seasoning for noodles, 369
Italian Plum *Clafouti*, 520
Italian Rice Pudding, 502

Jack Chicken, 212
Jardinière of Vegetables, 322
Jus, 80
Jus de veau (Brown Veal Stock), 80

Kamman's Onion Soup, 90
Kamman's Veal Stew, 204
Kasser, Selma, 406
Key Lime Sauce, 131
Kidney(s), 227–231
  beef, 228
  Beef-Kidney and Mushroom Pie, 232
  beef, to sauté or braise, 230
  freezing and defrosting, 228
  lamb, 227, 228
  Lamb, Skewered, 231
  pork, 228, 230–231
  veal, 227–228, 229
  Veal, in Mustard Sauce, 232
  Veal, Tio Pepe, 231

veal, to broil, 229; to pot-roast, 229; to sauté, 229–230
Kids' Bread, The, 424
Kir, 526
Kitchen towels, 12
Knives, 11
  how to use, 11–12
  to clean carbon-steel blades, 11
Krebsbutterhühner, 209
Kugelhupf, Abgeschlagener, 432
Kulebiak of Trout, 308

Ladyfingers, 454
Lamb
  Abbacchio e Finocchi, 206
  Chops, Marinated, 181
  heart, *see* Heart
  kidney, *see* Kidney(s)
  Leg of, Poached, English, 219
  leg, to bone, 156
  liver, *see* Liver(s)
  Moussaka Soufflé, 471
  Nuggets, Broiled, and Basil Butter, 175
  Rack of, Persillade, 169
  roasting, 163–164; thermometer readings, 164
  Shoulder, Mountain Style, 197
  Shoulder of, Poêled, with Herbs, 215
  sweetbreads, *see* Sweetbread(s)
  tongue, *see* Tongue(s)
Lapin de Mémère (pot-roasted rabbit), 214
Lard
  Crust, 303
  in pastry doughs, 390
  Pastry, English, Mrs. Reeves', 392
Larding, 191–192
Lardoir (larding needle), 191
La Varenne, François de, 340
Lazy Cook's Brown Sauce, 113
Leavening in cakes, 438
Leeks, 26
  Braised, 331
  Cream of (soup), 99

Leeks (*continued*)
Gratin, 355
Topping (for potato pancakes), 343
Lemon
juice in pastry doughs, 390
-Lime Fish Steaks, 252
-Lime Mousse, 487
Zabaglione, 67
Lettuce, Braised, 331
Lettuce Purée, 326
Liaison of sauces, 110, 111
Liaison for soup thickening, 88
Liederkranz Chicken Cutlets, 187
Lime
Avocado-Lime Cream Tart, 409
Éclairs, 528
Key Lime Sauce, 131
Mousse, *see* Lemon-Lime Mousse
Rum Shrub Cake, 455
Upside-Down Custard, 499
Zabaglione, 67
Liqueur(s), 33–34
Buttercream, 446
Mousseline Buttercream 447
Pastry Cream, 449
Stirred Custard, 63
Liver(s), 233–235
beef, 234
calf's, broiled, 234; *Fegato*, 235; preparing for cooking, 233; Terrine of, *see Note*, 307; *Walliseller Spiessli*, 236
chicken (or other poultry), 235; Crêpes, 513; Fritters, 190; Sautéed, 237; skewered, *see Note*, 236; *Walliseller Spiessli*, 236; Terrine of, 306
foie gras, 29
lamb, 234
pork, 234; braised, 234; Terrine of, *see Note*, 307
poultry, Poor Man's *Mousse de Foie Gras*, 491
Loaf, Loaves, 494
baking, 495
Fish, 504
meats, 494

preparing, 495
Spinach, Quick, 503
vegetables, 494
Lobster, 272–273
Baked, 272
Boiled, 272
and Caviar Mayonnaise, 138
Civet, 273
Ouzo, 275
sizes, 272
Soufflé, *see* Alaskan King-Crab Soufflé
tails, 273
Thermidor, 274
to cut for stew, 273
Louis XIV, 109
Louisiana Strawberry Patch, 456
Lyonnaise Potatoes, 341

Macaroon Soufflé, 475
Mackerel, Baked, *à la Croque au Sel*, 266
Madeira Bavarian Cream, 501
Madeira Sauce, Classic, 118
Maître d'Hôtel Butter, 146
Maltaise Sauce, 130
Mandoline, 8
Maple Mousse, 488
Maple Walnut Crêpes, 517
Marble slab, 8, 391, 449
Margarine, 18–19
for omelets, 45
in pastry doughs, 390
Marie Becker's Green Beans, 336
Marinade, Red-Wine, 193
Marinade, White-Wine, 192
Marinating meats, 192
Mario's Escarole (salad), 363
Mayonnaise, 133–138
Apple, Swedish, 138
Avocado, 138
Blender, 135
Caviar and Lobster, 138
Dill, 136
Gribiche Sauce, 137

Mayonnaise (*continued*)
  Handmade, 135
  Hard-Cooked Egg-Yolk, 137
  Mousquetaire Sauce, 137
  oil for, 134
  separation, 134
  stabilizing, 134
  Watercress, 136
Measuring cups, 10
Meat(s)
  aging, 154–155
  autolysis in aging meat, 154
  braising, 190–196; defattening and thickening the juices of a braise, 194; *fonds de braise,* 191, 193, 195; red meats, 193–194; reheating and freezing, 196; searing, 193; stock for, 194, 195; white meats, 195
  broiling, 173–174; preparing for broiling, 173; to check doneness, 174
  buying, 153
  in a Crust—*Pâté Pantin,* 308
  curing, 155
  cutting and boning, 156
  deep frying, 187–189
  flambéing, 158
  freezing, 13
  Glaze (*glace de viande*), 79
  grading, 153
  larding, 191–192
  loaves, 494
  marinating, 155, 192
  panbroiling and panfrying, 176–178; *Anglaise* and Breading (for panfrying), 178; breaded meats, 178; preparing meat, 177; red meats, 177; white meats, 177
  poaching, 216; sauces with, 217
  pot-roasting, 207–209
  roasting, 158–161; resting a roast, 161; tying a roast, 159
  stewing, 202–203
  storing, freezing and defrosting, 156
  variety, 224–242; *for details see* Brains; Heart; Kidney(s);

Liver(s); Sweetbread(s); Tongue(s); Tripe
  See also Beef; Lamb; Pork; Veal
Melanie's Stuffed Zucchini, 352
Mikado Sauce, 130
Milk *Court-Bouillon,* 257
Milk, soured, in pastry doughs, 390
Mincemeat Pasties, *see* Puff-Paste Pasties
Mint Butter, 148
Mirepoix, 12
Mistake Cake, 452
Monosodium glutamate (MSG), 24
Montagné, Prosper, 44, 120, 249, 357
Montmireil, 175
Mornay sauce, 110
Morvandelles, 514
Moses, Claire and Warren, 255
Moules (Les) de la Mère Pin, 282
Mousquetaire Sauce, 137
Moussaka Soufflé, 471
Mousse, 484
  Fish, 493
  Ham, 492
  Poor Man's *Mousse de Foie Gras,* 491; to mold, 492
  Poultry, 492
  Shellfish, 493
  as stuffing for buffet dishes, 484
Mousse—Dessert, 482
  Apricot, 485
  Banana, 485
  base, 482; fruit-flavored purée, 482; liqueur-flavored, 482; nut-flavored, 482
  Coffee, 486
  Cream-Cheese, 486
  gelatin as a stabilizer, 482
  Lemon-Lime, 487
  Maple, 488
  Orange, *see* Lemon-Lime Mousse
  poaching egg-yolk bases and whole-egg bases, 484
  Praline Chocolate, 488
  Strawberry, 489
  Tangerine, *see* Lemon-Lime Mousse
  whipping cream for, 484

Mousseline Buttercream (Sugar-Syrup Cream), 446
Mousseline Sauce, 129
  Caviar, 130
  Curry, 130
  Irish Sauce, 130
  Roquefort, 129
Mrs. Reeves' English Lard Pastry, 392
Muscatel Sabayon, 68
Mushroom(s)
  and Artichokes Gratin, 356
  Butter, 142
  Caps, Deep-Fried, 346
  Creamed, 339
  Duxelles, 340
  à la Grecque, 359
  and Ham Roulade, 472
  Mustard, 339
  panfrying, 337
  -Potato Gratin, 355
  Sautéed, 338
  Tart, 403
  Velouté (soup), 97
Mussel(s)
  Boats, Cape Neddick, 282
  cleaning, 281
  importance of freshness, 281
  Moules (Les) de la Mère Pin, 282
  steaming to open, 281
Mustard
  Butter (cold), 147
  Butter (warm), 141
  Gratin, 355
  Hollandaise, 129
  Mushrooms, 339
Mutton, 163

Nectarines, to remove skins, 376
Noisette Butter, 145
Noisette Potatoes, 342
Noodles
  German-Alsatian-Austrian Dough, 368
  Italian Dough, 368

Seasonings for, 369–370
  to make, 369
Nova Scotia Quiche, 402
Nuts, 22
  Ground Nuts Mousseline Buttercream, 447
  Puff-Paste Pasties, 410
  to mince, 12

Obermayer, Judy, 223
Oeufs Mollets (eggs cooked in the shell), 43
Oeufs à la neige (meringue eggs), 64
Oil, 19
  for deep frying, 188; temperature, 189
  for mayonnaise, 134
  for panfrying moist vegetables, 337
  for salad dressings, 360
Old-Fashioned Spongecake, 440
Old Giovanni's Rabbit Cutlets, 186
Olive and Anchovy Sauce, 118
Omelets, Omelettes, see Egg(s)
Onion(s)
  Five Onions Soup, 92
  Gratin, 355
  Minced, Sautéed, 344
  Sauce, 468
  Soup, Kamman's, 90
  Soupe à l'Oignon comme aux Halles, 73
  Steaks, 179
  to dice, 11
  White, Braised, 332
  Whole, Glazed, 344
Orange
  Maltaise Sauce, 130
  Mousse, see Lemon-Lime Mousse
  Sauce, 385
  Zabaglione, 67
Orange-flower water, 23
Our Family Sauerkraut, 333
Oxtail (soup), Alan's, 99
Oysters, 281
  importance of freshness, 281

Oysters (*continued*)
  Without a Name, 283

Pain d'Épices, American Style, 450
Panbroiling—Dry-Heat Procedure
  meats, 176–178
Pancakes and Crêpes, 505
  Batter for Basic Savory Crêpes, 506
  Batter for Cornmeal Crêpes, 506
  Blini Batter, Basic, 510
  Blini and Caviar, 515
  Breakfast Folly, 511
  buttering the pan for crêpes, 507–508
  Carrot *Blini*, 516
  Chicken-Liver Crêpes, 513
  Chive *Blini*, 516
  cooking *blini*, 510
  cooking crêpes, 508
  cooking pancakes, 510
  Cotton Cakes, 509
  Crêpes Americana, 514
  Flambéed Crêpes, 509
  Herr Kraemer's Palatschinken, 512
  Morvandelles, 514
  pan for crêpes, 507
  Shah's Pannequets, The, 511
  Shredded Potato Pancakes, 343
  Souffléed Crêpes, 514
  storing and freezing crêpes, pancakes
    and *blini*, 511
  turning over a crêpe, 508
Pancakes and Crêpes—Dessert
  Batter for Dessert Crêpes, 507
  Cherry Brandy Flambéed Crêpes, 518
  Crêpes Flambéed South Pacific, 518
  Maple Walnut Crêpes, 517
  Raspberry Souffléed Crêpes, 519
  Typsy Dixie, 519
Panfrying—Dry-Heat Procedure
  fish, 268; *à la meunière*, 268
  margarine not recommended, 19
  meats, 176–178
  vegetables, 336–337
Paprika *Chaud-Froid* Sauce, 296

Parisienne Potatoes, 342
Parsley, 24–25
Parsley and Garlic Sauce, 119
Pastry—Basic
  acid in pastry doughs, 390
  Basic Pastry Crust or Short Paste,
    391
  Butter Crust (for pâtés), 303
  chiqueter (to make indentations at
    the edges of pastry), 310, 399
  Cream-Cheese Pastry, 393
  eggs in pastry doughs, 390
  equipment for pastry making, 390–391
  fat for pastry doughs, 389–390
  flour for pastry doughs, 389
  fraiser (to flatten pastry dough),
    392
  glazes, 399, 421
  Lard Crust (for pâtés), 303
  Mrs. Reeves' English Lard Pastry,
    392
  pastry bag, 10
  pastry brushes, 10
  pastry cutters, 10
  Pastry for Pâtés, 302
  patty shells, dinner size, cocktail size,
    404
  pie plates, 393
  pies and tarts, blind-baked and one-
    operation, 394
  Puff Paste, 395–400
  rayer (to decorate tops of pastries
    with lines), 399
  rolling out pastry doughs, 392, 394
  sabler (reduce to sand), 391
  Sandy Pastry, 393
  Sour-Cream Pastry, 393
  storing and freezing pastry doughs,
    392
  Sweet Pastry, 393
  Tartlet Shells, 395
  trimming dough, 394
  vol-au-vent, 403
  water and other liquid ingredients
    for pastry doughs, 390
Pastry Cream, *see* Fillings and Icings

Pastry—Dessert
  Berry Cream Puffs, 527
  Blueberry Napoleons, 409
  Butterscotch Cream Puffs, 528
  Grapefruit Ring, 529
  Profiteroles Pontresina, 530
  Puff-Paste Pasties, 410
  See also Pies and Tarts—Dessert;
    Yeast Pastries
Pastry—Entrée and Hors-d'Oeuvre
  Beef Wellington, 311
  Blue Cheese or Roquefort Turnovers,
    405
  Burgundy Gougère, 526
  Cape Neddick Mussel Boats, 282
  Dutch Cheese Puffs, 527
  Hickory-Smoked Gougère, 526
  Pastry Ramekins (with fillings),
    524–525
  Salmon Pâté Lutèce, 309
  See also Pies and Tarts
Pâte à Choux, 521
  for gnocchi and fritters, 521
  for pastries and shells, 522
Pâtés and Terrines, 302
  building a pâté, 304
  building a terrine, 305
  Duck Pâté, see Note, 306
  Pastry for Pâtés, 302
  Pâté in Crust (basic mixture), 303
  pâté mold, 7, 302
  pâté pantin—meats in a crust, 308
  Salmon Pâté, Cold, 307
  Salmon Pâté Lutèce, 309
  spiced salt for pâté mixtures, 304
  Terrine of Chicken Livers, 306
  Terrine of Duck, 305
Paton (dough and butter package),
    396–397
Peaches
  Flambéed, Auguste Escoffier, 382
  Kotja, 379
  poaching, 374
  to remove skins, 376
Pear(s)
  Bavarian Cream, 501
  Dubonnet, 378

  peeling, 376
  poaching, 374
  Poires Belle Dijonnaise, 378
  Tart, Black-Currant, 406
  West Coast Fruit Salad, 381
Peas
  and Artichokes, Ragout of, 335
  boiling or blanching, 321
  Purée of, 324
Pecan-Praline Frozen Soufflé, 490
Pecan Torte, Creole, 458
Pepper (Nigrum), 26
  effects on meat in broiling, 174
  Pepper Steak, Modern, 180
Petits Pains au Chocolat, 428
Pies and Tarts
  Beef-Kidney and Mushroom Pie, 232
  blind-baked, 394
  Endive Pie, Deep-Dish, 401
  Mushroom Tart, 403
  Nova Scotia Quiche, 402
  one-operation, 394
  pie plates, 393
  Potato Pies, 401
  Sweetbread Tourte, 400
  tartlet shells, 395
Pies and Tarts—Dessert
  Avocado-Lime Cream Tart, 409
  Black-Currant Pear Tart, 406
  Cantaloupe Tart, 408
  Chestnut Tarts, 407
  My Apple Tart, 405
  Raspberry Tart, 408
  Strawberry Tart, see Raspberry Tart
  Zwetschkeweihe (prune tart), 406
Pike Fillets, Baked, for Good Friday,
    267
Pike Quenelles, 289
Pinching (browning meats for stock),
    81
Pistachio(s)
  Chicken Cutlets Quattrocento, 222
  Raspberry Roll, 458
  to skin, 22
  Upside-Down Custard, 500
Poaching—Moist-Heat Procedure
  fish, 248–249; cooking temperatures,

Poaching—Moist-Heat Procedure (*continued*)
249; fillets and small steaks, 248; small pieces in small amount of liquid, 248–249; whole fish or large pieces in a *court-bouillon*, 256–257
fruits, 373–374
meats, 216
Poêlage, French, 208
Point, Fernand, 262, 280
Poires Belle Dijonnaise, 378
Pojarski, 185
Polish Butter (polonaise sauce), 149
Pompano Fillets with Florida Butter, 269
Poor Man's *Mousse de Foie Gras*, 491; to mold, 492
Pork
    fatback, unsalted, for larding, 192; for pâtés, 303
    kidney, *see* Kidney(s)
    liver, *see* Liver(s)
    Loin of, Braised in Milk, 199
    Loin or Shoulder in Crumb Coat, Roast, 170
    Our Family Sauerkraut, 333
    rind for *fonds de braise*, 193, 195
    roasting, 164–165
    and Sprouts, 215
Potato(es)
    Anna-Corning, 354
    Baked, Gratiné, 352
    boiling or blanching, in jackets, 321; peeled and cut, 322
    cooked, panfried, 340; Home Fries, 341; Lyonnaise, 341; Swiss *Rösti*, 341
    Dauphine, 349
    French Fries, 347; to keep warm until serving, 348
    Gratin of, 354; variations, 355
    how to purée, 323
    Mashed, 323
    Nests, 348
    Omelet, 53
    Pies, 401

Purée, 323
Salad, 321
scalloped, baked, 350
Shredded, Baked, 353
Shredded, Pancakes, 343
Souffléed, 349
Straw, 348
uncooked, panfried, 342; Château, 342; *Noisette*, 342; Parisienne, 342
Potato starch, for sauce binding, 104, 105
Pot-Roasting—Dry- and Moist-Heat Procedure
    chicken, 208–209
    French casserole roasting, 207–208
    French *poêlage*, 208
    meats, 207–209
    vegetables, 334
Pots and pans, 5
    aluminum, 5
    bean pot for *daube*, 202, 242
    cast iron, 5
    copper, 5; to clean, 5–6
    copper bowl and wire whip for egg whites, 9, 59
    necessary supplies, 6–7
    omelet pan, 44; to condition, 44–45
    pan for emulsified sauces, 123; for panfrying fish, 268
    pot for braising, 191; for pot-roasting, 207, 208
    sauteuse, 207, 209, 218
    stainless-steel, 5
Poularde Demi-Deuil, 219
Poularde Piemontaise, 220
Poultry
    buying, 154
    grading, 154
    livers, *see* Liver(s)
    Mousse, 492
    Quenelles, 290; Poaching, 291
    roasting, timetable, 167
    Soufflé, 468
    storing, freezing and defrosting, 156
    to bone, 157

Poultry (*continued*)
   See also Chicken; Duck(s); Goose;
      Rock Cornish Game Hens;
      Squab(s); Turkey
Poundcake, *see* Cake(s)
Praline
   buttercream, *see* Creole Pecan Torte
   Chocolate Cake, 453
   Chocolate Mousse, 488
   Mousseline Buttercream, 447
   Pecan-Praline Frozen Soufflé, 490
   Powder, 23
   Stirred Custard, 63
Preparation tray, 13
Profiteroles Pontresina, 530
Provençal Butter, 142
Pruneaux Pinot, 381
Prunes
   Italian Plum *Clafouti*, 520
   Pruneaux Pinot, 381
   Zwetschkeweihe (tart), 406
Pudding, Rice, Italian, 502
Puddings, Souffléed, 475
Puff Paste, 395–400
   Blueberry Napoleons, 409
   Blue Cheese or Roquefort Turnovers,
      405
   chiqueter (to make indentations at
      the edges), 310, 399
   cocktail shells, 404
   cutting, 399
   détrempe (flour and water paste),
      396
   freezing and defrosting, 399
   half turn, 398
   Pasties, 410
   paton (dough and butter package),
      396–397
   patty shells, 404
   rayer (to decorate tops with lines),
      399
   rolling out, 399
   Semi-Puff Paste, 400
   to prevent scorching on the bottom,
      399
   turns I and II, 397
   turns III to VI, 398

vol-au-vent, 403
Purée Gloria (soup), 95

Quatre épices (four spices), 27
Quenelles, 289
   molded, poaching, 291
   Paste, 290–291
   Pike, 289
   poaching in the oven, 291
   poaching in stock, 291
   Poultry, 290
   Salmon, 290
   of Salmon Nordic, 292
   Sole, 289
   of Sole Lexington, 292
   Veal, 290
Quiche, Nova Scotia, 402

Rabbit
   Cutlets, Old Giovanni's, 186
   Fricassee, California, 204
   Lapin de Mémère, 214
Radish-Green Soup, 91
Raisin(s), 23
   Bread, 422
   Poundcake, 450
   Rum Raisin Soufflé, 476
Raspberry(ies)
   Berry Cream Puffs, 527
   Madeleine, *see* Strawberries Made-
      leine
   Pistachio Raspberry Roll, 458
   Sauce, 384
   Soufflé, 479
   Soufflé, Frozen, 490
   Souffléed Crêpes, 519
   Tart, 408
Ratatouille Gratin, 351
Ravigote Butter, 145
Rayer (to decorate tops of pastries with
   lines), 399
Red Snapper, Broiled, with Basil, 214
Red Snapper, Poached, 259
Red-Wine Fish *Fumet*, 83

Red-Wine Marinade, 193
Rice
  Boiled, 364
  Braised, Pilaf Method, 365
  Braised, Risotto Method, 365
  Bruno's Risotto, 367
  molded: Braised Rice, Pilaf Method, 365
  Pudding, Italian, 502
  Saffron Pilaf, 366
  Shellfish Pilaf, 366
Roasting—Dry-Heat Procedure
  beef, 161–162
  chickens, 165–167
  ducks, 167
  geese, 167
  lamb, 163–164
  meats, 158–161
  pork, 164–165
  poultry, timetable, 167
  turkeys, 165–167
  veal and calf, 162–163
Robert, Claire, 140
Robert sauce, 118
Rock Cornish Game Hens
  Krebsbutterhühner, 209
  poached, 221
  pot-roasted, *see* Squab(s), Pot-Roasted
Roll Dough, Semisweet, 430
Roquefort, *see* Cheese
Roulades (soufflés), 467
  Ham and Mushroom, 472
Roux (cooked mixture of fat and flour), 105, 106
Rum, 34
  Lime Rum Shrub Cake, 455
  Raisin Soufflé, 476
Russian Filling (for pastry ramekins), 525
Rutabagas, *see* Turnips, Yellow

✾

Sabayon, 499; *see also* Custards—Dessert
Sabler (reduce to sand), 391

Safety pointers, 13–14; for deep frying, 187–188
Saffron Pilaf, 366
Salad, 360–364
  Alan's Folly, 364
  beverage to accompany, 361
  Curried, 362
  Fruit, West Coast, 381
  Gloria's, 361
  Goody's Favorite, 363
  Green, 360
  Mario's Escarole, 363
  Potato, 321
  Sam's, 362
  Vegetables *à la Grecque,* 357
Salad Dressing, 360–361
  mayonnaise, *see* Mayonnaise
  oil for, 360
  shallots in, 361
  Vinaigrette, 360
  vinegar for, 360
Salmon
  Creamed Salmon Omelet, 56
  Nova Scotia Quiche, 402
  Pâté, Cold, 307
  Pâté Lutèce, 309
  Quenelles, 290
  Quenelles, Nordic, 292
  Russian Filling, 525
  Scallops Drei Könige, 269
  Shah's Pannequets, The, 511
  Steaks in Mushroom Butter, 254
  Steaks Zinfandel, 253
  Whole, Poached, 258
Salt
  effect on deep-fried vegetables, 345
  effect on gluten in dough fermentation, 418
  effect on meat in broiling, 174; in roasting, 160
  to balance sweetness, 24
Sam's Salad, 362
Sandy Pastry, 393
Sauces
  aïoli, 134
  Aïoli the American Way, 137
  aluminum pans for white sauces, 6

Sauces (*continued*)
  Anchovy Hollandaise, 128
  Anchovy and Olive, 118
  aurore, 110
  Béarnaise, 132; Brazier, 133
  Béchamel, 110; thickening, table of measures, 109
  bercy, 110
  beurre blanc, 139
  binding with a slurry, 104; table of measures, 105
  bordelaise, 118
  Brandy Glaze, 320
  Brown, 112; enrichment, 117; thickening, table of measures, 115; variations, 114
  Brown, Classic, chef's method, 115; home method, 114
  Brown, Lazy Cook's, 113; Short-Cut, 113
  Butter Sauces, 139–140; emulsified on an acid base, 139; emulsified on a glaze base, 139; keeping and freezing, 144
  Caper Butter, 143
  Caper Hollandaise, 128
  Caviar Mousseline, 130
  Chaud-Froid, Brown, 297
  Chaud-Froid, White, 296; variations, 296–297
  Choron, 133
  cooking a brown *roux,* 106; table of measures, 107
  cooking a white or golden *roux,* table of measures, 106
  cream, for vegetables, table of measures, 317
  Curry Mousseline, 130
  Custard, 144
  deglazing caramelized proteins, 139, 161
  Demi-Glace, 115, 117; quick version, table of measures, 117
  emulsified, cold, 133–135
  emulsified, warm, 121–125; serving, 125
  emulsion, 122

  Espagnole, 115, 116
  for fish, 247, 249
  Fish Velouté, 504
  flour-bound, 105–108; freezing, 108
  French White Butter, Classic (*beurre blanc angevin*), 140
  Garlic Hollandaise, 128
  Geneva Butter, 141
  gravy made from deglazing a roast, 161
  Green Butter, 143
  Gribiche, 137
  Herb, 469
  Hollandaise, Blender, 123, 126; Cold Butter, 123, 126; curdling, 125; Double-Boiler, 124; Professional, 124, 127; separation, 124; stabilizing, 125
  Horseradish Hollandaise, 127
  infusion, 122
  Irish, 130
  Key Lime, 131
  liaison, 110, 111
  Madeira, Classic, 118
  Maltaise, 130
  mayonnaise, *see* Mayonnaise
  Mikado, 130
  Mornay, 110
  Mousquetaire, 137
  Mousseline, 129
  Mushroom Butter, 142
  Mustard Butter, 141
  Mustard Hollandaise, 129
  neutral, 103
  Onion, 468
  Parsley and Garlic, 119
  with poached meats, 217
  Provençal Butter, 142
  Robert, 118
  Roquefort Mousseline, 129
  roux, 105; adding liquid to a *roux,* 107; freezing cooked *roux,* 107
  sauce mère, 103
  separation, 112
  skimming a flour-bound sauce, 107
  slurry, 104, 105
  starch-bound, 103-105

Sauces (*continued*)
suprême, 110
thickening with *beurre manié*, 119
thickening with a *roux*, 105
Tomatoes, Essence of, I, 120; II, 121
Tomato, Spiced, 121
Valois, 133
for vegetables, *see individual vegetables*
Velouté, 108; in white stews, 203
Virgin Butter, 140
White, Basic, 108; enriching and finishing, 110–111
White-Wine Fish, 131
See also Butters—Flavored or Compound
Sauces—Dessert
Almond Milk, 22, 478
Apricot, 384
Cherry, 385
flavorings, 23
Orange, 385
Raspberry, 384
Sabayon, 499
Strawberry, 384
Zabaglione, 66
Sauerkraut, Our Family, 333
Saupiquet, 395
Sauteuse, 207, 209, 218
Savarin, Old-Fashioned, 432
Savory Fritter Batter, 189
Scallops, 276
Clam-Juice *Court-Bouillon* for, 277
cooking, 276
Gratin of, 280
Gratiné, 277
Oporto, 278
au Pernod, 278
Schnecken, 427
Searing, 193
Seasonings, 24; for Noodles, 369–370
Sel épicé (Spiced Salt), 27; for pâtés, 304
Shad, Whole, Broiled, 264
Shah's Pannequets, The, 511
Shallots, 25
for salads and dressings, 361

storing, 9
to dice, 11
Sheedy, Charlotte, 431
Shellfish, 272–286
Bar Harbor Chowder, 93
Green Fish Pot (soup), 92
Krebsbutterhühner, 209
Mousse, 493
Pilaf, 366
Short Paste or Basic Pastry Crust, 391
Shrimp(s), 276
Clam-Juice *Court-Bouillon* for, 277
cooking, 276
Fritters, 280
Gratin of, 280
Istanbul, 279
Ouzo, *see* Lobster Ouzo
Soufflé, *see* Alaskan King-Crab Soufflé
Tomato Timbales, 505
Sieve (*tamis*), 8, 87, 323
Simon, Ellen, 205
Skewered Dishes
calf's liver, 234
Lamb Kidneys, Skewered, 231
Walliseller Spiessli, 236
Slurry (watery mixture of starch and liquid for sauce and soup thickening), 88, 104
Small utensils, 9–10
Smelts, Fried, 271
Snail(s), 285
Butter, 146
Lo Cagaraulo, 285
Omelette Cagouillarde, 55
Sole
Dover, 246
Fillets of, Meunière, 268
Fillets of, Prosper Montagné, 249
Goujonnette of, 271
Quenelles, 289
Quenelles, Lexington, 292
Soltner, André, 180, 309
Sorrel Soup, 91
Soufflé, 463–467
Alaskan King-Crab, 471
baking after freezing, 466

Soufflé (*continued*)
  Blue-Cheese, 470
  collar mathematics, 464
  dish, 464
  filling the dish, 465
  Fish, 469
  freezing, 466
  garnish in, 465
  Ham and Mushroom Roulade, 472
  Hickory-Smoked Cheese, 470
  Lobster, *see* Alaskan King-Crab Soufflé
  Moussaka, 471
  oven temperature, 466
  Poultry, 468
  Roulades, 467
  round-hat, 465
  sequence of procedures, 465
  serving, 467
  Shrimp, *see* Alaskan King-Crab Soufflé
  Souffléed Crêpes, 514
  top-hat, 465
  yields, 467
Soufflé—Dessert, 473–475
  Almond, Snow-White, 477
  Apricot, 478
  Avocado, 477
  bouillie or stirred pudding base, 474
  Cappuccino, 480
  Chocolate, 479
  Dried-Fruit Souffléed Pudding, 481
  egg-yolk base, 474
  Macaroon, 475
  pastry-cream base, 473
  Raspberry, 479
  Raspberry Souffléed Crêpes, 519
  Rum Raisin, 476
  souffléed puddings, 475
  sugar-syrup and fruit-purée base, 474
  Tea, Spiced, 476
  yields, 467
Soufflé—Dessert, Glacé or Frozen, 463, 481, 482–483
  Blueberry, 489
  freezing, 483
  fruit-flavored, 483

liqueur-flavored, 483
Pecan-Praline, 490
poaching egg-yolk bases and whole-egg bases, 484
Raspberry, 490
whipping cream for, 484
Soup
  Avocado Velouté, 98
  Bar Harbor Chowder, 93
  bisque, 86
  Bisque of Tomato, Spanish, 100
  canned stock for creamed soups, 87
  chowder, 85; technique of poaching for, 256
  clarifying consommé, 89
  clear, 85
  consommé, 85
  Consommé Double, 89
  Consommé Simple, 89
  cream, 85, 86
  Cream of California Wheat, 98
  Cream of Leeks, 99
  enriching, 87
  fish, 85
  Five Onions, 92
  freezing, 88
  garnishes, 90
  Green Fish Pot, 92
  Indian Purée, 95
  Mushroom Velouté, 97
  Onion, Kamman's, 90
  Oxtail, Alan's, 99
  purée, 86; puréeing, 87
  Purée of Carrot, 96
  Purée of Cauliflower, 94
  Purée of Chestnut, 97
  Purée Gloria, 95
  Radish-Green, 91
  serving, 88
  Sorrel, 91
  Soupe à l'Oignon comme aux Halles, 73
  Spinach, *see* Sorrel Soup
  straining, 87
  thickening with liaison, 88
  vegetable, 84
  velouté, 86

Sour-Cream Pastry, 393
Sour cream in pastry doughs, 390
Spanish Bisque of Tomato, 100
Spatulas, 9
Spiced Salt (*sel épicé*), 27; for pâtés, 304
Spiced Tea Soufflé, 476
Spice mixtures, 27
Spices, 26
Spinach
    Braised, 332
    Loaf, Quick, 503
    Soup, *see* Sorrel Soup
Spirits, 32–34
Spit-roasting, 162
Squab(s)
    Brown Sauce, Classic, 115; Short-Cut, 114
    Confit de Pigeons, 201
    Pot-Roasted, 213
    to truss, 166
    whole, to bone, 157
Squash
    Butternut, Sautéed, 338
    Summer, Basilico, *see* Zucchini Basilico
    Summer, *à la Grecque*, 359
    Winter, Gratin, 356
    See also Zucchini
Starch, 103
    hydrolysis of starch gel, 104
    See also Cornstarch; Potato starch
Stewing—Moist-Heat Procedure, meats, 202–203
Stews
    Beef, Guinness, 203
    brown, 202
    California Rabbit Fricassee, 204
    Catfish, 255
    Chicken and Artichokes, Fricassee of, 205
    Lobster Civet, 273
    Veal, Kamman's, 204
    white, 202–203
Sticky Buns, 431
Stock
    for braising, 194

for braising white meat, 195
Brown, 78
Chicken, *see* White Stock, 76
Fish *Fumet*, 81, 83, 247
Fish Glaze, 83
freezing bones and meat scraps for stock, 13
in a Hurry, 79
jus, 80
Meat Glaze (*glace de viande*), 79
pinching (browning meats), 81
for poaching, 216
Quick Broth, 74; bouillon cubes, 74; canned stocks, 75; granules, 74; meat extracts, 74
Red-Wine Fish *Fumet*, 83
to freeze, 76
varieties, 74
Veal, Brown (*jus de veau*), 80
Veal, White, *see* White Stock, 76
Vegetable Broth (*bouillon de légumes*), 75
White, 76
White-Wine Fish *Fumet*, 83
Storing utensils, 9
Stoves, 13, 46
Strainers, 8; *see also Tamis*
Strawberry(ies)
    Berry Cream Puffs, 527
    Louisiana Strawberry Patch (cake), 456
    Madeleine, 383
    Mousse, 489
    Sauce, 384
    Tart, *see* Raspberry Tart
Straw Potatoes, 348
Succotash Chicken, 211
Sugar, 21
    adding to beaten egg whites, 59, 61; table of measures, 60
    adding to ribboning eggs, 58
    brown, 21
    in cakes, 437
    candy thermometer, 374–375
    confectioners', 21
    cooking sugar syrup, 374–375; table of temperatures and stages of

Sugar *(continued)*
    cooking, 375
    fructose, 374
    glucose, 374
    granulated, 21
    powdered or superfine, 21
    to prevent recrystallization, 374
    Vanilla Sugar, 27
Summer squash, *see* Squash
Suprême sauce, 110
Swedish Apple Mayonnaise, 138
Sweetbread(s), 237–238
    blanching, 238
    braising, 238
    Cara Mia, 239
    Filling for *Vol-au-Vent* or Patties, 404
    lamb, 237
    preparation for cooking, 237
    Tourte, 400
    veal, 237
Sweet Pastry, 393
Sweet-Potato Gratin, 356
Sweet-Potato Purée, 324
Sweet Yeast Dough, 431
Swiss Filling (for pastry ramekins), 525
Swiss *Rösti*, 341
Swordfish, Fish Steaks *au Persil*, 250
Syneresis in baked custards, 495
Syneresis during defrosting, 108

❀

Tabasco Butter, 148
Tait, Elaine, 403
Tamis (sieve), 8, 87; for puréeing vegetables, 323
Tangerine
    Mikado Sauce, 130
    Mousse, *see* Lemon-Lime Mousse
    Zabaglione, 67
Tante Else's Gans, 171
Tarragon
    Butter, 147
    Chaud-Froid Sauce, 297
    Chicken *Chaud-Froid* (with truffles),

298; with tarragon leaves, *see Note,* 299
    Roast Chicken, 170
Tarts, *see* Pies and Tarts; Pies and Tarts—Dessert
Taylor, Walter, 30
Terrines, *see* Pâtés and Terrines
Timbales, 494
    Shrimp Tomato, 505
Tomato(es)
    -Basil Butter, 148
    Bisque of, Spanish, 100
    Chaud-Froid Sauce, 297
    Deep-Fried, 347
    Essence of Tomatoes (sauce), I, 120; II, 121
    Fried, 344
    Sauce, Spiced, 121
    to remove skins, 376
Tombage à glace (reducing stock for braising), 195
Tongue(s), 239–240
    poaching, 239
    Veal, Braised, 240
Torten (flourless cakes), egg-white, whole-egg, 442
Tripe, 240–241
    blanching, 241
    boiling in *court-bouillon*, 241
    honeycomb, 241
    pocket, 241
    smooth, 241
    Tripes (Les) en Amérique, 241
Trout
    Forelle Blaue, 259
    Kulebiak of, 308
    Poached, in Aspic, 301
    Truites (Les) de Monsieur Point, 262
Truffles, 28
    black, 28; to revive taste after canning, 28; to store or freeze, 28
    Chaud-Froid Sauce, 297
    freezing, 13
    peelings, to use, 28
    Poularde Demi-Deuil, 219
    Poularde Piemontaise, 220

Truffles (*continued*)

Sheet (aspic), 295

white, 29; to revive taste after canning, 29

Truites (Les) de Monsieur Point, 262

Trussing poultry, English method, 166; French method, 166

Tschudi's Scaloppine, 182

Turkey

roasting, 165–167; timetable, 167

to truss, 166

whole, to bone, 157

Turnips, Yellow (rutabagas), Purée of, 327

Typsy Dixie (crêpes), 519

Uncooked Icing, 449

Valois Sauce, 133

Vanilla, 26

Buttercream, 446

Mousseline Buttercream, 447

Sugar, 27

Variety meats, *see* Brains; Heart; Kidney(s); Liver(s); Sweetbread(s); Tongue(s), Tripe

Veal

Brown Sauce, Classic, 115; Short-Cut, 114

Cordon Bleu, Zürcher, 183

heart, *see* Heart

kidneys, *see* Kidney(s)

liver, *see* Liver(s)

Loin, Braised, 197

Loin Tante Claire, 168

meat glaze, *see* Brown Veal Stock

Pojarski, 185

Quenelles, 290; poaching, 291

roasting, 162–163

Scaloppine, Tschudi's, 182

Shoulder of, Poêled, with Herbs, 215

Stew, Kamman's, 204

Stock, Brown (*jus de veau*), 80

stock, white, *see* White Stock

sweetbreads, *see* Sweetbread(s)

tongue, *see* Tongue(s)

Top Round, Braised, 197

Vegetable(s), 315–358

baked in heavy cream, 350; in their skins, 350

boiling or blanching, 315–316

braising, 327–328

Broth, 75

creaming, table of measures, 317

deep frying, 345

flavoring, 25

fonds de braise, 191, 193; for fish, 260; for white meats, 195

freezing, 13

garnish for scrambled eggs, 42

Jardinière of, 322

leafy green, to cut into chiffonnade, 12

loaves, 494

Marinated or *à la Grecque,* 357

panfrying, 336–337; moist vegetables, 337; mushrooms, 337; starchy vegetables, 336

pot-roasting, 334

purées, 323

scalloped, baked, 350

slicer, 8

soups, 84

Succotash Ramekins, 52

to cut into *brunoise,* 12

to cut into julienne, 12

to cut into *mirepoix,* 12

to dice, 11

to mince, 12

to slice, 11

See also names of individual vegetables

Vegetable shortening in pastry doughs, 390

Velouté (sauces), 108

fish, 504

thickening, table of measures, 108

in white stews, 203

Venison Brown Sauce

Classic, 115

Venison Brown Sauce (*continued*)
Short-Cut, 114
Viennese Bread, 422
Viennese Custard, 498
Vinaigrette, 360
Vinegar
added to egg whites, 59
Court-Bouillon, 258
for emulsified sauces, 123
in marinating, 192
in pastry doughs, 390
in salad dressings, 360
to make vinegar from wine, 360
Virgin Butter, 140
Vol-au-vent, 403

Walliseller Spiessli, 236
Walnuts, Maple Walnut Crêpes, 517
Watercress Mayonnaise, 136
West Coast Fruit Salad, 381
Wheat, Cream of California (soup), 98
White Stews, 202–203
White Stock, 76
White-Wine Fish *Fumet,* 83
White-Wine Fish Sauce, 131
White-Wine Marinade, 192
Whitings, Braised, 260
Wiener Kipfeln or *Spitzwecken,* 425
Wine, 29–32
American, 30–31
Chaud-Froid Sauce, 296
for cooking fish, 248–249
Court-Bouillon, 257
European, American Equivalents, 31
fortified, 32
generic, 30
Labrusca grapes, 30
for marinating, 192
in stock making, 81
table wines, 29–31
varietal, 30
Vinifera grapes, 30
in white sauces, 111
Wine and Food Society, Philadelphia

Chapter, 201, 292
Winter-Squash Gratin, 356
Wooden spoons, 9; for use in aluminum pans, 6

Yams Gratin, 356
Yams, Purée, 324
Yeast Dough, 415–421
activation of a batter, 415; direct method, 415; rapid-mix method, 416; starter method, 415
baking, 419
basic proportions, 420–421
browning, 419
completion of fermentation, 418
cool rise, 418–419
crashing rich doughs, 417
effects of mechanical action on an activated batter, 416
fermentation of the dough, 417–418
freezing, baked, 420; unbaked, 419
glazes, 421
kneading, 416
lean, 416
proofing or proving the dough, 418
punching down, 418
rich, 416–417; fermentation, 418
sourdough breads, 418
types of breads, 420
yeast, 415
Yeast Pastries
Abgeschlagener Kugelhupf, 432
Babas, 433
Danish Pastry, 426
Savarin, Old-Fashioned, 432
Schnecken, 427
Semisweet Roll Dough, 430
Sweet Yeast Dough, 431
See also Bread

Zabaglione, Classic, 66
to stabilize for chilling, 66
variations, 67

Zucchini
  Basilico, 334
  Deep-Fried, 347
  Fried, 345
  Fried Eggs Saint Vincent, 53
  à la Grecque, 359
  Stuffed, Melanie's, 352
  See also Squash
Zürcher Cordon Bleu, 183
Zwetschkeweihe (prune tart), 406

About The Author

Born in Paris and educated in modern languages at the Sorbonne, Madeleine Kamman has diplomas from the Cordon Bleu Academy and is a member of the Escoffier Foundation Society. A food consultant and cooking instructor in Philadelphia for ten years, she also operated her own school, Modern Gourmet, Inc., and the affiliated restaurant, Chez La Mère Madeleine, in Boston. After teaching in Annecy, France, for several years, she returned to live in Glen, New Hampshire where she taught and launched a new restaurant. Madeleine Kamman is now the director of the School for American Chefs at Beringer Vineyards in St. Helena, California. *The Making of a Cook* is her first book; she is also the author of *Dinner Against the Clock, When French Women Cook, In Madeleine's Kitchen, Madeleine Cooks*, and, her most recent, *Madeleine Kamman's Savoie*. She is also the host of her own national PBS television cooking series.